The Teacher In A Democratic Society

The Teacher In A Democratic Society

An Introduction to the Field of Education

Adam M. Drayer

King's College
Wilkes-Barre, Pennsylvania

Charles E. Merrill Publishing Company
A Bell & Howell Company
Columbus, Ohio

The Coordinated Teacher Preparation Series
Under the Editorship of
Donald E. Orlosky
University of South Florida
and
Ned B. MacPhail
Depauw University

International Standard Book Number: 0-675-09328-7

Library of Congress Catalogue Card Number: 72-115888

1 2 3 4 5 6 7 8 9 10 — 75 74 73 72 71 70

Printed in the United States of America

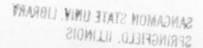

To *Mike* and *Barb*

Preface

The purpose of this book is to provide the prospective teacher, or any interested person, with insights into what the profession of teaching in America was, is, and ought to be. More specifically, it attempts to help the reader 1) to recognize the pervasive influence of philosophy in education; 2) to become aware of the importance of a democratic philosophy of education; 3) to understand how the various levels of American education evolved, and the influences affecting that development; 4) to become familiar with local, state, and federal roles in controlling and financing education; 5) to learn of the requirements and opportunities in the teaching profession; and, 6) to gain some insight into the problems in the field of education.

Introductory textbooks in the field of education can include a broad range of topics, as shown by an examination of the books written on that subject. It is the author's opinion that an introductory textbook should not attempt to range over the whole field of education, because it marches the student through a host of vague generalities which are not meaningful to him. For this reason, the topics included in this work are limited to those that are directly related to the above-stated aims. The realization of these aims should provide the student with enough professional development to enable him to study more meaningfully the specialized professional courses which follow the introductory course. At the same time, uncommitted students are provided with enough information to help them decide whether or not they are suited for, or interested in, the profession of teaching. The topics included in this book are discussed in a reasonably comprehensive manner, with the hope that the added details will aid students in the understanding, appreciation, and correlation of the material.

Because of recent developments in the profession, certain topics, heretofore treated briefly, are given chapter status. Thus, the progress made in teacher education, and the developments in teacher certification, are deemed important enough to be given separate treatment. Similarly, since higher education has expanded rapidly, separate chapters are devoted to the development of higher education, and to the requirements and opportunities in college teaching. Also, because the federal government has become heavily involved in education, its role has been given more detailed treatment than it usually receives in introductory textbooks.

The chapter on philosophy of education is discussed from a practical viewpoint, to show the student that a teacher's philosophy of education is a living thing, permeating all of his activities. Because of existing differences in philosophies of education, it is expected that this chapter will prove somewhat controversial; yet, it should serve as a starting point for a discussion of the importance of philosophy in education, and of the evolution of our democratic philosophy of education.

The historical chapters are of special importance in showing that a knowledge of what *was* in education is indispensable to an understanding of how education came to be what it *is*, and that an understanding of what American education is, cannot be reached without a knowledge of the European influences that affected it. Throughout the discussion, an attempt is made to correlate these influences.

Of interest and importance to future teachers are the requirements and opportunities in the teaching profession. Therefore, the personal and educational requirements for teachers are discussed, supply and demand for teachers is shown, and information is provided on the monetary and intangible benefits to be found in teaching.

Finally, the student is introduced to a sampling of today's problems, controversies, and innovations in the field of education. This not only exposes him to some of the current issues he will meet in the field, but also should help him to understand that there are, and always will be, unsettled problems in the field.

The author gratefully acknowledges the permissions received from the many publishers whose works have been cited herein. He is indebted to Mrs. Patricia Carda, of the Charles E. Merrill Publishing Company editorial staff, whose deft blue pencil and provocative pink slips added immeasurably to the effectiveness of this work. Special thanks are due, too, to Mary Jane Donnelly for her cheery work in compiling the index, and to Margaret S. Knorr for her total involvement in typing the manuscript. Lastly, it is a tribute to the patience of the authors' wife that this manuscript was written at all.

A.M.D.

Contents

The Teacher In A Democratic Society

1

The Importance of Philosophy in Education

Most of us shudder a bit when we are confronted with the word "philosophy", because we tend to think of it as an abstract field of study which can be understood only by the intellectually gifted. Although elaborate, abstract thought processes are required to study many of the fine points of philosophy's several branches, it is equally true that each of us has a philosophy which we apply either consciously or habitually in our daily living. Even the person who is without formal education has formulated a philosophy, although he does not label, or even recognize, it as such. The field of philosophy, therefore, is not confined to long-haired scholars in ivory towers. It is the most basic and practical piece of intellectual equipment that each person possesses.

This chapter will demonstrate the intimate relationship that exists between philosophy and our daily living, between our philosophy of life and a philosophy of education, and between a teacher's philosophy of education and his work as a teacher. The discussion of these relationships is necessarily brief and general, but it should show that philosophy pervades all aspects of education.

RELATIONSHIP BETWEEN PHILOSOPHY AND EDUCATION

Philosophy may be defined as the study of the ultimate causes of all things through the use of reasoning. It pushes questions concerning reality back to the last *who, what, why,* or *how.* By *reason alone,* the

1

individual attempts to discover the final answer to questions such as the existence of God, the nature of the universe, the norms of behavior, and the origin, nature, and destiny of man. For example, the individual discovers that everything on earth and in the universe moves continuously, even the smallest particle of matter. He notices that some things are put into motion by others, but what causes these things to be in motion? He tries to push his questions and answers back to the point where he can explain all motion, or as we have stated previously, he seeks the *ultimate* cause of motion. It is in this manner that philosophy studies all of reality.

Because of the tremendous scope of philosophy, and because it would help to discuss these questions more logically, philosophy has several branches, each branch specializing in a certain type of knowledge. Thus, the following divisions have been made in the study of philosophy:

Psychology: the science of the mind
Theodicy: the science of God
Cosmology: the science of the universe
Epistemology: the science of the ability of the mind to attain
                            truth
Ethics: the science of correct conduct
Ontology: the science of being, as such
Logic: the science of correct thinking
Aesthetics: the science of beauty

A glance at these divisions shows the magnitude of the field of philosophy. It poses, and tries to answer, a seemingly endless number of questions. It is apparent that a person, left to his own resources, could spend his lifetime pursuing these questions without obtaining answers to all of them.

Building a Philosophy of Life

Since the field of philosophy is so broad, one might challenge the statement that every individual has a philosophy which he applies in daily living. Actually, the average layman does not pose questions in all the branches of philosophy, nor does he exhaust the questions in any one branch of philosophy; nevertheless, each individual does reach conclusions to questions that are important to him. He reaches points in his thinking at which he definitely concludes that "This is true," or "This is false." For example, he comes to accept or reject the existence of God; he either concludes that man has a spiritual soul, or that he is a purely material being; he either believes that there is a life hereafter, or that the end of this life is the end of all things for him. In other words, as he grows, studies, and thinks, he arrives at a basic set of principles that he has accepted as true.

There are many influences that help to shape an individual's philosophy of life. As a child, he is first exposed to the influence of his parents. From them he learns ways of acting and reacting, and to a large degree, through imitation, he begins to reflect their ideas, attitudes, and beliefs. As he begins to attend school, he adds to, and modifies, his basic set of values. Around the age of seven, he becomes capable of reasoning, and, as this power develops, he begins to raise questions, challenging many of the principles he accepted from his parents, teachers, and others. During this period, his reasoning sometimes confirms what he had accepted, but at other times he is not able to substantiate his previous convictions. His church also has contributed to his outlook on life, by interpreting for him the purpose of life, by trying to show him that the apparent conflicts between faith and reason can be resolved and by demonstrating to him that some truths he may have to accept on faith alone because of the limitations of the human mind.

Besides the educational influence of the home, school, and church, the individual is exposed to many informal agencies of education. He watches television, listens to the radio, reads periodicals and books, exchanges ideas with friends and acquaintances, and becomes a member of various types of organizations. These, and other influences, add to his background of knowledge, and help him to reach a fuller understanding of human relationships.

Obviously, the individual does not seek the answers to his questions alone, for he has the help and influence of many educational agencies. As he grows and matures, a sifting-out process takes place. "This I can accept." "This is unreasonable." "This is not incompatible with my principles, but I need more proof." This process continues, and through experience, through study, and through authority he increases his knowledge of the world and of man. He gradually formulates a basic set of principles which constitutes his personal philosophy. Once he has acquired these principles, he applies them in his daily living to govern his actions, and to interpret everything with which he comes into contact. His philosophy gives his life its meaning, its directions, and its goals. It gives him perspective, by helping him put first thing first. It provides him with principles for living as a person, as a member of society, and, if he acknowledges a Creator, as a creature of God. Hence, an individual's philosophy is the most intangible and the most practical of his possessions.

A person's actions reflect his philosophy of life, because his actions usually are based on his convictions. If we study a person's behavior and speech, we can infer with some accuracy his philosophy of life. What we think of that person is, in turn, dependent on our philosophy of life. The following examples should illustrate this process.

Mr. Smith is a cheerful person. He has a ready "Hello" for everyone he meets. Whenever a neighbor is in need of help, or whenever the community is sponsoring a project, he usually helps. His employer has noted that he takes great pride in his work, and that he often expends extra effort and energy to see that things are done properly. He is anxious to get ahead, but tries not to do so at the expense of his co-workers. When he has made a mistake, he admits it and profits by it.

Mr. Jones is also a cheerful person who is always ready with a handshake and a slap on the back. He maintains good relationships with his neighbors, but does not take a personal interest in their problems. He appears at community projects where he is an excellent conversationalist, but somehow manages to avoid becoming involved in the actual work. In his occupation, he does the work required of him steadily, putting forth an extra burst of energy whenever he thinks that it will be noticed by his employer. He has insinuated covertly to his employer that others in the firm are not carrying out their responsibilities, and, on occasion, has blamed them for his errors.

Even this brief description demonstrates that Mr. Smith and Mr. Jones do not share the same philosophy of life. Mr. Smith sincerely believes that he has a responsibility to do his best to improve himself and society without impeding or trampling on anyone in the process. He is basically honest, unselfish, and truthful. In contrast to him, Mr. Jones is selfish. His basic motivation centers around self-advancement which he promotes with a minimum of effort. He is deceitful when he thinks it will go unnoticed. He apparently believes that he would be foolish not to take everything he can get, even though he must occasionally bend the principles of socially acceptable behavior. His philosophy is one of "Everyone for himself."

Because our actions reflect our philosophy, while our philosophy determines our actions, we evaluate the philosophy of others in terms of our own convictions. Mr. Smith, because of his convictions, undoubtedly could not bring himself to act like Mr. Jones, while Mr. Jones undoubtedly would think that Mr. Smith is an altruistic fool. In the eyes of each, the other is living according to a false philosophy. The reader, in turn, as he followed this discussion, has already evaluated Mr. Smith and Mr. Jones in terms of his own basic principles.

Building a Philosophy of Education

Everyone who expresses an opinion on education has a philosophy of education, even though it may be incomplete or inaccurate. The layman does not hesitate to speak his mind on educational problems. Perhaps this is because we consider education everybody's business. In one way or another, the entire citizenry is intimately concerned with what is done in the schools. Many people have children in school, and are anxious that they have the best possible education; everyone is taxed to maintain the schools, with the result that some feel that they are entitled to say how the money will be spent. Others, aware that education determines the quality of our future citizenry, express their ideas on the type of education that should be given in a democracy. Comments such as "That is a good school," or "What they are teaching is a lot of nonsense" are simply expressions of individual philosophies.

The layman, not having any formal training in philosophy of education, formulates his ideas incidentally as he goes through life. He has been exposed to varying periods of schooling, ranging from an elementary education to graduate and professional training, depending on his ability and circumstances. During these years of schooling, he has built up definite ideas about education, but always from the viewpoint of a student; rarely does he see things as a professional educator does. Consequently, his convictions are limited to his experiential background, so that he does not fully appreciate the ramifications of the problems encountered in the field.

The real formulation of a total philosophy of education occurs when the individual who has decided to become a teacher, begins his program of professional education. At this time he learns what was and is happening in the field of education; simultaneously he starts to crystallize a professionally oriented set of convictions about what *ought* to be in education.

He will discover immediately that his philosophy of education is inextricably bound to his philosophy of life. In formulating his philosophy of education the prospective teacher must, before he can do anything else meaningfully, answer two fundamental questions, one relating to the individual's nature and the other to his destiny.

In education, we try to bring about certain desirable changes in an individual. However, before we attempt to bring about planned changes in *anything*, it is necessary for us to know the nature of the raw material we are dealing with; otherwise, we would be proceeding in haphazard fashion. The first question, then, is: "What *is* the nature of the individual?" Is he a purely material being? Or, does he also have spiritual qualities? Does he have an animal nature? If so, how does he differ from other animals? What types of powers does he have? The answers to these questions will come from the prospective teacher's philosophy, and the kind of answers he gives will depend on the type of philosophy to which he subscribes.

Once the future educator has decided on the nature of the individual, he must decide what he will seek to accomplish with him. In other words, he must set up his objectives of education. Again, in order to do so, he must resort to philosophy. "I know the individual should be prepared for life, but what is life all about? What should I do while I am here? Where am I going?" What he tries to do with his pupils will depend on his answers. Persons may, of course, answer these questions in different ways, a point which will be discussed later in this chapter.

As the individual progresses in his teacher education program, he elaborates on his philosophy of education. Through formal classes, informal seminars and discussions, reading, and some experience in teaching, he follows a process similar to that through which he formulated his philosophy of life. There are ideas which he finds reasonable, therefore intellectually acceptable, and there are other ideas which are repugnant to him because they are incompatible with his basic principles. He works from the broad principles which he has accepted toward particular applications; at the same time, through observation and experimentation he may arrive at generalizations. Thus, through induction and deduction he formulates his philosophy of education.

Philosophy of Education in Action

The teacher's philosophy of education is important because it will affect his entire approach to education. Certainly if he conceived of the nature of the individual as purely animal, he would try to train him differently from the training he would use if he believed that human beings are rational animals. Similarly, if he felt that life on earth were the only life, he would believe in a system of education that would be different from the system of an educator who holds that there is an after-life. Philosophies do not have to be totally different to produce conflicting theories in education. Sometimes, teachers may accept the same basic principle, but interpret it so differently that they disagree on methodology.

All teachers agree that pupil-activity is necessary in learning. Yet, they may disagree on the degree of pupil-activity that produces best results. Teacher A, for example, may believe that effective learning will take place in direct proportion to the amount of pupil-activity. Teacher B also believes that pupil-activity is necessary, but he may feel that it can be overdone. Implicit in Teacher A's philosophy is the idea that pupils have within themselves the ability to formulate and reach desirable objectives. Teacher B's philosophy, however, is based on the premise that immature individuals need direction and guidance from mature, experienced persons.

This disagreement on the amount of pupil-activity necessary to produce desirable results will affect the type of procedures used by these two teachers. If Teacher A followed his belief to its logical conclusion, he would allow his pupils to become completely self-active by permitting them to determine what they would like to do, and how they would like to do it. If he does not go to that extreme, he would at least adopt procedures that emphasize maximum pupil participation and planning, such as individual and group projects, committee work, panel discussions, symposiums, and field trips. Even though Teacher B believes in pupil-activity, he believes that it should always be under the direction and guidance of the teacher. Consequently, he would plan the objectives and procedures for his classes. Although he might use some of Teacher A's procedures, he would maintain a higher degree of control. Also, he would be likely to use more teacher-guided procedures, such as explanation, illustration, question and answer, drill, review, and class discussion.

Thus, even though two teachers may accept the same basic principle, their different interpretations can cause major differences in their approach to education. In the case of pupil-activity, these approaches may range from complete permissiveness to rigid domination by the teacher.

Conflicting Philosophies of Education

One of the problems that complicates the process of formulating a philosophy of education is the fact that educators do not agree among themselves on a basic, generally acceptable philosophy of education. Because of the disagreement on a basic philosophy, there is disagreement on objectives, contents, and methodology, which are influenced by the former.

This disagreement is evident in many ways. One educator will hold that the ultimate aim of education is the full development of the individual; another will state that the individual's development is only as important as its contribution to the welfare of society. Regarding man's nature, some educators believe that man is purely a material being; others believe that man is composed of a material body *and* a spiritual soul. Many educators believe in the essential goodness of man, believing that if he is unencumbered by external influences he may eventually approach perfectibility; still others feel that man has a darkened intellect, a weakened will, and a tendency toward disorder, and because of these he needs discipline, guidance, and instruction. There are conflicting ideas on every phase of educational theory and practice. This conflict, and the resulting confusion, has been described in effect by the sentence: "In education we are rushing along toward undetermined goals."

Since there is conflict and contradiction, it is reasonable to conclude that not all of these ideas can be sound. It would follow logically that any system of education which is rooted in a false philosophy would itself be erroneous. We are therefore forced to conclude that, because some philosophies of education are in error, the educators subscribing to them are teaching in error. The problem, then, is to find and implement a true philosophy of education.

DEMOCRATIC PHILOSOPHY OF EDUCATION

Our democracy has been built upon certain principles which have been accepted by most Americans throughout the years. It has been built upon the recognition of a Creator, from Whom each of us has received inalienable rights, and to Whom we are responsible. It has been built upon the recognition of the dignity of the individual, and on the principle that the state exists for the good of the individual. These principles were clearly stated in the Declaration of Independence, as follows:

> We hold these truths to be self-evident, that all men are created equal, that they are endowed by their Creator with certain inalienable Rights, that among these are Life, Liberty and the pursuit of Happiness.—That to secure these rights, Governments are instituted among men, deriving their just Powers from the consent of the governed.—That whenever any Form of Government becomes destructive of these ends, it is the Right of the People to alter or to

abolish it, and to institute new Government, laying its foundation on such principles and organizing its powers in such form, as to them shall seem most likely to effect their Safety and Happiness.

It will be noted that the Founding Fathers held these principles to to be *self-evident;* i.e. these rights were given to them by their Creator. Their rights were not received from the state, and could not be taken away by the state, but rather were to be protected by it. They assured the protection of their rights in the articles of the Constitution and the Bill of Rights.

The basic principles of our Founding Fathers were reflected, of course, in their philosophy of education. They felt that education was necessary for intelligent citizenship and good government, and they expressed their aim of education in terms of producing the moral man. The idea of the moral man as a goal in citizenship education was introduced as early as 1787 in the Congressional Ordinance on the Northwest Territory.

Religion, morality, and knowledge being necessary to good government and happiness of mankind, schools and the means of education shall ever be encouraged.

In view of these specific statements, it should be evident that if our educational system is to preserve the ideas and ideals of our democracy, it should be built upon these fundamental concepts stated by those responsible for its establishment. It is true that the Constitution mentions nothing specific concerning education and that education was therefore left to the states. It would be unreasonable, however, to apply the philosophy of the Founding Fathers to all areas of living except education, since education is the means by which we train individuals to know, to live, and to perpetuate our basic democratic principles. If we interpret a democratic philosophy of education only in terms of the thinking of our Founding Fathers, good citizenship training would begin with an acceptance of the self-evident truths enunciated by them. The goal of this training would be to develop an individual of good moral character who worships his Creator, understands his relationships with his fellow-men, and has achieved enough self-dicipline to respect the rights of others and work for the common good. This, indeed, has remained the broad objective of our educational system throughout the years.

As our public school system expanded, certain other basic ideas have taken root as representative of education in our democratic society. These include equality of opportunity in education, public support of schools through taxation, compulsory attendance, and the separation of church and state.

Equality of Opportunity

In a democracy, it would be natural to assume that every citizen, regardless of race, color, creed, or economic status should have an equal opportunity to develop his potentialities. We have been progressing for three centuries toward the achievement of that goal, but, as we know, we have not yet fully realized it. There are still wide differences in educational opportunities, represented by the differences in physical equipment and facilities, quality of teachers, variety of curricular offerings, length of school year, and per pupil expenditures. Perhaps these differences will never be completely equalized, but progress has been made and will be made in closing the gap that exists between the extremes.

The statement that "all men are created equal" must not be misinterpreted to mean that all men are equal in their potentialities and abilities. Human beings differ widely in their mental ability, and, therefore, in their ability to profit from education. Some can absorb only a few years of schooling, while others have the capacity to continue their education into colleges and graduate schools. Human beings also differ in their interests and aptitudes, so that some, with training, can become skilled mechanics, accountants, musicians, or physicians, while others could never become proficient in those fields.

Those differences among human beings present problems in providing an equal opportunity in education. If all human beings are to be provided with the opportunity to develop their special talents, a variety of school programs must be made available to them. To the extent that this is not done, there exists an inequality of opportunity.

Public Support Through Taxation

Even in early colonial days measures were taken to provide schooling through public support, although this practice was not prevalent throughout the colonies. The earliest legislation was the Massachusetts Law of 1642, which required that children learn to read and know the laws of the country. It also provided for a fine on each town which did not comply with the law. Although progress was slow, gradually the idea of free, tax-supported schools took hold, but it still was not until the end of the nineteenth century that the practice became prevalent. It is now taken for granted that all people, even those who do not have children, or who for various reasons do not send their children to public schools, must contribute to the support of public education.

Compulsory Attendance

If the welfare of a democracy depends upon an educated citizenry, it is logical for the government to institute compulsory attendance for a period of time which would be regarded as minimal for the development of their basic capacities. The Massachusetts Law of 1642 embodied the idea of compulsory education, but the first compulsory attendance law was not passed until 1852. Massachusetts then passed legislation requiring children between the ages of eight and fourteen to attend school a minimum of twelve weeks each year. Gradually other states followed suit, so that today all states have laws regulating the attendance of children.

Separation of Church and State

Although there was a union of church and state in colonial Massachusetts, and although early education was religious in purpose, a gradual separation of church and state has occurred. There now is a "wall of separation", based on the First Amendment's "establishment of religion" clause and reinforced by Supreme Court decisions. It was common to use public funds to support private schools during the early years, but in the beginning of the nineteenth century New York declared it illegal, and other states gradually passed similar legislation. Not only is it illegal to use tax money to support schools of religious denominations, but also the Supreme Court has ruled that public schools cannot be used to instruct children in religion. However, the Supreme Court has deemed it constitutional to release school children for religious instruction outside of the school premises. Furthermore, the Supreme Court has ruled it constitutional to use public funds for the provision of services to parochial school children, such as lunches and transportation. The judges based their ruling on the premise that *all* children are entitled to these services, and that this aid does not directly promote the establishment of a religion. More recently, the United States Supreme Court, in 1962, ruled it unconstitutional to compel the recitation of a state-prescribed non-denominational prayer in public schools. In 1963, the Supreme Court ruled it unconstitutional to read the Bible as a religious practice in public schools.

The trend in our democracy, then, has been to separate religion from the public schools to an ever greater degree. Our schools are therefore faced with the difficult task of educating the "moral man" without any reference to specific religious doctrines or practices, except those that are examples of inspirational literature or occur in the history of religions.

It should be noted that all of the preceding restrictions apply only to public schools. The national government recognizes the right of private schools, unsupported by public funds, to include religion in the curriculum. It also recognizes the right of parents to send their children to the type of school of their choice, public or private.

AIMS OF EDUCATION

Throughout the years there have been many statements of the aims of education in our democratic society. The ideas and contributions of Europeans such as Quintilian, Rousseau, Pestalozzi, Herbart, and Froebel, have been prolifically reported in histories and philosophies of education. Similarly, extensive treatment has been given to the role of Americans such as Parker, Mann, Barnard, Hall, and Dewey in the development of our school system. Any historical review of the objectives of education will reveal a lack of agreement on the desired goals. Generally speaking, the pendulum swings between an emphasis on *individual* development, and an emphasis on *social* efficiency. Often the argument on these broad objectives has been on an "either-or" basis, rather than on a recognition that *both* are important; i.e., social aims cannot be achieved without the proper development of indvidual members of society.

A statement of the Educational Policies Commission of the National Education Association in 1938 clearly distinguishes the relationship between social institutions and the individual:

> Social institutions are convenient systems of relationships among individuals, the lengthened shadows of groups of individual men and women. The State, for example, consists of its members. Destroy all the members and the State is gone; but destroy the State and the members remain. Apart from these individuals the social organization has a merely fictional existence. There can be no such thing as the welfare of "the State" at the expense of, or in contrast with, the general welfare of the individuals who compose it. Man is not made for institutions. Institutions are made by and for mankind.[1]

[1]National Education Association and American Association of School Administrators, Educational Policies Commission, *The Purposes of Education in American Democracy* (Washington, D.C.: the Commission, 1938), p. 17.

This statement re-affirms the idea of government "of the people, by the people, and for the people", which was the underlying principle of the Declaration of Independence and the Constitution, previously set forth. Yet, in our desire to "improve society", we sometimes overlook the fact that it is necessary to first improve the individuals who make up society.

In our democracy, therefore, the focus is on the individual. Our system of education aims to provide the opportunity for every individual to develop his unique potentialities in a way that contributes to his personal well-being, and through this, contributes to the general welfare of all. In order to achieve this general objective, it is necessary to formulate particular aims which contribute to the realization of the major objective. Again, the report of the Educational Policies Commission is an illustration of modern thinking on the broad and specific objectives of education in a democratic society. The Commission stated:

> The general end of education in America at the present time is the fullest possible development of the individual within the framework of our present industrialized democratic society. The attainment of this end is to be observed in individual behavior or conduct.[2]

Most of the Commission's report then outlined and explained the more particular aims through which the general objective might be realized. The Commission categorized the specific objectives into four general groups: self-realization, human relationship, economic efficiency, and civic responsibility. These objectives take into account personal development, relationships in the home and community, production and consumption of income, and duties of citizenship.[3] Because these objectives have been widely quoted and accepted, they are included here as a representative statement of aims of American public education:

I. *The Objectives Of Self-realization*[4]

> *The Inquiring Mind.* The educated person has an appetite for learning.
> *Speech.* The educated person can speak the mother tongue clearly.
> *Reading.* The educated person reads the mother tongue efficiently.

---

[2]*Ibid.*, p. 41.
[3]*Ibid.*, p. 47.
[4]*Ibid.*, p. 50.

Writing. The educated person writes the mother tongue effectively.

Number. The educated person solves his problems of counting and calculating.

Sight and Hearing. The educated person is skilled in listening and observing.

Health Knowledge. The educated person understands the basic facts concerning health and disease.

Health Habits. The educated person protects his own health and that of his dependents.

Public Health. The educated person works to improve the health of the community.

Recreation. The educated person is participant and spectator in many sports and other pastimes.

Intellectual Interests. The educated person has mental resources for the use of leisure.

Esthetic Interests. The educated person appreciates beauty.

Character. The educated person gives responsible direction to his own life.

II. *The Objectives Of Human Relationship*[5]

Respect for Humanity. The educated person puts human relationships first.

Friendships. The educated person enjoys a rich, sincere, and varied social life.

Cooperation. The educated person can work and play with others.

Appreciation of the Home. The educated person appreciates the family as a social institution.

Conservation of the Home. The educated person conserves family ideals.

Homemaking. The educated person is skilled in homemaking.

Democracy in the Home. The educated person maintains democratic family relationships.

III. *The Objectives Of Economic Efficiency*[6]

Work. The educated producer knows the satisfaction of good workmanship.

Occupational Information. The educated producer understands the requirements and opportunities for various jobs.

Occupational Choice. The educated producer has *selected* his occupation.

---

[5]*Ibid.,* p. 72.
[6]*Ibid.,* p. 90.

Occupational Efficiency. The educated producer succeeds in his chosen vocation.

Occupational Adjustment. The educated producer maintains and improves his efficiency.

Occupational Appreciation. The educated producer appreciates the social value of his work.

Personal Economics. The educated consumer plans the economics of his own life.

Consumer Judgment. The educated consumer develops standards for guiding his expenditures.

Efficiency in Buying. The educated consumer is an informed and skillful buyer.

Consumer Protection. The educated consumer takes appropriate measures to safeguard his interests.

IV. *The Objectives Of Civic Responsibility*[7]

Social Justice. The educated citizen is sensitive to the disparities of human circumstance.

Social Activity. The educated citizen acts to correct unsatisfactory conditions.

Social Understanding. The educated citizen seeks to understand social structures and social processes.

Critical Judgment. The educated citizen has defenses against propaganda.

Tolerance. The educated citizen respects honest differences of opinion.

Conservation. The educated citizen has a regard for the nation's resources.

Social Applications of Science. The educated citizen measures scientific advance by its contribution to the general welfare.

World Citizenship. The educated citizen is a cooperating member of the world community.

Law Observance. The educated citizen respects the law.

Economic Literacy. The educated citizen is economically literate.

Political Citizenship. The educated citizen accepts his civic duties.

Devotion to Democracy. The educated citizen acts upon an unswerving loyalty to democratic ideals.

Although the preceding objectives are comprehensive on many phases of individual development, they do not emphasize moral-spiritual values. There is no specific mention of man's relationship to his

---

[7]*Ibid.*, p. 108.

Creator, although there are references to character development, social justice, and loyalty to democratic ideals.

In 1951 the Educational Policies Commission filled this gap with its report entitled *Moral and Spiritual Values in the Public Schools.* This report included emphatic statements on the necessity of teaching moral and spiritual values to school children:

> This report deals with a problem of utmost importance. Intelligent and fervent loyalty to moral and spiritual values is essential to the survival of this nation. The Commission hopes that this report will encourage in homes, churches, and schools a nationwide renaissance of interest in education for moral and spiritual values. Out of such interest the public schools should receive a clear mandate to continue and to strengthen their efforts in teaching the *values which have made America great.*[8]

> The development of moral and spiritual values is basic to all other educational objectives. Education uninspired by moral and spiritual values is directionless. Values unapplied in human behavior are empty.[9]

The Commission's report outlines the values that have been generally accepted by the majority of Americans. These values, they indicate, find their political expression in the Constitution and Bill of Rights, and their religious expression in the tenets of major religious groups.[10]

According to the Commission, the following values have found common acceptance:

1. Among the values here proposed, the first is fundamental to all that follow. The basic moral and spiritual value in American life is the supreme importance of the individual personality.
2. If the individual personality is supreme, each person should feel responsible for the consequence of his own conduct.
3. If the individual personality is supreme, institutional arrangements are the servants of mankind.
4. If the individual personality is supreme, mutual consent is better than violence.
5. If the individual personality is supreme, the human mind should be liberated by access to information and opinion.

---

[8]National Education Association and American Association of School Administrators, Educational Policies Commission, *Moral and Spiritual Values in the Public Schools* (Washington, D.C.: the Commission, 1951), p. vi. Italics by the author.
[9]*Ibid.*, pp. 6-7.
[10]*Ibid.*, p. 18.

6. If the individual is supreme, excellence in mind, character, and creative ability should be fostered.
7. If the individual personality is supreme, all persons should be judged by the same moral standards.
8. If the individual personality is supreme, the concept of brotherhood should take precedence over selfish interests.
9. If the individual personality is supreme, each person should have the greatest possible opportunity for the pursuit of happiness, provided only that such activities do not substantially interfere with the similar opportunities of others.
10. If the individual personality is supreme each person should be offered the emotional and spiritual experiences which transcend the materialistic aspects of life.[11]

The Commission stated that these values should permeate the entire school program, and should be integrated with the instruction in every course, because ". . . the entire life of the school, every classroom, every teacher, every activity, makes its contribution, plus or minus, to the understanding and appreciation of moral values."[12] In addition, "Teachers can, without promoting any religious creed, encourage pupils to regard with approval participation in religious activities appropriate to their home and family background."[13] Similarly, "Although the public schools cannot teach denominational beliefs, they can and should teach much useful information about the religious faiths, the important part they have played in establishing the moral and spiritual values of American life, and their role in the story of mankind."[14] This, however, the Commission cautions, is not to be regarded as a substitute for direct religious instruction which either the home or the church can provide. The home, states the report, can be the greatest single factor in forming character, because parents, by precept and example, can exert a powerful influence in inculcating proper values. The influence of the church is well summarized, as follows:

> The churches and other organized institutions of religion play a major role in the development of moral and spiritual values. The great systems of religious belief reject a mechanistic view of the nature of man. They teach that a power exists above the material universe. They deny that man is merely another educable animal, whose behavior can be fully explained and rightly directed by the

---

[11]*Ibid.*, pp. 18-29.
[12]*Ibid.*, p. 59.
[13]*Ibid.*, p. 76.
[14]*Ibid.*, p. 78.

laws of science alone. They seek to understand and teach the relation of man to God. They grapple with the enduring problems of the meaning of human life, aspiration, suffering, and death. In these transcendental terms, religion adds a unique emphasis to moral and spiritual values. For many Americans, the teaching of their church provides the only sure foundation for moral standards and the best single guide to moral conduct.[15]

When the 1938 and 1951 reports of the Educational Policies Commission are combined, they form a comprehensive statement of aims, that should be acceptable to nearly all people, in American public education. These aims are cognizant of the many-sided development of the individual: physical, intellectual, social, aesthetic, and moral-religious. Moreover, they are in harmony with the basic principles upon which our democracy was built and has thrived. All of these aims have not yet been achieved by all of the people, but the goal is there, visible to all, and increasingly closer to the grasp of all.

AGENCIES OF EDUCATION

Who is responsible for the education of children? Until the time the individual reaches maturity, he is exposed to a variety of educational influences. Some of these influences are in the form of conscious instructional programs which are directed toward the achievement of set goals. These influences are designated as formal agencies of education and consist of the family, the church, and, through its schools, the state. There are other educational influences which are important but which are not systematic in their influence on individuals. They are designated as informal agencies, such as television, radio, and the press. The education of children belongs to the formal agencies, each of which has rights and responsibilities in their training of children.

The Family

The individual is born into the family, so that the family has the first right, a natural right, to provide for its children's education. Parents, to the best of their ability, have a corresponding duty to provide for the temporal and spiritual welfare of their children. It should be evident, however, that in our complex society the family does not have all the

---

[15]*Ibid.*, p. 87.

means necessary to bring about the full development of the child. To discharge their responsibility properly, parents seek the cooperation of two other agencies: the church, and the state.

Since the state exists for the welfare of its members, it must take measures to promote that welfare. It is obvious that education could promote the welfare of our democracy by developing a citizenry that can make intelligent, informed, moral decisions, and elect capable people as representatives. The state, therefore, can insist that all of its members receive the amount and quality of education deemed necessary for good citizenship. Simultaneously, the state has the responsibility to provide the means necessary for each individual to develop his particular capacities, which will assure his temporal welfare. In other words, the educational systems set up or approved by the state, should contribute to the welfare of the people as a whole, and at the same time should meet the temporal needs of each individual.

Yet the state cannot go quite far enough to assure the complete development of its members. The cravings of man's moral-religious nature must be satisfied; for this he must look to the religion and church of his choice. In his religion, and in the teachings of his church, he will find the means to participate in a supernatural life which will fulfill his destiny.

Thus, the home, the state, and the church cooperate in the education of the individual. Each has its rights in the realm of education, which cannot be infringed upon nor usurped by the others. The family, for example, can choose the type of education it wishes for their child, provided that minimum state standards are met. It can choose either private or public school education, and cannot be compelled by the state to send children to public schools. The Supreme Court in the Oregon School Case of 1925 upheld this right:

> The fundamental theory of liberty upon which all governments in this Union repose excludes any general power of the state to standardize its children by forcing them to accept instruction from public teachers only. The child is not the mere creature of the state; those who nurture him and direct his destiny have the right coupled with the high duty to recognize and prepare him for additional obligations. (Supreme Court of the United States, 1925, Pierce vs. Society of Sisters.)

On the other hand, if the family is unwilling or unable to discharge its responsibility in education, the state has the right to assure the child of the minimum amount of education required by law.

Similarly, in church-state relationships, each must act within its own sphere. Because each individual is assured religious freedom, the state cannot establish an official religion for its members. Thus, the First Amendment of the Constitution states that "Congress shall make no law respecting an establishment of religion, or prohibiting the free exercise thereof."

The state assures the right of each individual to worship as he pleases. The church, in turn, cannot interfere in the functions of civil government, i.e., "Render unto Caesar the things that belong to Caesar, and to God the things that belong to God." If each agency acts within its own sphere, and respects the rights of the others, there should be no conflict about who has the right to educate our children.

Informal Agencies of Education

In addition to the home, church, and school, the child is exposed to many incidental influences which are formative and informative in nature. These informal agencies of education should not be underestimated, for they can add a great deal to, or detract from, the education provided through formal agencies. The more important informal agencies are television, radio, motion pictures, periodicals, newspapers, books, clubs, and various types of social, civic, and church organizations.

Whether or not some of these informal agencies exert a healthy influence on the individual depends on the selections he makes. There are many programs or articles from these agencies that are informative, inspirational, patriotic, cultural, and wholesomely entertaining; there also are other themes that emphasize crime, violence, and immorality, and may have an unwholesome influence on individuals during their formative years. Although the home, church, and school condemn these negative influences, the child is often exposed to them inadvertently or covertly, or through parental negligence. Selectivity and supervision will reap beneficial results from these informal media of education.

THE CHANGING VERSUS THE UNCHANGEABLE

Throughout history, philosophers have debated whether or not there is such a thing as objective truth, that is, whether there are certain things that have always been, are, and always will be true. As far back as the fifth century B.C., there have been doubts about the permanency of things. The Greek Sophists, Heraclitus and Protagoras, held that everything is constantly in a state of change and that, therefore, nothing is permanent. Gorgias reached the pinnacle of frustration and doubt among the Sophists. He in effect stated that there is nothing, and that if there were anything we could not know it, and if we could know it we could not express it. Conversely, Aristotle, who founded the science of logic, reasoned to truths which he said were immutable. Through the following centuries the question of man's ability to arrive at objective truth continued to be argued. One of the most recent expressions of a philosophy of change has been found in the experimentalism of John Dewey, who is regarded by many as one of the outstanding philosophers of the twentieth century.

Finding an acceptable answer to the question of change is extremely important to American democracy. Indeed, the survival of our way of life may depend on the answer. To find the answer it is necessary to break the question of change into two parts.

Are *some* things changing all of the time? When we consider the facts of observable experience, the answer is an emphatic "Yes!" We notice changes taking place everywhere. Changes take place in the growth and development of every human being; the face of the earth is continuously being altered; new ways of doing things are being discovered in every phase of human endeavor; our style of clothing, hairdress, and transportation keep changing; and even governments change.

However, we must ask a second question: are *all* things changing all of the time? When we consider fundamental principles and the essence of things, the answer would have to be "No". Even though we observe changes occurring in every phase of life, we also recognize that the *nature* of man has remained unchanged. Man has always been a rational animal, which distinguishes him from other forms of life. Similarly, we notice changes taking place in matter, liquids changing to gas, gas to liquids, solids to gas, but, at the same time, we arrive at the law that the amount of mass, together with its energy, never changes although its form may do so. Again, man's rational nature has led the majority of men of all time to believe in a creator. It also has led them to believe that certain types of conduct, (such as murder and theft), are always wrong. It is unreasonable to assume that all men of all time could have erroneously accepted these unchanging principles, but even if they had, they still have been acting on what they regard as unchanging truths. For individuals who believe that their Creator made truths known through Revelation, the acceptance of unchanging truths is even easier. They believe certain things to be true because God said so, and their God cannot be wrong. Whether men have accepted things on reason alone, or bolstered reason with Revelation, the fact remains they have always regarded certain basic principles as unchangeable.

In our previous discussion we have shown that our Founding Fathers believed certain truths to be *self-evident*. They believed in a Creator, in the dignity and equality of man, in government of the people, by the people, and for the people, and in the inalienable rights of man which are protected by the government. These basic, unchangeable principles have guaranteed, among other things, the individual's right to disagree with these ideas, and, of course, many do disagree.

We have mentioned that it is very important to American democracy that we find an answer to the question of whether or not there is objective truth. If there is no such thing as objective truth, then the self-evident truths mentioned by the Founding Fathers are a fantasy, and there are no such things as inalienable rights. A philosophy of change does not admit objective truth, and would not admit to rights that could never be taken away from the individual. A philosophy of change would hold that what we now regard as true, and what we now regard as rights, may not apply in the future. Consequently, if this philosophy became prevalent in our democracy, it is conceivable that changes could be legislated in the Constitution that would legally remove our inalienable rights, if it were deemed expedient. Therefore, if we are to preserve our rights and insure against the possibility of the individual becoming subservient to the state, we must continue to plant our educational system in a democratic philosophy of education which is based on *permanent* basic values and principles. If we do not, we will erode the principles of our democracy.

THE IMPORTANCE OF A TEACHER'S PHILOSOPHY

It has been said that a landlord is interested in the financial status of a prospective tenant, but even more interested in the prospective tenant's philosophy; i.e., whether or not his principles include meeting his responsibilities and obligations. In the field of education, it is important to know whether or not a teacher is well versed in his subject and the techniques of teaching. It is even more important to know his basic philosophy.

The teacher's philosophy will affect his entire approach to education. His philosophy will determine how he will try to influence his pupils, what kind of character he will help to form, what kind of ideas, attitudes, ideals, and habits he will try to inculcate, and how he will interpret and evaluate his subject matter. Educators feel, without exception, that a sound philosophy should be a basic qualification possessed by a teacher. If it is not a sound philosophy, the teacher's aims, procedures, and interpretation of his subject matter will be faulty, and his pupils may receive a damaging type of education.

In our democratic society we should have as teachers, individuals who have been grounded in, accept, and are loyal to our democratic principles. Our teachers should keep an open mind to new developments in education, but should keep their democratic principles, and should evaluate new developments in terms of our basic philosophy. Teachers should not feel that they are old-fashioned if they do not accept new practices. The latest is not always the best, and sometimes it can be the worst.

Until he is convinced that a new idea in education is philosophically sound, the teacher can adhere to proven methods in education. Frequently he can combine new ideas with the old. For example, although he may recognize that interest and "felt needs" are powerful motivating forces, he also may realize that these can and should be stimulated from the outside environment when they do not come from within the pupil. He can urge his pupils to be as active as possible in learning because he knows that no learning can occur without self-activity. At the same time he knows the importance of bringing this activity under the mature, experienced guidance and direction of the teacher. He recognizes that education is a privilege whereby latent talents can be developed, but he can help his pupils to realize that they are not permitted indiscriminate expression of their interests and desires.

The teacher's philosophy of education then, will determine what principles are taught, and how they are taught, to our future citizens. If pupils are influenced by teachers who believe in a God, who accept and respect the idea of the dignity of the individual, who know, communicate, and live the principles of democracy, there is a most potent force operating in educating pupils for good citizenship.

However, the function of the teacher goes beyond the knowledge and the teaching of these things. Pupils learn by example. If a teacher hopes to inculcate high ideals and worthy principles in his pupils, he must exemplify them in his daily living. He cannot, for example, teach freedom of expression, but stifle legitimate expressions of opinion in the classroom. He cannot hold up freedom of worship as an ideal, and at the same time belittle the religious practices of his pupils. He cannot point out the equality of individuals, and make distinctions on the basis of nationality, religion, or race. If he *does*, his *teachings* will fail.

Teachers have an opportunity, challenge, and responsibility in educating our future citizens. As long as they remain in the profession they have no alternative: they *must* accept that role. The preservation of our democracy depends upon *how well* they discharge their responsibilities.

SUMMARY

Philosophy, which is the study of the ultimate causes of things through the use of reason, permeates our entire existence. Each individual, through his own resources and through external influences, arrives at certain principles which he uses to interpret and evaluate the meaning of life and life's activities. His principles will determine his character, and, as he lives in accordance with these principles, his character will be reflected in his daily activities.

A philosophy of education is built upon a philosophy of life. Before we can do anything in education, it is necessary to set up objectives; before we can formulate objectives, we must consider our philosophy of life for an interpretation of the nature of the individual and the purpose of his existence. Only then can objectives lead to the proper development of the individual and to the fulfillment of life's purposes. Our philosophy of life not only influences the objectives of education but also permeates the entire educational process, including content and methodology.

Not everyone accepts the same philosophy of life. Because of differences in philosophy, we have many philosophies of education, some of which are conflicting. Of these, some must, of necessity, be in error. Therefore, there are, in operation, erroneous philosophies of education which do not train the student according to his true nature toward proper goals.

In our democracy, one of the purposes of education is the transmission and perpetuation of our democratic heritage. Our objectives of education, therefore, should reflect the principles upon which our democracy was founded: the equality of all men in the eyes of their Creator, from Whom they have received inalienable rights which must be protected by the state. The Founding Fathers believed that informed, moral citizens were necessary to good government, and they felt that education should help to produce the moral man who would work toward his own development and contribute to the common good.

As our republic developed, the following ideas and practices took root: equality of educational opportunity, public support of schools through taxation, compulsory attendance, and separation of church and state. Throughout the years, there have been many expressions of educational objectives which differ because of the diverse interpretations of the nature and destiny of man. In modern times, the 1938 and 1951 reports of the Educational Policies Commission of the National Education Association may be taken as a representative statement of the objectives for our public schools.

Education is conducted by formal agencies (the family, the church, and the school), but informal agencies (radio, press, television, etc.) also considerably influence the individual. The family may choose the type of education it wishes for its children, but it should cooperate with the church and the state for the temporal and spiritual welfare of the child. The state may insist on certain standards of education, but it can not usurp the authority of the family by insisting on a standardized type of education. Neither the family nor the state can develop fully the individual's moral-religious nature; this may be accomplished by the church of the individual's choice. Informal agencies of education exert a positive or negative influence on the development of the person; whether or not the influence is beneficial depends on parental supervision and the individual's self-control.

The question of objective or relative truth is important to the maintenance and continuation of our democratic ideals and ideas. Our democracy rests on an acceptance of objective truth. Yet proponents of philosophies of change believe that everything is in a constant state of change. The prevalence of this type of philosophy might endanger the survival of our democratic society because it does not admit unchanging inalienable rights.

A philosophy of education is possessed by every teacher. It affects his entire approach to education and determines the individuals we will leave behind us to carry on our democratic way of living. It is extremely important, therefore, that our teachers possess a philosophy of education which is in harmony with our democratic principles.

Questions for discussion:

1. Contrast the rights of the individual in a democratic society with the rights of an individual in a totalitarian state.

2. Think of a specific example of a teacher's philosophy influencing his interpretation of subject matter.

3. What does John Dewey's idea that education is a continuous recon-struction of experience mean?

4. How do moral principles penetrate the "wall of separation" that has arisen between church and state?

5. Find published evidence that philosophies which are inimical to our democracy are sometimes taught in our schools.

For further reading:

Brubacher, John S., ed., *Eclectic Philosophy of Education*. New York: Pren-tice-Hall, Inc., 1951.

Carron, Malcolm, and Alfred D. Cavanaugh, ed., *Readings in the Philos-ophy of Education*. Detroit: The University of Detroit Press, 1963.

Dewey, John, *Democracy and Education*. New York: The Macmillan Com-pany, 1916.

Henry, Nelson B., ed., *Philosophies of Education*, Forty-First Yearbook, Na-tional Society for the Study of Education, Part I. Chicago: National Society for the Study of Education, 1942.

Maritain, Jacques, *Education at the Crossroads*. New Haven: Yale University Press, 1943.

National Education Association and American Association of School Admin-istrators, Educational Policies Commission, *Moral and Spiritual Values in the Public Schools*. Washington, D.C.: the Commission, 1951.

_____*The Purposes of Education in American Democracy*. Washington, D.C.: the Commission, 1938.

Park, Joe, ed., *Selected Readings in the Philosophy of Education*. 2nd ed., New York: the Macmillan Company, 1963.

Woelfel, Norman, *Molders of the American Mind*. New York: Columbia Uni-versity Press, 1933.

2

European Backgrounds of American Education

Education in the colonies began in a vacuum, as the colonists did not have a system of education awaiting them on their arrival. However, when they turned to the problem of education, the vacuum was filled by the inflow of ideas, traditions, and beliefs brought from Europe. Because the colonists tried to organize education after their European pattern, we did not have, to begin with, a uniquely American system of education. Consequently, to understand and appreciate the development of education in the United States, it is necessary to become familiar with the European educational practices and influences that were brought into the colonies.

Obviously, a complete exposition of European education can be found only in books devoted to the history of education. Yet, it is possible in a brief summary to describe the highlights of its history. This chapter will concentrate on these highlights, general trends and influences in European education, which affected, in the seventeenth century, the people who were to colonize our country. We also will note later European ideas, which have influenced American education during the last three centuries.

HEBREW, GREEK, AND ROMAN INFLUENCES

We seldom realize that our present civilization is a selective cumulation of ancient history. Although many things that happened did not make a permanent impression on the minds of men, some people and ideas from the past continue to influence us. The Hebrews, Greeks, and Romans, made important contributions which have helped to mould western civilization and education into its present shape. Changes, of course, took place, but parts of the foundation of the future, and even some of its superstructure, were built and still remain. The important contributions of the Hebrews, Romans, and Greeks occurred over a period of a thousand years, from about 500 B.C. to the collapse of the Roman Empire in 476 A.D.

Hebrew Contributions

The early history of the Hebrews extends over a period of about 2,000 years before the birth of Christ. The last five hundred years of this period exposed them to the influence of the Greeks and Romans.

Since the Hebrews regarded themselves as the people chosen by God to reveal His wishes, the religious element predominated in their way of life and their education. The prophets, said to be divinely inspired, and the scribes, who were regarded as lacking divine inspiration were their teachers. Religion and religious training permeated everything in Hebrew society. The major objective of education was to train an individual who would please his Creator. Although vocational training was important, because an untrained boy would become a parasite on society, preparation for an after-life overshadowed everything else. During the period of Graeco-Roman influences they evaluated these influences in terms of their religious beliefs, resisting anything that they felt would jeopardize their religion.

Interestingly enough, the Hebrews developed many practices in education which are commonplace today. For example, they believed that teachers should be selected with great care, a matter receiving much attention today. The following are other ideas held by them, and substantially acceptable today: class size should be limited to twenty-five pupils; learning is more effective if it appeals to several senses; mnemonic devices aid memory; drill is necessary to fix learning; the content of elementary education should include the 3 R's, history, religion, and vocational training; and, education should be compulsory, although only male children received it.[1]

However, western civilization and education is chiefly indebted to the Hebrews for their emphasis on and maintenance of moral-spiritual

---

[1]Stephen Duggan, *A Student's Textbook in the History of Education* (New York: Appleton-Century-Crofts, Inc., 1948), pp. 11-12.

values. The Hebrews kept these values in spite of their exposure to the pagan beliefs and practices of the Greeks and Romans. By doing this, and by preserving their literature, they paved the way for another moral-spiritual force which was to have profound effects on western civilization: Christianity.

Contributions of the Greeks

It should be noted that two very different types of societies and educational practices existed among the Greeks. In Sparta, which was a socialistic society, the individual was submerged to the good of the state, and education consisted of rigorous, and sometimes brutal, physical training. Conversely, education in Athens, a democratic society (although there existed a large slave population), was largely intellectual and aesthetic. It was the Athenian society that left a rich legacy to western civilization.

The most significant contributions were made after Athens became a republic in 509 B.C. Under the republic, any talented citizen could participate in state affairs. To do so, however, he needed skill in public speaking and argumentation. This created a need and a demand for teachers who could prepare individuals for careers in public affairs. A group of philosophers and teachers known as Sophists, discouraged by their inability to arrive at ultimate truth, turned their attention to teaching public speaking, debate, and specious reasoning. Believing that "man is the measure of all things", and that everything is a matter of opinion, they criticized everything in Greek society, including religion and conduct. Their movement set the stage for a higher religion and the development of the science of ethics. They stimulated others through their faulty argumentation to develop the science of logic. They themselves founded the science of grammar, because it was needed as a preparation for teaching effective speech. The Sophists conducted private schools, and charged for instruction. One of the greatest Sophist teachers was Isocrates (436 B.C.–338 B.C.) who conducted a school which attracted students from all over the Greek-speaking world.

In addition to grammar, rhetoric, and politics, many Sophists taught other subjects such as mathematics, geography, astronomy, history, music, art, and athletics. Although early attempts were made to organize a definite curriculum, it was a gradual process which was not completed until around the time of Christ. When completed, it consisted of what was later termed by Cassidorus (480–575) as The Seven

Liberal Arts,[2] and was accepted as the standard curriculum for a liberal education in preparation for the study of philosophy. This curriculum influenced the content of education, with varying degrees of emphasis, for over fifteen hundred years. Its influence was felt throughout western Europe; it became the content of medieval university education, and was still an influence during the colonial period in America.

Although the subjects of the Seven Liberal Arts can be identified readily, the content of the subjects, of course, varied with the knowledge and needs of the times.[3] The following outline is only an indication of the content in these studies.

Content of The Seven Liberal Arts
Ancient and Medieval
Trivium

Grammar: technical grammar (the rules of grammar) and exegetical grammar (the study of literature.) Philosophical grammar, concerned with logic, was also taught as part of the subject.

Rhetoric: the science and art of effective speech. Included in this were composition, public speaking, and debate during Greek and Roman life. During the Middle Ages, it also came to be applied to writing letters, documents, and study of law. In the curriculum, the study of rhetoric was connected with the study of literature. Literature also included the study of history.

Dialectic: the science of correct thinking (logic). Logic was required everywhere for a degree in medieval universities. Scholastic philosophy developed around logic.

Quadrivium

Arithmetic: the Greeks taught practical arithmetic and theoretical arithmetic. During the Middle Ages, it was taught mainly in connection with the use of the calendar and church seasons. There was no great progress in practical arithmetic until the 13th century; with the rise of commercial life and cities, stress was laid on keeping accounts. After the publication of the first printed arithmetic book in 1476, progress in arithmetic was very rapid.

Geometry: the study of the elements of Euclid. It also embraced some study of geography and surveying.

---

[2]Paul Abelson, *The Seven Liberal Arts* (New York: Teachers College, Columbia University, 1906), p. 9.

[3]*Ibid.* Abelson gives a detailed and scholarly discussion of the content of the Seven Liberal Arts.

Astronomy: local and general geography, and natural science were taught as a preparation for astronomy.
Music: both practical and theoretical music were studied.

Note: the study of philosophy was considered to be the capstone of The Seven Liberal Arts.

Subjects were divided into two groups: trivium, embracing what might be termed literary subjects, and the quadrivium, including the mathematical studies. For approximately fifteen centuries, the subjects of the trivium received the dominant emphasis; only within the last two centuries have the sciences received emphasis.

Although the Sophists had given up their search for ultimate truth, some philosophers continued this type of speculation. The three outstanding Greek philosophers were Socrates, Plato, and Aristotle. They, too, taught their theories, but were not professional teachers, as were the Sophists, because they did not charge for instruction.

Socrates (469 B.C.–399 B.C.) was concerned with improving the moral character of the people. He is credited with founding the science of ethics, and formulating "universal definitions", i.e., definitions that could be applied to a whole class of things. He is known for his use of the question and answer teaching method, which became known as the "Socratic method." In this method, Socrates used the knowledge his pupils already had, and through a series of questions and answers led his pupils to the desired conclusion. This method still is used in classrooms throughout the world.

Plato (427 B.C.–347 B.C.), a pupil of Socrates, established a school of philosophy in Athens, where he taught for most of his life. He felt that an ideal state could be brought about through education. Although he set forth his educational theories in his *Republic,* they were never put into practice. His theory of education was socialistic, but his plan did provide for individual differences in training individuals for their roles in the state. The study of Plato's philosophy formed a part of the content in education for many centuries, and, for a time, was a dominant influence in philosophical thought.

Aristotle (384 B.C.–322 B.C.) studied under Plato, and eventually came to outshine his teacher. In fact, he has been regarded by many as "The Master" among philosophers, as he developed the syllogistic form of logic. He believed that education should be determined by the nature of the individual, which he regarded as dual (body and soul), and by the nature of the state to which the individual belongs. He held that the state should be concerned with the education of its members because they contributed to the welfare of the state.[4] He also felt that the family should play an important part in the education of their children. The best type of education, he felt, was a liberal education.[5] Aristotle had little influence in his own time, but his philosophy became an important part of scholastic philosophy after the twelfth century. It can be seen, too, that his broad ideas still dominate the thinking of many people today.

In addition to making contributions to the content of education, the Greeks also organized schools into elementary, secondary, and higher. They had private elementary and secondary schools, schools of rhetoric, and universities, all of which formed the basis for the later refinements of this type of organization.

The Greeks also made great contributions to the field of fine arts. Their architecture is still a source of admiration. They produced many capable dramatists, such as Aeschylus, Sophocles, and Euripides in tragedy; and Thucydides in comedy. Heroditus also is well known as an historian, while Demosthenes always is mentioned as an outstanding example in oratory.

Greek education was a training for a life of elegant leisure, with a large slave population to do the work. The Greeks succeeded in achieving their objective, but their progress was halted (although their influence remained) by the Roman conqueror.

Roman Education

Whereas the Greeks were speculative, the Romans were a practical people. Their important contributions to western civilization were in law and social organization.

In early Roman education, from 753 B.C. (when Rome was founded) to about the middle of the third century B.C. (when Greek influence began to be felt), the home was the chief educational agency. The emphasis was on the practical development of the individual so that he could better serve the state as a worker, citizen, and soldier. The objective of education was the cultivation of the *vir bonus*, the "good

---

[4]The acceptance of this idea forms the basic justification for compulsory education today.

[5]At present, there is again emphasis on the desirability of a liberal education as part of all types of professional training. Aristotle held that liberal education was education for its own sake, and not for the sake of something else.

man", who developed and exercised practical virtues such as industry, honesty, prudence, fortitude, piety, and obedience.

In 509 B.C., Rome became a republic and the common people (plebeians) struggled to obtain the same rights which were held by the nobles (patricians). They partially succeeded when the codification of Roman law into the Laws of the Twelve Tables began in 451 B.C. These laws stressed a philosophy of self-discipline. However, as the Romans conquered the Greeks, and absorbed Greek educational ideas and practices, a philosophy of pleasure and self-indulgence became evident in Roman education. After 146 B.C., when Rome had completed the conquest of Greece, education became Graeco-Roman. The Latinized version of Homer's *Odyssey* (translated by Livius Andronicus, a Greek slave) was a major influence in changing the Roman philosophy of education.

Later Roman education continued its objective of the *vir bonus*, but changed the training for the "good man". Earlier training of the *vir bonus* meant the training of the orator, an individual who was morally good, an effective speaker, knowledgeable and competent in the affairs of state. Later, as Tacitus (50–117 A.D.) indicated training of the orator declined, became superficial because of its artificial imitation of form, and minimized moral training.

Among the many persons who could be mentioned in Roman education two must be mentioned as figures of outstanding importance: Cicero and Quintilian. Both of these men remained an influence on education for centuries.

Cicero (106–43 B.C.) outlined his idea of the orator in his *De Oratore* (55 B.C.). An accomplished orator, he was widely imitated. He greatly influenced the style of oratory not only in his time but also during the Renaissance, thirteen centuries later. The term "Ciceronianism" has been applied to narrow imitations of his style.

Quintilian (c. 35 A.D.–c. 100 A.D.) was also a highly respected orator. He too outlined his ideal training of the orator in his *De Institutione Oratoria*, which began with the education a boy should receive before entering a school of rhetoric. A study of the principles of education advocated by him shows how advanced he was. Many of the principles he advocated are still widely accepted and practiced. For example:

1. Relaxation and play, in moderation, are necessary for children.
2. The child can learn much during his pre-school years.
3. Learning should be made attractive for the child.
4. Individual differences should be considered.

5. Sensory impressions are important in learning.
6. Attention span of children is short because they fatigue readily.
7. There should be no corporal punishment.
8. The qualifications of teachers should be high.
9. Care should be taken in the selection of teachers.
10. There should be close contact between the teacher and his pupils.

Quintilian's principles exerted an influence in his own time, but he was forgotten throughout the Middle Ages. His ideas were resurrected when Roman manuscripts were again studied during the Renaissance period; his ideas were incorporated into the educational theories of da Feltre and Vives. From the Renaissance to the present, Quintilian's principles have been stated and re-stated in different ways. Rusk comments on Quintilian's influence as follows:

> Quintilian's *Institutes* is the most comprehensive, if not the most systematic, treatise on rhetoric in existence; it doubtless appeared too late to influence Roman education greatly, but it was regarded by the renaissance educators as the standard and authoritative work on education, and through them it assisted in fashioning educational training throughout Europe up to quite modern times.[6]

It can be seen that the Hebrews, Greeks and Romans contributed to much of our basic framework of modern education. Their broad contributions consisted of: emphasis on moral training by the Hebrews; intellectual and aesthetic progress by the Greeks; and, the development of law and social organization by the Romans. Their schools were organized into three levels, the content of education was organized into specific subjects, and many sound principles of education were formulated. Professional training could be obtained in the Universities of Rome, Athens, and Alexandria in law, medicine, architecture, and philosophy.

THE INFLUENCE OF CHRISTIANITY

Five centuries before the fall of the Roman Empire and the closing of its schools, Christ came to earth. With the acceptance of His teachings, the objective of Christian education became the salvation of souls.

---

[6]Robert R. Rusk, *The Doctrines of the Great Educators* (London: Macmillan & Co., Ltd., 1954), p. 50.

New ideas and forces were accepted by the Christian: all men were regarded as equal in the eyes of God; each individual would attain everlasting happiness or punishment in an afterlife; and Christ to carry on His teachings, established a church which would offer the individual supernatural aids in achieving his destiny.

The Romans, however, suppressed Christian education. Nevertheless, the Christians established cathechumenal schools in which instruction prepared the learner for baptism. They also conducted catechetical schools, which gave a higher form of instruction, enabling Christians to support and defend their faith. It was not until the Edict of Milan, in 313, that the Christians were freed from persecution.

In the interim, many Christians attended the Graeco-Roman schools, as they were the only schools in existence at the time. Some Christians frowned on this attendance, feeling that it would jeopardize their faith. Other Christians felt that their faith was strong enough to ward off any pagan influences.[7]

Christianity exerted a powerful influence on education and society. In Christian schools, religion and theology became dominant in the curriculum, and the ultimate objective of education became eternal salvation. A variety of Christian schools developed during the Middle Ages, and Christian education was to remain a major influence thereafter.

Contributions of the Middle Ages

The Roman Empire gradually crumbled under the onslaught of barbarian invaders, and Rome fell in 476 A.D. Chronologically, its fall marked the beginning of the Middle Ages. With the Graeco-Roman schools gone, the Christians concerned themselves with the problem of education. Because they lacked experience and money, their progress was slow. However, if it were not for the educational efforts of the Church during this period, organized education would not have developed. The Middle Ages began as a period of darkness, with an occasional bright light shining through, reached a period of relative splendor, and was again overcast with shadows.

Early in the Middle Ages, monasticism developed. A group of laymen formed a community under the religious vows of poverty, chastity, obedience, and, occasionally, stability, which bound the individual to his particular monastery. Each monastery was autonomous and adopted

---

[7]Today this argument takes the form of separation of church and state in education.

its own rules. Since there was no common organizational or administrative bond between the monasteries, monastic life became lax and ineffective. The Rule of St. Benedict, a set of rules written at Monte Cassino in 520 improved this situation. Simple and appealing, the Rule emphasized the dignity of labor, obedience, and the spirit of Christian democracy. It was adopted by thousands of monasteries in Europe, however, each monastery remained autonomous.

The Rule of St. Benedict specified (among other things), that the monks had to read daily. Since many of them were unable to read, it became necessary to establish schools, and monastic schools came into existence. Eventually both internal schools, for the training of monks, and external schools, for the education of the laity, developed. At first only elementary education was offered, but gradually secondary education was also given.

Besides conducting schools, the monks preserved the literature of the past, copying the manuscripts in the writing room (scriptorium), and keeping them in the library (armarium). In addition, many monasteries became the centers of commerce, with the monks building roads, reclaiming swamp lands, and fostering trade and industry. Monasticism, then, was an important influence in education and medieval society.

Although the Rule of St. Benedict provided a practical guide for the administration of monasteries, the rules were not always observed, and, at times, there was considerable degeneration among the members of individual monasteries. Yet, on the whole, monasticism made distinct, positive contributions during those early centuries.

The Decree of Vaison in 528, a Church edict, called for the establishment of rural parishes and the maintenance of schools in those parishes. Cathedral schools were also established, at each bishop's seat, in order to train future clergymen. Some cathedral schools had external schools for the education of the laity and became important seats of learning. Later, during the Middle Ages, some of these schools developed into universities.

One of the bright lights of the Middle Ages occurred around 800 under the leadership of Charlemagne who welded together most of Europe under his rule. Having little education, but great respect for it, he felt that it would better knit his empire. To help promote education, he imported from England a monk named Alcuin, headmaster of the York cathedral school.

Alcuin, who arrived at Charlemagne's palace school at Aachen in 782, was a diligent, sincere, humble individual and an excellent teacher. The palace school under him became famous, attracting as students not only Charlemagne's family but also notable personages from all over the empire. In addition, Alcuin personally supervised the correction of errors in liturgical literature. He introduced script writing, and a system of punctuation to make the manuscripts more legible and readable.

To promote education throughout his empire, Charlemange employed Alcuin in issuing a series of capitularies, urging the monks to become literate, and urging the establishment of schools throughout the empire. His attempt at universal education was not successful, even though he sent out inspectors to see how well his orders were followed.

After Charlemagne's death, Europe once more entered a period of darkness. Society disintegrated and feudalism arose as the means of social organization. Although this system fostered social inequality and permitted each lord the right of warfare, it helped to prevent complete anarchy in Europe.

It was not until the tenth century that more light filtered through the darkness with the Cluniac Reform which began in a monastery at Cluny. The Cluny monastery, founded by Berno in 910, provided the social organization and moral reform that Europe needed. Berno persuaded five other monasteries to accept the central authority of Cluny. Gradually, other monasteries voluntarily submitted to Cluny's authority, and by the twelfth century 314 Benedictine houses were under the rule of Cluny.[8] In addition to bringing about a stable social organization, Cluny was responsible for widespread moral reform. Inspired by the example of the monks, who led truly holy lives, the moral tone of Europe was raised among clergy and laity alike.

The eleventh century brought a revival of interest in things intellectual. An immediate stimulus to intellectual education came from the monastery at Bec, where Lanfranc, a learned Italian monk, taught in 1042. From Bec, through Lanfranc, intellectual curiosity spread to other parts of Europe.

Much of the material for intellectual education came from the Saracens who had gradually spread their domain across northern Africa, advanced into Spain, and were contained there after the Battle of Tours of 732. The Saracens had developed an amazingly advanced culture during the period that Europe stagnated. Beginning about 650, Saracen education made rapid progress, and reached its peak in Spain around the middle of the eleventh century. An acquisitive and inquisitive people, they made advances in mathematics, physical sciences, art, literature, philosophy, medicine, law, and the crafts. They had pre-

---

[8]William T. Kane and John J. O'Brien, *History of Education* (Chicago: Loyola University Press, 1954), p. 84.

served many of the ancient classical writings; including the writings of Aristotle, with commentaries by Avicenna an eleventh century Persian, and Averroes a twelfth century Spaniard.

Much of the Saracen culture seeped into Europe from Spain, and flooded Europe after the Christians had reconquered Spain. Just at the time the European mind was ready for an intellectual revival, the content was provided.

The institution of chivalry and the crusades were further educational influences and contributing factors to an exchange of ideas. Much of the training for future knighthood was moral, and the individual went through definite stages of training as a page, squire, and knight. His training, which culminated at the age of twenty-one with a religious ceremony, usually involved personal service to a lady or lord, as well as preparation for warfare. Important educational effects resulted from the Crusades to the Holy Land. The study of geography, astronomy, and navigation became important. Chivalry and the crusades inspired literary effort, and an eastern influence in art and literature became discernable. New products and inventions were brought to Europe by the returning knights, thus stimulating commerce and industry. Towns arose to meet the needs of the crusaders, and others arose to process or manufacture the new products.

The new towns were, by agreement or struggle, free from church and feudal authority. Within the towns, guilds, associations of individuals who were engaged in certain types of work, were formed. There were guilds of various types, but the most numerous were the craft guilds, which were similar to our present trade unions. The individual who aspired to become a weaver or goldsmith, for example, went through three stages of training: apprentice, journeyman, and master. The apprentice was taken into the home of a master, where he spent from two to ten years, depending on the craft he was learning. After his apprenticeship, he spent an average of three years as a journeyman, at the end of which he submitted to the guild a sample of his work (his "masterpiece"). If his work measured up to guild standards, he then became a master, who, in turn, would be eligible to train apprentices. In addition to the training given by the master craftsman, guilds conducted schools in which the guild chaplain gave elementary instruction to children. Burgher schools, supported by the town, also provided children with an elementary education. Song schools were established by patrons who wanted Masses sung, but in many of these schools the priest instructed children in rudimentary learning.

Perhaps the greatest contribution to intellectual education during the Middle Ages was scholasticism, which consisted of a vigorous intellectual training centering around logic. It was an attempt to support faith with reason. The schoolmen held that there could be no contradiction between faith and reason, because all truth originated with God Who cannot contradict Himself. If one reasoned logically, they held, he should be able to support, on a rational basis, those truths which were believed to have been revealed by God.

Scholasticism gained momentum during the eleventh century, reached its most fruitful period under Thomas Aquinas during the thirteenth century, and declined during the fourteenth century. During its growth, the schoolmen built up a complete system of philosophy, which rested heavily on the teachings of Aristotle and Aquinas and was known as scholastic philosophy. Unfortunately, scholasticism during the Middle Ages fell out of touch with the times. In succeeding centuries, scholastic philosophers turned their attention to the interpretation and solution of contemporary problems. Nevertheless, scholastic philosophy, especially as formulated by Thomas Aquinas, still has widespread acceptance today.

There have been heated discussions over the relative merits of scholasticism. A dispassionate appraisal will show that it had both advantages and disadvantages. Monroe states:

> That scholasticism was a tremendous advance in intellectual life beyond that of the early Middle Ages is evident; that it possessed some decided merits peculiar to itself is at least suggested by the previous discussion; that it served as the only education of the higher or intellectual type for several centuries, and produced a succession of great men unsurpassed in their intellectual acumen, has been noted. For all that, by the fifteenth century scholasticism reached its limits, degenerated into mere form, and became an obstacle to further progress, so that it had to be cast aside as outgrown and useless by the Renaissance movement of that period.[9]

With the increase in knowledge, the inclination to probe beyond the accepted formulas, and the trend toward more detailed knowledge in specific fields, higher institutions of learning developed: the universities. Some universities grew out of existing cathedral schools, for example, the University of Paris. Some began as a result of the migration of students from one university to another location. Others simply sprang up where a group of students and teachers gathered together to form a university. These universities were granted a charter by the Church or

---

[9]Paul Monroe, *A Textbook in the History of Education* (New York: The Macmillan Company, 1933), p. 307. For a more detailed evaluation, see pp. 302-313.

by the town in which they originated. Both students and teachers enjoyed special privileges, such as freedom from military service and taxation, and trial by university personnel for any offenses they may have committed. Although the exact date of origin is unknown for many universities, Bologna, Salerno, Oxford, and Paris were among the first to be founded. Bologna is said to have been chartered in 1158, and Paris was fully recognized by 1200.[10] In England, Oxford was known to exist in 1189, and Cambridge in 1231, although they may have been established earlier.[11] Between 1100 and 1250, there were fourteen or fifteen universities in Europe. By the time of the Reformation this number had increased to about eighty.[12]

The universities systematized knowledge and gave vigorous intellectual training. As time went on, however, their inordinate concern with logic resulted in a narrow, superficial type of intellectual education. Logical distinctions and sub-distinctions were so fine that one author classified the schools as "logic-chopping machines."[13] Yet their basic organization is still in use today.

The people of the Middle Ages slowly trudged upward from the darkness, in which they found themselves after the collapse of the Roman empire. By the thirteenth century, they had reached a relatively high plateau of civilization and learning. They had evolved a variety of schools at all levels; and their universities would stand as their greatest educational achievement. Education was reaching more and more people, not only through the schools but also through guild training. In the churches and cathedrals they built, they had made great contributions to architecture. They preserved and revived the learning of the past, and made some contributions of their own to it, such as the distinctly medieval drama. The "Dark Ages" or the Middle Ages were only dark at some times; at other times, they were positively brilliant.

Various factors contributed to the break-up of medieval solidarity. The Church had been the unifying force of society. Most education had been carried on under her auspices. However, considerable dissention arose among the churchmen; some of them set their authority above the authority of the Church. Corruption in politics and morals developed among them, and with the appearance of rival Popes, the authority and prestige of the Church was further weakened. Latin had been

[10]*Ibid.*, p. 316. Hastings Rashdall disagrees, placing the date of Paris at 1210.

[11]Arthur F. Leach, *Educational Charters and Documents* (Cambridge: Cambridge University Press, 1911), pp. xxiv-xxv.

[12]William T. Kane and John J. O'Brien, *op. cit.*, p. 102.

[13]*Ibid.*, p. 142.

the universal language in education, but the growing spirit of nationalism introduced and spread the use of the vernacular. Scholasticism became sterile, and the universities, sometimes so influenced by politics that a doctorate degree could be bought, did not show the same enthusiasm for learning as they did before. Wars in England, France, Germany, and Italy during the fourteenth century had a further disintegrating influence. Finally, the Black Death plague decimated the population of Europe, killing nearly half of the people. This plague killed thousands of priests, who taught in the majority of schools; ordained men without sufficient training, took their place. With all of these contributing factors, it is small wonder that the Middle Ages came to an end and yielded to new forces and influences.

The Renaissance

The factors that contributed to the end of the Middle Ages were, in reality, some of the conditions which brought about the Renaissance. The social and economic conditions brought about by the crusades and the guilds, the growing importance of the free cities and the merchant class, the advent of printing and the greater availability of books further contributed to the arrival of the Renaissance.

Often the Renaissance is described as a rebirth of learning, a return to the study of Greek and Roman classical literature. As a movement, it lasted for about two centuries, from about 1350 to 1550. It began in Italy and gradually spread to northern Europe, where it was different in spirit and approach. The Italian Renaissance stressed the individual, and individual development. The objective of education became worldly. Fame, pleasure, and individual success were sought. In northern Europe, the Renaissance emphasized religion and social reform.

Petrarch (1304–1374) is considered to be the prime mover of the Renaissance in Italy. He reacted strongly against the Church and scholastic philosophy, substituting for it a devotion to the Latin classics. As he especially admired Cicero, he was instrumental in reviving Ciceronian Latin.

Manuel Chrysoloras, who came from Constantinople in 1397 to teach Greek at the University of Florence, really revived classical Greek. He was a successful teacher, had many prominent scholars as his students, and aroused a widespread interest in reviving Greek language and literature.

In northern Europe, the spirit of social reform received impetus from the Brethren of the Common Life who devoted themselves to teaching among the poor. Adapting their methods to the needs of their pupils, they were successful in their teaching and spread their work from their native Holland to France and Germany. Gradually, some of their members went to Italy to study, and absorbed the spirit of the study of the classics.

The return to classical antiquity for the study of man and his problems became known as humanism. Depending on how the classics were approached, various classifications of humanism evolved: broad, narrow, Christian, or pagan. *Broad* humanists studied the classics and built upon the knowledge therein; *narrow* humanists accepted the views or style of the classical writers as their goal in learning and life. Similarly, *Christian* humanists held to their religious beliefs and evaluated the classics from the Christian point of view; *pagan* humanists adopted the ideals expressed in the classics. Various combinations of these forms of humanism were possible, so that there were broad and narrow Christian humanists, as well as broad and narrow pagan humanists.

Three of the many educators who might be mentioned as representative of the Renaissance period, deserve special consideration: da Feltre, Erasmus, and Vives. Da Feltre and Vives were representatives of board, Christian humanism, while Erasmus is an example of narrow Christian humanism.

Vittorino da Feltre (1378–1446) ran one of the most famous schools of the Reniassance at Mantua. Opened in 1423, it was called *Casa Giocosa* (Pleasant House), which reflected the atmosphere and environment of the school. Da Feltre believed that education should take place in pleasant surroundings, and that study should be interspersed with games and other recreational activities. Feeling that humanistic education should combine the classics and Christian faith, much time was spent in oral reading, declamation, and composition.The following represent a few more of his ideas. A strong body is necessary for mental efficiency; subjects should be varied, and should be adapted to the mental level of pupils. The teacher, he felt, should uncover a pupil's potentialities, and liberal education should precede his vocational training. Although young children should be carefully supervised in order to avoid bad habits, discipline should be mild. Da Feltre was a model of pious and reverent life he encouraged his pupils to lead.

Da Feltre's school, of course, was not typical of Renaissance schools; it was an outstanding school, and for that reason always receives mention in histories of education.

Juan Luis Vives (1492–1540) is recognized as the most thorough educator of the Renaissance period. Born in Spain, he was educated at the University of Paris and the University of Louvain, where he exchanged ideas with Erasmus and other notable humanists of the time. Following his education he became a teacher and a prolific writer. His greatest educational writing was entitled *De Tradendis Disciplinis,* which not only criticized contemporary education but also offered positive suggestions.

Most of his ideas were not new; da Feltre and Quintilian had stated many of them previously. However, Vives attempted to apply his educational principles to contemporary life, by, for example, emphasizing the study of the vernacular before studying the classics. This, and the emphasis he placed on sensory impressions and the use of the inductive method, classify him not only as a verbal realist but also as a sense realist.[14] Vives recommended minimizing rote memory in learning. Instead of studying the rules of grammar, he advocated learning them through their usage in reading. He emphasized obtaining and training teachers of high caliber and believed in teacher consultations on the progress of pupils. For girls, he advocated a separate curriculum. Throughout his educational theory, he stressed character formation.

Although he borrowed many of his ideas, later writers quoted occasionally verbatim, his ideas as their own, without acknowledging him. Some authorities considered him to be the founder of educational psychology, because his *De Anima* used inductive methods to apply psychology to education. Thus, Kane can state:

> A long lifetime before Francis Bacon, a century before Comenius, a dozen years even before there had begun, with Copernicus, the great era of scientific discoveries, Vives urged the importance of nature studies carried out by new methods of observation and experiment. He was not merely the precursor of Francis Bacon in demanding a wider use of the inductive method but vastly his superior in applying that method. All the authors who have studied Vives show that he was the real founder of educational psychology.[15]

Erasmus (1466–1536) was typical of northern Renaissance humanists who worked for social reforms but did not break with the authority of the Church. He is considered in the category of narrow humanism, because of his insistence upon a classical education for boys as well as girls. He felt that Latin should be taught as a living language and

---

[14]See pp. 46–47 for an explanation of these terms.
[15]William T. Kane and John J. O'Brien, *op. cit.,* p. 208.

the study of grammar deferred to a later time. Latin scholarship and education became synonymous to him. He favored establishing public schools, but limiting schooling to those who had the ability to profit by it. He further recommended mild discipline, and the use of concrete illustrations in teaching. Although a prolific writer, he is not as famous for his educational theories as for his satires of the clergy and contemporary society.

During the Renaissance, as in the Middle Ages, the Seven Liberal Arts continued to be the basic curriculum. However, the emphasis had changed. Whereas the dialectic had received chief emphasis during the Middle Ages, grammar moved to the forefront during the Renaissance. In both instances the curriculum was unbalanced, and the result the same. The Renaissance began with vigorous intellectual inquiry, but by the end of the sixteenth century it had become too concerned with the form of grammar in imitations of the classics: education was rendered sterile. Yet, the movement, before it declined, had enriched education with its new emphasis on the development of the individual, its new methods, and its additions to content of education.

The Reformation

As there are in most major movements, there were many contributing causes to the Reformation. Nationalism, which emphasized state supremacy, weakened the authority of the Church. The prestige of the papacy had already been lowered, and there were abuses of power and office among Churchmen. The Renaissance had revived pagan ideals which had appealed to many, and the exaggerated individualism which developed was leading to the rejection of authority.

The Reformation began in 1517, when Martin Luther posted his famous 95 Theses on the church door in Wittenberg. Luther's criticisms of certain church practices were the sparks that produced the tremendous explosion. Luther was excommunicated, yet supported by German princes. Eventually the Reformation spread to Switzerland, the Netherlands, England, and Scotland.

The immediate effect of the Reformation was detrimental to education. The confiscation of Church property closed many schools that were conducted by the Church. Gradually, of course, the number of schools again increased under other auspices. Futhermore, with the Reformation came the gradual secularization of education. By the end of the sixteenth century Europe was solidly split into Protestant and Catholic.

Luther's contributions to education consisted of three main ideas. Education should be free and compulsory. However, under his plan, children would have attended school for only an hour or two a day, devoting the rest of the time to vocational training. The more intelligent students would have attended school for a longer time. Secondly, he advocated state support and control of education, an idea which was to prevail not only in Europe but also in the United States. Finally, because of his principles of private interpretation and individual justification in religion, he stimulated historical research consulting primary sources in religion.

Another important educational Reformation figure was the German, Melancthon. He undertook the task of surveying the school system which resulted in the organization of secondary schools into a state system.

The Counter Reformation

Many sincere churchmen attempted reformation before the Protestant Revolution, but these attempts were not organized nor crystallized until the Council of Trent, which met in twenty-five sessions from 1545 to 1563. The Councils succeeded in defining the dogma of the Church and issued many disciplinary decrees. Its educational effects were found in the establishment of seminaries, the encouragement of elementary education, and the establishment of teaching congregations.

The best known of these teaching orders was the Society of Jesus (Jesuits), which was established by Ignatius Loyola (1491–1556) in 1534. They outlined their method of organization and teaching in the *Ratio Studiorum* (an extension of the constitution), which appeared in its final form in 1599, after Loyola's death. The Jesuits were very successful teachers because of their efficient organization, good training, effective methods, and for a while free schools. Their method of instruction was to follow three basic steps: prelection—an explanation of the passage being studied; erudition—general information which could be related to the passage; and repetition, or drill. They also made extensive use of rivalry.

A great number of seminaries, colleges, and universities were founded by the order. By 1600, there were 200 of these institutions, and by 1700 the number had grown to 769.

Another later, but effective teaching congregation was the Christian Brothers, founded in 1682 by Jean Baptiste de la Salle (1651–1719). La Salle made several important contributions to education. He organized elementary schools for both poor boys and delinquent boys. He established the first normal school in 1684, for the training of teachers. Also, he economized instruction by using the "simultaneous method" of instruction; children were graded according to their capacity, and those in each grade followed the lesson under one teacher. This was in contrast to the individual method of instruction which had been prevalent.

At La Salle's death, the Christian Brothers numbered 274, with a school enrollment of approximately 9,000 pupils in 26 communities. By 1778, the number of brothers increased to 760, teaching 31,000 children. At the present time, their pupils are in excess of 300,000, and they maintain over 100 schools in the United States.[16]

The Catholic Revival or Counter Reformation came too late to preserve the solidarity and authority of the Church. Gradually a multiplicity of religions, with their consequent effects on educational theories, developed in Europe. It was this type of transplant that took place in colonial America, as we shall see in the next chapter.

Realism in Education

As the Renaissance progressed, humanistic education became formalized. By the seventeenth century it had often degenerated into narrow Ciceronianism. Just as the Renaissance was a reaction to the extreme formalism of late scholasticism, realism arose as a reaction to formalized humanism.

The realists felt that the classics were important, but their objectives of education went beyond the classics. They believed that education should prepare a student for the realities of life. Of course, there were different interpretations of the realities of life, so three types of realism developed: verbal, social and sense.

Verbal realism. Verbal realists stressed the importance of the studying the classics, but emphasized the content rather than the form of those works. They believed that, along with the study of religion, the classics contained most of the knowledge that would help in dealing with the realities of life. Erasmus and Vives, already mentioned in this chapter, were leading representatives of verbal realism.

Social realism. The social realists, largely members of the aristocracy, held that education should prepare the student for a career in world affairs. They felt that the schools neglected foreign languages

---

[16]Luella Cole, *A History of Education* (New York: Rinehart and Company, 1950), pp. 366-67.

and sciences and, therefore, gave an inadequate preparation for careers of state. Social intercourse and travel were deemed essential to this preparation. They also believed that a private tutor was superior to group instructions.

The leading exponent of social realism was Michel de Montaigne (1533–1592). He advocated education by travel and by a tutor rather than in school. He recognized individual differences, minimized book learning, advocated self-expression and activity, and stressed the importance of physical exercise. Montaigne influenced the later theories of John Locke and Rousseau. He was also influential in establishing academies in France, England, and Germany.

Sense realism. The sense realists emphasized studying the realities of nature by the inductive method (sometimes called the "scientific method") and by extensive observation, investigation, and analysis. They advocated using the inductive method in the classroom and held that instruction should proceed from the concrete to the abstract, from things to ideas. The vernacular, they felt, should be the first language taught since it is the natural medium of instruction. Although a great many names can be associated with sense realism, there are a few that stand out as contributing "firsts" to the movement. These are Mulcaster, Bacon, Ratke, Comenius, and Francke.

Richard Mulcaster (1531–1611) emphasized education for contemporary life, and recommended that the vernacular be taught first. Consequently, he is usually mentioned as a forerunner of sense realism.

Francis Bacon's (1561–1626) emphasis on the use of the inductive method is regarded by many as the beginning of the modern scientific movement. He felt that all previous knowledge should be reconstructed on the basis of scientific investigation. The nature of things, he believed, should be studied through induction. Being a theorist and not a teacher, Bacon did not have the opportunity to apply his theory in education.

Wolfgang Ratke (1571–1635), a failure who ended in prison, is considered to be the originator of educational realism. Having read Bacon's ideas, he developed a method of teaching which he shrouded in secrecy. Among his ideas were the following: the teacher should follow the "order of nature"; individual experience should replace authority; and, nothing should be learned by rote. Like his predecessors, he felt that the vernacular should be studied first, and that grammar should be studied inductively. He was given an opportunity to practice his principles in a school in Germany, but the school failed after a year and a half because of mismanagement, and Ratke was thrown into prison as an imposter. However, he did influence Comenius, who became the leading representative of sense realism.

John Amos Comenius (1592–1670), a Moravian, is the best known exponent of sense realism. He set forth his educational theory in his *Great Didactic* (1632). Sensory experience, he claimed, is important because knowledge originates in the senses. Learning should appeal to the child's interests, and teachers should make every effort to motivate the children and introduce interesting material. Furthermore, all instruction should be compatible with the nature of the child and school work should be related to life's activities. Comenius wrote textbooks for various levels of study, and was the first writer to illustrate textbooks. His *Orbis Pictus* (1658), an elementary reader, was the first illustrated textbook ever written.

Comenius also presented a plan for the organization of schools, with suggestions for the curriculum at each level. He divided education into four levels: School of the Mother's Knee, to the age of six; the Vernacular School, ages six to twelve; the Latin School, from twelve to eighteen; and the University, eighteen to twenty-four.

Although Comenius traveled considerably in Europe, and although his textbooks were used widely, he had little impact on educational practices during his own time, perhaps because Europe was in a period of upheaval. It was not until the middle of the nineteenth century when the political and religious turmoil had ended, that his works were revived in Germany. Speaking of the *Great Didactic*, Monroe states:

> So sane and far-seeing are the precepts of this work that it may even yet be read with greater immediate profit to the teacher, sufficiently intelligent to avoid many minor errors, than the majority of contemporary educational writings.[17]

August Hermann Francke (1663–1727) most thoroughly applied the principles of sense realism in his schools. He was responsible for the founding of many types of schools, such as a school for the sons of the wealthy, a people's school, an orphan school, an advanced elementary school, a higher school for girls, and a training school for teachers. As Francke was a Pietist, the aim of his schools was both religious and practical. The courses were taught according to the principles of sense realism and introduced biological and natural sciences. Francke's

---

[17]Paul Monroe, *op. cit.*, p. 495.

schools exerted a widespread influence in Germany, but they gradually lost their religious character.

Thus, over a period of a century, from the time of Bacon to the time of Francke, sense realism made little progress. There were only scattered attempts at introducing the sciences in elementary schools. Better progress was made at the secondary level, with the inclusion of realistic studies in the academies of England, France, and Germany. This movement received slow acceptance in higher education. Some sciences were taught during the seventeenth century, but it was not until the middle of the eighteenth century that the natural sciences were emphasized.

The Enlightenment

The period of the Enlightenment was a return to the primacy of reason over authority and religion. It was not a new emphasis. Five centuries before Christ the Greek Sophists had maintained that "man is the measure of all things", asserting the primacy of man's reason for determining truth, or right and wrong. The emphasis placed on reason under scholasticism, which did not divorce itself from religion, produced, in its later stages, individuals who placed their conclusions above the authority of the Church. More emphasis of this kind came with the Reformation and its principle of private interpretation of the Scriptures. In philosophy, John Locke (1632–1704) helped to promote the idea that authority should be replaced by reason and investigation. His theories contributed to bringing about the Enlightenment, and he has been called the founder of empirical psychology. His major influence came after his death, when Rousseau popularized many of his and Montaigne's ideas.

Voltaire (1694–1778), the best known representative of the rationalists, characterized his life, thoughts, and writings with contempt for all the authority inherent in the Church, state, society, and morality. He and the other rationalists attempted to build up an aristocracy of intellect to replace the aristocracy of birth. Voltaire despised Christianity, and did his best to destroy it with his clever ironical wit. Contributing largely to the rationalistic movement were the Encyclopedists (*illuminati,* as they termed themselves). The most prominent of these men was Diderot (1713–1784), editor of the *Encyclopedia* which contained his and other criticisms of existing abuses.

The inevitable reaction to this extreme rationalistic tendency came during the latter part of the eighteenth century. At this time, the emphasis shifted from appeal to reason to appeal to the emotions, and the

movement has been termed sentimentalism. The sentimentalists substituted for Christianity a morality devoid of supernatural elements.
The broad term "naturalism" has been used to categorize this type of
belief. In substance, it is based on the assumption that "nature" is the
source of, and can be used to explain, everything.

Jean Jacques Rousseau (1712–1778), a speaker for sentimentalism
and naturalism, greatly influenced education and many other fields.
Because of his importance we shall consider him in more detail than
the other theorists. His theory of education appears in *Emile* (1762).
Rousseau stated that man, as made by nature, is good, but that society
has a corrupting influence on him, and produces inequalities of all
kinds. Consequently, he felt that education should be natural and according to the child's nature. If man developed his own resources in a
natural way he would be good, i.e., uncontaminated by the bad influences of society. Anything interfering with natural development should
be avoided.

This doctrine of natural goodness conflicted with the concept of
original sin and its effects which had been taught by the churches for
centuries. Rousseau believed that original sin, and consequently its
effects, do not exist in man. Instead, each individual is born good, and
becomes bad only through the corrupting influences of others. To avoid
these influences, he advocated educating children away from society in
natural surroundings.

In his *Emile*, Rousseau divided education into four periods:

1. Infancy and early childhood (to age 5)
2. Childhood (to age 12)
3. Boyhood (to age 15)
4. Youth (to age 20)

During infancy and early childhood, Emile would be taught by his
mother, who would allow him complete freedom. In his freedom of
movement he would be allowed to experience the hardships of hunger,
thirst, heat, and cold. During his childhood he would come under the
guidance of a tutor, but would continue his free development. The
tutor would try to guide Emile without him realizing it. Emile's body
would develop, and he would gather sense information. He would receive no systematic instruction in religion, morality, or any other subject. Similarly, he would receive no training in discipline, except that
offered by nature—a discipline of natural consequences. When he
reached boyhood, he would have a sound body with well-trained
senses. At this point, he would begin his intellectual education, learning only what interested him, and what might prove to be useful to

him in life. Even though Emile was wealthy, he would learn a trade, so that he could sympathize with the working class, and, if he lost his wealth, he could rely on his trade to live. He would learn the natural sciences from nature and not from books. He would be challenged to solve problems as they arose in their natural surroundings to develop his reasoning powers. At the age of fifteen, having reached youth, he would begin to mingle in society. Emile's tutor would help him to develop a natural sympathy for his fellowmen and acquire a sense of morality.

The influence of Montaigne and Locke on Rousseau's ideas in education is obvious. Also, a brief biography of his life may help to explain his ideas. Rousseau's mother died when he was young, and he was raised by his father with very little training and discipline. He left home, led a vagabond life, tried several occupations, but relied on a woman for his subsistence. He went to Paris where he mingled, and exchanged ideas, with many people. He then took as his common law wife a poor woman named Therese Levasseur, by whom he had five children. Immediately after their birth, Rousseau put each of these children into an orphan asylum. Rousseau gradually won recognition in the literary world. When he published *Emile*, however, he was ordered arrested. For eight years he was a fugitive in France, Switzerland, and England, and then he safely returned to Paris, where he had many sympathizers. He spent his last years with a tormented mind and body, and died in 1778.

His life is reflected in some of the things recommended for Emile's upbringing. He himself had lived an undisciplined, vagabond life, learning much from nature and from experience, which was the basic theme underlying Emile's education. There were some sound ideas in Rousseau's educational theory. Modern psychology has confirmed his division of the periods of a child's development. Furthermore, the child should not be treated as a miniature adult, and the methods used to teach him should be based on his psychological development. Education should give the child some experience with his natural surroundings; and practical preparation for life should be one of the objectives of education.

On the negative side, Rousseau's basic principle of the natural goodness of man is illogical. He stated that the individual is good, but that society is corrupt. Yet society is made up of individuals. If his principle were true, society would necessarily be good. History shows, and experience confirms, that each individual is a mixture of good *and* bad, the proportion varying with each person. Although Rousseau stated that education should follow the individual's natural development,

Emile's education was unnatural in many respects. Emile's intellectual education did not begin until the age of twelve; yet we know that children begin to reason around the age of seven, or even sooner. Intellectual education should have begun much earlier for Emile. Similarly, Rousseau withheld social education and the development of feelings until the age of fifteen, but feelings and social development manifest themselves long before that time. Also, Rousseau felt that moral education would occur through a discipline of natural consequences. Although this type of experience may have merit in some situations, it would expose the child to many needless dangers if applied universally. Finally, it would be impractical to try to supply a tutor for each pupil.

Rousseau's influence in education was out of proportion to the value of his plan for education. As a theorist, he did not have the opportunity to note the inconsistencies of his plan by applying it to a practical situation. However, his basic principles, the natural goodness of man, natural education, and education according to natural development, influenced a long line of educators who modified and applied his ideas. Pestalozzi, Herbart, Froebel, and Spencer were influenced by him. In recent years, some of the theories in Progressive Education bear a striking similarity to Rousseau's theories. As Rusk states,

> Rousseau nevertheless stands to modern education as Plato to ancient education; the heading of almost every chapter in *The Schools of Tomorrow* is a quotation from Rousseau.[18]

The period of the Enlightenment did somewhat influence the field of education. Tradition and authority were further weakened by the emphasis on reason, and the philosophy of naturalism made inroads on the teachings of Christianity. The naturalists considered man as a product of nature rather than as a creature of God with a supernatural destiny. This led to greater emphasis on natural science and scientific investigation. Rousseau's ideas later would stimulate further study of child development, which would result in the movement known as developmentalism.

Developmentalism

During the nineteenth and twentieth centuries, the idea grew that education should be a process of unfolding from within, rather than an imposition of adult standards. This idea sometimes has been called the

[18]Robert R. Rusk, *op. cit.*, p. 185.

"child-centered movement" or the "psychological movement" and shows the influence of Rousseau's ideas. In order to apply the theory to education, it was found necessary to study and understand the unfolding process, or the process of growth and development.

Johann Basedow (1723–1790), in Germany, made the first practical application of Rousseau's "back to nature" and "education according to nature" theories. Basedow opened a school, the Philanthropinum, in 1774, in which he applied his methods. The school aroused considerable interest as an educational experiment, but closed in 1793, because of Basedow's personal shortcomings and his unsupported claims for the school. However, the interest in educational experimentation found further expression in other men, notably Pestalozzi, Herbart, and Froebel.

Johann Heinrich Pestalozzi (1746–1827) led a life consisting of an amazing series of failures and fresh beginnings. When he was five years old, his father died, leaving him under the influence of three women: his mother, sister, and a servant. For the next four years, before he entered school at the age of nine, he spent most of his time daydreaming in and around the house. When he entered school, he was subjected continually to the practical jokes of his classmates, who derisively referred to him as Harry Oddity of Foolborough. Although meek and trusting, he is reported to have actively championed the poor and the oppressed. This sympathy for the downtrodden was the dominating force behind his life's activities.

When he entered the University of Zurich, he hoped to become a minister, but his personality, physical appearance, and speech were unsuitable for that profession. He then hoped to bring about reforms by studying law, but gave this up after being branded as a revolutionary for advocating the political ideas of Rousseau. He finally turned to agricultural reform, but, since he was impractical and inefficient, he again failed. Paradoxically, even though he and his family were destitute, he turned his farm into a home for destitute children. This experiment at Neuhof, in which he used a modification of Rousseau's educational ideas, was at first successful, and brought him some donations. However, as he increased the number of children on his farm, Pestalozzi's inefficiency caused the project to collapse. Fortunately for him, a servant named Elizabeth Naef offered to him her services. A capable woman, she brought order and stability to the household, and raised enough food to sustain the family. Shortly thereafter, Pestalozzi wrote *Leonard and Gertrude*, using Elizabeth Naef as a model for Gertrude. This book was received favorably and brought Pestalozzi some recognition.

After he had spent eighteen years writing his theories, the Swiss government placed Pestalozzi in charge of an orphanage at Stanz. His relationship with the children was based on love, and he tried to allow each child to develop his individual potentialities. Although he was achieving some success, the citizens suspiciously regarded him as a heretic, and the visiting government inspectors, not understanding his method, reported that the institution was in a state of confusion. After five months, the orphanage was converted into a needed hospital, and this project also came to an end.

Within a short time, Pestalozzi was granted a teaching position in a school at Burgdorf. Here, he was transferred first to an infants' school, and then back to a larger school at Burgdorf. There he was joined by Hermann Krusi and two other teachers. With their dedicated aid, the school became a success, and attracted many pupils. At this point, Pestalozzi wrote *How Gertrude Teaches Her Children*, published in 1801. The book, which outlined his educational theories, was a success, and his reputation spread. However, he again was forced to leave Burgdorf for political reasons.

In 1805, Pestalozzi moved his school to Yverdon, where he remained for approximately twenty years. This school became famous as a training school in Pestalozzian principles. Teachers, pupils, administrators, and legislators from several European countries and the United States visited it. Yet, Pestalozzi still was incapable of efficient management. Consequently, the years at Yverdon were characterized by disorder, confusion, and dissension and quarrels among his teachers. Finally, in 1825, Pestalozzi was removed from Yverdon by the government. He returned to Neuhof, where he died in 1827.

Pestalozzi gave himself credit for "psychologizing" education. He felt that education should be based on the nature and development of the child, and that a teacher should proceed from the concrete to the abstract in teaching. Stressing that knowledge must be founded on sensory impressions, learning through observation was a basic procedure. He advocated the use of concrete aids in learning, devised a table of units, used clay models, slates, and objects and specimens of various kinds. As a teacher, he loved his pupils and did not believe in severe discipline. Rather, he felt that the relationship of pupils and teachers should be based on love. He undoubtedly achieved this type of relationship. However, whether or not he actually developed a method of teaching is obscure. Even the teachers who worked for him

were sometimes mystified by what was taking place.[19] Although Pestalozzi had stimulated interest in educational psychology, he had over-
emphasized the role of sense perception in education.

Pestalozzi's principles and "method" spread throughout Europe, and
later the United States. He influenced the following men among others:

Froebel, in the development of kindergarten

Herbart, in the field of educational psychology

Fellenberg, in industrial education

Mann, in educational reforms in the United States

Sheldon, in the Oswego movement in teacher training, which
spread throughout the United States in the last half of the nineteenth century

Johann F. Herbart (1776–1841) helped to overcome Pestalozzi's deficiencies. One of Herbart's contributions was his *theory of apperception,* in which he denied that the mind had several faculties or powers.
Rather, he believed, the mind was simple and had only the power of
interacting with an individual's environment through the sense impressions received by the nervous system. These impressions, he held, sank
into the subconscious until other impressions aroused them, modified
them, and fused with them. This process was continuous, with the new
impressions arousing and modifying the old "apperceptive mass". How
well new material was received by the mind would depend on the
material with which it could fuse. For this reason, he believed that it
was necessary for new materials of instruction to be well-selected, well-
presented, and coordinated. Also, it was important for the teacher to
know his subject matter and his pupils' capacity for learning.

Furthermore, Herbart considered it important for the teacher to
develop in his pupils *many-sided interests,* a variety of interests. He
felt that the pupil should be well-rounded in many fields and a "vir-
tuoso" in one field. The formation of good character, he claimed, was a
major objective of education, and knowledge would lead to virtue.
Many-sided interests would drive the pupils to seek knowledge which
would lead them into virtuous action. By his insistence that the teacher
stimulate interests, Herbart differed from other developmentalists who
tried to capitalize only on the interests that manifested themselves from
within the child.

---

[19]William T. Kane and John J. O'Brien, *op. cit.,* p. 336.

As an aid to proper instruction, Herbart outlined four formal steps for the teacher to go through: clarity of presentation, association with previous knowledge, assimilation of knowledge acquired, and application of what had been learned. Later Herbartians elaborated them into the following *five formal steps:*

1. Preparation: making certain that the pupil has the proper apperceptive background for the task at hand
2. Presentation: ideas are clearly presented and analyzed so that they can be grasped
3. Comparison: material is correlated with previously learned material
4. Generalization: a synthesis of what has been analyzed
5. Application: through practice the information is impressed on the mind

Herbart undoubtedly had intended his formal steps as an instructional aid, but his followers exaggerated their application. The steps were used as stilted, standard procedure in classroom recitations.

During the latter half of the nineteenth century, Herbart's influence was widespread in Germany and the United States. In 1892, the National Herbart Society was formed and the name later changed to the National Society for the Study of Education. By 1900, Herbart's principles were taught widely in the normal schools of the United States. Today, the principles of association, stimulating interests, and lesson planning are remnants of Herbartian ideas.[20]

Friedrich Wilhelm August Froebel (1782–1852), like Herbart, was influenced by Pestalozzi. While teaching in Switzerland, he spent considerable time at Pestalozzi's institute at Yverdon. He became interested in the problem of the education for pre-school children, returned to Germany, and founded the first kindergarten at Blankenburg in 1837. His theories are set forth in his *Education of Man.*

Following the developmentalist tradition, Frobel believed that education should be a process of unfolding from within, not an imposition of adult standards. He felt that there should be self-activity in learning, and that the development of the child should be brought about through the free expression of impulses and instincts. In kindergarten, the development of motor activity, creative expression, and social cooperation were to take place. Play, being the main instinct, would dominate the kindergarten activity. There would be play, songs, and simple tasks with concrete objects, and religion would permeate all activities.

---

[20]Luella Cole, *op. cit.*, p. 505.

Frobel developed both songs and materials which were called "gifts" and "occupations" for use in the kindergarten. The "gifts" were objects of various shapes that could be manipulated, while the "occupations" consisted of clay for modeling, paper for drawing or coloring, and materials for sewing among other things. Activities were carried on in the "play circle".

Although the idea of pre-school education was not original with Froebel (Quintilian had stressed learning in early years, and Comenius had advocated the School of the Mother's Knee), "Froebel was really the first to give a philosophical and psychological basis to such an institution."[21]

After Froebel's death, the kindergarten movement spread throughout Europe, with the exception of Germany, where it was banned for a time. In the United States, the first kindergarten was established in Watertown, Wisconsin by Mrs. Carl Schurz in 1855. It was a private, German-speaking kindergarten. The first English-speaking kindergarten, which also was private, was established in Boston by Miss Elizabeth Peabody in 1860; and the first public school kindergarten was established in St. Louis in 1873.

During the nineteenth and twentieth centuries, many Americans became more concerned and involved in formulating educational theories, and European influences waned. Horace Mann, Henry Barnard, G. Stanley Hall, William James, Edward L. Thorndike, and John Dewey provided the leadership in American education. Some of these men further evolved the ideas of the developmentalists, while others concerned themselves with the scientific measurement of the results of education. Their ideas and influence will be discussed in Chapter Three.

In reading over the general trends of educational history outlined in this chapter, two facts have re-occurred:

1. Many of the ideas and practices that might have been thought to be of recent origin are, in reality, many centuries old
2. New ideas, when they first appeared, were often carried to extremes, with the result that they produced reactions which, in turn, became extremes

The student of history of education will notice that most of the *basic principles* (sound and unsound) we find in education today were expressed at some time in the past. Yet new and more detailed knowledge

---

[21]Elmer H. Wilds and Kenneth V. Lottich, *The Foundations of Modern Education* (New York: Holt, Rinehart and Winston, Inc., 1961), p. 321.

has been discovered that elaborates some of these principles. For example, Quintilian stated that sensory impressions are important in learning. His statement was stated and restated by educators throughout the centuries. It was emphasized especially by the sense realists, and has never been discredited. Today we have courses in audio-visual aids as a development of this principle; we also have developed new devices (such as radio, motion pictures, and television) to aid learning, but the *basic principle* has remained unchanged. Today we recognize the importance of individual differences; so did Plato, Quintilian, Vives, and many others. We have devised new ways of dealing with the individual differences, but the basic principle (adapting instruction to individual differences) has always been with us.

We also have seen the shift between extremes in some of the major movements in recent centuries. The Renaissance was a reaction to medieval authority, and the superficiality into which university education had lapsed; yet, the reaction eventually ended with a superficial and stilted concern for grammar. This, in turn, resulted in the development of sense realism. It was followed by rationalism with its complete rejection of authority, and its emphasis on reason; and sentimentalism became a reaction to rationalism. The more recent "child-centered" movement eventually brought on some of the extremes of Progressive Education, to which there was again a strong reaction. The pendulum of opinion has swung back and forth throughout the centuries, and, of course, at any particular time, there have been minority deviations from contemporary popular opinions.

SUMMARY

American education had its early roots in European educational ideas and practices. American colonists brought over, and put into practice, the theories that were familiar to them when they left Europe. In order to understand and appreciate the evolution of American education, it is necessary to re-trace the steps of the educational history of Europe.

The Hebrews, Greeks, and Romans made distinct contributions to education and society. The Hebrews, regarding themselves as the chosen people of God, emphasized and preserved the moral-religious aspects of life, thus paving the way for Christianity. The Greeks, as represented by Athens, made lasting contributions to the intellectual and aesthetic aspects of civilization. The Sophists arose as teachers, helped to popularize learning, graded schools into three levels, and added to the content of education by teaching the subjects which later became The Seven Liberal Arts. The Greek philosophers also made important contributions. Socrates, a great teacher who used the question and answer method, founded the science of ethics. Plato's philosophy was to become an influence on education for many centuries. Aristotle, founder of the science of logic, so advanced philosophical thought that he was regarded by many people, even in the present day, as "The Master" among philosophers. The Romans expressed their educational ideal as the *vir bonus*, the orator who was an educated and moral man. However, as they were exposed to Greek influences, their philosophy of self-discipline gradually gave way to the Greek philosophy of self-indulgence. Their code of law and their methods of social organization are their major contributions to civilization. Cicero and his style of expression was imitated greatly during his own time, and during the Renaissance period.

With the coming of Christ, and the establishment of the Church, the chief objective of education became the salvation of souls. Outliving its early centuries of persecution under the Romans, the Church became an increasingly powerful influence in all spheres of individual and social life.

After the fall of Rome, the Church assumed, almost exclusively, the task of education for approximately nine centuries during the Middle Ages. Monastic, cathedral, and parish schools slowly developed. Charlemagne and Alcuin made great efforts to improve education, and through the capitularies issued by Charlemagne they attempted to bring about universal education. However, these efforts were not sustained by their successors, and education once again lapsed. The Cluniac Reform in the tenth century brought religious reform and social organization. An intellectual revival emanated from the monastery of Bec in the eleventh century, with much of the content supplied by the Saracens through Spain. Other educational influences were chivalry, the crusades, the rise of towns, and the guilds. Chantry, venture, guild, and burgher schools arose. Under scholasticism, universities began to spring up. Among the first universities were Bologna, Salerno, and Paris. These universities offered vigorous intellectual training, but by the end of the Middle Ages their training became superficial and overly concerned with logical distinctions. Although progress had been made in education during the latter half of the Middle Ages, many factors contributed to its break-up. The abuses among churchmen, the rising spirit of nationalism, the increased use of the vernacular in languages, wars, and the Black Death were the chief causes.

The Renaissance, described as a rebirth of learning, was a return to the study of classical literature. It began in Italy, where Petrarch revived the study of Latin, and Manuel Chrysoloras popularized Greek. Although it was pagan in nature in Italy, the northern European Renaissance contained the elements of religious and social reform. The study of the classics became known as humanism, which was classified as broad or narrow, Christian or pagan, depending on the interpretation of the classics. Da Feltre and Vives, broad humanists, were outstanding educators whose ideas were influenced by Quintilian. Da Feltre ran the most famous of Renaissance schools, Casa Giocosa, while Vives gave the most thorough exposition of the principles of education during that period. The Renaissance stimulated learning and resulted in an increase in schools, but it later stagnated and over-emphasized the study of grammar.

The Reformation which began with Martin Luther, was an attempt to reform the Church but ended in revolt against it. It spread from Germany to other European countries. For a while education suffered because Church property, including educational facilities, was confiscated. Gradually these schools were supplanted in Protestant countries by private and state supported schools.

The Catholic Counter-Reformation beginning with the sessions of the Council of Trent, attempted to remedy abuses by issuing disciplinary decrees and defining dogma. It also encouraged education and resulted in the foundation of religious teaching congregations such as the Jesuits and the Christian Brothers. They were, and still are, effective teachers in many countries. LaSalle, founder of the Christian Brothers, established the first normal school and emphasized using the simultaneous method of instruction. Although the Counter Reformation was good, it could not stem the Protestant Reformation.

By the seventeenth century, humanistic education had become formalized into a narrow imitation of the classics. As a reaction to this came realism, which believed that education should be concerned with the realities of life. Verbal realists, such as Vives and Erasmus, stressed the content rather than the form of the classics. The social realists, of whom Montaigne is the major example, held that education should include travel, instruction by a tutor, knowledge of foreign languages, and preparation for a career. Sense realism was the third form of realism. The sense realists stressed the study of nature through observation and the use of the inductive method; they also recommended studying the vernacular first. While Mulcaster was a forerunner of the movement, Bacon is regarded as father of modern science because of his emphasis on the use of induction in seeking knowledge. Ratke tried to apply the principles of sense realism in his schools, but failed. Comenius, the best known sense realist, was the author of the first illustrated textbook. Francke best applied the principles of sense realism in the schools. Although the movement paid more attention to scientific studies in the curriculum, its progress was slow until the eighteenth century.

The first half of the eighteenth century, through the influence of Locke, Voltaire, and the Encyclopedists, brought reasoning to the fore once again with a consequent denial of tradition and authority. Reacting to this extreme rationalistic tendency, the sentimentalists of the last half of the eighteenth century appealed to the emotions, substituting a naturalistic form of religion for the supernatural elements of Christianity. Rousseau, with his doctrine of the natural goodness of man, was the chief exponent of naturalism. In *Emile,* he outlined his plan of education, and influenced educational thought even to the present day.

One of Rousseau's ideas found expression in the movement known as developmentalism, which stressed education as a process of unfolding from within, instead of imposing standards from without. Greater attention was given to studying the growth and development of children from that time forward. Pestalozzi stressed education based on the natural development of the child. He influenced Froebel who was concerned with the education of pre-school children and instituted the kindergarten. Further contributions were made by Herbart with his theories of apperception, many-sided interests, and steps in teaching. American educators and psychologists during the last two centuries, influenced by European theories, made contributions to the development of educational theory and practice. These contributions were based on a study of child development, and also attempted scientific measurements of the results of education.

Questions for discussion:

1. What general educational ideas and practices in ancient Greece survived throughout the subsequent centuries?

2. How would modern educators regard Quintilian's principles of education?

3. Show how Christianity has affected educational objectives and content throughout history.

4. What were the strengths of later medieval education? What were its shortcomings?

5. In what sense was the Renaissance a "rebirth of learning"? In what sense was it not?

6. How did the Reformation affect education?

7. Rationalism is based on the premise that truth should be discovered through reason alone. To what extent would you agree with the proposition that "the child should discover his own truth"?

8. How far back can you trace the belief that education should be based on the nature of the pupil?

For further reading:

Abelson, Paul, *The Seven Liberal Arts*. New York: Teachers College, Columbia University, 1906.

Cole, Luella, *A History of Education*. New York: Rinehard & Company, 1950.

Cubberley, Elwood P., *The History of Education*. Boston: Houghton Mifflin Company, 1948.

Duggan, Stephen, *A Student's Textbook in the History of Education*. 3rd ed., New York: Appleton-Century-Crofts, Inc., 1948.

Graves, Frank P., *A Student's History of Education*. New York: The Macmillan Company, 1936.

Kane, William T. and John J. O'Brien, *History of Education*. Chicago: Loyola University Press, 1954.

Leach, Arthur F., *Educational Charters and Documents*. Cambridge: Cambridge University Press, 1911.

McCormick, Patrick J. and Francis P. Cassidy, *History of Education*. Washington, D.C.: The Catholic Education Press, 1946.

Meyer, Adolphe E., *An Educational History of the Western World*. New York: McGraw-Hill Book Company, 1965.

Meyer, Frederick, *A History of Educational Thought*. Columbus: Charles E. Merrill Publishing Co., 1960.

Monroe, Paul, *A Textbook in the History of Education*. New York: The Macmillan Company, 1933.

Mulhern, James, *A History of Education*. New York: The Ronald Press Company, 1959.

Power, Edward J., *Main Currents in the History of Education*. New York: McGraw-Hill Book Company, Inc., 1962.

Rusk, Robert R., *The Doctrines of the Great Educators*. London: Macmillan & Co., Ltd., 1954.

Wilds, Elmer H. and Lottich, Kenneth V., *The Foundations of Modern Education*. New York: Holt, Rinehart and Winston, Inc., 1961.

3

The Development of American Elementary Education

The first permanent white settlement in America was at Jamestown, Virginia, in 1607. A short time later, in 1620, the Pilgrims landed at Plymouth Rock in Massachusetts. Thereafter, the colonists began to arrive in large numbers, settling all along the eastern seacoast.

What was happening in Europe at the time America was settled? The Middle Ages had ended but had left their imprint on succeeding centuries. The Renaissance had revived ancient knowledge and an interest in learning, but had spent itself as a movement at the time of colonial settlement leaving its legacy to education. The Reformation had been in progress for nearly a century, resulting in the establishment of many religious sects, the increased emphasis on state control in education, and growing individualism. Realism had just begun as a reaction to narrow humanism, and Francis Bacon had just published his *Novum Organum* which emphasized the inductive method.

It is impossible to state the extent to which the past influenced the people of the early seventeenth century, but the influence was there. Ciceronian Latin was taught in the schools, the ideas of Aristotle and Quintilian were studied, Christianity continued as a way of life but in different forms, the apprenticeship system was still used, and the scholastic philosophy of the Middle Ages was still taught in the universities, although the emphasis had now shifted to the classics. These and other later influences affected the colonists and therefore, the development of American education.

Although there were many nationalities represented among the early colonists, the English exerted the greatest influence on the development of the educational practices in America. A brief look at the conditions in England during the early seventeenth century will therefore provide a better understanding of the beginnings of American education.

SEVENTEENTH CENTURY ENGLAND

England's economic conditions were poor at the turn of the seventeenth century. During the preceding century, the monasteries had been suppressed, and their wealth confiscated. Even the religious endowments of the guilds were taken over by the crown, yet the country remained in financial difficulty. Taxes were increased, and the currency was devaluated. By the time of James I, half of the population of England was dependent on begging. Begging was regarded as a way of life. These conditions prompted the passing of tax laws for the relief and education of the poor.

Politically, England was a monarchy, subscribing to the doctrine of the "divine right of kings". However, early in the seventeenth century there were rumblings of discontent in Parliament over the lack of civil rights for the people. Parliament petitioned the king for the rights which had been outlined in the Magna Carta several centuries earlier. After many years, Parliament attained a degree of success through the Bill of Rights of 1689.

By 1533, Henry VIII had broken with the Catholic Church and gradually had established the Church of England as the official church of the country. In addition to the Anglican Church, there still remained many Catholics who continued their allegiance to the Pope. There slowly developed, before America was colonized, two other major religious groups: the Puritans and the Separatists. The Puritans believed in a greater strictness in daily life; a simpler form of worship; and a greater distinction between the religious practices of the Anglican Church and the practices of the Catholic Church. The Separatists (Congregationalists) frowned upon the idea of a state church, and favored the autonomy of local congregations. All religious groups deviating from the Church of England suffered varying degrees of oppression and persecution under their English rulers.

Several reasons prompted many people to sail for America; some people embarked to try to improve their economic status, while other people fled from political oppression or religious persecution. Many people may have gone for all three reasons.

Education in England

In England, education was mainly for the upper classes, not the masses. Higher education was an individual, not a state, affair. The aristocratic element in society received their elementary education through a private school or tutor, then proceeded to a Latin Grammar School for secondary education, and culminated their education with college training. The poor could receive the rudiments of an elementary education from: dame schools, in which spelling and reading instructions were given to neighborhood children for a small sum of money; writing schools, in which writing and perhaps some arithmetic were taught; or charity schools, operated by religious groups. For the majority of people the most widespread form of education was vocational, in the form of apprenticeship training. The "poor laws" provided payment to masters who took in poor children or orphans to teach them a trade.

In England, the attitude that education was an individual and church affair lingered from medieval times, when the church was the chief educator. After the Reformation, church properties, monasteries, and schools were confiscated, leaving England virtually without facilities for educating the people. Civil authorities did not provide substitute facilities for the ones which were confiscated. The aristocracy believed that educating the masses would be dangerous to the continuation of their superior position in society and might result in heresies. The Puritans, however, adopted the Calvinistic concept of state control of education and belief in free education for all.

ATTITUDES TOWARD EDUCATION IN COLONIAL AMERICA

There was a substantial difference in the educational ideals and efforts of the three geographical sections of the Atlantic seacoast, New England, the Middle States, and the South. New England and southern education was the most direct transplant of English ideas, although the influence took different forms in each of these sections. In the Middle Atlantic colonies, for example Pennsylvania, educational practices differed from the other sections.

New England.   Most of the colonists in New England were Puritans. During the reign of Charles I alone, from 1629 to 1640, it is estimated that twenty thousand Puritans migrated to New England.[1] Although they were English, they subscribed to the Calvinistic ideas of state control in education, and favored education for the masses. However, even though the Puritans believed in a state control of education, the types of schools they established were English in form, namely, dame schools, writing schools, Latin grammar schools, and colleges of the European pattern.

Middle States.   Pennsylvania is usually regarded as representative of educational practices in the Middle Atlantic States. Because William Penn had adopted an "open-door" policy of religious freedom, many nationalities and religions were represented in Pennsylvania. The following list gives an indication of the diversity among Pennsylvania colonists:

English: Quakers, Episcopalians, Baptists, and Methodists

Germans: Mennonites, Pietists, German Baptist Brethren, Schwenkfelders, Moravians, and later Lutherans and German Reformed

Scotch-Irish: mostly Presbyterians

Welsh: Quakers, Baptists, and Episcopalians

Early French: mostly Huguenots

Scotch: largely Presbyterians

Irish: Catholics

Dutch: Reformed Church

Swedish: Swedish Lutheran Church

With such an amalgamation of people it would be difficult to establish common schools that would satisfy the needs of all groups. Consequently, the European practice of establishing church related schools was adopted. Through these schools, the religion, traditions, and customs of each group were perpetuated. In addition, the apprenticeship system and some private schools were established. However, the predominant type of school was the parochial school.

The South.   The southern colonies presented yet another situation. The colonists in this area were communicants of the Church of England, so they did not come to Virginia to escape religious persecution.

---

[1]Edgar W. Knight, *Education in the United States* (Boston: Ginn and Company, 1951), pp. 71-73.

Instead, they migrated for economic reasons. Virginia was suited to agriculture, and it was not long before tobacco was raised for profit, and a plantation economy arose. Towns, therefore, did not arise as they did in the northern colonies. Work on the plantations was done by poor people, by slaves (introduced in Virginia in 1619), and by indentured servants. The indentured servants were individuals who had pledged themselves to work for a specified number of years to pay off their debts, or criminals who were deported from England. Therefore, in the south there developed three classes of people: the well-to-do, or aristocrats, slaves, and poor whites.

Education in Virginia duplicated the educational practices in England. The wealthy either had tutors for their children, or sent them to private schools and colleges either in the colony or in England. For poor children, either religious charity schools, or pauper schools financed by taxes, were established; the apprenticeship system for poor children and orphans provided vocational training. Education was not considered to be a responsibility of the state. However, by the nineteenth century, two centuries later, the New England attitude toward education predominated in the country.

The development of education in America will be better understood if we remember the conditions in England at the time of the colonial period, and the three different predominating views of education in this country. Although the discussion in this chapter is confined to elementary education, much of the background data also applies to the development of secondary and higher education, which we will discuss in later chapters.

Although the English exerted the greatest influence in the development of American education, other nationalities and religions played a vital role in our early and subsequent development. Many other nationalities accepted the Calvinistic idea of state control, education for all, and the importance of religion in education. It simply happened that the Puritans who settled in New England took the initiative in state educational legislation, and were followed by other states until finally those few basic ideas, with adaptations, became universal in the country.

Important Early Legislation

Two early Massachusetts laws are considered the first steps toward compulsory education and compulsory schooling: the Massachusetts Law of 1642 and the Massachusetts Law of 1647. The Puritan leaders respected education because they, themselves, were well educated and because they wanted their children to read the Scriptures. They encouraged education early in their settling. In spite of their belief, however, there were parents and masters who were not devoting the desired attention to their children's education. They then passed laws to improve educational conditions.

The first of these laws, the Massachusetts Law of 1642, stipulated that the selectmen[2] of every town periodically inspect the schools and children's training "in learning and labor" for the good of the Commonwealth. This concept was inherent in the apprenticeship laws of England. However, the Massachusetts law went beyond that as it specifically required that children be able ". . . to read and understand the principles of religion and the capital laws of the country." A fine of twenty shillings was levied on those people who did not comply with the law. It was the first American law requiring the compulsory education of children, and recognizing the right of the state to prescribe for children a minimum amount of education to preserve the welfare of the state. Furthermore, the 1642 law recognized the authority of the state to penalize those who did not comply with it. It became a precedent for other colonial and state legislation.

Yet the law of 1642 did not require the the establishment of schools. It simply prescribed that children learn certain basic things. It did not state how, where, or by whom the instruction would be given to children. Parents and masters were left to provide the instruction themselves, or to see that someone did it for them. Although some towns had established schools, others had not; although some parents and masters had the ability and means to provide instruction, others did not. These deficiencies were remedied partially with the passage of another historic law, five years later.

The Massachusetts Law of 1647 (known as the Old Deluder Satan Act because of its opening words), provided for compulsory schools on the elementary and secondary levels in towns that exceeded a specified population. Every town of fifty families had to appoint a teacher of reading and writing, whose salary was to be paid by the parents or masters, or by the town. It further provided that every town of one hundred families had to establish a grammar school to prepare children for college. Failure to comply with the law resulted in a fine of five pounds. The full text of the 1647 law, with a modernized spelling, follows:

> It being one chief object of that old deluder, Satan, to keep men from the knowledge of the Scriptures, as in former times by keep-

---

[2]The town officials.

ing them in an unknown tongue, so in these latter times by per-
suading from the use of tongues, that so at least the true sense and
meaning of the original might be clouded by false glosses of saint-
seeming deceivers, that learning might not be buried in the grave
of our fathers in the Church, and Commonwealth, the Lord assist-
ing our endeavors,

It is therefore ordered, That every township in this jurisdiction,
after the Lord hath increased them to the number of fifty householders, shall then forthwith appoint one within their town to teach
all children as shall resort to him to write and read, whose wages
shall be paid either by the parents or masters of such children, or
by the inhabitants in general, by way of supply, as the major part
of those that order the prudentials of the town shall appoint:
Provided, Those that send their children be not oppressed by paying much more than they can have them taught for in other towns;
and

It is further ordered, That where any town shall increase to the
number of one hundred families or householders, they shall set up
a grammar school, the master thereof being able to instruct youth
so far as they may be fitted for the university; *Provided,* That if any
town neglect the performance hereof above one year, that every
such town shall pay five pounds to the next school till they shall
perform this order.[3]

Like the law of 1642, the law of 1647 is an historic "first" in America:
it is the first law to make compulsory the establishment of schools. The
law of 1647 had another important implication, namely, that the state
has the right to require the establishment of schools for the education
of children, and the right to impose sanctions for failure to comply with
law. Both the law of 1647 and the law of 1642 acted as precedents
which were followed by other colonies and states.[4]

Purpose of Early Education

Colonial education was religious in purpose as the colonists of the
New England and Middle Atlantic colonies felt that education was a
means of perpetuating their religions. There was, of course, an economic aim in apprenticeship training, and a civic aim in stating that
education was for the benefit of the commonwealth, but the religious

---

[3]As quoted by Edgar W. Knight, *op. cit.,* p. 105.
[4]Edgar W. Knight, *op. cit.,* p. 85, disagrees. He states: "Instead of being a foundation stone upon which the American school system has been constructed, as is so
often claimed for this law, it seems rather to have been an effort to restrict the influence of Catholics and adherents to the English Church and to impose the Puritan
creed upon this first generation of native-born New-Englanders."

aim embodied in the Massachusetts Law of 1642 predominated the elementary, secondary, and higher education levels. The purpose of teaching reading was to enable children to read and interpret the Bible. Grammar schools prepared children for college and because the major purpose of the early colleges was the training of ministers, the religious theme permeated all levels of education. In the southern colonies, however, religious motives were not as important as they were in the other colonies.

ELEMENTARY EDUCATION DURING THE COLONIAL PERIOD

In New England, two types of elementary schools came directly from England: the dame school and the writing school.[5]

The dame school was conducted by a neighborhood woman in her kitchen. She would accept children from other families, and, with her own children, would teach them reading, religion, and spelling, for a small fee. Sometimes, a little arithmetic also would be taught in these schools. The amount of instruction varied with the knowledge possessed by the teacher. This type of school was widespread, as a town sometimes would contribute to its support rather than establish a more costly town school.[6]

The writing school, as the name implies, taught pupils to write, figure, and keep simple accounts. These schools did not become numerous or popular. Instruction often depended on a teacher who taught one or more of these subjects while wandering from one place to another as his services were demanded.

Town Schools. The town school, found in New England was a tax supported elementary school in which the 3 R's and some religion were taught. Dame schools were considered town schools if the towns contributed to their support. However the genuine town school was conducted by a male teacher whose salary was paid out of public funds.

In the early colonial days, when a town's population was confined within a small area as a precaution against Indian attacks, children could easily reach the schools. However, after King Philip's War (1675–1678) the fear of Indian attacks was diminished and the colonists moved their settlements farther from town. In many instances it be-

---

[5]Ellwood P. Cubberley, *Public Education in the United States* (Boston: Houghton Mifflin Company, 1919), pp. 25-26.

[6]Edwin E. Slosson, *The American Spirit in Education* (New Haven: Yale University Press, 1921), p. 19. From the Yale Chronicles of America. Copyright Yale University Press. United States Publishers Association, Inc., sole distributors.

came impossible for children to walk to school. These more remote districts, therefore, established their own pay schools for children, causing the decline of the town school's enrollment. As it became more difficult to maintain the schools financially, the town levied a property tax on all of their members. The more distant members of the town demanded that, in return for the taxes they paid, their children should attend the town school. The result was the "moving school" which moved to different districts of the town and stayed the length of time that was proportionate to the amount of taxes contributed by the district. In the first quarter of the eighteenth century this had become a common practice in New England. As the towns began to return the taxes to their districts, the districts were given the authority to appoint school officials who had the right to levy school taxes and appoint teachers. By the latter part of the eighteenth century, the school district system evolved and from there spread throughout the rest of the country.

Parochial schools. Because there were so many religious denominations in the Middle Colonies, the educational ideas of any one group could not predominate. Consequently, church schools were established, and were taught by the minister or any qualified person of the religious denomination. The four R's, reading, writing, arithmetic, and religion, constituted the curriculum, and instruction was given in the vernacular of the country of the group's origin. Those who favored parochial schools were opposed to state control of education.

The Society for the Propagation of the Gospel in Foreign Parts conducted much of the parochial educational work. Established in England in 1701, it was a missionary society of the Church of England, which supported the society's ministers and teachers. The society operated many schools in the middle and southern states, giving instruction in the four R's to children of the Anglican faith.

Charity schools. While the majority of the early colonial schools were pay schools, the poor laws cared for children who could not afford the fees. In some cases, they attended private schools, and their fees paid for them. In other instances, special schools were established for them. These charity or pauper schools were not popular, because parents hesitated to be labelled as paupers or as recipients of charity.

Private tutors. Widespread use of tutorial education was found in the southern colonies. The children of the well-to-do received their education from private tutors, or were sent to school in England. The qualifications of their tutors varied greatly. Some of them were refined gentlemen who had graduated from college in England. Others, however, were indentured servants who possessed only a minimum ability in reading and writing. The first teacher of George Washington was an indentured servant who ". . . was a slow, rusty old man by the name of Hobby."[7] Yet much of the education which took place on the plantation was not academic.

> Plantation life itself was a liberal education in agriculture, business management, horsemanship, and the conventions of polite society —subjects as essential in those days to a well-rounded career as any of the more academic branches.[8]

Apprenticeship training. Apprenticeship training began in the guilds of the Middle Ages and was practiced throughout Europe at the time of American colonization. Although it was vocational training, the master craftsman was responsible for both the moral and civic training of his apprentice, as well as some training in the 3 R's.

The individual went through three stages of training: apprentice, journeyman, and master. As an apprentice he lived in the home of the master craftsman, who was to treat him as one of his family, providing him with food, clothing, shelter, and necessary training. The apprentice received no wages, but he was expected to do his work conscientiously and respect the authority of the master. After completing a period of apprenticeship, he became a journeyman and was paid for his work. Finally, if his work met guild standards, he became a master craftsman.

The length of the apprenticeship varied with the occupation being learned. However, in 1562, a statute was passed in England limiting the apprenticeship to a minimum of seven years. The individual, by law, had to be at least twenty-one years old before he was released from his apprenticeship. The practice of apprenticeship continued in the colonies, and was the most widespread type of education for orphans or children who could not afford an academic education. Even one of our most famous Americans, Benjamin Franklin, went through apprenticeship training.

Early Teachers

Elementary school teachers during the colonial period varied in their qualifications. Many of them were ministers with good educational backgrounds. If the minister did not teach, he often would judge the

---

[7]Clifton Johnson, *Old-Time Schools and School-Books* (New York: The Macmillan Company, 1904), p. 33.

[8]Edwin E. Slosson, *op. cit.*, p. 43. From *The Yale Chronicles of America.* United States Publishers Association, Inc., sole distributors.

qualifications of teachers who were hired. These qualifications usually consisted of good character and a knowledge of the fundamentals, reading, writing, and some arithmetic. Women who conducted dame schools had similar qualifications. Indentured servants, used widely as teachers in the middle and southern colonies, did not always prove effective or desirable, which is shown by the following newspaper advertisement: "Ran away: a Servant man who followed the occupation of a Schoolmaster, much given to drinking and gambling."[9] There were, of course, many effective teachers among them, but in general they were not as good as schoolmasters who were hired and paid.

The chief qualification of a colonial teacher was his ability to maintain discipline. In the dame school, the offender frequently was pinned to the teacher's skirt, or rapped on the head with a thimble. Male teachers resorted to whipping students either "on the run" or while tied to a whipping post. There were other forms of punishment, such as isolation, the dunce cap and chair, holding a heavy object at arm's length until fatigued, public exhibition of the errant pupil, and other methods depending upon the imagination of the teacher. The right of the teacher to discipline children was unquestioned by the parents, although they could request him not to be so severe.

Besides instructing children and maintaining discipline, the schoolmaster had to make and mend the goose-quill pens that were used in writing. It was a time consuming task. Indentured servants who served as teachers or tutors often were required to work in the parish or on the plantation, as caretakers, sweepers, or even grave-diggers. Some town schoolmasters worked their own land from spring until fall, and then taught to supplement their income.

The wages early teachers received were small. Many teachers were paid "in kind" with barley, peas, corn, rye, lumber, iron, or other products of the particular location. Their wages were sometimes supplemented by land grants, room and board, or exemption from taxes. It has been estimated that a teacher's salary was in the neighborhood of sixty to seventy dollars a year.

School Buildings

In many New England towns, the meeting house was also used as the school house. Sometimes it was built of sawn timber; otherwise logs were

---

[9]Clifton Johnson, *op. cit.*, p. 33.

used. It consisted of one room with a fireplace, windows that may have been fitted with greased paper to keep out the weather, and backless wooden benches. When buildings were erected specifically as schools, they were usually log buildings in a centrally located spot on land that was not otherwise valuable. Along the inner side walls a continuous plank board could serve as a desk for the pupils who were seated on the long wooden benches. The fireplace heated the building with wood that had been donated by the pupils' parents. Older boys were responsible for maintaining the fire, and girls were charged with sweeping out the school. Little attention was given to keeping the school in good repair, with the result that many of them were in a deplorable condition.

Curriculum

A full curriculum in a colonial elementary school consisted of the previously mentioned four R's. Yet arithmetic was infrequently taught. Many towns were satisfied to hire teachers who possessed no knowledge of arithmetic.

Reading and religion were studied hand in hand because of the form of the reading material. Spelling also was studied with reading. The first reading material was the *Hornbook*, which was not a book at all. It consisted of a printed page covered with a transparent sheet of horn protecting it from soiling or mutilation, and mounted on a square board. A handle from the board enabled the pupil to hold it up easily. The printed page of the *Hornbook* began with the alphabet, in capital and small letters. The alphabet was followed by the vowels, separately and then in combination with the consonants. After this came the Lord's Prayer. Some hornbooks included the Roman numerals at the end. When the child had mastered his A,B,C's and the *Hornbook*, he progressed to Catechism and the Bible. This was the extent of his instruction in reading. Until the end of the seventeenth century, his reading instruction extended no farther than the Bible.

The New England Primer was issued in 1690, and helped to mould the minds of children for over a century. Primers had been published in England as books of devotion, the content of which varied with the publisher's beliefs. *The New England Primer* was one of these early variations, and went through several changes during the century that it was used. Its content was religious, but it became the chief instrument of learning to read. An estimated three million copies of it were sold during the time it was used.

The Primer included syllables, and religious and moral rhymes and prose. It had an illustrated alphabet, accompanied by the following rhymes:[10]

A   In Adam's fall
    We sinned all.

B   Heaven to find,
    The Bible Mind.

C   Christ crucified
    For sinners died.

        . . . .

X   Xerxes did die,
    And so must I.

Y   While youth do cheer
    Death may be near.

Z   Zacchaeus he
    Did climb the tree
    Our Lord to see.

With its religious, moral, and philosophical observations read by millions, *The New England Primer* was obviously a formative influence on generations of children.

Writing first was taught in writing schools and dame schools. As town schools were established, the skill was taught with the other subjects, making the writing schools unnecessary. Goose-quill pens were dipped in homemade ink to write on paper, which was costly and not always obtainable. As a substitute for paper, the children often used birch bark. Examples of the children's writing show that they achieved a commendable degree of proficiency.

Arithmetic, when taught, was usually taught without a textbook. The teachers used sum-books, which were collections of notes, that they had compiled when they were taught arithmetic. Rules, problems, and exercises were assigned from these. It was not until after 1743, when Thomas Dilworth published his *The Schoolmaster's Assistant*, that the study of arithmetic became more popular.

EDUCATION IN TRANSITION

For several years before the Revolution, and for many years after, Americans turned their attention to independence. Schools and school-

---

[10]*Ibid.*, as quoted by Johnson, pp. 78-79.

ing were neglected since the war was costly, and money was scarce. Except for large population centers, schools became increasingly rare.

A change in thinking, however, occurred in educational matters. The influence of the New England church had been weakened and greater secular control of education took its place. Before the Revolution there were established religions in nine colonies. After the Constitution of the United States was adopted, most of these states did away with established religions, and their state constitutions prohibited the establishing of a state religion. This, coupled with the fact that the Constitution neglected to mention education (therefore leaving it to the states), laid the basis for the complete secularization of education in the years ahead.

Federal Land Grants for Education

At a time when educational conditions were poor, the federal government passed two ordinances which encouraged and supported education. Congress received control of the Northwest Territory between the Allegheny Mountains and the Mississippi River in 1785. The territory was surveyed and organized into townships, six miles square, divided into thirty-six sections, each one mile square.

The Ordinance of 1785 stated that "There shall be reserved the lot No. 16 of every township, for the maintenance of public schools within the said township." Later, the Ordinance of 1787 stated in part: "Religion, morality, and knowledge being necessary to good government and the happiness of mankind, schools and the means of education shall be encouraged." An extension of the 1787 ordinance also provided for the donation of two townships for purposes of a university.

Beginning in Ohio in 1802, each new state was given the sixteenth section for the maintenance of schools; in return, the states agreed not to tax federal lands within their borders. The only new states not receiving this grant were Texas, which possessed its own land, and Maine and West Virginia, which were formed from other states. In 1850, when California was admitted to the union, the sixteenth and thirty-sixth sections were given to it and other new states thereafter. The only exceptions to these grants were Utah, Arizona, and New Mexico, which received four sections because of the low valuation of their land. In time, these land grants amounted to over 80,000,000 acres. Since only the income produced from the rental or sale of the land could be used, a permanent income for the maintenance of education was established.

The End of the Colonial Period

As the Revolutionary War years passed, prominent Americans expressed themselves on the importance of education. Jefferson advocated the education of the common people as the best means of preserving freedom. A national university was recommended by George Washington, while John Adams and James Madison favored an informed citizenry. However, their recommendations were not put into effect until many years later.

In the meantime, the Massachusetts Law of 1789 crystallized some past practices and set a more realistic population standard for the establishment and maintenance of schools. The district system that had been in use for so many years was given a legal basis, and a provision was made for supervision of schools. The following provisions were enacted for the establishment of schools.

Towns of fifty families: to maintain an English school for six months a year

Towns of one hundred families: to maintain an English school for an entire twelve months

Towns of one hundred and fifty families: to maintain an English school for twelve months, and a grammar school for six months

Towns of two hundred families: to maintain an English school and a grammar school for twelve months

The law of 1789 tried to raise the teacher qualification standards by prescribing that all elementary teachers obtain certificates and be United States citizens. All teachers in the higher schools had to be college graduates or certified by a highly qualified minister. Although these requirements slightly improved educational standards, education continued to lag for another half-century.

PROGRESS IN THE NINETEENTH CENTURY

By the nineteenth century, free tax-supported schools had taken root in New England, but not in the Middle Atlantic and southern states. Even though the spirit of democracy was growing in the middle and southern states, class distinctions remained to block progress. Education still was considered a private matter. Public funds, it was thought, should be used only for the education of the poor. Several states had legislated the use of public funds for education, but they usually stipulated that these funds should be used for indigent children.

Private philanthropic societies established in larger cities made important contributions to the education of poor children. The most influential of these societies was the New York School Society, which later became The Public School Society of New York. Organized in 1805, one of the society's founders was Dewitt Clinton. Although a private society, it received support from public funds, a procedure which was protested by religious groups who felt that they should share in the funds. Governor Seward ended the dispute in 1842, by terminating financial support. In that same year, New York City established public schools. Ten years later the Public School Society disbanded and turned its facilities over to the city.

Free school societies were established in other cities such as Washington, Baltimore, and Philadelphia. Founded by private subscription, and receiving some support from public funds, the societies represented a transition from private to public support of education. In 1849, the New York state legislature passed an act that required school support by local taxation, supplemented with state funds; however the act was repealed. It was not until 1867 that New York state required free public schools for all children.

Pennsylvania in 1834 had passed a law requiring free education throughout the state. Here again there was pressure for the repeal of the law, but the efforts of Thaddeus Stevens on its behalf kept the law alive. The legislation was permissive, and many sections of the state, where the belief in private schools was still strong, did not take advantage of it.

Influence of Lancastrian Schools

At the turn of the nineteenth century, two Englishmen, Andrew Bell (1753–1832) and Joseph Lancaster (1778–1838), simultaneously introduced the monitorial system of instruction. Their plans were similar, and a controversy developed over which man was the originator of the plan. Both plans had their adherents in England, but Lancaster's plan became popular in the United States.

Under the monitorial plan, one teacher instructed brighter pupils, who then instructed a group of ten pupils placed under their care. A monitor (bright pupil) was assigned for each subject, and for each level of a subject. The regular pupils were classified by their subject and ability level, after which they were assigned to the proper monitor for instruction. When the regular pupils had completed the requirements under one monitor, they were promoted to the next level and another monitor. Under this system a single teacher could instruct many pupils since he taught only the monitors; the actual number of pupils taught in Lancastrian schools may have varied from a hundred to a thousand. Lancaster, who had great organizational ability, planned everything in detail, therefore any teacher could use the system without difficulty.

The Lancastrian system was first introduced to the United States in New York City in 1806. From there it spread to many other cities in various parts of the country. In 1818, Lancaster came to the United States, and spent the rest of his life helping to organize schools based on his method.

There were many advantages to the monitorial system. Until its introduction, the schools used individual instruction which made education slow, uneconomical, and created many motivational and disciplinary problems. Lancaster's system was economical, quickened instruction, and kept pupils active and more interested, causing disciplinary problems to become minimal. Furthermore, it graded and promoted pupils according to their ability. Introduced at a time when there was still considerable opposition to public education, it helped to arouse interest in the value of education, and made education available to many individuals who would not have received it otherwise.

Yet, the monitorial system had its shortcomings. It was a mechanical, superficial type of instruction. Obviously, the monitors could not take the place of their more qualified teachers, which caused complaints about the inadequacy of instruction. Gradually interest in the system decreased, and by 1840, the Lancastrian system had been discarded. It, however, had brought education to public attention.

At this time when interest in education was quickening, several gifted, dedicated educational reformers made important contributions which improved the quality of education. James G. Carter laid the groundwork for reforms which were extended by Horace Mann and Henry Barnard.

James G. Carter (1795–1849) had laid considerable groundwork for educational reform in Massachusetts. He had succeeded in having enacted in 1826 a law which gave towns the power to appoint a school board for the purpose of supervising districts within their borders. The school board was also given the authority to select textbooks and appoint teachers. Carter was also instrumental in having a state school fund established in 1834, and the country's first state board of education appointed in 1837. It was generally felt that Carter would become the first secretary of the board, but Horace Mann received the appointment in his place.

Horace Mann (1796–1859) was an individual with seemingly inexhaustible energy directed toward education. A native of Massachusetts, he held many important positions during his lifetime: lawyer, state senator, secretary of the Board of Education of Massachusetts, United States representative, and college president. His greatest contributions to education, however, were made while he was secretary of the State Board of Education.

The State Board of Education in Massachusetts did not have administrative powers. Through its secretary, the board was to investigate conditions in education, and then make recommendations to the legislature. Some of the corrections needed, according to Mann, were:

> (1) In two-thirds of all the towns in the State teachers were allowed to commence school without being previously examined and approved by the committee as required by law. (2) In many cases teachers obtained their wages from the treasurer without lodging any duplicate certificate with him, as the law required. (3) The law required committees to prescribe text-books. In one hundred towns—a third part in the Commonwealth—this duty was neglected, and all the evils incident to a confusion of books suffered. (4) The law required committees to furnish books to scholars whose parents were unable or had neglected to provide them. In forty towns this was omitted, and poor children went to school without books. (5) The law required committees to visit the schools a certain number of times. From their own statements it appeared that out of three hundred towns about two hundred and fifty did not comply with the law. (6) On an average one-third of all the children of the State between the ages of four and sixteen were absent from school in the winter, and two-fifths of them in the summer.[11]

For twelve years, Mann devoted himself to reforming education in Massachusetts. Each year he published a report of his findings and his recommendations. He traveled, lectured, debated, and won many of his reforms, sometimes against strong opposition. He established the *Common School Journal*, for the dissemination of professional ideas among teachers and others interested in education. He spent several months in Europe studying the educational systems of various countries. Of the schools he observed, he preferred the Prussian ones, and incorporated many of their ideas and practices in his recommendations. Mann's reports were read throughout the United States, and his views

---

[11]As quoted by Paul Monroe, *Founding of the American Public School System,* I (New York: The Macmillan Company, 1940), p. 248.

influenced educational practices far beyond Massachusetts' borders. His major contributions to education might be summarized as follows:

1. He helped popularize the idea that education should be universal, free, and non-sectarian.
2. He led the organization of schools into a state system.
3. The school year was lengthened by a month.
4. Appropriations for public schools were doubled.
5. Salaries of teachers were increased more than fifty per cent.
6. A great number of inadequate school buildings were replaced.
7. He recommended compulsory attendance laws.
8. He organized three normal schools in Massachusetts, which were the first in America.

Mann also made recommendations for the improvement of teaching methods which were based on his *Seventh Report* in 1843 describing his findings in European education. Some of his recommendations show the influence of Rousseau and Pestalozzi, who was influenced originally by Rousseau. Prussia enthusiastically had adopted Pestalozzi's ideas. Consequently, the Swiss educator's influence was brought to the United States by Mann. Mann recommended the elimination of corporal punishment; the substitution of love and kindness for fear in the classroom; the stimulation of the child's interests; the use of the inductive method in the classroom; and the classification of pupils into grades.

Judging by his results, Mann exerted a monumental influence on the development of the American public school system. His reforms, brought about in Massachusetts, spread to other states, and what he did not accomplish was achieved by others who fought to reform education.

Henry Barnard (1811–1900) accomplished in Connecticut what Mann accomplished for Massachuetts. The public schools of Connecticut were in a state of decline when Barnard took an interest in the problems of education. Like Mann, he went to Europe to study European schools, and stayed there for two years, from 1835 to 1837, giving special attention to Pestalozzian practices.

After his return to Connecticut, he began a whole series of educational activities that were to occupy the rest of his life. During his career, Barnard was secretary of the Connecticut State Board of Commissioners for Common Schools which he had helped to create as a member of the state legislature. He also was State Commissioner of Public Schools in Rhode Island, principal of a state normal school in Connecticut, president of the University of Wisconsin and St. John's College in Maryland, and the first United States Commissioner of Education.

As secretary of the State Board in Connecticut, he tried to arouse people to the need for better conditions in public schools. He lectured, traveled all over the state, addressed teachers' conventions, corresponded widely, established and edited the *Connecticut Common School Journal,* and issued annual reports on the schools. Apparently his attempts were too zealous to suit certain political elements, because, in 1842, after four years as secretary, his office was abolished.

Undeterred, Barnard went to Rhode Island where his efforts resulted in the creation of a state board of education, and he was appointed the first commissioner of schools in Rhode Island. Under his leadership, great improvements were brought about in the state: taxation for public schools was accepted, school libraries were established in the towns, teachers' institutes were conducted, and a demonstration model school was used to familiarize teachers with methods of teaching. His health failing, he left Rhode Island after five years and returned to Connecticut where, by this time, he received a warm welcome. He served as principal of a recently established normal school and as *ex officio* secretary of the state board of education.

In 1885, because of his health, he gave up these positions and began his monumental task of editing and publishing the *American Journal of Education,* which eventually ran to thirty-two volumes. This journal carried important articles on the history and other aspects of education, and remains a valuable primary source for the study of American education. The journal besides taking many years to complete, drained his personal financial resources. Rounding out his official life, Barnard became the first United States Commissioner of Education in 1867, an office which he had helped to create and in which he served for three years.

Although Barnard was instrumental in bringing about many educational reforms, he is considered more as "the scholar" among American educators. Besides his various journals, ". . . he published 52 works on the history and theory of education and accounts of European and American school systems . . . He gave America her earliest literature of education."[12]

By the middle of the nineteenth century, the work of Mann and Barnard, and many lesser-known reformers, gave momentum to the growing awareness of public education: people became more aware of education; taxation for the support of schools received wider acceptance; supervision of local schools improved, and the machinery was set

---

[12]Paul Monroe, ed., *A Cyclopedia of Education,* I (New York: The Macmillan Company, 1928), p. 325.

up for state supervision and administration of schools. More attention was given to the qualification of teachers, their training, and their improvement while in service. The old recitation method was challenged by newer methods of teaching, and there were the beginnings of more amicable relationships between teachers and pupils.

Curriculum Changes

By the middle of the nineteenth century, grammar, geography, and history found their way into an elementary school program of the four R's and spelling, although these new subjects, like arithmetic, did not appear in all schools.

Geography had been studied informally as a part of reading instruction during the eighteenth century. Early in the nineteenth century, it became a formal school subject. The first American geography textbook was published in 1784 by Jedidiah Morse in New Haven, Connecticut,[13] and others quickly followed it. The first books were unillustrated, but gradually illustrations, and sometimes accompanying atlases, were added. The globe was also used as an instructional aid. During the first part of the nineteenth century, the object lesson was used occasionally, but the Pestalozzian principles of observation were not employed widely until the end of the century.

Early teachers were not examined on their proficiency in grammar, and they were not expected to teach the subject. Although Lindley Murray's textbook on grammar was published in 1795, and became popular in America, the subject was seldom taught in the elementary schools. Grammar was regarded as a boring and useless subject by many, and there were few teachers qualified to teach it. By 1810 most schools were adopting it.[14] However, as late as 1843, in Provincetown, Massachusetts, officials noted that grammar was neglected even though the state law required its teaching.[15] A greater number of grammar textbooks displaying a determined effort to be more interesting in text and illustrations began to appear at this time. At mid-century, grammar was taught regularly in the larger towns, but still did not receive attention in the small town schools.

History, like geography, received some early attention as part of reading exercises. It was taught as a subject during the first part of the nineteenth century, although it was not widely taught before the Civil

---

[13]Clifton Johnson, *op. cit.*, p. 318.
[14]*Ibid.*, p. 366.
[15]Edgar W. Knight, *op. cit.*, p. 434.

War. As with other subjects, the lack of adequate textbooks was a problem in teaching history. The first popular American history text was published by Rev. C. A. Goodrich in 1822 and was followed ten years later by Noah Webster's *History of the United States.* Textbooks dealing with the history of other countries also began to appear. Vermont was one of the first states to insist upon teaching history. In 1827 it was added to the elementary school program.[16] Although Massachusetts also required history in larger schools, it was not until 1857 that history was required in elementary schools.

During the first half of the nineteenth century the evolution of the elementary school curriculum was completed. Cubberley's summary of it follows:[17]

> By 1830, certainly, we have the full curriculum of our elementary schools, as it was by 1860, clearly in use in our better city systems. The subjects were these:

For the younger children	*For the older children*
Letters and syllables	Advanced Reading
Reading	Advanced Spelling
Writing	Penmanship
Spelling	Arithmetic
Numbers	Geography
Elementary Language	Grammar
Good Behavior	Manners and Morals
	United States History (?)

For the girls

Sewing and Darning

During the last part of the nineteenth century, a few other subjects were added to the new curriculum. For example, Massachusetts in 1870 made drawing a mandatory subject, and, in 1885, added physiology and hygiene. In more recent years, of course, the elementary program has included subjects such as art, music, and science.

Development of the Graded School

The sorting and promoting of pupils by grades in an eight-grade elementary school developed only in the last one hundred years. Originally schools were either reading schools or writing schools, in which the

---

[16]Ellwood P. Cubberley, *op. cit.,* p. 307.
[17]*Ibid.,* p. 222.

teacher had pupils of all ability levels, ages and stages of process. Next, general divisions of instruction were established, and schools became either primary schools, intermediate schools, or upper schools. Many other names were given these schools, such as common, junior, and high school. These general classifications were in wide use by 1840. Grade classifications within these schools, however, had not yet occurred.

The monitorial schools had a semblance of classification by ability level as pupils were grouped and taught at their level by appropriate monitors before their promotion to the next higher monitorial group. This system, with its minute classifications, bears no resemblance to grading as we now know it. Exactly when grading began in our schools is not known. Monroe quotes Henry Barnard as saying that in 1848 the Quincy school of Boston was the first school to use graded classes.[18] It is recorded that in 1853 New York City schools had thirteen grades, which included secondary education. Presumably, grading began in the 1830's, was used in the cities in the 1850's, and was widespread by 1870. There was no uniformity in the number of grades in elementary schools, this number varying between seven and nine. Eventually, the eight-grade elementary school predominated.

Compulsory Attendance

Compulsory education laws date back to the Massachusetts law of 1642, but over two centuries elapsed before Massachusetts passed the first compulsory attendance law in 1852. The law of 1852 required children between the ages of eight and fourteen to attend school twelve weeks a year. Of these twelve weeks, six of them had to be consecutive weeks of attendance. Under the law which was weak and ineffective, poor children could be excused from attending. This law was soon followed by other laws with more stringent provisions.

Following the lead of Massachusetts, early compulsory attendance laws were passed in the District of Columbia in 1864; Vermont in 1867; New Hampshire, Michigan, and Washington, 1871; and Connecticut and New Mexico in 1872. By 1890 twenty-seven states and the District of Columbia had compulsory attendance laws. Most states required attendance until the age of fourteen, but a few extended it to the age of fifteen or sixteen. Connecticut was the only state to require attendance for the full term of the school year. By the early part of

---

[18]Paul Monroe, *op. cit.*, p. 257.

the twentieth century all forty-eight states had passed compulsory attendance laws. Mississippi was the last of these states to pass a compulsory attendance law in 1918.

The Beginning of the Child-Centered Movement in the United States

During the nineteenth century, the theory of developmentalism influenced European education. Pestalozzi, influenced by Rousseau, attempted to "psychologize" education by studying the nature of children and adapting teaching methods to the child's development. He recommended moving from the simple to the complex, using sensory impressions, proceeding from the concrete to the abstract, and felt that love should characterize the teacher-pupil relationship. Herbart built upon Pestalozzi's theories, modifying them and placing them on a more scientific basis. He developed the theory of apperception, urged the development of many-sided interests in the pupils, and formulated for teachers four formal steps of instruction. At this time, Froebel, also influenced by Pestalozzi, turned his attention to pre-school training and established the first kindergarten. These developments were taking place in Europe during the first part of the nineteenth century.

Mann and Barnard, both of whom had traveled to Europe and were impressed with many of the innovations they saw, tried to incorporate them into educational reforms in the United States. These men were an important, but not the only, means by which European ideas were transmitted to America.

William Maclure, a wealthy member of the United States commission to France, provided the United States with its first direct contact with Pestalozzianism. He brought back to the United States Joseph Neef, who taught in Pestalozzi's school at Yverdon. In the United States, Neef organized schools based on the Pestalozzian principles in Philadelphia and Village Green, Pennsylvania; in Louisville, Kentucky; in Harmony, Indiana, where he taught from 1825 to 1828; and in Cincinnati and Steubenville, Ohio. Neef spent the last twenty years of his life promoting Pestalozzi's principles through writing. However, he had little immediate success in his efforts.

Other Americans traveled to Europe and some published reports on their observations of European education. In 1819, John Griscom published *A Year In Europe* which stimulated a little interest in Pestalozzi's principles. A short time later, in 1820 and 1825–1829, William Woodbridge visited Europe and published his *Letters* on European conditions. He also wrote two geography textbooks which incorporated

Pestalozzi's methods. Victor Cousin's *Report on the Condition of Public Instruction in Germany, and Particularly Prussia* also exerted a great deal of influence on education. Cousin made this report which was printed in 1832 to the French government; it was reprinted in England in 1834, and in America in 1835. The report supported the idea of state control of education. It was followed by Calvin E. Stowe's influential report, *Report on Elementary Education in Europe,* made to the Ohio legislature in 1837. Stowe contrasted the educational practices of Prussia with those in Ohio, and advised the adoption of the Prussian practices where, incidentally, Pestalozzian principles were used widely. Finally, came the European visits by Barnard, 1835–1837, and Mann, 1843, with their subsequent reports.

These contacts with European ideas during the first half of the nineteenth century began to make an impression on American thinking. They served as a foundation for translating theory into practice toward the end of the century, when the ideas of Pestalozzi, Herbart, and Froebel were used in this country.

Although Pestalozzi's ideas had received some attention through various reports and textbooks which had incorporated his principles, the main impetus was given to them by the Oswego Movement in New York. Edwin A. Sheldon, superintendent of schools in Oswego, became interested in the Pestalozzian methods formalized by Charles and Elizabeth Mayo of England. In 1860, he established a normal school for training his teachers in the Pestalozzian methods. He brought from England teachers who were familiar with the methods to act as instructors in the normal school. The school received widespread recognition, and hosted many prominent visitors who, in turn, spread its fame. Other normal schools throughout the country followed the example of Oswego, and Pestalozzi's principles, with special emphasis on the "object lesson" and oral instruction, became regarded as a necessary part of a teacher's training. These ideas were carried forward by men such as William T. Harris, who organized elementary school science as a subject, and Colonel Francis W. Parker, whose efforts led to improved methods of teaching geography.

Herbart's theories also were revived in Germany about twenty-five years after his death, when Ziller published a book on them. A German society developed to study Herbartian ideas, and a pedagogical school was established at the University of Jena, with a detailed course of study including practice lessons incorporating Herbartian principles.

Americans who studied at Jena, returned with the Herbartian ideas taught there. Of books that began to appear, three were greatly responsible for the spread of Herbart's methods in United States normal schools. The first, *Essentials of Method*, by Charles DeGarmo, was published in 1889; the second, Charles A. McMurray's *General Method*, appeared in 1892; and, the third, a cooperative affair between Charles McMurray and his brother Frank, *Method in the Recitation* was published in 1897. In 1892 the National Herbart Society was founded to promote and discuss his ideas. The name was changed ten years later to the National Society for the Study of Education, as Herbart's influence waned.

During the last decade of the nineteenth century, Herbart's influence was impressive. Normal schools began to teach his ideas, devoted time to the five steps formalized by his followers in planning lessons, and gave new emphasis to methods of teaching history and literature. At the elementary level, the Herbartian influence was responsible for the introduction of history and literature as part of the curriculum and resulted in greater attention to the correlation between subjects. Although certain aspects of Herbart's psychology have been discredited, he advanced and stimulated further interest in psychology. In this connection, Cole makes some interesting observations:

> The Herbartian remnants in modern education are usually so much a part of what to Americans is traditional school procedure as to be almost unnoticed. A young teacher learns to make lesson plans, perhaps both inductive and deductive, without knowing of her debt to Herbart. Many teachers of today are convinced that they can make or remake their pupils according to the nature of their instruction, and they are quite sure that they can create interest where none grew before. Although the progressive movement of recent decades had tended to alter the relation of the teacher to the class, the teacher still remains the font of knowledge in most classrooms. Most teachers believe in using childish interests for the purpose of better adapting a child to his present environment. The mother who says that her child was a good boy under Miss X's teaching but has become a bad boy since being exposed to Miss Y's instruction is also being Herbartian without knowing it. Perhaps the greatest significance of Herbart's works, however, was his insistence upon pedagogy as a science, based upon the application of psychology to the procedures within the classroom. If this idea were not generally believed at the present time, the complex program of teacher training would hardly be necessary.[19]

Froebel, another disciple of Pestalozzi, also influenced education. He not only established the kindergarten as a new level of schooling, but

---

[19]Luella Cole, *A History of Education* (New York: Rinehart & Company, 1950), p. 505.

also he was responsible for the more careful study of the child's nature, and for emphasis on self-activity or "learning by doing." The kindergarten fostered play, motor activities, expression, and social cooperation, all of which were provided by Froebel through the use of his "gifts" and "occupations", the play circle, and the songs he composed for the pupils, allowing them as much free expression as possible.

The kindergarten became popular during the last quarter of the nineteenth century, although there were kindergartens before then. The first kindergarten established in the United States, a German-speaking private school, was begun in Watertown, Wisconsin, in 1855, by a former pupil of Froebel, Mrs. Carl Schurz. Five years later, Miss Elizabeth Peabody opened the first private English-speaking kindergarten in Boston. She also was influential in establishing a training school for kindergarten teachers in 1868. The kindergarten first became a part of a United States public school system in 1873, when William T. Harris, superintendent of schools in St. Louis, invited Miss Susan Blow to open one there. From then on, the kindergarten movement spread rapidly; however, private kindergartens outnumbered public ones. By 1880 there were approximately three hundred kindergartens and ten kindergarten training schools in the United States.[20]

By the end of the nineteenth century psychology and educational psychology were beginning to take form. Pestalozzi, Herbart, and Froebel had started the study of the child's personality and the adaptation of instruction to his personality. Since Froebel was concerned with the pre-school child, and Herbart with the adolescent, some beginnings had been made for all levels of schooling.

The effects of these new theories began to appear in American schools. Until this time, teachers had made little effort to understand the child. He usually was treated as a miniature adult by teachers who had only the minimum knowledge and qualifications. Now they were beginning to understand, through their training in the normal schools, that the child is different at various stages of growth and development. Until the end of the nineteenth century, too, instruction had been individual. The teacher's function was to hear lessons which the pupils recited in a parrot-like fashion; now, there were the beginnings of object lessons, pupil activity and expression, careful lesson planning in the formal Herbartian manner by the teacher, and better textbooks in all subjects. The tyrannical exercise of authority by the teacher was ending, and in its place was the recommendation for a relationship between the teacher and pupil based on sympathy and understanding.

These were only beginnings, however. The knowledge acquired was

---

[20]Ellwood P. Cubberley, *op. cit.*, p. 320.

still largely theoretical and lacked an experimental basis to prove its validity or falsity. This lack was partially closed during the last quarter of the nineteenth century.

In 1879 the first organized attempt at experimental psychology occurred when Wilhelm Wundt opened a psychological laboratory in Leipzig, Germany. Here they scientifically studied both the processes underlying the operation of the external senses and the mental processes involved in learning. The laboratory drew students from Europe and America, who in turn, made notable contributions of their own.

William James (1842–1910) who also spent thirty-five years as a professor at Harvard University was one of the greatest contributors to organizing psychology as an empirical science. James, a pragmatist, subscribed to the empirical approach in psychology. A prolific writer, his most influential work was *The Principles of Psychology,* published in 1890 and subsequently translated into many languages. This work contains, among other things, his famous explanation of the laws of habit formation; the advisability of appealing to natural instincts in learning; and his views on transfer of training. Later, in 1900, he published his *Talks to Teachers,* which exerted a widespread influence on educational practice.

G. Stanley Hall (1844–1924), an early student at Wundt's laboratory, also contributed to the study of children. Possessed of a broad educational background, including a Ph.D. from Harvard where he had studied under William James, he went to Europe to continue his studies at the University of Berlin and the Leipzig laboratory. He then taught at Johns Hopkins University, and later became president of Clark University in Massachusetts. Under his leadership, Clark University became a leading center for child study. Hall published several books for which he obtained much of his information through the use of the questionnaire method. *Adolescence,* published in 1904, helped to further the study of adolescent and child psychology, even though his findings were questioned because of his extensive use of the questionnaire method.

TWENTIETH CENTURY TRENDS

As we have seen, progress in education was woefully slow during the first two hundred years of American history, but it gathered momentum during the nineteenth century. In the twentieth century, this momentum has achieved an almost dizzying pace, with rapid progress occurring in almost all phases of education. Among the myriad details of this progress, at least two general trends deserve special consideration: 1) the continuation of the child-centered movement, reaching a climax with the theories of Progressive Education; and 2) an increased emphasis on science and the scientific method, including an attempt to measure quantitatively various aspects of the individual's growth and development.

The Child-Centered Movement

The twentieth century has brought the child under practically microscopic observation in behavioral and in learning situations. From the time of G. Stanley Hall to the present day an increasing number of studies and experiments have been conducted, resulting in an endless stream of publications by countless psychologists and educators. A mass of information (sometimes conflicting) has become available on learning principles, factors influencing learning, and the child's nature, growth and development. In recent years, Arnold Gessell and his associates at Yale University have made notable contributions to child development.

The study of twentieth century education inevitably will focus on the name of John Dewey, who has been described as the most influential philosopher and educator in modern times. Born in Burlington, Vermont, his life spanned almost a century, from 1859 to 1952. His education included undergraduate work at the University of Vermont and graduate work at Johns Hopkins University. He taught at the University of Michigan until 1894, when he left to become the head of the Department of Philosophy and Education at the University of Chicago. In 1896, he opened a laboratory school, in which he tried to implement his theories on socializing education. In 1903, he joined the staff of Columbia University, where he remained for the rest of his career.

During his formative years, Dewey was influenced by the philosophies of Hegel, Darwin, and William James. He accepted some ideas from them while rejecting others. Similarly, he concurred with some of the theories of Herbart and Froebel, but disagreed with much of what they said. Dewey himself stated that his philosophy was built in eclectic fashion, and that he yielded to many influences in the process.[21] Perhaps it is for this reason that many readers have found it difficult

---

[21]On this point, and for a general evaluation of Dewey's philosophy, see Robert R. Rusk, *The Doctrines of the Great Educators* (London: Macmillan & Co. Ltd, 1954), pp. 284-303.

to grasp his theories, and some followers may have misinterpreted his statements. It may also be the explanation for some inconsistencies between his earlier and later publications. Among his more important publications are the following: *School and Society*, 1899; *How We Think*, 1909; *Democracy and Education*, 1916; *Human Nature and Conduct*, 1922; and *Experience and Education*, 1938.

Dewey's philosophy combines pragmatism, socialism, and materialism. It has been labelled by some as experimentalism, by others as instrumentalism. Dewey's belief that objective truth does not exist makes up its pragmatic aspect. For him, the test of truth is its practical value in a given situation. In this theory, experience must always test truth. Yet, even if truth meets this test, an individual cannot assume that it will always do so; what is true today may not be true in the future. The concept of change is basic to Dewey's philosophy. Consequently, there can be no predetermined, fixed goal in his scheme of education, because the desirability or validity of the goal may change before it can be reached. Dewey held that education could not prepare a child for life; rather, education should be life, and should try to duplicate the conditions of the society in which the individual lives.

The objective of Dewey's education was the development of the individual for social efficiency. He advocated the socialization of education, which meant a departure from traditional principles, methods, and subject matter. The school in general, and each classroom in particular, was to become a miniature reproduction of the typical conditions in social life. Froebel's influence is evident in Dewey's ideas that the child should be self-active, expressive, cooperative, and learn by doing. The influence of Herbart is evident in Dewey's emphasis on interests, although in Dewey's theory only spontaneous interests (not interests artificially stimulated by the teacher) should be utilized in learning. Dewey also emphasized problem-solving as a means of stimulating thought. Translated into classroom procedure: the teacher would fade into the background, while the pupils, individually or collectively, would become self-active in activities determined by their spontaneous interests. Since industrial activities occupy a prominent place in producing social efficiency, more industrial activities were recommended for the school; the liberal or cultural arts were to occupy a position of secondary importance.

Besides containing elements of socialism and pragmatism, Dewey's philosophy was materialistic. Influenced by Darwin's theory of evolution, Dewey held that man is continuous with nature, that is, that man is purely a material being without a spiritual nature, differing in degree, but not in kind, from other animals. Since he did not believe in a spiritual soul, it was logical for him to believe that the objectives of education should be confined to a preparation for life in this society.

Dewey's philosophy won many zealous followers. His theories were accepted as the basis for the progressive education movement, which advocated self-development through self-activity in socialized classroom procedures, and included the notions of "free activity", "learning by doing", and "spontaneous interests" as the motivating and driving forces in learning. Dewey's followers may have carried his ideas to extremes; he did caution against extreme freedom of activity for children, and said that too many liberties should not be taken with the curriculum, yet he did not give any precise guidelines. Even Dewey's definition of education as a "continuous reconstruction of experience" was a generality which has been interpreted in various ways.

In 1918, the Progressive Education Association was formed, with William Heard Kilpatrick as one of its most influential leaders. Kilpatrick, a professor at Colombia University from 1909 to 1938, was an outstanding spokesman of Progressive Education; he had authored several books outlining his views, and was the champion of the "project method". Other prominent names in the movement are: George Counts, Boyd Bode, John Childs, Harold Rugg, Thomas Briggs, Ross Finney, and Stanwood Cobb.

The progressive education movement grew in the 1920's, and found expression in the "Activity Movement" of the 1930's. It received wide attention by educators, and many experimental schools were founded throughout the United States in which children were allowed to express themselves happily in social activities. Some of Dewey's followers carried his ideas to extremes in keeping the child self-active. Pupil self-direction was expressed in the form of socialized recitations, projects, panel discussions, self-government. Ingenious means were devised for democratic action among children, but in many cases not enough foresight was given to the educational results.

Various objections to the progressive movement arose: children were turning freedom into license; essentials were neglected; work lacked direction because goals were not set; too much emphasis was given to the gratification of desires, and not enough emphasis was given to meeting responsibilities; furthermore, the curriculum was not well organized. William C. Bagley, who taught at Columbia University, later served as editor of *School and Society* represented the voice of the opposition. Gradually the opposition prevailed, and in 1944 the Progressive Education Association became the American Education Fellowship, and, in 1955, disbanded. John Dewey's death, three years earlier, had crumbled its foundation.

The basic ideas of progressive education were not new. Self-activity, expression, motivation through interests, use of concrete experience, all these can be traced to Rousseau, Pestalozzi, Herbart, and Froebel, and before them to Renaissance educators who in turn had repeated many of the ideas of Quintilian. However, even though the ideas were not new, and even though they unfortunately were carried to extremes, progressive education helped education. It carried forward the study of the child's growth and development. It stimulated many educators to use some of the newer procedures in moderation, and it demonstrated that cooperative effort can produce beneficial effects for the individual and for society. Both extremes in education regressed toward the middle road: some extremely conservative educators became more progressive, while some extreme progressives became more conservative.

Although John Dewey and the Progressive Education Association have died, their influence undoubtedly will linger. Generations of pupils have felt the impact of their practices. Countless teachers and educators attended Teachers College, Columbia University, where for a half-century Dewey and his followers taught their theories. Of course, not all the teachers who attended Teachers College accepted Progressive theories. However, the possible extent of the influence of these views is illustrated in the following quotation:

> The mecca of U. S. public schoolmen, T.C. has turned out a fourth of the nation's big city (over 50,000 population) school superintendents. It lists among its alumni nearly a third of all U. S. deans of education and presidents of teacher-training institutions. As such, it has been more than any other campus the creator of the modern public school.[22]

The Beginnings of Measurement in Education

During the latter part of the nineteenth century, there was a greater demand for the introduction of sciences into the curriculum. The demand was due in part to Herbert Spencer (1820–1903). To the question "What knowledge is of most worth?" Spencer's answer was "Science". A materialist, he believed that man was primarily an animal, with life beginning and ending in nature. He felt that nature should be investigated more thoroughly through the introduction of science into the school's curriculum. Spencer's emphasis on the importance of science

---

[22]"Change on 120th Street", *Time*, Vol. 63 (May 3, 1954) 63.

resulted in its wider acceptance. Furthermore, educators began to feel that the scientific method could be used profitably in the field of education, and soon began to use experimentation, laboratory methods, and statistical procedures to determine the content and methods in education.

By the end of the nineteenth century, psychologists in Germany and England began to develop standardized tests to try to measure mental processes, and applied statistical procedures to interpret the results of these tests. In the United States, J. McKeen Cattell had devoted his attention to the measurement problem as early as 1890 with his publication of *Mental Tests and Measurements*. Later, in 1894, J. M. Rice's study of achievement in spelling through the use of a list of fifty words attracted a great deal of attention. Perhaps the greatest early stimulus to the measurement movement was the 1905 publication in France of an intelligence scale by Alfred Binet and Thomas Simon. Binet revised this scale in 1908 and 1911; the Stanford Revision of the Binet Scale was accomplished by Lewis M. Terman of Stanford University in 1916.

It remained for Edward Lee Thorndike, however, to develop statistical procedures for the interpretation of the results from the early scales. By 1908 with Stone's Arithmetic Reasoning Tests and with his own Handwriting Scale in 1909, he had developed these procedures. Several of Thorndike's students at Columbia University then developed scales in other subjects under his direction. Since then statistical procedures in education have undergone continuous refinement.

The importance of the sciences has steadily increased with the advance of technology. In 1957, when Russia beat the United States into space with Sputnik, the teaching of sciences was bolstered with a speed that rivaled that of the circling satellite.

INNOVATIONS IN EDUCATION

Increased federal and philanthropic financial support of educational experimentation and research introduced new procedures and media. There has been increased emphasis on the use of audio-visual aids in instruction. *Educational television* has extended the services of outstanding teachers to large numbers of pupils, has brought world events into the classroom as they occur, and has provided adults with the opportunity to continue their education. Auto-instructional devices in the form of *teaching machines* and *programmed instruction* have made their debut, as means of relieving the teacher of teaching things that pupils can learn for themselves, and as means of providing for individual differences. Both Skinner, with his linear programed instruction, and Crowder, advocating the branching programed instruction have received some support; however, some educators support neither. At the present time, there are experiments with *computer-assisted instruction*, and it is likely that the "mechanical brain" will be important in future educational programs.

As usual, the early research on these innovations has produced conflicting claims of their merits. More extensive research and experimentation eventually will show their proper function in the educative process.

The *ungraded primary* has received greater attention in recent years. Under this arrangement, the first three elementary grades are eliminated, and pupils are permitted to finish these first three years of work as soon as their ability permits, then enter fourth grade. There also has been some experimentation with ungraded schools in which grading is eliminated at various levels of elementary and secondary schooling. The advantages claimed for this procedure are that it allows each pupil to progress according to his ability, and that it eliminates the stigma of "failing a grade".

Experimentation with *team teaching*, as contrasted to the "self-contained" elementary classroom is also relatively recent. In the self-contained classroom one teacher instructs a group of pupils in all of the subjects of a particular grade. In team teaching, several teachers cooperatively plan the work of a given level, and each one teaches his speciality to the same group of pupils. In this way, some educators claim individual differences among pupils are given more attention and, at the same time, the pupils benefit from superior instruction in each field.

Culturally disadvantaged children have begun to receive greater attention. These children, brought up in a culturally deficient environment, are handicapped when they enter school because their apperceptive background does not embrace the knowledge pre-supposed by the school and possessed by children from an average environment. To remedy this deficiency, some pre-school children are given special instruction in the *Head Start program*. Carrying pre-school instruction one step further, the Educational Policies Commission in 1966 recommended that the age for starting school should be reduced from six to four. They theorized that all children can profit by earlier schooling, especially the culturally deprived, those who are victims of racial prejudice, those who are unloved or who lack companionship, and those who are physically handicapped.

Education is moving in many directions to meet the needs of today's society. There has been a gigantic explosion of knowledge and of population which has made it necessary to explore new approaches to education. Some of these explorations will be fruitless; others may bring about effective means to elevate all people to a higher plane of knowledge.

SUMMARY

Early colonial education in America was a transplant of European ideas and practices, with the greatest influence coming from England. The English Puritans, accepting the Calvinistic idea of state control of education and favoring education of the masses, established these ideas in New England. The Middle Atlantic States, which had a greater diversity of nationalities and religions, favored church-related schools to satisfy the needs of the individual religious and national groups. The southern colonies, settled by members of the Church of England, favored the English idea that education was an individual responsibility. The well-to-do had tutors for their children, or sent them to private schools, while the poorer class of people attended religious charity schools or tax-supported pauper schools. New England ideas were to prevail in the United States, but the process took over two hundred years.

Two early laws were important to American education. The Massachusetts Law of 1642 was the first compulsory education law, and the Massachusetts Law of 1647 was the first law requiring the establishment of schools. These laws recognized the right of the state to promote its welfare through an educated citizenry.

During the colonial period, several types of elementary schools were established; most of them were a direct transplant of European schools. Dame schools were conducted by neighborhood women who taught reading, religion, spelling, and sometimes arithmetic. Writing schools, not very numerous, taught writing, arithmetic, and keeping simple accounts. Town schools supported by taxes arose chiefly in New England. In the Middle Atlantic colonies, schools were usually parochial, established by various religious denominations. The southern colonists, believing that education was an individual responsibility, made wide use of private tutors. Charity schools were established for indigent children in the south as well as in other colonies. Apprenticeship training also was used throughout the colonies, giving vocational training as well as instruction in the 4 R's.

The qualifications of teachers varied from excellent to mediocre. The usual qualifications consisted of good character, a knowledge of the fundamentals, and the ability to maintain discipline. Wages were small, which caused teachers to depend on other types of work for support.

School buildings usually were simple, log structures of one room, with a fireplace, backless benches for children, and a long plank which served as a desk. The buildings were generally in poor repair.

The curriculum consisted of the 4 R's, although arithmetic was taught infrequently. Reading, religion, and spelling were studied together. The first reading material was the *Hornbook*. After 1690, the *New England Primer*, religious in content, became the chief instrument in reading. Writing was sometimes taught in dame and writing schools, but later was taught in town schools. Arithmetic received little attention in the early days, but became popular after the publication of Dilworth's *The Schoolmaster's Assistant* in 1743.

Education declined before and after the Revolution, because the colonists were occupied with the fight for independence, and because money was scarce. During this time, religious authority in educational and state matters weakened. Moreover, the new Constitution forbade the establishment of state religions, and laid the basis for the secularization of education in future years. The federal government gave some stimulus to education through the Ordinances of 1785 and 1787, which provided land grants for the maintenance of education. The Massachusetts Law of 1789 provided a legal basis for the district system, crystallized some past practices, and raised the qualifications of teachers, but there was little progress in education during the next fifty years.

The free school societies of the early nineteenth century did much to educate poor children, and they represented a transition from private to public support of education. Early in the century the Lancastrian schools aroused more interest in education, and made an economical education available to thousands of pupils. However, because of its shortcomings the system was discontinued by 1840.

The work of Horace Mann in Massachusetts, and Henry Barnard in Connecticut and Rhode Island, brought about many needed reforms in education in the nineteenth century. Through their efforts, state boards of education were established, the standards and facilities of education were improved, and free, universal education was expanded. In addition, Barnard was instrumental in creating a United States Office of Education and became its first commissioner in 1867.

Expansion of the elementary school curriculum occurred during the nineteenth century. In addition to the 4 R's and spelling, geography, grammar, and history were added by the middle of the century. By the end of the century, drawing, physiology, and hygiene were also mandatory subjects in Massachusetts.

The grading of schools occurred during the middle of the nineteenth century, from about 1830 to 1870. The number of grades varied from seven to nine, with the eight-grade elementary school becoming the predominant type. Compulsory attendance began with the Massachusetts Law of 1852.

The child-centered movement had its beginnings in the nineteenth century. The theories of Pestalozzi, Herbart, and Froebel were brought to the United States by Americans who went to Europe to study them. Horace Mann and Henry Barnard were the most prominent and influential of these travelers. Others who were important in transmitting European ideas to America were Joseph Neef, John Griscom, Victor Cousin, and Calvin Stowe. Pestalozzi's principles received their impetus through the Oswego Movement in New York. The ideas of Herbart became popularized after the publications of DeGarmo and the McMurray brothers. Froebel's kindergarten was transplanted by his disciples, Mrs. Carl Schurz and Miss Elizabeth Peabody. Thus, child-study, psychology, and educational psychology began to take a definite form. Contributing greatly to child-study were Wundt's psychological laboratory in Germany, and the writings and studies of William James and G. Stanley Hall.

During the twentieth century, education moved ahead rapidly. The child-centered movement reached its climax toward mid-century. John Dewey, whose philosophy of experimentalism was accepted as the basis for progressive education, was the most influential educator of the century. The progressive education movement won many influential followers during the 1920's and 1930's. It also had many influential opponents. Its influence began to wane toward the middle of the century, and in 1955 the American Education Fellowship (formerly the Progressive Education Association) disbanded. Although many of its ideas were carried to extremes, the movement stimulated a more intensive study of the nature of the child and the nature of the educative process.

The twentieth century also emphasized science and the scientific method in obtaining information on the learner and the educative process. Science received greater emphasis in the curriculum. Tests were devised to attempt to measure the various abilities of the child, and Thorndike's statistical procedures were used to interpret test results. Today, standardized tests and statistical interpretation of their results are used universally in American education.

Recently, many innovations and new ideas have been introduced into education. The more prominent of these have been educational television, programed instruction, computer-assisted instruction, ungraded schools, team teaching, the teaching of culturally disadvantaged children, and the recommendation that children start school at an earlier age.

Questions for discussion:

1. Explain the differences in the attitudes toward education during the colonial period.

2. How did the curriculum in colonial elementary schools differ from the curriculum of today's schools?

3. Cite examples of the religious aim of education from the history of American education.

4. State Horace Mann's contributions to education, and evaluate them in terms of present educational ideas and practices.

5. Defend or refute the statement: "Education should be child-centered."

6. Today some educators believe that children should begin school at the age of four. Do you agree or disagree? Why?

For further reading:

Cubberley, Ellwod P., *Public Education in the United States*. Boston: Houghton Mifflin Company, 1919.

Good, H. G., *A History of American Education*. New York: The Macmillan Company, 1962.

Hillway, Tyrus, ed., *American Education*. Boston: Houghton Mifflin Company, 1964.

Johnson, Clifton, *Old-Time Schools and School Books*. New York: The Macmillan Company, 1904.

Knight, Edgar W., *Education in the United States*. Boston: Ginn and Company, 1951.

Lucio, William H., *Readings in American Education*. Chicago: Scott, Foresman and Company, 1963.

Monroe, Paul, *Founding of the American Public School System*. New York: The Macmillan Company, 1940.

Rusk, Robert, *The Doctrines of the Great Educators*. London: Macmillan and Co., Ltd., 1954.

Slosson, Edwin C., *The American Spirit in Education*. New Haven: Yale University Press, 1921. From *The Yale Chronicles of America*. Copyright Yale University Press. United States Publishers Association, Inc., sole distributors.

4

Development of Secondary Education

Once the colonists had provided for the elementary education of their children, they turned their attention to higher education and provided for the establishment of secondary schools. These schools, they felt, would prepare their children for college, where their future ministers and leaders would be trained.

In the preceding chapter, the European ideas and practices that affected the development of American elementary education were described. These influences also were felt in the development of secondary and college education and should be kept in mind during this chapter. Additional influences and their relationship to the objectives and content of secondary education will be described presently.

Secondary education in America developed in three stages. The first type of secondary school was the Latin grammar school, which was a direct transplant from Europe. Following it was the academy which also originated in Europe but underwent certain modifications in America. Finally, during the nineteenth century, the high school, a distinctly American institution, gradually replaced the academy as the primary type of secondary school.

THE LATIN GRAMMAR SCHOOL

It will be recalled from Chapter II that, approximately two centuries before the American colonization, European education came under the influence of the Renaissance. This influence emphasized Greek and

103

Roman classical literature as the content of secondary and college education. Gradually, Renaissance education deteriorated into a study of the form and style of classical literature, rather than its content. Latin and Greek grammar was studied endlessly in the Latin grammar schools to prepare boys for college admission. In college, although the curriculum ostensibly consisted of the seven liberal arts, the greatest emphasis was on the trivium (grammar, rhetoric, and dialectic), and within the trivium itself, grammar again received the greatest emphasis.

The Latin grammar school, then, was preparation for college, and the chief subject of study was Latin, with some attention also given to Greek and Hebrew. In England, St. Paul's, established in London during the the first decade of the sixteenth century, was a representative grammar school. It admitted boys at the ages of seven or eight, after they could read and write Latin and English well enough to read and write their own lessons. At St. Paul's, Greek was not studied extensively. Most of the boys' time was spent with Latin, which was spoken exclusively in the classroom, and was even encouraged during recreational activities. The regulations of the school stated that the course of study should center around authors who had joined wisdom with "pure chaste eloquence". The curriculum also included the study and practice of religion.

It has been estimated that there were approximately three hundred grammar schools in England during the middle of the sixteenth century. The majority of their students came from middle class families. The quality of instruction naturally varied with the school and the teachers. Usually, they followed the program found at St. Paul's, which prepared boys to enter college at the age of fourteen. Although some attention was given to Greek and religion, the boys first studied Latin (accidence, grammar, construction) through rote memorization, after which they learned meanings. Discipline in these schools was extremely severe, sometimes even discouraging intelligent boys from further education. This was the English grammar school, and, making allowances for modifications within individual schools, this also was the grammar school that was transplanted to colonial America.

Early American Latin Grammar Schools[1]

The first plans for a Latin grammar school in America were made in Virginia in 1621. Funds for a school in Charles City were raised, but the Indian massacre of 1622 ended this ambition.

---

[1]Although these early secondary schools were most frequently called Latin grammar schools, they have sometimes been referred to as endowed schools, or free schools (free in the sense of offering a liberal education).

The dates for the first Latin grammar schools in America are obscure as some elementary schools provided a little Latin grammar and therefore claimed status as secondary schools. It is generally conceded that the first known Latin grammar school was the Boston Latin Grammar School, established in 1635.[2] This school, still in existence, was once run by Ezekiel Cheever, a famous early schoolmaster who became associated with the school in 1670, and whose text book, *Accidence,* was used widely in the study of Latin.

Other towns quickly followed the example of Boston. Brown has stated that in its first sixteen years of existence Massachusetts developed Latin grammar schools in seven or eight towns.[3] The Massachusetts Law of 1647, which required the establishment of this type of school in every town of one hundred families, provided an incentive, and a legal basis, for other towns to establish grammar schools.[4] Other colonies began to make similar provisions. Yet the grammar school remained more popular in New England than in the Middle Atlantic and southern colonies.

Early Latin grammar schools led an uncertain existence. Many of them, especially in larger towns, were well endowed and assured of financial support. In smaller towns it was difficult to raise funds, and many schools had to close their doors. Frequently, the Latin grammar school was in the same building as the elementary school. In some cases, a single teacher provided instruction for both levels. Even in Massachusetts, where a fine of five pounds was imposed on towns not complying with the law of 1647, many towns ignored the law, or simply paid the fine, considering it a more economical measure than financing a grammar school. Moreover, the number of pupils in these towns seeking admission to college was small, and in some towns there were no college-bound pupils at all. In these cases, the law was fulfilled if a qualified teacher were available to instruct an occasional pupil who wished college preparation. For these reasons, grammar schools developed slowly.

The American Latin grammar schools like the English Latin grammar schools admitted only boys, and their purpose was strictly college preparatory. Boys were admitted at the age of seven or eight, after learning to read and write in the elementary school. The course of study took seven years, so that by the age of fourteen the pupils were ready to enter college.

---

[2]Records indicate that the school's first financial support came in 1636.
[3]Elmer E. Brown, *The Making of Our Middle Schools* (New York: Longmans, Green and Co., 1902), p. 42.
[4]See Chapter III for text of the law.

Curriculum

Since the Latin grammar school offered a college preparatory course, college entrance requirements determined the curriculum of the secondary schools. Harvard, therefore, founded in 1636, and the only college in America for over a half-century, set the curriculum pattern for any boy who wished to attend a colonial college in the seventeenth century. Only one other college, William and Mary, was founded in that century, and even then not until 1693. During the eighteenth century, however, approximately twenty new colleges were established. The increasing number of new colleges, however, did not change the entrance requirements set by Harvard. Admission requirements remained similar to Harvard's during the entire colonial period, and even beyond it. A student had to be able to translate into English the works of classical authors and have some knowledge of Greek grammar. Yale first added one other admission requirement, arithmetic, in 1745.

There are no records of the particular subject matter taught in the earliest grammar schools. It is known that at the time Ezekiel Cheever was teaching in the Boston Latin School (1670–on) the following were studied:[5]

Cheever: *Accidence*

Lily's grammar

Aesop: *Fables*

Corderius: *Colloquies*

Virgil: *Aeneid*

Cicero: *De officiis* and orations

Cato

Ovid: *Metamorphoses*

By the time of the American Revolution, Greek began to receive more emphasis. Pupils now studied some Homer and Xenophon. There were also other variations, such as the study of Erasmus, Caesar, and Justin, but the preceding list is typical of the education in a Latin grammar school.

During the eighteenth century, as the population expanded and commercial life increased, there was a demand for the inclusion of more practical subjects in the schools' curriculum. Many grammar schools refused to include them because they did not fit the concept of a

---

[5]Elmer E. Brown, *op. cit.*, p. 130.

classical education. However, later in eighteenth century, some grammar schools introduced subjects such as arithmetic, bookkeeping, geometry, surveying, and navigation. Yet the Latin grammar school remained essentially college-preparatory.

From their beginnings the grammar schools taught religion, and morality, and tried to build character in the boys. Morning and evening prayers were said at school. Masters examined the pupils on the sermon they had heard on Sunday, instructed them in their catechism, and tried to inculcate good manners and "dutiful behavior towards all." In a negative way, the whipping post was an incentive for self-discipline and good conduct. It further helped the boys to refrain from offenses such as name-calling, fighting, bickering, tardiness, and truancy.

Organization

Both the school day and school year was long for the Latin grammar school student. One student in the class of 1773 stated that, during the summer session, school lasted each day from 7 to 11, and from 1 to 5, while during the winter, the morning session began an hour later.[6] Pupils were organized into seven classes, with each class occupying a separate bench. The school building usually consisted of one room, although sometimes it was provided with a room in the loft for the master. When it did not, the teacher lived with a near-by family, or he was provided with a dwelling of his own.

Until 1789, boys were admitted into the Boston Latin School for a seven year course of study, at the age of seven. After 1789, the entrance age was raised to ten, and the course was reduced to four years. Other changes in entrance age and the length of the course of study were made in later years.

In Massachusetts, school affairs were handled through the town meeting. The town's citizens voted on the selection of teachers, and provided for the school's supervision. As early as 1645, Dorchester elected a board to oversee the schools. In the case of endowed schools, the donor or his representative became the overseer and made periodic visits to check on the school's management and funds. These overseers were also known as "visitors" or "wardens".

Teachers

The teachers in the Latin grammar schools were of high caliber. Many of them were college graduates, or graduates of Latin grammar

---

[6]*Ibid.,* p. 132.

schools. Before they were appointed, they were examined on their knowledge of the classics and their soundness of faith, the latter task usually done by a clergyman. Quite often, the minister of a town also acted as a teacher, preparing a few boys for admission to college. Many ministers who had not yet received assignments, or were still divinity students in colleges, were appointed as teachers.

The well qualified Latin grammar school teacher was held in high esteem. "To their names was prefixed the title Mr., then allowed only to the chosen few in a society where Goodman or Goodwife marked their sober address."[7] Besides Ezekiel Cheever, other outstanding colonial schoolmasters were Elijah Corlett, John Levell, and Nathan Tisdale. The influence and fame of these early schoolmasters may be judged by the following statement about Tisdale, who taught in Lebanon, Connecticut:

> For thirty years the master of the school was Nathan Tisdale, a man whose assiduity and fidelity became so widely known that he not only had pupils from the New England and Northern colonies, but from those of the remotest South and from the West India Islands.[8]

Unfortunately, some incompetents were found among colonial schoolmasters, but on the whole they were educated men of good character.

Teachers' salaries approached those of ministers, another indication of the high prestige they held. They were paid in currency or "in kind", or both. Sometimes the fees paid by students were added to their salary. Occasionally they may have received the fringe benefit of a dwelling and plot of land. The range of salaries received during the seventeenth century was from twenty to sixty pounds a year. During the eighteenth century, the salaries of some teachers were as high as one hundred pounds. There was considerable range in the salaries paid, and in the method of payment. The following are known examples of salaries paid by some Massachusetts towns:[9]

Roxbury: twenty-five pounds a year in 1668, three quarters of which was to be paid in Indian corn or peas, and the other fourth in barley.

[7]Paul Monroe, *Founding of the American Public School System,* Volume I (New York: The Macmillan Company, 1940), p. 154.

[8]Clifton Johnson, *Old-Time Schools and School-Books* (New York: The Macmillan Company, 1904), p. 40.

[9]Summarized from Elmer E. Brown, *op. cit.,* pp. 124-125.

Hadley: until 1709, thirty to forty pounds a year, payable in produce. After 1709, salaries were paid in province bills.

Northampton: up to the Revolution, salaries paid were equivalent to eighty dollars, plus board.

Decline of the Latin Grammar School

Except in large towns, the enrollment in the grammar schools remained small. Some towns had no pupils who were interested in becoming Latin scholars, while a town the size of Boston frequently had an enrollment of one hundred. Most of the pupils in the school were from the higher social and financial classes. Many of them, however, were unwilling learners. In fact, it was said that a master's eyes sparkled when he found a pupil who showed promise of becoming an apt scholar.

There was an increasing need and demand for a secondary education which included "practical subjects". Pupils who had no intention of going to college wished to receive preparation for the increasing commercial life of the time. The Latin grammar school could not meet this need, partly because it was financially incapable of expanding its program. As its popularity decreased, another type of secondary school, the academy, arose. It offered a more diversified program, and gradually replaced the Latin grammar school as the major type of secondary school. In spite of the limitations of the Latin grammar school it did help to shape the characters and minds of many colonial leaders and statesmen.

THE ACADEMY

A definition of the academy will make it easier to classify these schools and to trace their development in America. The academy was then a private secondary school, chartered by the state, but independent of state control even though it often received financial aid or support from the state. The academy was usually governed by a board of trustees.

During the early part of the eighteenth century there were many private schools and private teachers who taught practical subjects. They taught all branches of mathematics, surveying, navigation, geography, bookkeeping, languages, and fine arts. They also conducted schools for girls which ". . . specialized in reading and writing, French, music, dancing, painting, embroidery, sewing, millinery, and hairdressing."[10] Although this type of specialized instruction does not necessarily classify the schools as academies, the next organizational step led to a chartered private school which made available practical as well as classical curricula.

The Academy in England

John Milton used the term "academy" as a name for a school in his *Tractate On Education* (1634). He was a critic of the existing grammar schools in England and proposed that academies replace them. The curriculum of an academy, although classical, would prepare the individual for the realities of life, by including the study of pure and applied sciences, fine arts, physical education, social intercourse, and travel with humanistic studies. In 1697, Daniel Defoe in his *Essay on Projects* recommended the establishment of three types of academies: one for the study of language; one for military sciences; and one for women.[11]

During the seventeenth century, the dissenters in England began to establish schools of their own and called them academies. The first academy was established in 1665.[12] By the time of the American Revolution there were over thirty academies in England.[13] One main purpose of these schools was to prepare students for the ministry although they also accepted students preparing for other occupations. During the five- or six-year course that was given, these academies tried to give their students social intercourse, travel, along with humanistic studies. Yet many of the schools were not well equipped for this task. For this and other reasons they declined toward the end of the century. However, their introduction of realistic studies in the curriculum exerted an influence on the grammar schools.

Two of the dissenting academies deserve special mention. Under the administration of Dr. Phillip Doddridge from 1729 to 1751, the academy at Northampton conducted instruction in the vernacular and included in the curriculum preparation for a variety of occupations. The other important dissenting academy was at Warrington, where Joseph Priestly lectured from 1761 to 1767. Priestly was instrumental in introducing into the academy ". . . the study of English literature

---

[10]Newton Edwards and Herman G. Richey, *The School in the American Social Order* (Boston: Houghton Mifflin Company, 1963), p. 109.

[11]Frederick Eby and Charles F. Arrowood, *The Development of Modern Education* (New York: Prentice-Hall, Inc., 1934), pp. 312-313.

[12]Elmer E. Brown, *op. cit.*, p. 161.

[13]*Ibid.*, p. 162.

and grammar, history, chemistry, geography, anatomy, and natural science. . . . The course in natural science at Warrington became noted. Priestley's influence was felt over all of Great Britain and the United States. Noah Webster and Thomas Jefferson corresponded with him."[14]

The Academy in America

Several influences contributed to the rise of the American academy. The Latin grammar schools offered a curriculum that was too narrow, strictly college preparatory, and limited to boys only. The demand for a secondary education that would offer practical courses to students who wished to enter commercial life, was only partially met by private teachers. The dissenters academies in England had already been established and were beginning to influence American education. By the middle of the eighteenth century, there was a favorable atmosphere for the establishment of American academies.

Benjamin Franklin founded the first academy in the American colonies. Dissatisfied with the quality of American grammar schools and undoubtedly influenced by Daniel Defoe, Franklin drew up a plan in 1743 for the establishment of an academy in Philadelphia. This plan was followed by his publication of *Proposals Relating to the Education of Youth in Pennsylvania* in 1749. In this pamphlet he described his plan for an academy.

Franklin proposed the establishment of an academy, governed by a board of nonsectarian trustees, which would be located in pleasant surroundings where the students could participate in sports to maintain their physical well-being. The school would have a rector, who would be in charge of a sufficient number of teachers for the entire student body. The curriculum would be varied according to the future vocational plans of the students. Ideally, Franklin said, the curriculum should include everything that would be useful and ornamental; however, because of the amount of knowledge and the shortage of time, only the *most useful* and the *most ornamental* would be taught to the students. He emphasized in his proposals the teaching of English, history, and natural history. Languages would be optional, again depending on the vocational plans of the students.

Franklin received wide support for his academy shortly after distributing his pamphlet. Funds were raised, a building was secured, and the academy was opened in 1751. Two years later it was chartered as

---

[14]Frederick Eby and Charles F. Arrowood, *op. cit.,* p. 607.

the Academy and Charitable School and organized into three schools: Latin, English, and Mathematical, with a rector for each school. In 1755, the Latin school was reorganized into the College of Philadelphia, and in 1779, became the University of Pennsylvania.

Although Franklin had envisaged a school in which Latin was subordinate to English, Latin became more emphasized as time progressed. Franklin pointed out that

> . . . the English school suffered from systematic discrimination in favor of the classical studies, until the English master had been reduced to the position of a mere assistant to the Latin master, whose pupils he instructed in the English branches, or of a teacher of little boys in the elements commonly taught in a dame school.[15]

In spite of this the introduction of realistic studies into the curriculum continued.

The Growth of the Academy Movement

During the last quarter of the eighteenth century many academies appeared in New England and the Middle Atlantic States. In Maryland, Lower Marlboro Academy was incorporated in 1767, and Washington Academy in 1779. A few years later the two famous Phillips academies were founded: Andover in Massachusetts (1778), and Exeter in New Hampshire (1781). The Phillips academies, regarded as excellent educational institutions, were widely imitated in other parts of the country. During Washington's second term as president, the number of academies in the United States was enumerated as follows:[16]

New Hampshire: 6

Massachusetts: 6

Maine: 4

Rhode Island: 2

Connecticut: 5

New York: 8

New Jersey: 7

Pennsylvania: 8

---

[15]Elmer E. Brown, *op. cit.*, pp. 189-190.

[16]*Ibid.*, pp. 199-202. These figures represent, in most cases, academies that were singled out by name. It is implied that others, unnamed, were in existence at the time. The above listing is extracted from Brown's lengthier summary of data taken from W. Winterbotham's *View of the United States of America*, Vol. 24 (Extracts in *American Journal of Education*), pp. 137-157.

Maryland: provision for one in each county.

Virginia: several

North Carolina: 5 or 6

South Carolina: several in Charleston, and several others.

Georgia: provision for one in each county.

Specific evidence has shown that by 1790 there were academies in all parts of the United States. During the nineteenth century, Cubberley reports, the number of academies further increased:

> By 1830 there were, according to Hinsdale, 950 incorporated academies in the United States, and many unincorporated ones, and by 1850, according to Inglis, there were, of all kinds . . . a total reported for the entire United States of 6085, with 12,260 teachers employed and 263,096 pupils enrolled.[17]

With the amazing growth of the academy movement, it rapidly became the leading type of secondary school in the United States for approximately the first three-quarters of the nineteenth century.

Financial Support

Academies were supported in various ways. Because they were fee schools, one steady source of their income was the tuition they charged. Many academies owed their existence to patrons who had provided the original endowment, and sometimes continued to support the school with either land grants or money, or both. Individual states encouraged the foundation of academies through land grants, funds, tax exemptions, lotteries to raise funds, and other special privileges. "To speak generally, the states subsidized the academies by one plan or another, leaving them, for the most part, to self-perpetuating boards or other forms of local control."[18] Although they received financial support in many ways, the academies relied heavily on tuition fees for their support.

Organization

The academies were privately controlled by a board of trustees. Although a religious element pervaded all academy training, they could become nonsectarian by appointing to the board of trustees representa-

---

[17]Ellwood P. Cubberley, *Public Education in the United States* (Boston: Houghton Mifflin Company, 1919), p. 185.

[18]Paul Monroe, ed., *A Cyclopedia of Education*, Vol. 1 (New York: The Macmillan Company, 1928), p. 23.

tives of several religious groups which became the prevailing practice. There were, however, many academies that were, and remained, denominational in character.

The Latin grammar school offered one curriculum, usually taught by one teacher; the academy developed parallel programs which were taught by two or more teachers. The college preparatory curriculum was still retained to satisfy students who wished to go to college, but more emphasis was placed on the "English school", where a great variety of subjects were taught to meet the vocational needs of students who were not going to college. Each curriculum had one or more teachers, depending on its enrollment.

Because they did not limit their enrollment to local pupils, the academies developed as boarding schools. In the early years, when boarding facilities were limited, pupils boarded in town. Gradually the academies began to provide their own dormitories and dining facilities.

The length of the school day remained similar to the school day in the grammar schools. In 1790, the school day at Andover began at eight o'clock, and apparently did not end until evening. In 1820, the schedule at Leicester called for classes from eight to twelve, and from two to six. However, at the same school in 1834, the school day was reduced; classes were held from eight-thirty to twelve and from one-thirty to four-thirty.[19]

One of the academies' most important innovations was the admission of girls as students. Some academies became coeducational. In these cases, a separate female department was organized which provided separate instruction for the girls. Other academies taught certain subjects to both sexes at the same time. Some schools had men teachers for the girls, while other schools provided female teachers. There were also academies that were established exclusively for girls. One of the first of these academies was established in Philadelphia as early as 1780. Many other female seminaries were established later. Perhaps the most famous of these early academies was the Troy Academy founded in Troy, New York, in 1821.[20] The influence of this school can be seen from the statement, "It is said that two hundred schools for girls, one-half of them in the southern states, have come into existence as a result of the influence of this one institution."[21] The academy movement, therefore, conformed with democratic ideals more than the Latin grammar schools because secondary education became available not only to a greater number of boys but also for the first time, to girls.

[19]Elmer E. Brown, *op. cit.*, pp. 245, 261.
[20]Some claim this to be the first college for women.
[21]Elmer E. Brown, *op. cit.*, p. 254.

Curriculum

The academies provided two curricula for their students. The "Classical Department" provided a curriculum for those planning to attend college, while the "English Department" provided a curriculum for those who planned to enter commercial life.

In their early years, the academies' classical curriculum was similar to the curriculum of the Latin grammar school. Since college admission requirements demanded the study of Latin, Greek, and arithmetic, these subjects were taught to college-bound students. During the first half of the nineteenth century, college admission requirements expanded to include geography, English grammar, algebra, geometry, and ancient history. The classical departments of academies added these subjects to their curriculum. The curriculum, however, was not governed exclusively by college requirements. The academies freely added other subjects in their English, history, and natural sciences departments. Since the academies were sometimes thought of as the "people's college", college level courses occasionally were taught in the academies.

The English departments of the academies excluded the study of classical languages and literature. English grammar, composition, and literature were emphasized. English grammar, as a subject, was not well formulated until the publication of Lindley Murray's *English Grammar* in 1795. This book became the chief text for many years, and ranked in popularity with Webster's spelling book.[22] Among the other subjects taught in the English department were mathematics, geography, history, surveying, navigation, and natural science.

The difference between the curricula of the two departments may be seen in the course of study given at Exeter in 1818:[23]

Classical Department

For the First Year

Adam's Latin Grammar; Liber Primus, or a similar work; Viri Romani, or Caesar's Commentaries; Latin Prosody; Exercises in Reading and making Latin; Ancient and Modern Geography; Virgil and Arithmetic.

For the Second Year

Virgil; Arithmetic and Exercises in Reading and making Latin, continued; Valpey's Greek Grammar; Roman History; Cicero's

---

[22]Charles Carpenter, *History of American Schoolbooks* (Philadelphia: University of Pennsylvania Press, 1963), p. 97.

[23]Elmer E. Brown, *op. cit.*, pp. 237-238. As quoted from Charles H. Bell, *Phillips Exeter Academy in New Hampshire* (Exeter, New Hampshire, 1883), pp. 93-94.

Select Orations; Delectus; Dalzel's Collectanea Graeca Minora; Greek Testament; English Grammar and Declamation.

For the Third Year

The same Latin and Greek authors in revision; English Grammar and Declamation continued; Sallust; Algebra; Exercises in Latin and English translations, and Composition.

For the Advanced Class

Collectanea Graeca Majora; Q. Horatius Flaccus; Titus Livius; Parts of Terence's Comedies; Excerpta Latina, or such Latin and Greek authors as may best comport with the student's future destination; Algebra; Geometry; Elements of Ancient History; Adam's Roman Antiquities, etc.

English Department

For admission into this department the candidate must be at least twelve years of age, and must have been well instructed in Reading and Spelling; familiarly acquainted with Arithmetic, through Simple Proportion with the exception of Fractions, with Murray's English Grammar through Syntax, and must be able to parse simple English sentences.

The following is the course of instruction and study in the English Department, which with special exceptions, will comprise three years.

For the First Year

English Grammar including exercises in Reading, in Parsing, and Analyzing, in correction of bad English; Punctuation and Prosody; Arithmetic; Geography, and Algebra through Simple Equations.

For the Second Year

English Grammar continued; Geometry; Plane Trigonometry and its application to heights and distances; mensuration of Sup. and Sol.; Elements of Ancient History; Logic; Rhetoric; English Composition; Declamation and exercises of the Forensic kind.

For the Third Year

Surveying; Navigation; Elements of Chemistry and Natural Philosophy, with experiments; Elements of Modern History, particularly of the United States; Moral and Political Philosophy, with English Composition, Forensics, and Declamation continued.

Changes in the curricula of the academies appeared continuously, as new subjects were added. Records from the board of regents of New York show the number and variety of subjects that were taught. "From

1787 to 1870 the regents' reports show 149 different academic subjects. . . . The list for 1837 includes more than 60 subjects . . ."[24] Aside from the subjects required for college admission, the curriculum was not standardized among the academies. As new subjects were added, older subjects were displaced. In turn, some new subjects were replaced by still newer subjects. In the natural sciences departments, especially, many new subjects such as physics, chemistry, botany, zoology, geology, and astronomy, were introduced. Subdivisions of these subjects were taught as separate courses, greatly increasing the total number of courses.

The early academies were permeated with a strong religious spirit. Occasionally, religion was taught as a school subject; classical departments of the academies read the Bible. Objections arose to teaching the doctrines of any *one* religious body because there were so many religious sects in existence. These objections became particularly strong in the early nineteenth century. It was recommended that the academies teach general religious doctrines that were acceptable to all sects. Also, because the academies had appointed to the board of trustees representatives of several sects, the domination of any one sect was avoided. Instruction in "morals and manners" continued through personal contact between teachers and pupils in the classroom and in the dormitory. For example, during the first decade of the nineteenth century, in the academy at Deerfield, Massachusetts, "It was ordered that 'the precepters and ushers, besides teaching the arts and sciences, should instil into the minds of the pupils moral and Christian principles, and form in them habits of virtue and the love of piety.' "[25]

Apart from the formal curriculum, students also participated in extracurricular activities. There were rhetorical and debating clubs, exhibitions, and school plays in which the pupils took part. At Exeter, they played a modified form of football in the fall, and, in the spring, competed in "bat and ball".

Teachers

The quality of teachers varied, as it does today. The trustees of the Phillips academies in Exeter and Andover attempted to select the best possible persons for their schools. The accounts left by pupils indicate that the board of trustees did indeed select excellent teachers, for they

---

[24]Paul Monroe, *Founding of the American Public School System*, Vol. I (New York: The Macmillan Company, 1940), p. 407. Monroe lists the sixty subjects taught in 1837.

[25]Clifton Johnson, *op. cit.*, pp. 148-149.

are described in varied terms of admiration, affection, and respect. Undoubtedly many other academies were equally well staffed, but certainly some had only mediocre teachers. As private schools, the academies were independent, and received supervision only from their board of trustees. Many academies were one-man private ventures that did not last more than a year. Others went out of existence after a few years. Probably their failure to survive was because the instruction was of poor quality.

In the better academies, the teacher was a capable, informed man who confined his instruction to his specialty or specialties. He decided on the methods and techniques of instruction he wished to use. Usually he used lectures, demonstrations with whatever apparatus and concrete aids were available, recitations and declamations, and drill. The teachers were strong disciplinarians, and many academies had a graduated scale of fines for various infractions of rules. However, because the average age of the students in the academies was higher than it was in the Latin grammar schools (some students in the academies were "late beginners", or resumed an interrupted education), discipline did not need to be as severe as in the grammar schools.

Contributions to Teacher Education

During the nineteenth century there was a growing awareness of the importance of education. As population grew, many new elementary schools were needed. Yet, there was an acute shortage of qualified teachers. Prominent people urged the founding of additional academies to educate people who would become qualified elementary school teachers. In 1821, the New York board of regents regarded the academies as the means for easing the teacher shortage. After this decision the number of academies sharply increased and, from 1830 on, became the major suppliers of elementary school teachers.

Since there were no formal courses in pedagogy, the academies simply taught subject matter to their pupils who, after their graduation, taught it to elementary school pupils. The New York academies again adjusted themselves to an existing need by introducing classes for teachers in 1833. Shortly thereafter, in 1839, state normal schools came into existence.

Period of Rapid Expansion

By 1790 there were approximately fifty academies sprinkled throughout the thirteen states. During the first half of the nineteenth century, the academy movement rapidly increased. Between 1830 and 1850, the number of academies increased from 950 to 6085.[26] During this period, the pure Latin grammar school had almost gone out of existence, and the public high school was just beginning its existence. Numerically, therefore, the academy was the primary type of secondary school for approximately one hundred years after the Revolution.

Contributions of the Academy Movement

Obviously the academies made substantial contributions to the development of education in the United States. These contributions may be summarized as follows:

1. They offered curricula suitable for those not going to college; and they extended secondary educational opportunities to boys who otherwise would have possessed only an elementary education.
2. The academies admitted girls, further increasing the number of people receiving secondary schooling. As the number of female students increased, the prejudice against higher education for girls decreased. The academies were undoubtedly a stimulus to to the later foundation of girls' colleges and coeducational colleges.
3. They were responsible for important curriculum changes. The curriculum of the academies varied to suit the needs of the time. Their introduction of realistic studies, scientific subjects, and emphasis on the vernacular helped to change curricula in the Latin grammar schools and the colleges.
4. Although many academies remained strictly denominational, the majority became nonsectarian, while at the same time they provided moral and religious training. They represented a transitional stage between early sectarian schools and later secular schools.
5. The academies supplied elementary school teachers at a time when they were badly needed.
6. They provided a terminal education of good quality for many people. The better academies sometimes taught their pupils college-level courses and gave them the practical training they needed to take their place in society.

---

[26]Ellwood P. Cubberley, *op. cit.*, stated that the period of greatest development was from 1820 to 1830, although the statistics he presented indicated otherwise.

Decline of Academies

Even though the academy was better than the Latin grammar school, it was criticized as a secondary school. Early in its beginning, voices were raised against the use of public funds to help support the private academies. This use of funds, it was believed, deprived the public schools of the money needed for support and expansion and therefore acted against the common good. Samuel Adams, governor of Massachusetts, stated the typical point of view in 1795:

> It is with satisfaction that I have observed the patriotic exertions of worthy citizens to establish academies in various parts of the Commonwealth. It discovers a zeal highly to be commended. But while it is acknowledged that great advantages have been derived from these institutions, perhaps it may be justly apprehended that multiplying them may have a tendency to injure the ancient and beneficial mode of education in town grammar schools.
>
> The peculiar advantage of such schools is that the poor and the rich may derive equal benefit from them; but none excepting the more wealthy, generally speaking, can avail themselves of the benefits of the academies. Should these institutions detach the attention and influence of the wealthy from the generous support of the town schools, is not to be feared that useful learning, instruction, and social feelings in the early parts of life may cease to be so equally and universally disseminated as it has heretofore been?[27]

His statement also contains another prominent criticism of the academies. Although they made secondary education available to more people, they did not reach everyone who could profit from education. Since the academies charged tuition, most of their pupils came from the middle class who could afford to pay the fees. The tuition fee alone automatically prevented the children of poor families from attending academies, unless special provisions were made to admit a few children on a non-paying basis.

The demand for a free, public, tax-supported secondary school that could be attended by all children grew, and resulted in the highschool. With the developement of the high school movement during the nineteenth century, the number of academies began to decrease. An increasing number of pupils began to attend the free public schools, even when they could afford to pay the tuition charged by the academies.

---

[27]Elmer E. Brown, *op. cit.*, p. 241, as quoted from George H. Martin, *The Evolution of the Massachusetts Public School System* (New York: D. Appleton and Company, 1894) pp. 128-129.

The academies continued to decline as the high schools and normal schools began to provide the education and training that was previously given only in the academies. As the academies lost pupils to the public schools, they dropped some of their previous functions and began to concentrate on providing a college preparatory curriculum of high quality. Although their number has been reduced to a small fraction of what it was, many academies are still in existence today.

THE HIGH SCHOOL

The high school movement began in the second decade of the nineteenth century, shortly before the academy movement experienced its greatest growth. Because the idea of taxation for maintaining free secondary schools was only slowly accepted, the academies continued their rapid growth. It was not until the high schools rested on a firm legal basis, which took half a century to accomplish, that they were able to multiply rapidly.

The term "High School" was new to American education. The Boston school committee first used it in 1824, but how they came to use it is shrouded in mystery. It is thought that John Griscom introduced it. Among the places Griscom visited in Europe was the Edinburgh High School in Scotland. Upon his return to the United States he published his obsevations which were reviewed in the *North American Review* in January, 1824, and it is through this source that the name "High School" received attention in Boston.

Beginning of the High School Movement

The first high school was established in Boston in 1821. It was supported by taxes, free to all children and considered an upward extension of elementary education. In its recommendation for a new type of secondary school, the Boston school committee stated that English grammar schools taught only elementary subjects. In their opinion, the pupils could complete the instruction in five years instead of seven. The committee maintained that the existing grammar schools did not teach their graduates to meet responsibilities in their later lives and therefore, parents sent their children to the academies for an adequate education. In order to make public education available to all children, the committee recommended the establishment of the English Classical School, a "seminary" (secondary school).

The new high school in Boston admitted only boys who were twelve
years old, and who had learned reading, writing, English grammar, and
arithmetic as far as simple proportion. Admission was by examination,
the course of study lasted three years, and the teachers were required
to be college graduates. The subjects studied during each of the three
years were outlined as follows:[28]

The Studies of the First Class to be as follows:

Composition.	English authors,
Reading from the most approved	their errors & beauties
authors.	Declamation.
Exercises in Criticism; com-	Geography.
prising critical analyses	Arithmetic continued.
of the language, grammar,	
and style of the best	

The Studies of the Second Class.

Composition.		Geometry.
Reading.		Plane Trigonometry; and its
Exercises in		application to mensuration
Criticism.	continued	of Heights and Distances.
Declamation.		Navigation.
Algebra:		Surveying.
Ancient and Modern History		Mensuration of Superficies
and Chronology.		& Solids.
Logic.		Forensic Discussion.

The Studies of the Third Class.

Composition;		Natural Philosophy,
Exercises in		including Astronomy;
Criticism;		Moral and Political
Declamation;		Philosophy.
Mathematics;	continued	
Logic;		
History;		
particularly		
that of the		
United States;		

The curriculum included the courses that also were taught by the
academies of the time. In fact, a comparison between the high school's
curriculum and the curriculum of the English department at Exeter in

---

[28]*Ibid.*, pp. 300-301, as quoted from the records of the Boston school committee.

1818[29] will show the similarity between the two. The Boston high school, however, did not originally include the classics that were taught in the classical departments of the academies.

Inexplicably, the name of the Boston school was changed to English High School in 1824 (Griscom's review had appeared earlier that year and may have influenced the school committee). In June of 1824, the school committee passed a resolution to appropriate a building for the "English High School", but the records show no previous authorization to use that name. The school committee of 1832, lacking this authorization, reverted to the original name, and in 1833, returned to the name of "English High School". School officials in other cities and states imitated the Boston title, designating their secondary schools as "high schools". What may have been originally an unofficial use of the term resulted in its eventual use throughout the United States.

Massachusetts Law of 1827

The Massachusetts Law of 1827 which required the establishment of a high school in every town having five hundred families partially helped to stimulate the development of high schools. The law provided for instruction in United States History, algebra, geometry, bookkeeping, and surveying; if the population of the town exceeded four thousand people, Latin, Greek, history, rhetoric, and logic also were required in the curriculum. Although several high schools were established on the basis of this legislation, the law was not well observed or enforced. For example, in 1840, there were 114 academies, and only 18 high schools in Massachusetts; if the law had been observed there would have been 44 high schools.

In other states, the development of the high school movement was just as slow. High schools were established in large cities such as Philadelphia (1838), Baltimore (1839), Charleston (1839), and Providence (1843), but these schools were relatively few in number. Estimates on the number of high schools established prior to the Civil War vary greatly. For example, one source states that there were 80 high schools in the United States in 1851, while another source states that in 1852 there were 64 high schools in Massachusetts alone. Another conservative estimate claims that in 1860[30] there were only 40 high

---

[29]See pp. 115-116.

[30]*Ibid.*, p. 313. See Brown's footnotes for the particular sources of these several statistics. Ellwood P. Cubberley, *op. cit.* p. 198, quotes a report of the U. S. Commissioner of Education as stating there were approximately 321 high schools in 1860.

schools in the whole United States. Apparently, the statistics varied according to the definition of a high school. Yet, even assuming that the highest figures are correct, it becomes apparent that high schools developed slowly when their increase is compared with the over 5,000 new academies established during the period of 1830–1850 alone.

After the Civil War, the number of high schools increased steadily. According to a report of the United States Commissioner of Education, there were 800 high schools by 1880. This was a substantial growth, but not what it could have been. By the time of the Civil War, most states had passed legislation to provide for secondary education. In some states secondary education was mandatory, but, as we have seen, the laws were not well enforced; in other states the legislation was permissive, and there was still enough opposition to prevent rapid growth of high schools.

Much of the opposition came from people who objected to being taxed to provide secondary education for everyone. They felt that a free elementary education would provide a sufficient foundation for citizenship. Other people still believed that education should be private, not a state concern. People without children felt that they should not be taxed to educate the children of others. Moreover, a large group of people were interested in the foundation and perpetuation of private academies; these people opposed the high school movement because they sensed that free education would decrease the enrollment in academies and threaten their survival.

Yet, in spite of opposition, there were social, political, and economic forces at work favoring the high school movement. During the nineteenth century, there was a growing feeling of democracy, especially among the people who migrated westward where social distinctions were not as great as they were in the East. More emphasis was placed on equality of educational opportunity for everyone in order to produce an educated and informed citizenry, necessary for the survival of a democracy. Because of the large number of immigrants flowing in from Europe, and the rapid expansion of our industrial life, the need for a secondary education which would prepare individuals for occupational and leadership roles in society increased. At the same time, our increasing wealth made more money available for the support of education. There were more and more demands for free educational opportunities, including a free college education. As early as 1816, the constitution of Indiana stated that a free education should be provided from the the elementary through the state university level. This idea received even more support as the eighteenth century progressed.

The Kalamazoo Case

The Kalamazoo Case, brought to the courts in 1872 and decided in 1874, was perhaps the greatest stimulus to the development of high schools. It questioned whether or not a local school board could levy taxes for the support of high schools. In 1872, the school board of Kalamazoo, Michigan voted to establish a high school and, at the same time, raised the tax rate to maintain the school. Charles E. Stuart, a citizen of Kalamazoo, brought a suit against the district, challenging its right to levy additional taxes for this purpose. The Supreme Court of Michigan rendered a decision in favor of the school district. The court stated that school districts are not restricted with regard to the branches of knowledge that may be taught, and that, therefore, public funds could be used to maintain high schools, if the voters gave their consent. The Kalamazoo Case also concerned the right of the board to appoint a superintendent of schools. Again the court ruled that this was a matter for the board and people to decide.

The Kalamazoo decision of 1874 was important not only because it stimulated the growth of high schools in Michigan, but also because other states used it as a legal precedent for expanding their secondary systems. After this decision the secondary school movement, unfettered by the question of legality, made the rapid strides, shown in the following statistics.

Year	Number of public secondary schools
1860[31]	321
1880[32]	800
1890	2,526
1900	6,005
1910	10,213
1930[33]	23,930
1940	25,123
1950	24,542
1960	25,784
1964	26,431

[31]*Ibid.*, p. 198, Figure 35.

[32]Paul Monroe, ed., *op. cit.* Vol. 3, p. 263 for statistics from 1880 to 1910.

[33]Statistics from 1930 on are from U. S. Bureau of the Census, *Statistical Abstract of the United States: 1967*, 88th Edition (Washington, D.C.: U. S. Government Printing Office, 1967), Table 146, p. 109.

These figures show that by the end of the nineteenth century, the high school had become the major secondary school in the United States. From 1850 on, the number of academies decreased, and by 1890 their number was exceeded by the number of high schools. The number of high schools continued increasing until 1943, when they began to decrease. This was followed by upward and downward fluctuations. The decreases may have been due to consolidation of schools, while the subsequent increases were due to the building of new schools for a rapidly increasing enrollment.

Organizational Changes

It is difficult to establish precisely when the four year program prevailed over the original three year program, but by 1880 so many new courses were introduced to the curriculum that the course was extended to four years. Educational systems were organized on an 8-4-4 basis, with eight years of elementary school, four years of high school, and four years of college. This type of organization soon was criticized and changes were recommended.

The Committee of Ten in 1893 was the first to recommend a greater articulation between the different levels of schooling. Other committees pointed out that the organization of schools should consider the transitional stage of growth and development between childhood and adolescence. The 6-6 plan in which there would be six years of elementary education and six years of secondary education was proposed as a departure from the 8-4 system. Other variations such as 7-5, 7-4, 6-2-4, and 6-3-3 plans were proposed. The 6-3-3 plan eventually won the widest acceptance, calling for a junior high school of three years between elementary school and senior high school. During the first decades of the nineteenth century these plans for reorganization received wide attention. Today the 6-3-3 plan is used extensively, and sometimes the junior high school is located in the same building as the high school.

Curriculum Changes

Although the first high school, established in Boston in 1821, was originally called the English Classical School, its curriculum did not include any classical studies. The Boston school committee undoubtedly did not originally envision preparation for college as one of the aims of the high school. The committee's report had spoken only about fitting the child for an active life and giving him a foundation for his profession, whether it be "mercantile or mechanical". However, the Massachusetts Law of 1827 prescribed that towns with a population over four thousand persons add to their curriculum classical languages and other subjects necessary for college admission. The high school, therefore, became an all-purpose institution, building on the education received in elementary school. For some students it was a terminal point in education; for other students it was a stepping-stone to college.

The curriculum of any school is determined by its aims. The early high schools formulated two broad programs: one for those going to college; and one for those who would undertake an occupation after they completed high school. The admission requirements of the colleges determined the curriculum for the college preparatory course, while the needs of the times influenced the curriculum for others.

During the nineteenth century, the academies had increased their offerings. The high schools also had to increase their courses. If the high schools were to carry out their aims, they had to keep pace with the times. The colleges influenced the college preparatory curriculum of the academies and schools, but the secondary schools, having successfully introduced new subjects, gradually influenced the curriculum of the colleges. Between 1869 and 1875 the following subjects were introduced into the admission requirements of colleges: United States history, physical geography, English composition, physical science, English literature, and modern languages.[34] Although the content of the required subjects has been up-dated, the college preparatory curriculum of the high schools has remained relatively unchanged to the present time.

Aside from the college-preparatory curriculum, many changes have occurred in the high school program. During the twentieth century, society has become increasingly complex, and it has been necessary for the high school to diversify its offerings. Specialized curricula have been developed to enable pupils to choose the courses that best fit their future plans. In 1901, the schools of New York City had five curricula for the students to choose from, namely, classical, college and normal preparatory, scientific, modern language, and commercial. A limited number of electives were permitted in the senior years. Gradually, vocational, agricultural, technical, and home economics programs developed. In large high schools, designated as comprehensive high schools, most of these programs are still offered. Smaller high schools offer whatever their facilities permit. In densely populated areas, spe-

---

[34]Ellwood P. Cubberley, *op. cit.*, p. 234.

cial high schools were established, which offered courses in science, trades, arts, and music. Besides giving a variety of programs to suit the future plans of the individual, high schools have adapted programs for the various ability levels found among pupils. Superior students are offered an enriched curriculum so that they can develop their full potential. The below average pupils receive a curriculum of "minimum essentials" so that they can continue their secondary education to the extent that they are capable.

While high schools have tried to offer something suitable for everyone in the form of "common learnings", at the same time they have provided for individual interests, abilities, and future plans. It has been a difficult task, and they have had many problems, some of which are still unsolved. However, education has come nearer to the goal of "education for all". A great deal of progress has been made in providing an education suitable for each individual.

Teachers

In 1821, the Boston school committee stipulated that their high school teachers must be college graduates. Whether or not this qualification was enforced in Boston and other places cannot be ascertained. It is safe to assume that the requirement was not practiced universally. Students from many academies which were established to help train elementary teachers may have become high school teachers, on the basis of their graduation from the "peoples' college". After 1839, although the normal schools primarily concerned themselves with training elementary school teachers, some of them began to train high school teachers.

Surveys of teachers' qualifications, made at the end of the nineteenth century, show that a large percentage of high school teachers were college graduates, but many others had lesser qualifications. The following statistics give some indication of the educational background of high school teachers at the end of the nineteenth century.[35]

Degree of Education of High School Teachers

Massachusetts (1897)		New York (1898)	
College graduates	66%	College graduates	32%
Normal school graduates	13%	Normal school graduates	39%
Scientific school		High school graduates	19%
graduates	1%	Other	10%
Unclassified	20%		

[35]Elmer E. Brown, *op. cit.*, p. 428.

During the twentieth century various factors contributed to the improvement of teacher qualifications. Professional associations strongly recommended higher qualifications for high school teachers. In 1895, the Committee of Fifteen of the National Education Association stated that high school teachers should possess a college degree. During the first decades of the twentieth century, some normal schools were converted into teachers colleges. These conversions into degree-granting institutions increased rapidly after 1915. Accrediting associations, such as the American Asociation of Teachers Colleges, helped to standardize and improve the preparation of teachers. State departments of education raised the requirements for obtaining a teaching certificate. Professional education courses were strengthened. In fact, during the twentieth century, the quality of teacher education has undergone considerable change and improvement. Today's high school teacher is well-grounded in his subject matter, has a broad educational background, and a knowledge of professional education.

To give all the details of the improvements that have taken place in recent secondary schools would belabor the obvious. Education obviously takes place in a better environment than before. New physical plants that are attractive, functional, and well equipped are replacing outmoded and sometimes unsafe buildings. The curriculum has been so expanded that practically all children can have some secondary education. Beyond the formal classroom program, many extracurricular activities are available to further develop the individual's interests, personality, and character. Instruction is more effective because of a wide variety of appropriate audio-visual aids which are available to teachers: The expansion of knowledge, and the emphasis on evaluative thinking, contribute to the formation of well-informed, resourceful citizens upon whose shoulders will rest the responsibility for preserving our democracy.

SUMMARY

The development of secondary education in the United States went through three stages: the Latin grammar school, the academy, and the high school. The first two stages were influenced by European ideas, but the high school was a distinctly American institution.

The Latin grammar school was transplanted directly from England. Its purpose was preparation for college, and its chief subjects were the study of classical languages and literature. In 1635 Boston established the first Latin grammar school. Twelve years later, the Massachusetts

Law of 1647 required the establishment of a Latin grammar school in every town of one hundred families, but the law was not well enforced. Many towns ignored or circumvented the law because they could not raise funds for these schools. The development of Latin grammar schools was slow, although it was faster in New England than in the other colonies.

Although the schools accomplished their aim of preparing boys for college admission, they did not keep up with the times. During the eighteenth century, because of the expansion of commercial life, a demand arose for more practical subjects. Generally, the grammar schools resisted the addition of new subjects, but some of them gradually began to add a few practical courses to the curriculum. However, the course of study remained largely classical, and the grammar school continued to be strictly a college preparatory school.

Toward the end of the eighteenth century the grammar schools declined. They were criticized because their narrow curriculum confined them to college-bound boys. Thus, they made secondary education available to a relatively select number of boys.

During the early part of the eighteenth century private teachers and schools developed to meet the demand for practical training. Although they cannot be classified as secondary schools since they did not offer a full secondary program, they paved the way for the founding of academies. The academy was a private secondary school which was chartered by the state and usually governed by a board of trustees.

Academies existed in England during the seventeenth century. Many of them were established by the dissenters of England, in order to train ministers. However, their curriculum included besides the study of the classics, realistic studies using the vernacular, thus preparing their pupils for other occupations as well. The influence of these academies began to be felt in America.

In 1751 Benjamin Franklin established the first American academy in Philadelphia. In an attempt to make education more practical and available to more pupils, the school was organized into three divisions: Latin, English, and Mathematical. By 1790, academies had been established in every state. However, the greatest growth came in the nineteenth century, between 1830 and 1850 when the number of academies increased from 950 to 6,085.

The academies received financial support in many ways, through land grants, private endowments and funds, lotteries, and tax exemptions. There was a trend in their organization to make them nonsectarian by appointing a board of trustees representing several religious groups, but many academies remained strictly denominational in character.

The academies made secondary education available to more children because of their diversified courses of study, and because they admitted girls as well as boys. Many "female seminaries", or academies, were established for girls exclusively, while other academies admitted both boys and girls.

The curriculum of the academies unlike the Latin grammar schools changed with the passage of time. They offered a college preparatory program which introduced sciences, modern languages, English, and history. Because of their influence, colleges added these new subjects to their curricula.

The academies were generally staffed by competent teachers who were left to their own resources and initiative in the classroom. They were strong disciplinarians, but not as severe as teachers in earlier years. Before the establishment of normal schools in the nineteenth century, the academies provided an important service by training elementary school teachers.

Although they helped to modernize education, the academies declined in number and influence during the last half of the nineteenth century. A demand for free, public secondary education caused the development of the public high school and the subsequent decline of the academy.

The high school movement began in Boston with the establishment of the English Classical School in 1821. In 1824 the name was changed to English High School. Although the first high schools accepted only boys, they later became coeducation and made secondary education available for all children. In order to meet the needs of its students, the high school curriculum was expanded continuously. Originally offering a curriculum similar to the curriculum of the academies, which prepared some students for college and gave other students practical courses, the high schools became more specialized. Toward the end of the nineteenth century the high schools were offering parallel curricula in academic, commercial, and vocational fields to take care of individual differences in interests and abilities.

The high school movement progressed slowly during the middle fifty years of the eighteenth century, even though the Massachusetts Law of 1827, and similar laws in other states, required the establishment of high schools. Many people objected to being taxed for the maintenance of secondary schools; and, people who were interested in the survival of academies further opposed the establishment of high schools. It was not until the Kalamazoo Case in 1874, which legally upheld the right of the local school board to use public funds for the maintenance of high schools if the people consented, that the number of high schools multiplied rapidly.

By the end of the nineteenth century, the majority of public schools had settled into an organizational pattern of eight years of elementary school and four years of high school. This organization was criticized because there was not enough articulation between the elementary and secondary programs, and because it did not consider the transitional stages of growth and development in children. Consequently, other plans were proposed, such as divisions into 6-6, 6-2-4, and 6-3-3. The 6-3-3 plan became the most popular, providing for six years of elementary school, three years of junior high school, and three years of senior high school.

During the twentieth century the quality of secondary education improved continuously. The quality of teachers, diversification of curriculum, and physical plants, facilities, and equipment have all improved.

Questions for discussion:

1. Why did the curriculum of the Latin grammar school consist primarily of the study of the classics?
2. What were the advantages of the academies over the Latin grammar schools? What shortcomings did the academies have as secondary schools?
3. What factors influenced the development of high schools?
4. Why was the Kalamazoo Case so important in the development of the high school movement?
5. Compare the teachers in the academies with those in today's high schools.
6. What were the main differences between the curricula of the Latin grammar schools, the academies, and the high schools?
7. Show how the high schools of today are democratic in aims, content, and methods.

For further reading:

Brown, Elmer E., *The Making of our Middle Schools.* New York: Longmans, Green and Company, 1902.
Conant, James B., *The American High School Today.* New York: McGraw-Hill Book Company, 1959.

Cubberley, Ellwood P., *Public Education in the United States*. Boston: Houghton Mifflin Company, 1919.

Eby, Frederick, and Charles F. Arrowood, *The Development of Modern Education*. New York: Prentice-Hall, Inc., 1934.

Edwards, Newton, and Herman G. Richey, *The School in the American Social Order*. Second Edition. Boston: Houghton Mifflin Company, 1963.

Jacobson, Paul B., ed., *The American Secondary School*. New York: Prentice-Hall, Inc., 1952.

Krug, Edward A., *The Shaping of the American High School*. New York: Harper & Row, Publishers, 1964.

Monroe, Paul, *Founding of the American School System*, Vol. I. New York: The Macmillan Company, 1940.

5

Development of Higher Education

American higher education also dates back to the early colonial period, for the colonists saw the need of building upon their elementary and secondary levels of schooling to train their future leaders. Although a few colleges were established during the colonial period, the development of higher education remained painfully slow for approximately two centuries.

Early higher education, like early elementary and secondary education, borrowed heavily from European practices. The earliest colonial colleges in America duplicated the content and some of the organization of English colleges. Consequently, a brief exposition of the origin of the European universities and colleges should provide a better understanding of the development of American higher education. Universities in Europe developed before colleges did; yet in America, colleges existed long before the universities. American universities did not come into existence until the nineteenth century, lagging two centuries behind the colleges.

EUROPEAN BACKGROUNDS

Universities, as such, originated during the latter part of the Middle Ages. In keeping with the medieval practice of forming various kinds of guilds, or associations of craftsmen, groups of masters, or students, or both, banded together to form a corporation (*universitas*). The university, known as the *studium generale,* was simply one of many associations. They were chartered by the church or by the state, after which they were entitled by law to certain privileges and rights. Some early universities, however, were in existence for many years before they were chartered. Some universities, for example the University of Paris, were an outgrowth of cathedral schools.

The dates of the earliest universities are disputed because they were often chartered a century after they were founded. The University of Bologna was chartered in 1158, although it was founded earlier. Some authorities claim that Salerno was the first university in existence because it was founded during the latter part of the eleventh century, even though it was not officially recognized until 1231.[1] The University of Paris had its beginning around 1170 but was not recognized until 1210.[2] During the succeeding centuries, universities developed all over Europe. Their gradual increase may be seen in the following tabulation:[3]

Century	Number founded
Twelfth	6
Thirteenth	17
Fourteenth	22
Fifteenth	34
	79 Total at end of fifteenth century

The universities' course of study embraced four areas: arts, law, medicine, and theology. The term *faculty* was applied to each area of study, but eventually the term was used to designate the teachers of these areas instead, for example the "faculty of arts" or "faculty of law". It became customary for a university to offer the arts, with one or more of the other three areas. Some universities developed specialities, on which they based their reputations. In the early years, for example, Bologna specialized in law, Paris in theology, and Salerno in medicine.

---

[1]Hastings Rashdall, *The Universities of Europe in the Middle Ages,* Vol. I, edited by F. M. Powicke and A. B. Emden (London: Oxford University Press, 1936) p. 82.

[2]*Ibid.,* p. 292, 299-300.

[3]*Ibid.,* p. xxiv. Figures adapted from a table which lists the names of the universities founded.

Organization

There were two types of organization in European universities: "master universities" and "student universities". As the terms indicate, these schools were controlled either by the masters or by the students. The students at the University of Bologna who were older (similar to graduate students), controlled the university. They determined the courses to be offered, set their schedules, and paid the professors. At the University of Paris, where the students were younger, and most of them still in the arts course (similar to undergraduate students), the masters controlled the school. These two schools, Bologna and Paris, became the models for other universities, and "master universities" eventually predominated.

The professors, or masters, were organized into the faculties of arts, law, medicine, and theology, and each faculty elected its dean. The faculty deans and student representatives elected the *rector,* or head of the university.

Originally the course of study took seven years, but later it was shortened to six years. After four years, the student became a *baccalaureus,* which was not a degree. By the end of six or seven years, if he continued his studies, he became a master, doctor, or professor. These terms at first were used interchangeably.

Under their charters, or by decrees, universities acquired certain rights and privileges which applied to all university personnel. The universities themselves were given the right to license masters. University personnel were free from taxation and military service, and had the right to trial by university personnel rather than civil authority. Since confrontations between "town and gown", and between the students themselves, were not uncommon, this last right undoubtedly worked to the advantage of the students.

Origin of Colleges

University students organized themselves into nations, according to their geographical origin, and resided in halls which eventually were called *colleges.* Originally, instruction was not offered in the various colleges which were used as residence and study halls. For instruction, the students walked to the lecture halls of the university. However, a gradual tranformation took place. The masters who were assigned to the colleges gave the students individual instructional aid. As the number of students in the colleges increased, the masters gave group lectures to supplement the lectures the students heard at the university. As this practice increased, the universities began to officially sanction the instruction given in the colleges. Gradually the colleges became self-contained units within the university, where students slept, ate, studied, and received instruction in one of the faculties, under the auspices of the university. The last step in this evolutionary process was the establishment of colleges apart from and independent of, the universities. During the sixteenth century these changes occurred at Oxford and Cambridge universities in England, where

> . . . the colleges in both universities acquired functions and prestige which they had not enjoyed before. By the end of the period they were beginning to exercise such control of matriculation, the discipline of students, and instruction that their activities not only aided and supplemented the work of the universities themselves but duplicated it and seemed ready to supplant it.[4]

Instruction in Universities

All study in medieval universities was conducted in Latin. The master read or lectured from his textbook, while the students took notes. Sometimes, he added his own comments to supplement the textbook material. In addition, disputations (similar to debates) were carried on by the students under the direction of their master. *Ordinary* disputations were held weekly, and *extraordinary* ones were held annually. All disputations were conducted in Latin, and used the syllogistic form of reasoning.

Students in the college of arts studied the Seven Liberal Arts in which the trivium received the heaviest emphasis. Within the trivium, most attention was given to dialectic (logic). The quadrivium, which concerned the mathematical or scientific part of the curriculum was less emphasized. While the universities were in their prime, students received rigorous intellectual training. Unfortunately, after the thirteenth century the schools declined. Their emphasis on logic became superficial, and often dealt with trivialities. Kane, who has described these later universities as trade schools where students were taught logic-chopping, presents a graphic picture of this degeneration in fourteenth century universities:

---

[4]Mark H. Curtis, *Oxford and Cambridge in Transition 1558-1642* (London: Oxford University Press, 1959), p. 5. By permission of the Clarendon Press, Oxford.

Now it becomes petty, contentious, querulous, lost in insignificant details. The faculty of theology is a hotbed of intrigue. True zeal for study disappears before the trivial ambitions of vanity or greedy campaigning for ecclesiastical preferment. Political jockeying, and even bribery by money, make easy the approach to the 'doctorate'. In the faculty of arts the years of study are shortened, and 'beardless boys fill with infantile stammerings' the chairs of the masters. The students are sputtering dialectic; and the 'form' of a syllogism has become more important than the truth it may contain.[5]

Influence of the Renaissance

The Renaissance, emphasizing the study of Greek and Roman classics, produced a gradual change in the curriculum of the universities. Logic was deposed from its dominant place in the trivium, and grammar and rhetoric became the primary subjects of study. The style and thought of classical writers became the substance of education. The study of man (humanism), became the center of attention, and the universities began to prepare their students for secular as well as religious life. However, the religious base of education was retained, for even secularly controlled universities maintained their religious ties. The Reformation and the subsequent establishment of many religious denominations, exerting varying pressures on the universities located within their national boundaries, further influenced the movement toward secularism and nationalism.

Oxford and Cambridge

Because of the English influence on American education, it would be profitable to look briefly at what was happening in English universities before America was settled. During the sixteenth century, the universities of Oxford and Cambridge underwent the changes that affected all European universities during the Renaissance. The English humanists, More, Erasmus, Elyot, and Ascham, greatly influenced the universities. Education became based on humanistic principles, emphasizing the study of classical literature.

Similar to other European universities, Oxford and Cambridge also were controlled by the clergy, but after the Reformation the Crown

---

[5]W. Kane, *An Essay Toward A History of Education* (Chicago: Loyola University Press, 1935), footnote 2, p. 183.

began to influence changes in the universities. After the Act of Parliament of 1571, the very existence of the universities depended on the Crown. Yet, even though they became secular corporations influenced by the Crown, there still existed a close relationship with the church. In fact, ". . . the control of university affairs continued in the hands of clergymen."[6]

By the end of the sixteenth century, the status of the colleges at Oxford and Cambridge was greatly enhanced. Stately college buildings which housed students who had previously lived in halls and inns were constructed with money given by wealthy patrons. Parents of the students preferred these college residences for their children, because they offered supplementary lectures based on the needs of the students and provided closer supervision of the students. Furthermore, the colleges, unlike the halls, were more stable institutions since they were endowed with steady income. In the face of this competition, especially after the colleges began to admit fee-paying students, the number of halls gradually decreased.

By the end of the sixteenth century, the colleges had begun to admit the children of nobility and the wealthy who had previously received their instruction from private tutors. More and more of these students began to apply for admission because of the shift to a humanistic and secular type of education. Some of these students remained in the colleges only a year or two, taking the subjects that interested them, and then rounding out their education by travel or independent reading.

Although there were a few exceptions and dispensations, the A.B. degree required a residence for four years, or sixteen terms. The curriculum consisted of portions of the Seven Liberal Arts. Undergraduates were not required to work in all the subjects. It was thought that after a student had received his A.B. degree he would continue in the other arts and philosophy as part of the work for his master's degree. Toward the end of the sixteenth century, however, the undergraduate course achieved greater status. Instead of being regarded as preparation for higher studies, the bachelor's degree became an end in itself, and by the end of the century, it overshadowed the advanced work offered by the universities.

As a basis for comparison with the curriculum of early American colleges, which are discussed later in this chapter, we should consider the curriculum offered at Oxford in sixteenth century.[7]

---

[6]Mark H. Curtis, *op. cit.*, p. 32. By permission of the Clarendon Press, Oxford.
[7]*Ibid.*, compiled from pp. 86-87. By permission of the Clarendon Press, Oxford.

Grammar—2 terms
  Linacre's *Rudiments*
  Readings from Virgil, Horace, or Cicero's *Epistles*

Rhetoric—4 terms
  Aristotle's *Rhetoric,* or
  Cicero's *Praeceptiones* or *Orations*

Dialectic—5 terms
  Porphyry's *Institutions,* or
  Aristotle's *Dialectics*

Arithmetic—3 terms
  Texts by Boethius or by Gemma Frisius

Music—2 terms
  Text by Beothius

Obviously, the trivium received the greatest emphasis, for eleven of the sixteen terms were spent on those subjects. Within this area more time was spent on dialectic than on any other subject. During the seventeenth century, grammar and rhetoric received more emphasis, and the curriculum was expanded to include all of the Seven Liberal Arts, as well as other subjects.

Besides listening to lectures, the students were still required to participate in disputations, or debates. A controversial question was posed, and the students presented arguments for the side they upheld. These arguments were then evaluated by a moderator. Disputations were a regular part of student life. Not only did they help to train the students in thinking and expression, but also they were measurements of the students' progress in learning. Before a student could obtain his A.B. degree, he had to participate successfully in Lenten disputations, which were known as determinations (perhaps the equivalent of an oral final examination).

The tutor was an important part of a student's college education. He trained the student assigned to him in academic matters, and was an important influence in the development of the student's character. The effectiveness of this relationship naturally depended upon the tutor's personal qualities and qualifications. Sometimes the college tutor taught his pupils more than they learned at the university lectures they attended. Sometimes, too, the tutors did not limit themselves to the standard curriculum but ranged into other subjects such as history, politics, geometry, astronomy, and foreign languages other than Latin and Greek. A student's college education could be either an enriching or an impoverishing experience, depending on the tutor he had.

The preceding description of European universities and colleges in general, and Oxford and Cambridge in particular, is very brief. However, the European influence on American higher education will become evident in the organization, curriculum, methods, degrees, and terminology that were used in America during the early years, and, with modifications, are still in use.

EARLY COLONIAL COLLEGES

The colonists, having provided their children with elementary and secondary education, turned their attention to college education. The result of their activity was the establishment of Harvard, the only college in the colonies for over half a century. Because Harvard was the first colonial college and later colonial colleges had many things in common with it, some of the details of its development may be considered typical of college education during the colonial period.

The Development of Harvard

Harvard was established only six years after Boston was founded. On October 28, 1636 the General Court of Massachusetts passed a resolution appropriating four hundred pounds for the establishment of a college. A site was chosen at Newton (the name of the town was later changed to Cambridge, after the English university) the following year. In 1638, just after the first class was admitted, the Reverend John Harvard died and left his library of nearly 300 volumes, plus half of his estate of approximately 1,700 pounds to the college. Because of his bequest, the General Court named the college after him.

There was definitely a religious purpose in the founding of Harvard. The majority of Puritan clergymen were educated in English universities, especially in Cambridge University's Emmanuel College, where the sympathy for Puritanism was high. These Puritan clergymen felt that higher education was a necessity for the training of their future ministers and leaders. Their grave concern for this training was stated in the famous pamphlet, *New England's First Fruits,* which was written in 1643 by an unidentified author. The pamphlet states:

> After God had carried us safe to New England, and we had builded our houses, provided necessaries for our livelihood, reared convenient places for God's worship, and settled the civil government, one of the next things we longed for and looked after was to advance learning and perpetuate it to posterity, dreading to leave an illiterate ministry to the churches when our present ministers shall lie in the dust.[8]

With the establishment of Harvard, which was modelled after Emmanuel College, the Puritans felt assured of a future supply of educated ministers. Although this was the chief concern, the university did not limit its enrollment to divinity students.

Students were admitted to Harvard when they were approximately fourteen years old, after acquiring in the Latin Grammar Schools, the needed proficiency in Latin and Greek. The early admission requirements were stated as follows:

> When any scholar is able to read Tully or such like classical Latin author *extempore,* and make and speak true Latin in verse and prose *suo (ut aiunt) Marte,* and decline perfectly the paradigms of nouns and verbs in the Greek tongue, then may he be admitted into the College, nor shall any claim admission before such qualifications.[9]

Originally, the undergraduate program took three years to complete, but in 1654 it was changed to a four-year program. The curriculum consisted of the Seven Liberal Arts, with the exclusion of music, and, therefore, continued, with some modification, the tradition begun during the Middle Ages and still practiced at Oxford and Cambridge. In the early years, the curriculum at Harvard was the following:

Three-Year Course of Study at Harvard—1642[10]

First year

1. Logick
2. Pysicks
3. Disputes

---

[8]As quoted by Perry Miller, ed., *The American Puritans* (New York: Doubleday & Company, Inc., 1956), p. 323.

[9]Joshua L. Chamberlain, ed., *Universities and Their Sons,* Vol. I, (Boston: R. Herndon Company, 1898), p. 143.

[10]*Ibid.,* p. 10. As quoted from Peirce's *History of Harvard,* Appendix, 6, 7.

4. Greek—Etymologie
    and syntax; grammar
5. Hebrew—Grammar
    Bible
6. Rhetoric

Second year

1. Ethics and politics
2. Disputes
3. Greek—Prosodia
    and dialects;
    Poesey, Nonnus, Duport
4. Hebrew, etc.: Chaldee;
    Ezra and Daniel
5. Rhetoric

Third year

1. Arithmetic; Geometry;
    Astronomy
2. Greek—Theory, style
    composition, imitation
    epitome, both in prose
    and verse
3. Hebrew, etc.; Syriac;
    Trostius New Testament
4. Rhetoric
5. History
6. Nature of plants

Harvard's early curriculum reflects the changes that had occurred at Oxford and Cambridge by the end of the sixteenth century. The emphasis had shifted to grammar and rhetoric. Classical languages and literature now occupied a good portion of the curriculum. Disputations were a regular part of instructional procedures, and religion and religious exercises played a prominent part in daily activities.

During its early years, the faculty at Harvard consisted of the president and two tutors who received occasional help from graduate students. Each teacher was required to teach several courses, as departmentalized instruction, in which each teacher teaches his specialty, would not be introduced until 1766.

Although the students were examined by their teachers, a regular examination system did not appear until 1760. At that time the students were given oral examinations in the spring and fall. These were formal examinations and not to be confused with the daily oral questioning done by the teachers.

Since the Harvard students were only thirteen or fourteen years old when they were admitted, and were only sixteen or seventeen when they graduated, they were kept under strong discipline. Because the college was founded mainly for religious purposes, the students were required to attend daily services conducted by the president at six o'clock in the morning. Sometimes the morning service was used to announce offenses committed by individual students. Sometimes, too, these services were devoted to the students' public confessions of transgressions such as profanity, card-playing, and theft. With the long hours of study, complaints about poor food, strict discipline, and confining regulations which even prohibited attending a public function in town, periodic disturbances and rebellions occurred which often resulted in the suspension or expulsion of some students.

Enrollment at Harvard was small. Nine were graduated in the first class in 1642, and only four were graduated in the following year. The commencement exercises, attended by many prominent people, consisted of prayers, orations, and festivities. Apparently the students celebrated the occasion too enthusiastically, because by the end of the seventeenth century, the university issued prohibitions against the consumption of "plumb cake" and liquors. The necessity for subsequent regulations of a similar nature indicated that the students ignored the previous ones. Their celebrations continued unabated into the next century, and were never really eliminated.

Class Days, during which one of the students delivered a farewell to the college and its personnel in Latin, seem to have originated around the middle of the eighteenth century. James Russell Lowell said that these class days ". . . seem to have been restricted to an oration in Latin, sandwiched between two prayers by the president, like a criminal between two peace officers".[11] By the beginning of the nineteenth century, despite the objections of the faculty, the students began to deliver their orations in English.

Extracurricular activities during the eighteenth century included speaking, literary societies, and social clubs. Bats, balls, and footballs were in early use. Further physical exercise was provided by bear hunting, skating, wrestling, boating, swimming, and occasional skirmishes between freshmen and sophomores.

The students evidently had enough activities, academic and extracurricular, to fully occupy their time. The quality of their education,

---

[11]*Ibid.*, p. 192.

however, has been questioned. The faculty, other than the president, consisted of divinity students working for their master's degree or waiting for a ministerial assignment. These tutors were only slightly older than the students, which made for a precarious relationship. At least two European visitors to Harvard in 1680 were poorly impressed with the university.

> The first group of young men they encountered gave them the impression they were in a tavern rather than a college. The students, they reported, could hardly speak a word of Latin. Nor were they any more favorably impressed with the library, 'where there was nothing particular.'[12]

If true, this indictment not only indicates poor instruction, but also shows that admission requirements were not observed, because a knowledge of Latin was a prerequisite for admission.

Other Colonial Colleges

Harvard was the only college in America for over fifty years. By the time of the Revolution, however, eight additional colleges had been established. Their present names and the dates of their foundation are as follows:

Colleges Established Before 1776

College	Date Founded
Harvard	1636
William and Mary	1693
Yale	1701
Princeton	1746
Columbia	1754
Pennsylvania	1755
Brown	1764
Rutgers	1766
Dartmouth	1769

Life and study at the other colonial colleges was comparable to that at Harvard. Their purpose was to train ministers for their respective denominations. All of them, with the exception of the University of Pennsylvania, had a religious affiliation, and even at the University of

---

[12]Newton Edwards and Herman G. Richey, *The School in the American Social Order* (Boston: Houghton Mifflin Company, 1947), p. 118.

Pennsylvania some authorities point to a religious affiliation. Admission requirements in each school were similar and stressed a knowledge of Latin and Greek. The curriculum also was heavily weighted with classical studies.

By 1800 the number of colleges had increased to twenty-six, yet the enrollment continued to be small. Because the colleges were private institutions that largely depended on tuition for support, the small enrollment left them in an unstable financial position. Expenses were curtailed, and the improvement of facilities and instruction was forestalled. Lack of money prevented the hiring of a permanent, stable staff of teachers. The quality of education at these colleges was the same as the quality of education at Harvard. Thus, according to Hofstadter:

> The history of the early college is full of episodes of almost hysterical rebellion, malicious pranks, and even personal violence against tutors and college presidents of a sort that is unheard-of in the modern college. Many a provincial American college was little more than a high-grade academy with an intensive program of classical studies learned by rote.[13]

LATER DEVELOPMENT OF COLLEGES

One of the most important events for the later development of colleges was the Dartmouth College Case. The United States Supreme Court decision in 1819 helped to preserve the rights of private colleges. In 1816, the legislature of New Hampshire tried to obtain control over Dartmouth by attempting to appoint a state-controlled board which would govern the affairs of the college. Dartmouth's own self-perpetuating board of governors challenged the right of the state to interfere with its affairs, claiming that it was a violation of the college's charter. The case was tried in the courts of New Hampshire, and a decision was given in favor of the state. It was then appealed to the United States Supreme Court with Daniel Webster representing Dartmouth. He argued the case eloquently and passionately. The essence of his argument, as reported by an observer, was the following:

> *This, Sir, is my case!* It is the case, not merely of that humble institution, it is the case of every College in the land. It is more. It is the case of every Eleemosynary Institution throughout our coun-

---

[13]Richard Hofstadter and C. DeWitt Hardy, *The Development and Scope of Higher Education in the United States* (New York: Columbia University Press, 1952), pp. 17-18.

try—of all those great charities founded by the piety of our ancestors to alleviate human misery, and scatter blessings along the pathway of life. It is more! It is, in some sense, the case of every man among us who has property of which he may be stripped, for the question is simply this: Shall our State Legislatures be allowed to take *that* which is not their own, to turn it from its original use, and apply it to such ends or purposes as they, in their discretion, shall see fit![14]

In 1819, the United States Supreme Court reversed the decision of the state court, stating that a college charter, constituting a contract between a college and a state, could not be violated by the state. This Supreme Court decision permanently established that a state could not assume control of, or try to impose its views on, a private college.

It would be difficult to show the direct effects of the Dartmouth case. The Supreme Court ruling certainly made private institutions feel more secure from state interference. It may have given some impetus to the establishment of additional private colleges. Furthermore, it may have led to the establishment of state colleges when various states felt that the private colleges were not meeting the needs of the people.

Curriculum Changes

During the eighteenth century, there were gradual changes in the college curriculum. At Harvard the classical authors who were studied by the students, were periodically changed. French was taught sporadically. By the beginning of the nineteenth century, foreign language instruction was available in Spanish, Italian, German, and Portuguese.[15] At the end of the eighteenth century, the university not only offered natural science but also had established professorships in anatomy and surgery, "Theory and practice of physic," and chemistry and materia medica. These, however, were professional courses, apart from the regular college program.

Although the classical studies retained their prominence in the curriculum during the nineteenth century, modern subjects also were introduced. The country was expanding, wealth was increasing, and industrialization was taking place. There was a greater demand, which colleges began to meet, for more secular and practical subjects. Yale

---

[14]Richard Hofstadter and Wilson Smith, ed., *American Higher Education* (Chicago: The University of Chicago Press, 1961), as quoted on p. 212.
[15]Joshua L. Chamberlain, *op. cit.*, p. 146.

University added to its course of study French and political economy
in 1825, Kent's Commentaries on American Law in 1833, and modern
history in 1847. Scientific schools also were established during this time.
Rensselaer Polytechnic Institute was established in 1824, and Harvard, Yale, and Dartmouth had science departments by mid-century.
Nevertheless, the Seven Liberal Arts remained a major part of the
curriculum.[16]

The Yale Report of 1828 was the cause of the curriculum's immuta-
bility. Faced with mounting criticism and discontent with higher education, the Yale faculty launched an inquiry into education in 1827.
The inquiry became a full-scale investigation of the objectives and content of higher education in the United States.

In its report of 1828, the Yale faculty upheld the value of the old
classical and humanistic course of study. It defended Aristotelian psychology, the study of the "dead languages" as a necessity for forming
proper values and tastes, the importance of mathematics for developing
reasoning powers, and it upheld the efficacy of the old teaching methods. When Princeton with its formidable prestige also supported the
Yale Report, the critics were silenced. So influential was the report
that new colleges proudly announced that their curriculum was identical to Yale's curriculum. Rudolph commenting on the report's influence, maintained that "Behind it the American college curriculum
remained almost immovable until after the Civil War."[17]

One of the strongest proponents of curriculum changes was Francis
Wayland, president of Brown University, who stated that the colleges
were not meeting the needs of society. In 1850, in a report to the corporation of Brown University, he decried college education for its superficiality. The report stated, in part:

> We now have in the United States . . . one hundred and twenty
> colleges . . . All of them teach Greek and Latin, but where are
> our classical scholars? All teach mathematics, but where are our
> mathematicians? We might ask the same questions concerning
> the other sciences taught among us. There has existed for the last
> twenty years a great demand for civil engineers. Has this demand
> been supplied from our colleges? We assume the single academy
> at West Point, graduating annually a smaller number than many
> of our colleges, has done more towards the construction of rail-
> roads than all our one hundred and twenty colleges united.[18]

---

[16]*Ibid.*, p. 297 describes the course of study stated in the Yale catalogue of 1822.

[17]Frederick Rudolph, *The American College and University* (New York: Alfred
A. Knopf, Inc., 1962), p. 135.

[18]As quoted by Richard Hofstadter and C. DeWitt Hardy, *op. cit.*, pp. 24-25.

Although these strong arguments for change in the curriculum made some impression, the colleges were slow to offer a more practical education. As late as 1870, the president of Columbia criticized the colleges as being inflexible and out of touch with the needs of society. During this period of rising criticism, a new type of college, the land-grant college, came into existence, and affected the curriculum of the older established colleges.

Influence of the Morrill Act

During the first half of the nineteenth century there were sporadic attempts to introduce agricultural education into a few colleges. However, the farmers were not particularly interested in these courses. Nevertheless, it became increasingly apparent that more scientific methods of farming were needed to preserve the fertility of the soil. Equally evident was the need for scientific training in other fields if the industrial potentialities of the country were to be developed.

For many years, Justin Smith Morrill, a congressman from Vermont, had urged the colleges to substitute vocational training for a part of their existing curriculum. Since he could not persuade the colleges to change, in 1857, he introduced a bill in Congress which would have established colleges for technical training. The bill was vetoed by President Buchanan. In 1862, under Lincoln's presidency, Morrill again submitted the bill, and this time it was passed.

The Morrill Act of 1862 provided federal land grants for the establishment of colleges which would teach agriculture and the mechanic arts. Under the act, each state received 30,000 acres of public land, or land scrip, for each senator and representative the state had in Congress. This public land could be sold by the state, or the state could redeem the land scrip for cash from the federal government. Ten percent of the funds thus obtained could be used to purchase sites for colleges if necessary, but the remainder had to be invested, and the income from the investment had to be used for their maintenance. The income produced from land grants totalling 17,430,000 acres in all was used to finance new colleges, or to endow many existing public and private colleges to teach agriculture and mechanic arts.

The Morrill Act (supplemented by additional funds in 1890) resulted in the eventual support of sixty-eight colleges, many of them prominent universities today. The act did not stipulate the type of college eligible for support. Therefore, a variety of colleges were designated as land-grant colleges. In some states, new colleges were established; in other states, the land-grant funds were turned over to existing agricultural colleges or state universities. Even some private colleges, such as Yale, Dartmouth, Brown, and Rutgers became the designated recipients of the land-grant funds. In each case, however, the institution receiving the funds had to provide for education in agriculture and the mechanic arts.

There were mixed reactions to the land-grant colleges, especially in rural areas. While the value of mechanic arts was generally recognized, people were skeptical about the scientific study of agriculture. As one Philadelphia agricultural newspaper stated:

> Instead of introducing the students of agriculture to a laboratory and chemical and philosophical apparatus, we would introduce him to a pair of heavy neat's leather boots and corduroy pants, and learn him how to load manure.[19]

Shortly after the land-grant colleges were established, some educational leaders felt that they should offer more than vocational training. They, therefore, added a few traditional subjects to the curriculum. Critics then called the new colleges "dude factories." Agricultural courses continued to be poorly attended, not only because people distrusted their value, but also because there were no high schools in rural areas to prepare the children for college admission. During the last quarter of the nineteenth century, enrollment increased after the colleges lowered, and, in some cases, almost abandoned admission requirements.

The Hatch Act in 1887, which provided federal funds for the establishment of agricultural experimental stations, was an important factor in changing the farmers' attitude toward agricultural education. These stations applied scientific methods to solve the problems experienced by the farmers and, therefore, gradually won their confidence. From 1890 on, the land-grant colleges experienced increased acceptance, and the vocational objective in college education challenged the humanistic education that had dominated the college scene.

The Effect of Electives

Although the development of science courses and the demand for practical education affected the college curriculum, the elective system shattered the prescribed course of study. For approximately two centuries, the college curriculum, with minor variations, was a fixed pro-

---

[19]As quoted by Frederick Rudolph, *op. cit.*, p. 256.

gram which each student had to follow. Charles William Eliot who became president of Harvard University in 1869 was responsible for the radical change brought about by the elective system.

Elective courses had made some progress at Harvard before Eliot's appointment as president. As early as 1824, a committee appointed by the Overseers had recommended a partial elective system. Although the faculty opposed it, the Overseers adopted the recommendation. However, the modern language department under George Ticknor was the only department to promote it. In 1833, Tichnor reported that 103 out of 210 students took modern languages of their choice. Since he could not persuade other departments to use the elective system, and since he felt strongly about its use, he resigned. In 1841, Harvard sophomores, juniors, and seniors were permitted to take a few elective courses, but these offered fewer credits than the prescribed courses. Periodically, the policy on elective courses was revised, and by 1867, about half of the courses in the student's last three years of school were elective.

Number of Hours in Required and Elective Courses at Harvard, 1867[20]

Class	Required Hours	Elective Hours
Freshman	All	None
Sophomore	7	6
Junior	6	6-9
Senior	6	6-9

As soon as Eliot became president of Harvard in 1869, he made sweeping changes in the curriculum offered. In his inaugural address, he stated that he considered all courses equally important, that he would strengthen every subject and give it equal credit, and that students would be permitted to elect the subjects which best suited their capacities and interests. Each student, he believed, had different capacities which should be developed through the subjects which were appropriate for him, not through compulsory courses. In his speech, Eliot was merely restating the principle of individual differences which had been proposed from time to time throughout the history of education.

---

[20]Tabulated from Joshua L. Chamberlain, *op. cit.*, p. 152.

Eliot's principle of electives caused a furor among those people who believed in a prescribed curriculum. One of his more prominent debates on electives was with James McCosh, president of Princeton, in which both sides of the question were argued capably. However, a growing liberalism during the nineteenth century, and the theories of a long line of developmentalists helped to strengthen the elective system he had begun. American educators, who visited Europe, brought back with them theories of self-activity, individual differences, interests, and the idea that education was an unfolding process from within rather than an imposition of standards from without. Furthermore, new experimentation in psychology questioned the validity of the earlier faculty psychology. The elective principle was in harmony with all of these newer theories.

Eliot's progress and success with the elective system effected the abolition of required courses for seniors in 1872, for juniors in 1879, and for sophomores in 1884. In 1885, required courses for freshmen were reduced, and by 1897 the only required course for freshmen was a year of rhetoric. By 1897, Harvard offered 346 elective courses. The number of electives offered in each subject is shown in the following table.

Elective Courses at Harvard, 1897[21]

Semitic	14	Government	10
Sanskrit and Zend	5	Fine Arts	4
Greek	15	Architecture	10
Latin	18	Music	5
Classical Philology	12	Mathematics	24
English	27	Engineering	39
German	18	Military Science	2
Germanic Philology	7	Physics	9
French	14	Chemistry	13
Italian	3	Botany	6
Spanish	3	Zoology	8
Romance Philology	5	Geology	16
Comparative Literature	2	Mineralogy and Petrography	3
Philosophy	17	Mining and Metallurgy	1
Education and Teaching	5	American Archaeology	2
Economics	14	Anatomy, Physiology, etc.	5
History	18		
			346

[21]*Ibid.*, p. 156.

Outside of Harvard, the elective system was adopted in varying degrees. The enrollment in many small colleges increased as the schools added elective courses. Yet, because many of these schools were not well endowed financially, they could not begin the more costly elective system. For this reason, the elective system made more progress in large state and private universities and well-endowed small colleges. Among the older colleges, Cornell was as liberal as Harvard with its electives. Rutgers, Yale, and Princeton remained conservative. The status of the elective system at the beginning of the twentieth century may be seen in the following table.

Prevalence of Electives
in 97 Colleges, 1901

% of Electives Permitted	Number of Colleges
70	34
50-70	12
Below 50	51

Almost half of the colleges in 1901 permitted their students to elect half or more of their program, and over a third of the colleges permitted the students to choose at least seventy percent of their program.

By 1900 Harvard had gone from one extreme to the other, from the completely prescribed curriculum of earlier years, with no electives, to a curriculum which was completely elective except for one prescribed freshman course. Some colleges compromised between these two extremes. Yale, for example, permitted its students to elect one of the major sequences that were offered and even to select courses within those sequences. This type of compromise retained prescribed areas of study but made allowances for individual differences by permitting choices within these areas.

During the early part of the twentieth century, educators began to criticize the elective system. It was argued that:

1. The study of the classics was almost buried beneath the avalanche of electives, and many people still wanted to prescribe their study;
2. Vocationalism was becoming the dominant objective of education, with a consequent de-emphasis on spiritual values;
3. The standards of higher education were lowered, because many students concentrated on taking the easier courses;

4. It destroyed some of the cohesiveness of the student body because of the lack of common courses taken by all students;
5. The diversity of course offerings created problems of organization and administration.

As the century progressed, the critics of the elective system became more numerous, and gradually prescribed courses were returned to the curriculum. Between 1920 and 1940, there was a noticeable trend to restore the study of the humanities and require a prescribed number of courses considered important for a well-rounded development. Today colleges are still trying to achieve a proper balance between vocational and liberal education.

During the nineteenth century people became more aware of the value of a college education, yet only a small percentage of these people were able to receive it. The twentieth century brought new educational opportunity to the people of the United States. In 1869–1870, there were only 1.68 percent of college age persons going to college. This percentage rose to 4.01 in 1899–1900, 12.19 in 1929–1930, 25.70 in 1953–1954 and approximately 40 percent in 1968. During the decade 1955–1965, college enrollment doubled from 2,659,000 to 5,320,000. To accommodate this increase, higher education added more facilities in that one decade than during the entire preceding three centuries.

College enrollment will continue to increase in the immediate future. Educational and governmental agencies have made so many forms of financial aid available to qualified and deserving students that, today, most students can find a way of obtaining a college education. The prediction that college enrollment will rise to 9,000,000 by 1975 is an indication of the anticipated rise in enrollment. Part of this increase will come from the increased attendance at the graduate schools and junior colleges, which will be discussed next.

DEVELOPMENT OF AMERICAN UNIVERSITIES AND PROFESSIONAL SCHOOLS

The beginning of university education in America is clouded because the term "university" was used loosely until the twentieth century. During the eighteenth and nineteenth centuries, some colleges offered graduate and professional training but did not title themselves as universities. Other institutions were titled universities but provided only undergraduate instruction. These two situations further confused the issue. Harvard College, for example, gave advanced degrees and programs long before it was designated as a university in 1864. However, many state institutions were designated as "universities" from their founding without qualifying for that status.

European universities as we previously mentioned, were originally organized into four faculties: arts, law, medicine, and theology. After the students had studied the Seven Liberal Arts, they could take graduate work or professional work leading to a master's or doctor's degree. If we accept the European organization of a university then we would define the university as an institution consisting of "several colleges or schools and giving graduate or professional training."[21] Just as European universities did not necessarily offer advanced or professional work in all of the faculties, American universities, at least in the beginning, did not attempt to do so.

Many historians believe that the American university did not develop until the end of the nineteenth century because it was not until then that the universities began to model themselves on the German concept of a university; i.e., a school consisting of several faculties that prepare students for various professions, characterized by research, academic freedom, and service to the state. During the latter part of the nineteenth century American scholars traveled to Europe, studied European ideas, and then promoted them in the United States. These ideas were so widely accepted that American universities were described by some people as a "German university superimposed upon an English college". Yet, as late as 1898, Joshua L. Chamberlain, former president of Bowdoin College and ex-governor of Maine, complained about the lack of distinction between colleges and universities.[22] Chamberlain pointed out that some institutions claimed the title of university because of their extensive course offerings, while other institutions claimed the title because of the depth, rather than extent, of their studies. Still others, he said, assumed the title because they provided advanced training for various professions. This confused situation still exists today. Most large universities (with their varied schools, colleges, graduate and professional programs, and their emphasis on original research and intensive scholarship) deserve their title. Yet, some institutions use the title of university even though they offer only one or two programs at the master's degree level.

Because of these various interpretations, it is difficult to trace the early development of universities in the United States. If the discussion were limited to the "German type" institutions developed during the latter part of the nineteenth century, the early efforts toward

---

[21]Paul Monroe, ed., *A Cyclopedia of Education*, Vol. V, (New York The Macmillan Company, 1926), p. 665.

[22]Joshua L. Chamberlain, *op. cit.*, p. 41.

graduate and professional training would be ignored. Consequently, in spite of the difficulties with precise terminology, we will briefly describe early post-baccalaureate education.

Early Graduate and Professional Education

Because of the religious objectives of early colleges, the earliest post-baccalaureate program leading to a master's degree was in theology. The early colleges, then, had "divinity schools" from the start. The general requirement for a master's degree in theology was the completion of a year's work and the passing of an examination after the student had received his A.B. At Harvard, the Overseers in 1654 stated this requirement which remained unchanged until 1844. After 1844, any graduate of Harvard could receive a master's degree three years after he received his baccalaureate upon the payment of five dollars. Although it was hoped that the individual would follow some course of study during his three years, it was not required. In 1872, Harvard restored the academic requirements for the degree.

Until the second half of the nineteenth century, graduate study was meagre, unorganized, and often taken on an informal basis. A student could remain in college for an additional year as a graduate resident. Sometimes one or more faculty members directed the student in his readings and later discussed with him his findings. Too often, however, the graduate student was left to his own resources and profited little from his additional year of study. Because graduate education was not well organized in America, many students attended European universities for advanced work.

Professional education made more advances than graduate education, but its progress was also slow. Because the curriculum of American colleges remained relatively unchanged for two centuries, not admitting innovations or new subjects, it was common for an individual to serve an apprenticeship which would prepare him for a profession. For example, the prospective doctor would serve as an apprentice to a recognized physician. The prospective doctor would receive instruction from him, observe him in his work, and gain practical experience under supervision until he was qualified to practice on his own. Sometimes, as in the case of graduate study, the individual would attend a European university to learn his profession.

Only a few early American colleges offered a course or two in sciences related to professions. No college developed a formal program for a profession until the middle of the eighteenth century. In 1762, at the College of Philadelphia (University of Pennsylvania), a series of medical lectures was given by one doctor, who was joined by a second doctor in 1765. King's College (Columbia University) established a medical school in 1767; it first conferred the degree of Bachelor of Medicine in 1769, and in 1770, the degree of Doctor of Medicine. Harvard, trailing behind King's College, first awarded the degree of Bachelor of Medicine in 1785, and Doctor of Medicine in 1788. Dartmouth established its first medical school in 1798, and Yale in 1812. In the field of law, Harvard established its law department in 1818, and Yale in 1843.

These were small and slow beginnings in graduate and professional education. The question of "university" status can be raised again, using Harvard, because it is the oldest college as an example. Was Harvard a university from its beginning since it gave graduate work and a master's degree? Or did it become a university when it awarded the degree of Doctor of Medicine in 1788? Or, did it have to wait until the law department was established in 1818, thus giving it the four faculties of arts, law, medicine, and theology? The answer, of course, depends on the definition of a university.

Harvard first designated itself as a university in its catalogue of 1864, although it deserved that classification before then. The following enrollment statistics show the fields of study taught at Harvard just after the Civil War.

Student Enrollment at Harvard, 1869[23]

Classification of Students	Enrollment
Undergraduate	563
Graduate	6
Divinity School	36
Law School	120
Scientific School	43
School of Mining	9
Medical School	306
Dental School	16

These statistics not only reveal the fields of study into which Harvard had expanded but also the size of the enrollment in professional education. With an enrollment of 530, professional education constituted nearly half of the enrollment at the institution. Professional education was expanding, and within a few years this growth was followed by a great increase in the number of graduate students. Under Eliot's presi-

_____

[23]*Ibid.*, adapted from a table on p. 103.

dency from 1869 to 1909, Harvard added several graduate schools, and more than tripled its enrollment.

Similar changes were occurring in other private and state institutions. Other state universities followed the pattern set by the University of Michigan which was reorganized in 1852 to conform to the German concept of a university. The Morrill Act began to stimulate technical and scientific training, and since the progress of industry depended on new ideas and developments, the research concept was encouraged in the universities not only by scholars but also by businessmen.

Expansion of the University Movement

The modern idea of an American university received stimulus from, and seemed to coincide with, the first Ph.D. degree granted for graduate work. Until the Civil War, a Ph.D. degree had never been conferred by any American college or university. Yale University awarded the first Ph.D. in 1861, and within fifteen years twenty-five other institutions also awarded Ph.D.'s. The granting of this degree fostered the idea of scholarly achievement and pure research in graduate work. In fact, this type of work became one of the requirements for the degree.

Requirements for Degrees at Harvard, 1872[24]

Degree	Requirements
M.A.	A student must receive high grades in four advanced courses taken for one year.
Ph.D.	High attainment in a specialized branch of study, including a thorough examination and a thesis which makes a special contribution to knowledge. The degree could be taken in one of the following departments: philosophy, philology, political science, history, mathematics, physics (including chemistry), music, and natural history.
D.S.	Same requirements as the Ph.D., with the work confined to two subjects or fields in the general fields of mathematical, physical and natural sciences. The thesis must make a contribution to science or some special investigation.

[24]*Ibid.*, adapted from textual material, pp. 108-109.

There was no residence requirement or fixed period of study for a doctorate at Harvard in 1872. Normally the work took three years to complete, but some individuals completed it in two years.

The founding of Cornell in 1865 further stimulated the idea of free inquiry. Ezra Cornell, its founder, considered the school a place for vocational training, an idea that was fostered by the designation of Cornell as a land-grant institution for the state of New York. However, Andrew D. White, its first president, had a broader view of the objectives of the university, and stated that its programs would combine liberal and practical training. White also promoted nonsectarian control of the university, fostered scientific inquiry, favored the elective system, and hoped to make Cornell the outstanding institution in the state. Within ten years, Cornell's students won the intercollegiate academic contests held within the state, thus silencing some of White's critics, and considerably improving the school's image. Their victories also helped to promote the free inquiry which White had favored.

The founding of Johns Hopkins University was perhaps the greatest stimulus to the idea of a university as a place of free inquiry and research. Incorporated in 1867 and opened in 1876, Johns Hopkins was the first American institution which emphasized its graduate program more than its undergraduate program. Its president, Daniel C. Gilman, immediately surrounded himself with eminent and promising faculty members, and admitted only students who showed high potentiality. Gilman felt that the function of a university was to seek truth continuously, no matter how unpopular the search or the product might be. His spirit pervaded the faculty and the students, and was contagious, spreading to other institutions. This spirit, and its effects, were described by Rudolph:

> For the acceptance of revealed religious truth the new university in Baltimore substituted a search for scientific truth. For preparation for life in the next world it substituted a search for an understanding of this world. Johns Hopkins elevated man's reason to a position it had not before attained in the United States. It released the energies of scholarship, combined them with the national impulse to human betterment and material progress. The task it set for itself was immense and unending, and in time the spirit of Johns Hopkins would penetrate everywhere.[25]

The emphasis on graduate study at Johns Hopkins stimulated other institutions to strengthen their graduate programs. Furthermore, al-

---

[25]Frederick Rudolph, *op. cit.*, pp. 274-275.

though some institutions had earlier subsidized graduate study for their *own* graduates, Johns Hopkins expanded graduate work by awarding fellowships to promising students who had graduated from other colleges. This practice was adopted by other universities and therefore, increased the number of graduate students.

The development of universities gathered momentum during the last few decades of the nineteenth century. Some of the old colleges finally began to adopt the title of university. Yale designated itself as a university in 1887, twenty-three years after Harvard. Columbia and Princeton became universities in 1896. With the expansion of knowledge and the need for specialized training, the number of courses, programs, and degrees increased. By the end of the nineteenth century, Columbia University awarded the following degrees: A.B., LL.B., B.S. (mining, civil, and sanitary engineering), M.A., LL.M., M.D., and Ph.D. At the same time, Princeton offered graduate study in twenty departments and, in addition to the bachelor's degrees, awarded the degrees of M.A., M.S., D.Sc., and Ph.D. New universities were founded in all parts of the country at the turn of the century. Some of the better known schools include Vanderbilt (1875), Tulane (1884), Clark University (1889), Stanford (1891), and Chicago (1891). New state universities were founded, and existing ones were expanded.

Each succeeding decade of the twentieth century showed a substantial increase in college and university attendance. This is graphically demonstrated by the figures in the chart on page 162, showing the increase in enrollment and in the number of degrees conferred over a period of approximately eighty-five years.

Aside from temporary dips in enrollment that were brought about by the wars, and periods of decreased birth rate, college and university enrollment has shown a steady and remarkable increase during the twentieth century. The rapidly increasing birth rate during and following World War II, and the greater prosperity and expanded opportunities, have brought about a sharp increase in the college population during recent years. College enrollment doubled during the decade 1955–65. Further enrollment increases are anticipated; it is estimated that enrollment will rise to 7,000,000 in 1970, and that it will exceed 9,000,000 by 1975. (See Figure I, p. 163.)

To care for this increased enrollment, the last decade has been marked by the establishment of new colleges and universities, the expansion of facilities and personnel, and experimentation with innovations that might bring about more efficient and effective instruction. In 1953, there were 1,863 colleges and universities; of these 1,863 schools, 495 were junior colleges. By 1965, these figures had increased

College Enrollment and Degrees Conferred,
1889-90   to   1977-78[26]

	College Enrollment	Bachelor's or First Professional Degree	Master's or Second Professional Degree	Doctor's Degree
1889–1890	156,756	15,539	1,009	126
1899–1900	237,592	27,410	1,583	369
1909–1910	355,213	37,199	3,771	420
1919–1920	597,880	48,622	4,301	564
1929–1930	1,100,737	122,484	15,043	2,216
1939–1940	1,494,203	186,500	26,731	3,290
1949–1950	2,659,021	432,058	58,183	6,633
1959–1960	3,377,000	392,440	74,435	9,829
1969–1970	6,906,000	746,000	190,400	26,500
1977–1978	9,684,000	980,000	273,700	43,900

to 2,238 and 682 respectively, showing an increase of 375 in the number
of institutions of higher learning, with junior colleges accounting for
half of the increase. Although approximately two-thirds of colleges
and universities are private institutions, public institutions enroll about
two-thirds of all students.

THE JUNIOR COLLEGE

The junior college is strictly an American institution that originated
at the beginning of the twentieth century and has experienced amazing
growth since then. The term "junior college" was invented by William
R. Harper, the first president of the University of Chicago at the turn
of the century. Harper reorganized the university into two two-year
periods, and designated the freshman and sophomore years as a junior
college. He not only promoted the idea among colleges and universities, but also urged that separate two-year colleges be established.
Edwards and Richey summarized his reasons for promoting this type
of institution:

---

[26]*Biennial Survey of Education in the United States, 1952–54* (Office of Education, U.S. Department of Health, Education, and Welfare, 1957), figures for 1889–90
through 1949–50 extracted from Table 32, Chapter 1, p. 50. Enrollment figures for
1959–1960 through 1977–1978 are extracted from U.S. Office of Education, *Projections of Educational Statistics to 1977–1978* (Washington, D.C.: U.S. Government
Printing Office, 1969), Table 4, p. 12; figures on degrees conferred are from Table
18, p. 31. All figures for 1969–70 and 1977–78 are estimated ones.

The arguments advanced by Harper for the organization of the junior college as a unit of the American educational system were many: that many students whose best interests would be served by leaving college at the end of the two-year program would do so; that many would undertake the shorter course who could not afford the longer one; that many persons who enrolled for the two-year course would remain to complete the longer one; that high schools and academies would be improved through the acceptance and discharge of the added function; that the possibility of remaining at home during the first two years of college would lead to greatly increased enrollments for these years; and that many colleges poor in resources could become good junior colleges.[27]

Figure I

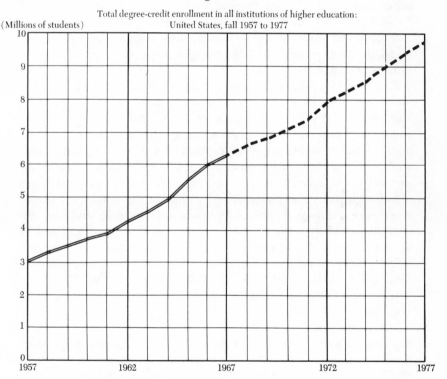

Total degree-credit enrollment in all institutions of higher education:
United States, fall 1957 to 1977

Source: Projections of Educational Statistics to 1977–78, 1968 Edition, U.S. Office of Education (Washington, D.C.: U.S. Government Printing Office, 1969), Figure 2, p. 8.

[27]Newton Edwards and Herman G. Richey, *The School in the American Social Order,* 2nd ed. (Boston: Houghton Mifflin Company, 1963), pp. 641-642.

Harper therefore conceived of the junior college as having a terminal as well as preparatory function. This type of institution, he felt, would make at least some higher education available to more people. His ideas were accepted by many prominent people, and the junior college movement was born.

The first junior colleges in existence were private institutions. Several existed prior to 1900. The earliest, listed in the sixth edition of *American Junior Colleges,* was Reinhardt College, organized in 1883 under the name of Reinhardt Normal College.[28] The first public junior college was Joliet Junior College, established in 1901 in Joliet, Illinois.

During the early years, the program offered by the junior colleges was similar to the program offered in the first two years of the liberal arts colleges. However, a vocational objective was soon advocated, and materialized in 1907 with the establishment of the Agricultural and Technical Institute of New York. Other technical schools were opened, and vocational programs were added by some junior colleges previously founded. Consequently, by 1920, the objectives of the junior colleges were considerably broadened.

From the viewpoint of control and financial support, three types of junior colleges developed: church-related, independent, and public. Various types of public junior colleges arose: local, municipal, district, and county, depending on their territorial organization and support; many of these were designated as "community colleges" rather than junior colleges. Academies, seminaries, technical institutes, and extension centers of universities have also been classified as junior colleges.

Although today the junior college is almost universally recognized as a two-year college, there have been advocates of three- and four-year institutions. Whereas the two-year college consists of grades 13 and 14, the advocates of the three-year college recommended that it include either grades 12-14, or 13-15. The four-year junior college extended from grade 11 through grade 14. Although the four-year plan was implemented in some school systems, it never received wide acceptance.

During the first decades of its existence there was considerable argumentation about the type of program the junior college should offer. Should its function be limited to preparation for the senior college, or should it offer terminal programs? Should it go beyond both of these objectives and offer service programs? Gradually, private colleges made individual decisions on the scope of their programs. Most schools

---

[28]Edmund J. Gleazer, ed., *American Junior Colleges,* 6th ed. (Washington: The American Council on Education, 1963), pp. 152, 494.

limited themselves to a two-year program that was of a college preparatory or general cultural nature. Those schools that offered vocational training usually limited the training to semi-professional training in fields such as business, merchandizing and nursing. Public junior colleges, which were more sensitive to meeting the needs of the community, offered college preparatory courses, general cultural courses, extensive and varied vocational programs, courses for special groups, and broad programs in adult education. A survey of 560 junior colleges made in 1952 showed the variety of terminal programs offered at the time.

The type of program offered in any particular junior college is determined by the demand for it. For example, New York City, as the center of the textile industry, has a technical institute offering courses in the textile industry which would not be given in other locations. Where several junior colleges exist in large cities, for example in California, highly specialized offerings usually are not duplicated.

Their rapid growth and increase in enrollment indicates that junior colleges, or community colleges, have been meeting a present need. In 1900–01, there were only 8 junior colleges, all private, each enrolling approximately 100 students. Private junior colleges outnumbered the public schools during their early decades, but, in 1921–22, the enrollment in public junior colleges (8,349) exceeded for the first time private enrollment (7,682), even though the private colleges still outnumbered the public colleges by 137 to 70. During the next twenty-five years the number of junior colleges rose sharply, but the majority of these new schools were public, so that, by 1947–48, the number of public ones exceeded the private by 328 to 323. There was also a corresponding larger surge of enrollment in the public colleges. Whereas in 1915 only 25 percent of the students were enrolled in public junior colleges, by 1959–60 the percentage had risen to 87 percent. In 1960 public junior college students numbered 712,000, as compared with 104,000 in private junior colleges.[29]

During the present decade there has been a continued emphasis on free public education beyond the high school. The two-year public community college may be the solution for providing some higher education for all people who can profit from it. Thus, the junior college movement continues to grow, and enrollment increases. The sixth edition of *American Junior Colleges* listed 655 junior colleges in 1962. The size of these schools varied from several small private ones that en-

---

[29]Statistics in this paragraph are from James W. Reynolds, *The Junior College* (New York: The Center for Applied Research in Education, Inc., 1965), p. 9.

*Frequency of Offering of Certain Terminal and Semiprofessional
Curriculums Among 560 Junior Colleges Listed in American
Junior Colleges*[30]

Curriculum	Frequency of Mention	Numerical Rank	Percentage of Colleges Offering
Business, Secretarial	260	1	46.4
Business, General	232	2	41.4
General Cultural	202	3	36.1
Music	170	4	30.4
Art	153	5	27.3
Home Economics	136	6	24.3
Journalism	121	7	21.6
Physical Education	112	8	20.0
Agriculture, General	101	9	18.0
Auto Mechanics	97	10.5	17.3
Drafting	97	10.5	17.3
Business, Salesmanship	95	12	17.0
Teaching, Elementary	94	13	16.8
Nursing	92	14	16.4
Medical Secretarial	91	15	16.3
Building Trades	80	16	14.3
Engineering, General	77	17	13.8
Woodwork	71	18	12.7
Architecture	59	19	10.5
Metal Work	58	20	10.4
Electronics	57	21	10.2
Agriculture, Forestry	52	22	9.3
Recreational Leadership	47	23	8.4
Engineering, Mechanical	45	24	8.0
Librarianship	42	25	7.5
Social Service	41	26	7.3
Engineering, Electrical	39	27	7.0
Business, Merchandising	34	28	6.1
Engineering, Civil	33	29	5.9
Aviation, Flight	31	30.5	5.5
Mechanical Technology	31	30.5	5.5

---

[30]Nelson B. Henry, ed., *The Public Junior College* (Chicago: The National Society for the Study of Education, 1956), p. 100. As compiled from Jesse P. Bogue, *American Junior Colleges* (Washington: American Council on Education, 1952).

rolled less than a hundred pupils to the unusually large Pasadena City College with an enrollment of 25,948. By 1967, there were 840 junior colleges enrolling approximately one and a half million students. It was estimated that these figures would increase to 1,000 and 2,500,000 by 1972.

Students completing terminal programs at junior colleges often receive associate degrees in arts or sciences. Other students, in preparatory programs, transfer to another college or university and work for their bachelor degree or even higher degrees. There have been many studies comparing the work of transfer students with the work of native students (those who have spent all of their time in the four-year college). The results of several of these studies, ranging from 1928 to 1954, have been summarized as follows:[31]

1. Junior-college transfers make records approximately the same as those made by transfers from four-year colleges and by native students, sometimes excelling slightly and sometimes being slightly excelled by the other groups. They usually show a drop in their grade average in the first term after transfer but then recover that loss.

2. Junior-college transfers retain the relative scholastic standing after transfer that they held before transfer. Those who originally have high scholastic standing tend to retain such relative standing. Likewise, those with relative low standing tend to remain in the lower groups.

3. There is clear evidence that junior colleges are salvaging a large number of students for success in advanced studies who would otherwise have missed them entirely.

4. There is variation, sometimes wide, in the findings in different senior institutions and also as between junior colleges in the same institution. It should be noted, in passing, that such variations present a problem to those senior institutions who seek to maintain a uniform policy for recognition of the public junior colleges of their state. By and large, however, the performance of junior-college transfers in senior colleges has proven to be so satisfactory that doubts about the quality of junior-college preparation for advanced study no longer exist.

Studies appear to indicate that, in general, the junior colleges are adequately preparing students for continuing their college work. This

---

[31]Nelson B. Henry, *op. cit.*, p. 85.

knowledge is especially important since increasing numbers of transfer students will be seeking admission to senior colleges and universities. A national advisory committee has found, however, that one of the greatest needs in the junior college today is a sound program of counseling and vocational guidance.[32]

Even this brief discussion of the junior college will show that it has become a considerable educational force in the United States.[33] It makes general, technical, vocational, and college programs available to millions of people who, without this type of institution, could not have continued their education. In providing this opportunity, the junior college, or community college, makes a considerable contribution to the development of the individual, and, through him, the betterment of society.

SUMMARY

Higher education in America, like elementary and secondary education, borrowed heavily from European practices. In Europe, the universities developed before the colleges, whereas in America universities, as we now know them, did not develop until the latter part of the nineteenth century.

European universities were first organized toward the end of the Middle Ages. The Universities were corporations of masters or students, really a type of medieval guild, who banded together for the purpose of learning. They received charters under which they were entitled to certain privileges and rights. The courses of study were organized into *faculties,* a term later applied to the teachers of these specialties, so that there developed the faculties of arts, law, medicine, and theology. Each faculty had a *dean,* and the deans with the student representatives, elected the *rector* of the university. Students from particular geographical areas banded together and resided in halls which came to be called *colleges.* At first no instruction was given in the colleges, but gradually as masters supplemented university lectures with individual tutoring, the colleges became self-contained instructional units within the university. The instructional methods used were *lectures* by the master and *disputations* by the students. The curriculum was the Seven Liberal Arts, which placed heavy emphasis on the trivium,

---

[32]"The Junior College and the Guidance Gap", *Carnegie Quarterly,* 15, Number 2 (Spring, 1967), 6.

[33]In May, 1967, the National Faculty Association of Community and Junior Colleges was organized. Associated with the National Education Association and with the Association for Higher Education, it will have a strong voice in American education.

especially on dialectic. At the end of four years of study the student became a *baccalaureus,* and if he continued his studies for two or three more years he became a *master, doctor,* or *professor,* terms which, at first, were used interchangeably. During the Renaissance, curriculum emphasis shifted from the dialectic to grammar and rhetoric. The style and thought of classical writers became the substance of education in the arts faculty. Although the religious base to education continued, the Renaissance, and later the Reformation, contributed to secularization of education.

Universities in England, from which came our ideas for colleges, were organized in much the same way as other European universities. During the sixteenth century, the English humanists influenced the curriculum at Cambridge and Oxford, and classical studies were introduced. By the end of the century the universities had come under the influence of the Crown and became secular corporations; yet even under this strong influence their control remained in the hands of the clergymen. During this period, too, the status of the colleges within the universities was enhanced, and the bachelor's degree became an end in itself rather than simply a preparation for higher studies. The curriculum for the bachelor's degree consisted of portions of the Seven Liberal Arts. During the seventeenth century, more emphasis was given to grammar and rhetoric than dialectic, and the curriculum was expanded to include all of the Seven Liberal Arts. The method of instruction was the same as at other universities, consisting of lectures and disputations, with each student placed under the guidance of a college tutor.

The first college in America was Harvard, established in 1636. It was patterned after Emmanuel College, Cambridge University, where many of the Puritan clergymen had been educated. The objective of Harvard, as well as other colonial colleges, was to train its students for the ministry. The curriculum and methods corresponded to the arts program taught in English colleges. By the time of the American Revolution eight other colleges were established, and by 1800 the number had risen to twenty-six. Enrollment and faculties were small in these early colleges. The Dartmouth College Case decision in 1819, protected the inviolability of a college charter, and stimulated the establishment of additional colleges, both private and public. By the end of the eighteenth century a few practical subjects were introduced into the curriculum, but the classical studies maintained their prominent standing until the Civil War. The Morrill Act of 1862, which provided the states with land grants for the establishment of colleges to teach agriculture and mechanic arts, was responsible for the foundation of many state colleges, some of which are now leading universities. These new colleges and other pressures, resulted in the introduction of more modern subjects into the curriculum of the old colleges. However, the elective system, popularized by Eliot of Harvard broke the old classical curriculum, required for over two centuries. By 1900, the elective system was in wide use. Some colleges went to extremes and almost completely abolished required courses. Around 1920, a reaction against this extreme occurred, and an effort was made to institute a proper balance between required and elective courses and vocational and liberal education. During the twentieth century, a steadily increasing number of students sought a college education, since more opportunities and financial aids were available to them than ever before. The 1960's especially were marked by a great increase in college enrollment and a rapid expansion of college facilities.

It is difficult to establish when the university movement began in America because the term "university" was used loosely. Some institutions designated themselves as universities even though they offered no graduate or professional studies. If a university is defined as an institution that offers an undergraduate arts program and, in addition, one or more graduate or professional programs, then Harvard and the other early institutions were universities from their beginnings, because they offered graduate programs in theology which led to a master's degree. If, however, a university is an institution consisting of several colleges or schools, and graduate and professional programs leading to the master's or doctor's degree (as European universities were organized), then American universities did not begin until the nineteenth century. Until the second half of the nineteenth century, graduate and professional work in American institutions was meagre and unorganized, with the result that many students traveled to Europe for their advanced studies. The last half of the nineteenth century saw the development of American universities along German lines, emphasizing research as part of the requirements for advanced degrees. The first Ph.D. degree was awarded by Yale University in 1861. After that, other institutions expanded their graduate and professional programs, becoming universities in the modern sense of the term. The establishment of Cornell in 1865, and Johns Hopkins in 1876, both of which emphasized free inquiry, further stimulated the growth of universities. Johns Hopkins was the first institution in America to allow its graduate program to overshadow the undergraduate program. By the beginning of the twentieth century, American universities were well established. They had increased in number and expanded their resources. Today many of them are among the most distinguished in the world.

Figure II

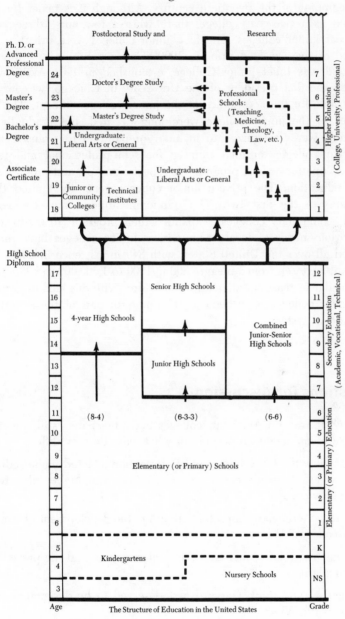

The Structure of Education in the United States

Source: U.S. Office of Education, *Progress of Public Education in the United States of America: 1967–68,* Figure 1, Page 1.

The junior college, a distinctly American institution, originated at the beginning of the twentieth century. Although it is generally recognized as a two-year college, there were a few one-, three-, and four-year junior colleges. The first junior colleges were private ones. Several of these existed prior to 1900. The first public institution of this kind was Joliet Junior College, established in 1901. William R. Harper, the first president of the University of Chicago, was largely responsible for the acceptance of the junior college concept. The objectives of the junior college were long debated, but gradually its programs were recognized to include: preparation for transfer to a four-year college; terminal training for semi-professional and technical occupations; short programs for special groups; and programs of adult education. The private junior colleges generally limited their programs to the first two. The public institutions, now frequently called "community colleges", expanded their programs to try to meet the various needs of local communities. Junior colleges have mushroomed all over the United States, with 840 in existence in 1967. Enrollment has risen from a meagre 800 in 1900 to 1,500,000 in 1967, with spectacular increases predicted for the future. With this kind of growth, the junior colleges have become an important part of the American educational system.

Questions for discussion:

1. In what way do American colleges and universities still resemble those of the medieval period? In what ways do they differ?

2. Show how the Renaissance and Reformation affected higher education. Were these effects evident in early American higher education? Did they persist?

3. What were the most important stimuli in the development of American colleges? Why?

4. Discuss the relative merits of the elective system and the prescribed curriculum.

5. When do you think Harvard first deserved to be designated as a university? Why?

6. Would you prefer to begin college work in a junior college, or a four-year college? Why?

For further reading:

Chamberlain, Joshua L., ed., *Universities and Their Sons*. Vol. I. Boston: R. Herndon Company, 1898.

Henry, Nelson B., ed., *The Public Junior College*. Chicago: The National Society for the Study of Education, 1956.

Hofstadter, Richard and C. DeWitt Hardy, *The Development and Scope of Higher Education in the United States*. New York: Columbia University Press, 1952.

Reynolds, James W., *The Junior College*. New York: The Center for Applied Research in Education, Inc., 1965.

Rudolph, Frederick, *The American College and University*. New York: Alfred A. Knopf, Inc., 1962.

Wahlquist, John T. and James W. Thornton, Jr., *State Colleges and Universities*. Washington: The Center for Applied Research in Education, Inc., 1964.

6

Progress in Teacher Education

The preceding chapters have shown that education in the United States developed extremely slowly until the twentieth century. Teacher education progressed even more slowly. In fact, there was *no* training in teaching during the first two centuries of American education.

Early elementary school teachers were people of varied qualifications. Some pupils were taught by well educated ministers or laymen. Other pupils were taught by men and women who knew little more than the rudiments they were trying to teach their pupils. Generally, teachers were individuals of good moral character, as judged by the minister who reviewed their qualifications. However, since it was sometimes difficult to obtain teachers, a variety of individuals including indentured servants, slaves, and part time teachers were pressed into teaching. The secondary school teachers of the Latin Grammar schools, and the academies, usually possessed higher qualifications than the elementary teachers. As a class, they were better educated, and many of them were college graduates. At the college level, the teachers, who were college graduates themselves, possessed the highest educational qualifications of all early teachers. Yet, tutors and graduate assistants who were not much older than the students themselves, were often used as teachers. Many of these young teachers could not maintain proper discipline, perhaps because they were not motivated toward teaching.

This situation did not change until the early nineteenth century. The only qualifications needed by teachers at all levels of schooling were good character, the ability to maintain discipline, and a knowledge of subject matter sufficient for the level taught. Not all teachers met even these qualifications, for there were some teachers whose character was marred by intemperance or profanity, whose disciplinary measures took the form of tyranny, and whose educational qualifications were below standard for the level they taught. However, there were also many great teachers who were an inspiration to their pupils and to the teaching profession.

For two centuries, it was thought that a good teacher was an individual who knew his subject matter well, and the better he knew his subject, the better teacher he was. Without the science of pedagogy, teachers received no training in the understanding of children, principles of learning, or methods of teaching. Teachers received the same education as everybody else. Judged by today's standards, early American education was wanting in many respects; yet, it produced many great leaders.

BEGINNINGS OF TEACHER EDUCATION

The idea that the regular secondary school or college program was suitable preparation for teaching in secondary schools persisted during the early part of the nineteenth century. Although it was considered desirable for elementary teachers to have completed their secondary schooling, many did not. Even so, a shortage of elementary teachers developed because the increased population, and the greater awareness of the importance of education caused enrollment to expand. A need arose for additional elementary schools, and for teachers to staff them. Two types of institutions, the academies and the Lancastrian monitorial schools, eased the shortage of elementary school teachers.

Academies

It was typical of academies to adjust their programs to meet the needs of the times. As concern about the lack of teachers grew, prominent people urged the establishment of more academies to help train better qualified elementary teachers. After the board of regents of New York formally encouraged the establishment of more academies, their number increased sharply. At first no pedagogical courses were offered or required, but in 1827, New York required academies receiving financial aid to give some teacher training courses. This requirement was followed by an 1834 law which formalized the requirement of a special class for teachers in one designated academy in each of the judicial districts in New York. After this law, many academies established separate departments for the training of students who would eventually teach in the common schools. Andover Academy was the first private academy to establish these departments without financial aid from the state. In 1830, it established an "English Department or Seminary for Teachers" under the direction of Samuel R. Hall. The program was discontinued in 1842 because of lack of financial support. Other academies, however, experienced more success than Andover, and they were among the major suppliers of teachers for the common schools.

Lancastrian Monitorial Schools

The monitorial system of instruction, in spite of its shortcomings, also helped to ease the shortage of teachers during the first part of the nineteenth century. This system, in which the teacher taught the brighter pupils who, in turn, taught other groups of pupils (see Chapter III), was economical and permitted one teacher to "teach" hundreds of pupils at the same time. Since it was a mechanical procedure which took the form of lesson-hearing, it cannot be classified as a genuine teacher education program. The system, however, after its introduction in New York City in 1806, met a definite need in American education for approximately a quarter-century. It made it possible to provide some education to large numbers of pupils who otherwise might not have been able to attend school.

Normal Schools

A normal school is an institution established for the purpose of training teachers. The term originated in France, and became popular in the United States during the 1830's.

The first normal school ever established was founded by Jean Baptiste de la Salle at Rheims in 1685. In 1696, August Hermann Francke founded the first normal school in Germany. During the eighteenth century several other normal schools were founded in these countries. These schools were later visited by American educators, and may have exerted an influence on their foundation in the United States.

Aside from the monitorial schools, the first school in the United States solely for the training of teachers was a private school established in Concord, Vermont by Samuel R. Hall in 1823. The program at his school included a review of elementary school work, some secondary school subjects, the art of teaching, and observations of teaching. The course took three years and, except for the courses on teaching, was similar to the programs given by other academies. In 1829, Hall published his *Lectures on School Keeping* which was widely read. The following year he transferred to Andover Academy and took charge of their program for preparation of teachers.

In the meantime, James G. Carter of Massachusetts published, in 1824–25, a pamphlet and various newspaper articles, appealing for educational reforms and recommending that the state establish teacher-training schools. His essay on *An Outline of an Institution for the Education of Teachers,* which offered a plan similar to that of Prussian "Teachers' Seminaries", later gave him the title of "father of normal schools". Unable to convince the legislature to establish state teacher training schools, Carter opened a private school in Lancaster, Massachusetts, in 1827, for which he tried, but failed, to obtain state aid. Carter continued his efforts for educational reform after he became a member of the state legislature in 1835. With the help of Horace Mann and others, he was influential in the passage of the Normal School Act of 1838. The following year, 1839, saw the opening of the first public normal school in the United States in Lexington, Massachusetts. The term "normal school", first used in Massachusetts, was later adopted throughout the country.

At the time the Normal School Act was passed, the conditions in the common schools had been under continuous criticism. The following description of existing conditions shows the basis for this deep concern.

> Except in the three cities (Boston, 80,000; Lowell, 18,000; Salem, 15,000) each school in the state had usually two teachers each year. A woman—frequently a girl of seventeen or eighteen—taught the summer term of about four months, at an average salary of $5.38 per month, and board; a man—frequently a youth under twenty—usually taught, or tried to teach, the winter term of ten or twelve weeks, at an average salary of $15.44 per month and board. The youth undertook the task at some peril; not seldom the winter school was broken up by unruly "big boys,"—often older than the teacher himself,—who came for the express purpose of "putting the teacher out." In 1837 about 400 of the 2,800 country winter schools were thus closed. The 5,600 teachers employed each year in the rural district schools of the state were a rapidly shifting

group, busy most of the year in other occupations. Most of them had no education beyond the spelling, reading, writing, English grammar, geography and arithmetic which they had themselves studied in the district schools. Many teachers were deficient even in these branches. School committees reported that they often accepted such candidates because no others were to be had at the "salaries" paid. As for "the science and art of teaching" and "school government," most teachers had never heard of such studies. After a survey of the situation Mann estimated that, of the 6000 teachers who were employed each year in the district schools, *including* the cities, not over 200 regarded teaching as a permanent vocation. Some of these, by long experience, or by being "born teachers," were of great excellence. Cyrus Peirce was one of them. But the lack of competent and fairly permanent teachers was the greatest single defect of the system of free public schools.[1]

Obviously, the quality of teachers in the common schools left much to be desired. The teachers were young and unqualified, and the children, even though they attended school, learned little. The short school term of three or four months attracted teachers on a part-time basis. Very few of them made a career of teaching. Although many reforms were needed in the educational system, it was felt that the improvement of the quality of teachers was basic to all other reforms. Carter, Mann, and other leaders felt that the establishment of normal schools precisely for the training of teachers was a fundamental step in the direction of reform. In fact, Mann felt so strongly about these schools that he said, "I believe Normal Schools to be a new instrumentality in the advancement of the race."

With these prominent supporters, and a gift of $10,000 from a member of the Board of Education, the Massachusetts legislature authorized the first normal school. The Board of Education fixed its location at Lexington, where it opened in July, 1839, but its site was later changed to Framingham. Two other normal schools were to be located at Barre (1839) and Bridgwater (1840).

Other states slowly followed the lead of Massachusetts and established state normal schools. The Connecticut legislature approved one school in 1846, but it did not open until 1849. By 1860, normal schools were opened in Michigan and New York, and by 1865, there were normal schools in California, Illinois, Kansas, Maine, Minnesota, New Jersey and Rhode Island. At the turn of the century, in 1900, there were

---

[1]Arthur O. Norton, ed., *The First State Normal School in America: The Journals of Cyrus Peirce and Mary Swift* (Cambridge: Harvard University Press, 1926), p. xliii.

127 state-supported normal schools located throughout the United States.[2]

Besides the state normal schools, there were private and city normal schools. In addition to these private schools, many existing private academies established "normal departments" for the training of teachers. These private normal schools increased in number and influence, but by the end of the nineteenth century they experienced difficulty in competing with the publicly supported institutions. Some larger cities, St. Louis, Philadelphia, New York, and Boston, established municipally supported normal schools to assure an adequate supply of teachers for their areas.

The training program for teachers varied with the type of institution offering it. However, the underlying theory of the early normal school programs has been summarized as follows:[3]

> 1. The purpose of such training is to prepare teachers for the ungraded district schools of the state. (At that time there were practically no other public schools in Massachusetts. The first public high school was established in Boston, 1821, and even in 1840 less than twenty others had been opened in the state. Nearly all were very small. A few communities had schools graded as primary, intermediate or grammar, and high schools; but these were the rare exceptions. The ungraded district school was the type.)
>
> 2. The studies included in professional training for teachers are—
>
> (1) A thorough review of the "common branches"—spelling, reading, writing, grammar, geography, and arithmetic—required by law to be taught in the "common schools."
>
> (2) Advanced studies (except ancient languages) so far as time permits.
>
> (3) The physical, mental, and moral development of children.
>
> (4) The science and art (i.e., principles and methods) of teaching each of the "common branches."
>
> (5) The art of school government; i.e., the organization of the day's work; rewards, punishments, and discipline in general.
>
> (6) Practice in teaching and governing a "model or experimental school."

As an example of the programs offered in early normal schools, the course of studies at the first normal school in Lexington is interesting. The following information comes from a letter written to Henry Bar-

---

[2]Donald P. Cottrell, ed., *Teacher Education for a Free People* (Oneonta, New York: The American Association of Colleges for Teacher Education, 1956), p. 23.

[3]Arthur O. Norton, ed., *op. cit.,* pp. xvii-xviii.

nard in 1841 by Cyrus Peirce, the normal school's first principal.[4] The subjects taught at Lexington were a review of all the "common branches" taken up "thoroughly" and "fully". In addition, the students studied composition, geometry, algebra, physiology, philosophy (natural, intellectual, and moral), natural history, botany, political economy, bookkeeping, vocal music, and the art of teaching. In the "art of teaching" course, Peirce stated that he first taught thoroughly the various subjects, after which, by his own example and by precept, he tried to show his pupils the best way to teach those subjects to others. A model school was annexed to the normal school and enrolled pupils aged six to ten from the various districts of the town. The normal school students who were considered sufficiently prepared, taught in the model school. Twice a day, Peirce visited the model school and observed the prospective teachers, or gave demonstration lessons for his normal school pupils. At the time he wrote to Barnard, Peirce was not only the principal of the normal school but also its only teacher, as well as the supervisor of the model school. He instructed approximately thirty-five normal school students and supervised the thirty children enrolled in the model school. With this load and responsibility, it is not suprising that he resigned in 1842 because of poor health. However, he returned two years later to give the school five more years of service.

The program at Lexington became typical of the programs offered at other normal schools. Pupils were admitted between the ages of sixteen and eighteen, after completing their work in the common schools. The applicants were required to pass an examination on their knowledge of the "common branches", and be of good character, but, in actual practice, very few applicants were denied admission. The level of instruction in the normal schools would be classified at the secondary school level since they taught the same subjects that were given in the academies with a few new additions, such as the "art of teaching" course and some training in a model school.

Although the normal schools made a beginning toward professional education for teachers, the hopes of the early reformers were not immediately realized. At the time of the Civil War, few teachers had taken advantage of the training offered by normal schools. Many students who did enroll left before they completed the program. Twenty-five years after the establishment of the first normal school, the quality of teachers in the common schools had only slightly improved.

After the Civil War, normal schools began to achieve greater stature. The last half of the nineteenth century brought a great increase in the

---

[4]*Ibid.,* pp. xlviii-lvi.

enrollment in the public schools. The elementary school population increased from 6,792,000 in 1869–70 to 14,984,000 in 1899–1900, more than doubling. The percentage of the increase at the secondary level was even more spectacular. The public high school was becoming accepted, and after the Kalamazoo Case established its legal basis, high school enrollment increased from 80,000 in 1869–70 to 519,000 in 1899–1900. With the upsurge in enrollment came new concern about the inadequate supply of qualified teachers. Normal schools, as the chief supplier of elementary school teachers, received renewed attention. During the last decades of the nineteenth century, the normal schools expanded their curriculum and raised their standards in response to the pressure exerted by professional groups and state departments of education. Eventually they brought their standards up to college-level instruction.

TEACHER EDUCATION IN COLLEGES AND UNIVERSITIES

Although normal school graduates usually taught in elementary schools, they occasionally taught in secondary schools and even in normal schools. Colleges and universities generally were the source of secondary school teachers. Here again because knowledge of the subject matter was the chief qualification for teaching, no special courses were introduced for those students who were considering entering the teaching profession. As state universities became more numerous and began to introduce courses in pedagogy, private colleges and universities reluctantly offered new courses also. Perhaps the most influential factor in the nineteenth century responsible for the introduction of education courses at the college level, was the gradual assembling of a scientific body of pedagogical knowledge.

The earliest college to consider introducing education courses into its curriculum was Amherst. In 1826, the faculty of the college discussed the possible introduction but did nothing about it. In 1831, Washington College in Pennsylvania became the first college to establish a department of education. New York University established its department of education in 1832. The education department established at Brown University in 1850 was discontinued after four years. In the midwest, education departments were established at the University of Iowa in 1855, the University of Michigan in 1879, and the University of Wisconsin in 1881. Teacher education in colleges and universities progressed to the point that ". . . chairs of pedagogy were established by

1890 singly or in combination in seventy-four institutions."[5] A further
indication of the growing importance of teacher education was the
chartering of Teachers College in 1889, which in 1893 became affiliated
with Columbia University, and in 1898 became a part of the university
although it retained its separate corporate organization.[6]

Foreign Influences on Teacher Education

Chapters II and III described the contributions of Pestalozzi, Herbart, and Froebel to the child-centered movement during the early part
of the nineteenth century. It was also noted that many prominent
Americans, including Mann and Barnard, visited Europe and brought
back various European theories of education. Furthermore, these chapters described the work of Joseph Neef, and the publications of Griscom, Woodbridge, Cousin, and Stowe, all of whom favored Prussian
practices in education and promoted the ideas of Pestalozzi. In the
United States, these theories were popularized through the normal
schools,[7] and were further developed by our educators. The combination of these events resulted in the dissemination of more precise information on methods, principles of learning, child development, and
history and philosophy of education. Pedagogy was developing content.

THE TEACHERS COLLEGE

During the twentieth century the state normal schools became four-
year degree-granting institutions, known as teachers colleges. The
increasing high school enrollment, the changing concepts on the preparation of high school teachers, and the rapidly developing science of
pedagogy were among the factors responsible for this change.

The high school movement, which had started early in the nineteenth
century, gathered momentum as the century progressed. By the turn
of the twentieth century, the high school was generally accepted as a
part of the public school system. High schools and high school gradu-

---

[5]Donald P. Cottrell, *op. cit.*, p. 26. The number of colleges and universities offer-
ing teacher education courses in 1890 is placed at 100 by C. A. Richardson, Helene
Brule, and Harold Snyder, *The Education of Teachers in England, France and the
U.S.A.* (Paris: UNESCO, 1953), p. 235.

[6]Joshua L. Chamberlain, ed., *Universities and Their Sons*, Vol. I (Boston: R. Herndon Company, 1898), p. 708.

[7]See Chapter III, pp. 86-90 for details.

ates became more and more common. As the number of high school graduates increased, the normal schools became more rigid in their requirement of high school graduation before admission into school. They no longer had to offer only high school subjects; now they were able to offer more advanced work in their programs.

At the same time, state departments of education and professional groups became more insistent on college graduation for high school teachers. Cities in which colleges were located had no problem in meeting this demand, but in less populated areas where there were no colleges, it was more difficult to obtain college graduates as high school teachers. State normal schools expanded their programs and became colleges to meet this need. In 1890 the normal school at Albany, New York, for example, was reorganized into the New York State Normal College. In Ypsilanti, Michigan, the normal school became Michigan State Normal College in 1897, and received authorization in 1903 to give the bachelor of arts degree. Other states began to imitate Michigan, but the greatest number of conversions did not occur until after 1915.

With the conversion of the normal school from a one- or two-year institution to a four-year college for the preparation of teachers, the resulting new teachers colleges were able to expand their curriculum. It had long been recommended that teacher preparation include general education, or liberal arts courses, to give the future teacher a well-rounded background. With the expansion of the normal school program to four years, it was possible for the schools to offer these courses. In addition, students received more advanced work in their specialties, and, as knowledge in pedagogy was broadened and systematized, they received more training in education courses. Eventually the problem was not to find enough courses for a four-year program, but rather to fit all of the knowledge needed by prospective teachers into four years. The solution to this problem was diversification of programs, in which the student chose his field of specialization.

State Colleges

The teachers college, transformed from the normal school, began as a single-purpose institution, namely, the training of teachers. However, just as the normal school was converted to a teachers college to meet the needs of future teachers, the teachers college expanded its programs to meet the needs of those students seeking training for other occupations. The broadened curriculum which included enough general education to make the program of the teachers college comparable to the program found in a liberal arts college, erased much of the difference that had existed between those two schools.

The greatest expansion of programs in the teachers colleges occurred after World War II. Many veterans who were eligible for benefits under the G.I. Bill and sought a college education, enrolled in teachers colleges to become teachers, or to receive training in a variety of occupations. To meet their needs, and the needs of an increasing number of non-veteran students, existing programs were expanded and new ones were added. Although ostensibly these institutions were still "teachers colleges", they had in reality, become multi-purpose institutions, training students for a variety of occupations. The state teachers colleges, recognizing their new role, began to drop the "teachers" from their name and instead designated themselves as state colleges. "Between 1935 and 1954, 76 state normal schools, teachers colleges, and normal colleges and universities were redesignated as state colleges or universities by authority of state legislatures."[8] By 1957, the single-purpose teacher-training colleges had almost disappeared from the American scene. Schools that retained the title of "teachers college" did so for sentimental or historical reasons.

Graduate Study of Education

During the twentieth century teacher education was obviously becoming important and assuming a truly professional status. With the rapid developments occurring in the profession, it was inevitable that advanced programs in the field would develop in the graduate schools of universities.

Historically, American secondary school teachers received their training in the colleges and universities, while elementary school teachers were prepared in the academies, high schools, or normal schools. However, the normal schools, toward the end of the nineteenth century, felt that they could develop programs for training of secondary as well as elementary teachers. The universities, which maintained that college-level training was essential for high school teachers contested this point. Moreover, the universities held that they were the only ones qualified to prepare administrators, a task which some normal schools had also undertaken. As a consequence of the growing need for high school

---

[8]Laurence D. Haskew, "Teacher Education—Organization and Administration," *Encyclopedia of Educational Research*, 3rd ed., (New York: The Mcmillan Company, 1960), p. 1454.

teachers and administrators, the universities began to give more attention to their teacher education programs.

Although some courses in the art of teaching were given earlier, the first permanent chair in education was founded at the University of Iowa in 1873.[9] During the last quarter of the nineteenth century, several other universities established chairs, departments, or schools of education:[10]

Early University Teacher Education Units

Iowa	1873
Michigan	1879
Wisconsin	1881
Johns Hopkins	1884
Missouri	1884
North Carolina	1884
Cornell	1886
Indiana	1886
Clark	1889
Stanford	1891
Chicago	1891
California	1892
Illinois	1893
Minnesota	1893
Nebraska	1895
Ohio	1896
Texas	1896
Northwestern	1898

During the twentieth century, graduate schools set the tone for teacher education in the United States. Previous chapters showed the influence of men such as G. Stanley Hall, John Dewey, J. McKeen Cattell, George Counts, Edward L. Thorndike, and William H. Kilpatrick in the fields of educational philosophy, psychology, methods, measurements, and child study. The graduate schools and departments of education generated new ideas which filtered down through the colleges and lower schools. Some of these ideas were widely accepted; others were opposed by people who held that the new ideas and practices were inimical to the welfare of the individual and of society.[11] The

---

[9]C. A. Richardson, Helene Brule, and Harold E. Snyder, *op. cit.,* pp. 234-35.

[10]All dates except that for Iowa are from Newton Edwards and Herman G. Richey, *The School in the American Social Order,* 2nd ed. (Boston: Houghton Mifflin Company, 1963), pp. 604-605.

[11]See Chapter I.

research function of universities made them the natural birthplace for new theories. Whereas in the early days of teacher education, techniques of teaching were heavily emphasized, twentieth century educational theory and practice has considered all aspects of the teaching profession. Graduate programs have been developed for teaching as well as nonteaching positions in the profession. In 1963–64, the U.S. Office of Education listed degrees earned in the field of education in the following categories:

Fields in Which Degrees Were Conferred
in Education, 1963-64[12]

EDUCATION

Specialized Teaching Fields
    Physical Education (separate curriculums; or combined curriculum with Health Education or Recreation)
    Health Education (separate curriculum)
    Recreation (separate curriculum)
    Education of Exceptional Children (all areas except Mentally Retarded and Speech correction)
    Education of Mentally Retarded
    Speech Correction
    Agriculture Education
    Art Education
    Business Education, Commercial Education
    Distributive Education, Retail Selling
    Home Economics Education
    Industrial Arts Education (nonvocational)
    Music Education
    Trade and Industrial Education (vocational)
    Specialized Teaching Fields, all others
General Teaching Fields
    Nursery and/or Kindergarten Education
    Early Childhood Education (through Primary Grades)
    Elementary Education
    Secondary Education (including Junior High School)
    Combined Elementary and Secondary Education
    Adult Education
    Other general teaching fields
Nonteaching Fields
    Educational Admin. and Supervision, Finance, Curriculum, Comparative Education, etc.

---

[12]*Summary Report on Bachelor's and Higher Degrees Conferred During the Year 1963-64,* (Office of Education, U.S. Department of Health, Education, and Welfare, 1965), p. 7.

Counseling and Guidance
Education, General (without specific concentration)—2d-level
  or higher degrees only
Other nonteaching fields
Education
Preprofessional bachelor's degree only
Education, not further classified

From the one- or two-year program that was offered in the old normal
school, teacher education has expanded to a four-year undergraduate
program, followed by offerings on the master's and doctor's level. In
1963–64, there were all types of degrees awarded in each of the fields
shown in the list. In a comparatively short time, the field of education
has become both broadened and specialized.

The number of institutions offering teacher education programs, and
the number of degrees conferred in education are further indications of
the rapid expansion and the increased importance of teacher education.
In 1949–50, there were 191 institutions offering graduate work in
teacher education; of these, 109 offered a doctoral program in education.[13] Including degrees at all levels (bachelor's, master's, or doctor's),
approximately three-fourths of the colleges and universities in the
country were offering teacher education programs by 1960.[14] An even
greater indication of the expansion of teacher education is seen in the
number of degrees conferred in the field. In 1963–64, there were more
bachelor's degrees conferred in education (112,503) than in any other
field; the nearest field to it was social sciences, with 76,964 bachelor's
degrees awarded. Similarly, the 40,710 master's degrees in education
were far ahead of the next field, engineering, in which 10,827 master's
degrees were awarded. The number of doctorate degrees (2,348), given
in education was exceeded by only one field, physical sciences, in
which 2,455 doctorates were earned.[15] Teacher education has quantitatively outdistanced all other disciplines taught in higher education.

TEACHERS INSTITUTES

The quality of teachers has been a matter of concern throughout the
history of education. It is evident that the quality of teachers, particu-

---

[13]Laurence D. Haskew, *op. cit.*, p. 1458.
[14]Newton Edwards and Herman G. Richey, *op. cit.*, p. 616.
[15]Statistics on earned degrees are from *Summary Report on Bachelor's and
Higher Degrees Conferred During the Year 1963-64, op. cit.*, Table 3, p. 5.

larly at the elementary level, was generally poor during the early centuries of American education. During the middle of the nineteenth century reformers such as Carter, Mann, and Barnard took many measures to improve the quality of education. The teachers institute was one of these measures.

Henry Barnard held the first teachers' institute in Hartford, Connecticut in 1839. In the previous year he had appealed to the Connecticut legislature for funds to finance a meeting of teachers at which they would learn about school management and methods of teaching the common school subjects. When the legislature failed to provide the needed funds, Barnard used his own money to conduct in Hartford a six-weeks meeting of young teachers. They were instructed in the subjects that were taught in the schools, and even visited some of the better schools in Hartford to observe the current teaching practices. Subsequent institutes were held under private auspices until 1847, when the state provided funds for teachers meetings.

The practice of holding teacher institutes gradually spread to other states. They were first held in New York in 1842, Rhode Island and Ohio in 1844, Massachusetts in 1845, and Pennsylvania in 1848. Eventually institutes were held in practically every county of every state. In some states, they were held by the state, while in others they were sponsored by the county or the city. The institutes originally gave instruction to teachers who had not received normal school training. As the population increased, and as additional normal schools were established, the need for instruction diminished. Therefore, the institutes were shortened to meetings of a day or two, and lectures on topics of general interest replaced instruction.

The value of teachers' institutes has been debated. It has been agreed that they fulfilled a need by providing teachers who did not have normal school training with instruction that improved their qualifications as teachers. As the normal schools increased, and as summer sessions in colleges and normal schools were introduced, many people felt that the institutes were no longer needed. The negative side of the argument is illustrated by the following twentieth century comment.

> Further, the programs are as a rule haphazard, unconnected, and require no preparation, and are followed by no discussion. Frequently, the lectures have become inspirational and entertaining in the worst sense.[16]

---

[16]Paul Monroe, ed., *A Cyclopedia of Education*, Vol. 3 (New York: The Macmillan Company, 1926), p. 469.

An example of a more favorable reaction to the value of institutes is the following which describes the institute of 1857:

> Institutes were normal schools on wheels, the superintendent and his high-powered itinerant lectures serving as the faculty and the earnest, hard-working teachers as the students. And they really were students; having accepted assignments in advance, they brought their books and carried on a systematic drill.
> . . . The institute was regarded as a means of educating the public as well as the teachers. Surprisingly large numbers of lay citizens attended, in many instances outnumbering the teachers three to one. Lectures on such topics as memory, emulation, patriotism, the teacher's influence, phonetics, cube root, discipline, the use of the blackboard, and on the various subjects evoked loud praises and favorable resolutions, including the frequent recommendation that the lecture be published.[17]

Probably, like today's institutes, some of the meetings were interesting and stimulating while others contributed very little to professional development.

Today, the programs of the teachers' institutes are almost the same as the programs conducted by professional associations. Both try to improve the professional competence of the teacher by discussing new trends and problems in the field of education.

Professional Associations

The organization of professional associations was another measure taken to improve the quality of education and teachers. Over a century ago, teachers voluntarily began to band together. Among the earliest associations were the American Institute of Instruction (1830), the Western College of Professional Teachers (1831), the American Lyceum Association (1831), and the American Association for the Advancement of Education (1849). None of these organizations became national. The first nation-wide association was the National Teachers' Association, founded in 1857, which became the National Education Association in 1870, and the National Education Association of the United States in 1906. Since the National Education Association, (NEA), was oriented toward public education, the personnel of private

---

[17]Edgar B. Wesley, *NEA: The First Hundred Years* (New York: Harper & Row, Publishers, 1957), p. 17.

schools also began to form professional associations, the largest of which is the National Catholic Education Association, (NCEA), founded in 1904.

Professional associations have multiplied so rapidly that space limitations prevent even a partial listing of them. The national associations, such as NEA and NCEA previously mentioned, are affiliated with state and local associations. Their membership became so large, and their problems so diversified, that they established many departments to deal with the special groups within the profession. In May, 1967, the membership in NEA reached 1,028,456, topping the million mark for the first time in its history.[18] As NEA progressed and grew through the years, new departments were added, some older departments were dropped, and the names of others were changed. At one time or another, over fifty departments were in existence. When NEA celebrated its centennial in 1957, it consisted of thirty departments, and this number had increased to thirty-four by 1968. The names of those departments, together with other organizational data, are given in the chart on page 192.

The national professional associations attempt to deal with the full range of problems experienced by all types of personnel at all levels of education. The state professional organizations also have a variety of departments within their framework, while the local associations are organized according to their available resources. The national, state, and local associations handle questions at their own level, but appeal to each other for advice and help. For example, the local group may seek the help of the state association, while the state association may use some of the national group's facilities. In some matters, all three groups may act in unison.

The National Commission on Teacher Education and Professional Standards, one of the commissions of the NEA, was established in 1946 and "was charged with responsibility for carrying on a continuing program for the profession in matters of selection and recruitment, preparation, certification, inservice growth, and the advancement of professional standards, including standards for institutions that prepare teachers."[19] The TEPS Commission has had many regional and national meetings dealing with the problems of education and professional standards and has made recommendations to its parent NEA, and

---

[18]*NEA Reporter,* 7, Number 1 (January 19, 1968), p. 4.
[19]Margaret Lindsey, ed., *New Horizons for the Teaching Profession* (Washington: National Commission on Teacher Education and Professional Standards, NEA, 1961), p. vii.

ORGANIZATION CHART*

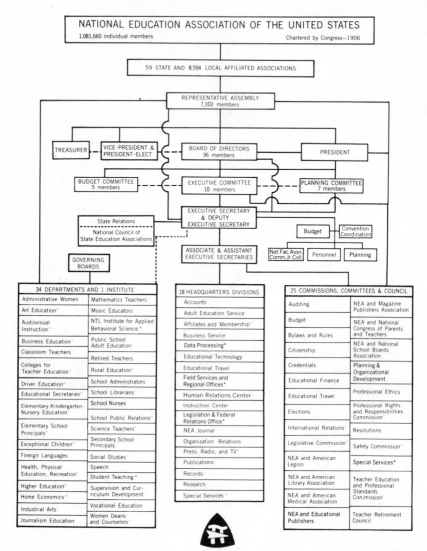

NATIONAL EDUCATION ASSOCIATION OF THE UNITED STATES	
1,081,660 individual members	Chartered by Congress—1906

59 STATE AND 8,594 LOCAL AFFILIATED ASSOCIATIONS

REPRESENTATIVE ASSEMBLY
7,103 members

TREASURER — VICE-PRESIDENT & PRESIDENT-ELECT — BOARD OF DIRECTORS 96 members — PRESIDENT

BUDGET COMMITTEE 5 members — EXECUTIVE COMMITTEE 10 members — PLANNING COMMITTEE 7 members

EXECUTIVE SECRETARY & DEPUTY EXECUTIVE SECRETARY

State Relations
National Council of State Education Associations

GOVERNING BOARDS

ASSOCIATE & ASSISTANT EXECUTIVE SECRETARIES

Budget — Convention Coordination

Nat.Fac.Assn. Comm.Jr.Coll. — Personnel — Planning

34 DEPARTMENTS AND 1 INSTITUTE		18 HEADQUARTERS DIVISIONS	25 COMMISSIONS, COMMITTEES & COUNCIL	
Administrative Women	Mathematics Teachers	Accounts	Auditing	NEA and Magazine Publishers Association
Art Education	Music Educators	Adult Education Service		
Audiovisual Instruction	NTL Institute for Applied Behavioral Science *	Affiliates and Membership	Budget	NEA and National Congress of Parents and Teachers
Business Education	Public School Adult Education	Business Service	Bylaws and Rules	
Classroom Teachers	Retired Teachers	Data Processing*	Citizenship	NEA and National School Boards Association
Colleges for Teacher Education	Rural Education	Educational Technology		
Driver Education	School Administrators	Educational Travel	Credentials	Planning & Organizational Development
Educational Secretaries	School Librarians	Field Services and Regional Offices*	Educational Finance	
Elementary-Kindergarten-Nursery Education	School Nurses	Human Relations Center	Educational Travel	Professional Ethics
	School Public Relations	Instruction Center	Elections	Professional Rights and Responsibilities Commission
Elementary School Principals	Science Teachers	Legislation & Federal Relations Office*		
Exceptional Children	Secondary School Principals	NEA Journal	International Relations	Resolutions
Foreign Languages	Social Studies	Organization Relations	Legislative Commission	Safety Commission
Health, Physical Education, Recreation	Speech	Press, Radio, and TV	NEA and American Legion	Special Services*
Higher Education	Student Teaching *	Publications	NEA and American Library Association	Teacher Education and Professional Standards Commission
Home Economics	Supervision and Curriculum Development	Records		
Industrial Arts	Vocational Education	Research	NEA and American Medical Association	
Journalism Education	Women Deans and Counselors	Special Services	NEA and Educational Publishers	Teacher Retirement Council

Units marked with asterisks have staffs at the NEA Headquarters

AUGUST 1968

---

*National Education Association, *NEA Handbook, 1968-69* (Washington, D.C.: the Association, 1968), p. 18.

through NEA, to the profession as a whole. In 1959-60, a task force appointed by the commission made an intensive study of the problems still facing the profession, and published a report in which it recommended specific action programs for the "complete professionalization of teaching".[20] Since its publication, many of its recommendations have been implemented.

In general, professional associations try to work for the welfare of everyone involved in the educative process: teachers, supervisors, specialists, pupils, and members of the community. They have encouraged higher standards to make the profession a respected one. At the same time, they have helped to raise, through their journals and other publications, the economic well-being of teachers to a level which is more commensurate with their training and responsibility. Ideas are spread through an ever-increasing number of meetings and conventions; indeed, if an individual had the time, interest, and money, he could spend all of his time attending these meetings for there is always at least one in session! Much of the improvement in education must be underwritten by legislation and the associations have added their weight to legislative proposals by lobbying.

Recently, to raise the standards of school system the NEA has imposed sanctions on districts in which sufficient improvement in educational conditions is not taking place. In these cases, the association begins by recommending desired changes. If the area involved does not take action, the association, then, widely advertises their lack of cooperation. NEA has imposed sanctions against an entire state, has advertised the poor conditions existing there, and has asked teachers not to accept positions in that area until the desired improvements have materialized. State education associations have taken similar action against particular districts within the state. Usually the areas involved begin to make concessions that lead to improved conditions.

When a new teacher enters the profession he is encouraged to become a member of a local, state, and national education association. In fact, he may feel obliged to become a member in districts that pride themselves on 100 percent membership in these professional groups. If a teacher becomes an *active* member, there is little doubt that it will help him grow professionally, and, depending on his zeal and energy, he may work through the associations to improve the profession.

---

[20]*Ibid.* This is a 243-page report replete with "definitive statements" in five areas: advancement of professional standards; teacher education, both pre- and in-service; accreditation; certification; and identification, selective admission and retention of professional personnel.

ACCREDITATION

Accreditation implies that an institution has met certain minimum standards that have been formulated by a professional group or legal body. Schools seeking accreditation for their teacher education programs are visited by a team of experts who evaluate it in terms of the standards adopted by the accrediting agency. The agency maintains and publishes a list of accredited schools. These accrediting bodies are of two types: voluntary, or legal.

Organizationally and geographically, there are national, regional, and state accrediting agencies. Institutions voluntarily apply to the first two organizations for accreditation, but in order to receive approval by the state, the institutions must meet the requirements legislated by the state and implemented by the state department of education.

The first professional association to accredit teacher education programs was the American Association of Teachers Colleges (AATC), now named the American Association of Colleges for Teacher Education (AACTE). This association began as the American Normal School Association in 1855, and became the Department of the Normal Schools in the NEA in 1870. In 1902, a group split off from the Department of Normal Schools, designated itself as the North Central Council of State Normal School Presidents, and met annually until 1917, when the American Association of Teachers Colleges was founded. In 1925, AATC became a department of the NEA, replacing the Department of Normal Schools, and, then, changed its name to the present AATCE in 1948.

In 1926, AATC published a set of standards for teachers colleges, followed this set in 1927 with a set of standards for accreditation and, in 1928, published its first approved list of colleges for teacher education. The first list included 63 four-year colleges and 10 junior colleges. "By 1940, 185 institutions were members and 158 were accredited."[21] After 1948, when the association became the AACTE, its membership increased to 284 by 1954, at which time AACTE surrendered its accreditation function to a new national accrediting body, the National Council for Accreditation of Teacher Education (NCATE). After 1954, AACTE became an important constituent member of NCATE. It performed research, provided consultative services, and evaluated the criteria used for the accreditation of teacher education programs. In recent years the membership of AACTE has risen sharply. From 284 member institutions in 1954, the number has increased to 775

---

[21]Edgar B. Wesley, *op. cit.*, p. 88, as quoted from NEA *Proceedings*, 1940, p. 337.

member institutions in 1967, and topped 800 in 1968. These members institutions now produce over 90 percent of the new teachers in the United States.

The National Council for Accreditation of Teacher Education (NCATE)

During the relatively brief period since its foundation, NCATE has had a very stormy, and at times, a precarious existence. It, however, has survived these periods and now is a most important national body for the accreditation of teacher education programs in the United States.

The AACTE was the first and only national association for accrediting teacher education programs. Its membership list, however, consisted largely of public teacher-training institutions. Although a small number of private liberal arts colleges and universities became members, most of the liberal arts institutions did not seek membership in AACTE. Consequently, the membership list was not representative of all teacher-preparing institutions.

In 1949, because of the increasing number of professional accrediting associations, the National Commission on Accrediting was established to coordinate their accrediting activities. The National Commission published a list of recognized accrediting bodies, but AACTE was not one of them. John R. Mayor gives the following explanation of why AACTE was not recognized:

> One reason for this exclusion of AACTE appears to have been the rumor that a new accrediting body for teacher education was about to be created. Another reason for not recognizing AACTE as an accrediting body was that it combined membership and accreditation. Also the National Commission on Accrediting may have doubted at that time whether teaching was well enough recognized as a profession to have an accrediting body.[22]

The action of NCA left the country without a recognized national accrediting association for teacher education. The proponents of a national accrediting body brought together in 1951–52 five professional associations to form NCATE. The original Council had 19 members, representing the five constituent organizations. This Council agreed to use the same standards for accreditation that had been used by

---

[22]John R. Mayor, *Accreditation in Teacher Education—Its Influence on Higher Education* (Washington: National Commission on Accrediting, 1965), p. 52.

AACTE. It also agreed that the first NCATE list of approved institutions would consist of the institutions that had been approved by AACTE. NCATE was ready to begin its functions on July 1, 1954.

During NCATE's organizational period, the opponents of a national accrediting body made their objections known. Liberal arts institutions which had opposed AACTE accreditation also opposed the NCATE. Their objections to NCATE have been summarized as follows:

> This opposition, stemming largely from liberal arts institutions, was based on three counts: first, to the extension of professional accrediting into an area which they insisted could be adequately served by the regional associations; second, to the acceptance of the argument that teaching is a profession like engineering or medicine; and third, to the relationship of the certification of teachers with the accrediting of liberal arts colleges by a national professional teacher education accrediting agency.[23]

The liberal arts colleges also objected to NCATE because they were not represented on the Council, and therefore, resented having this national body pass judgment on their programs.

As a result of this strong opposition, the National Commission on Accrediting refused to recognize NCATE. From 1954 to 1956, the two bodies negotiated their differences, and NCATE finally agreed to elect the majority of Council members from teacher-training institutions, and to work cooperatively with the six regional accrediting associations. NCA approved the new organization which became effective June 1, 1957, with the understanding that its structure and finances would be reviewed again by NCA in 1960.

NCA conducted a preliminary review in 1960, but it was felt that NCATE had not been in operation long enough to make a valid judgment. The review was therefore deferred until 1963. However, during the period 1960–63, NCA received a mounting number of criticisms on various aspects of NCATE's operations: it was too autonomous; it was too heavily weighted with "educationists"; there was danger of NEA control since approximately half of its funds came from NEA or its constituents; its methods in evaluation were inadequate; the standards of accreditation were too rigid and inflexible; the evaluation of academic departments was inadequate; some of the members of evaluating teams were inexperienced; and institutions did not have effective avenues of communication with NCATE.[24] In 1963, James B. Conant

---

[23]*Ibid.*, p. 53.
[24]*Ibid.*, pp. 65-83.

added his prestige to the criticism. He recommended that the Council "give greater power to (a) representatives of scholarly disciplines in addition to professional education, and to (b) informed representatives of the lay public."[25] He also recommended that "NCATE and the regional associations should serve only as advisory bodies to teacher-preparing institutions and local school boards. . . ."[26]

NCATE did not wither under these criticisms. Rather, during 1963–64 it held meetings with NCA and its constituent members to discuss ways in which teacher education accreditation might be improved. In 1963, NCA gave the NCATE recognition for another year to give them time to make the necessary changes. The following year NCA recognized that changes were being made but stated that recognition of NCATE beyond the spring of 1965 would depend upon "substantial progress" toward the attainment of the desired changes in structures, financing, and policies and procedures. By 1966 NCATE had revised its constitution which was later adopted by the five constituent members. The NCATE then made more changes in financing, policies, procedures, and gave AACTE the task of revising the standards for accreditation. After these changes, the NCATE received NCA's approval.

The constituent organizations and their number of representatives on the Council are as follows.

Council Membership

Constituent Organization	Number of Members
American Association of Colleges for Teacher Education	10
Council of Chief State School Officers	1
National School Boards Association	1
National Commission on Teacher Education and Professional Standards, NEA	6
National Association of State Directors of Teacher Education and Certification	1
Learned Societies	3

The total membership of twenty-two represents an increase of three members over the previous membership. The distribution of members,

---

[25]James B. Conant, *The Education of American Teachers* (New York: McGraw-Hill Book Company, 1963). Permission granted by Educational Testing Services, p. 69.

[26]*Ibid.*, p. 70.

changed in the 1965 constitution, gives more representatives to AACTE, and includes three members from learned societies. The new distribution of members on the Council somewhat appeased the liberal arts colleges.

NCATE can and will exert a powerful influence on teacher education. The kind of influence it will exert will depend on the standards that evolve during the coming years. Although it has been in existence only a short time, the number of NCATE-approved institutions has grown considerably, from 284 in 1954, to 462 in 1968–69.[27] The 1968–69 membership represents only about a third of the potential membership, but it trains approximately 70 percent of the students entering the profession.

Regional Associations

There are six regional accrediting associations in the United States, each of which includes several states. The regional associations do not accredit particular programs within an institution, but attest to the excellence of a school as a whole.

As the number of college applicants grew, at the end of the nineteenth century, college officials realized that the educational background of high school graduates differed in quantity and quality, thus presenting an admissions problem. Furthermore, some of the colleges established after the Civil War were offering programs of questionable quality, which created a problem when the students tried to transfer. College officials recognized the need for some standardization in the quality of programs, to allow high school graduates and college transfer students to meet at least minimum standards not only within the state but also in other states. To accomplish this, voluntary accrediting associations were formed. Four associations were founded at the end of the nineteenth century, and two during the twentieth century:

Regional Accrediting Associations[28]

Name of Association	Date Founded
New England Association of Colleges and Secondary Schools	1886

[27]*Annual List Number Fifteen: 1968-69* (Washington: National Council for Accreditation of Teacher Education), p. 6.

[28]John Forbes and Norman Burns, "Accreditation: Colleges and Universities", *Encyclopedia of Educational Research* (New York: The Macmillan Company, 1960), p. 12.

Regional Accrediting Associations—cont.

Name of Association	Date Founded
Middle States Association of Colleges and Secondary Schools	1887
North Central Association of Colleges and Secondary Schools	1895
Southern Association of Colleges and Secondary Schools	1895
Northwest Association of Secondary and Higher Schools	1917
Western College Association	1948

Regional associations evaluate an institution as a whole, giving attention to the institution's objectives, organization and administration, library, finance and facilities, programs, student personnel services, faculty and teaching, and outcomes. If the institution shows overall strength in these areas, it is accredited, even though it may be relatively weak in some one area. For example, it may have a weak Education department, or a weak English department, and still be accredited on overall quality. In these situations, of course, the association recommends removal of the deficiencies noted by the evaluators.

In the past, regional associations did not devote special attention to the teacher education programs in liberal arts colleges. In recent years, however, because of the interest shown in teacher education, and because of cooperative arrangements existing between NCATE and the regional associations, the associations have scrutinized these programs more closely. The Middle States Association of Colleges and Secondary Schools has made several strong statements on the courses offered in teacher education. The association has stated that

> . . . teacher education is not to be undertaken lightly. Unless a liberal arts college can establish, staff, conduct, and support it on a level of quality fully comparable to that of the best professional institutions, it has no right to offer teacher education at all.

> The task of giving teacher education philosophical and educational integrity is a congenial and rewarding one for liberal arts colleges, if they are willing to undertake it seriously and make it a central, rather than a peripheral, interest. If they are not, they had better leave it alone.[29]

---

[29]*Teacher Education in Liberal Arts Colleges*, Middle States Association of Colleges and Secondary Schools, Commission on Institutions of Higher Education, Document No. 4.65 (June, 1963), pp. 1-2.

These statements leave no doubt that regional associations, even though they do not accredit teacher education programs separately, are concerned about the quality of these programs in liberal arts colleges.

State Accreditation

Through certification requirements,[30] the states have increasingly influenced the nature of the teacher education programs offered within their borders. Toward the end of the nineteenth century and during the beginning of the twentieth century, the states began to assume the authority for setting standards in teacher education, and for issuing licenses to teach. Each state developed its own certification requirements. Although the requirements from state to state varied, they tended to specify a certain number of years of education, and to include professional education courses.

Obviously, the legal requirements set by the state would influence an institution's teacher education program. If certain courses are legally required for certification, the institution would feel obliged to make those courses available, and even mandatory for those students who wish to become teachers. Through certification requirements a state can determine the programs given in teacher education programs. The state, of course, acts on the advice of professional organizations and/or advisory boards which have been appointed for setting requirements.

During the last decade, there has been a definite trend to raise the standards for teacher certification. The legal requirements have been raised for the initial certificate, usually a provisional one. Furthermore, a year's post-baccalaureate work is becoming more common as a requirement for permanent certification.

In determining whether or not to accredit an institution for teacher education, the state employs criteria and procedures similar to those used by the professional associations. The institution usually must make a self-study and then prepare a report for the state. A team of experts, representing several disciplines, read this report before visiting the school to evaluate the programs offered. Accreditation is either given or denied on the basis of the reports submitted by the institution and the evaluators. Occasionally, if the school's weaknesses are not too grave, provisional accreditation may be given until school strengthens the program.

---

[30]Certification requirements are discussed in detail in the next chapter.

In recent years, the state departments of education have worked in close cooperation with regional associations and the NCATE. Members of the state departments of education are often invited to serve on the evaluation teams of regional associations and the NCATE. Thus, the state has not only the information provided by its own evaluation teams but also the information provided by two other types of accrediting bodies.

During the 1960's the "approved program" approach to certification was used by many states. In the past, the usual procedure in certification was to count the transcript credits in each field to be sure that certification requirements were met. Now, states have been approving the specific and individual *programs* an institution offers for the training of, for example, English teachers, or mathematics teachers, or guidance counselors. Once a program of the institution has been approved, the state automatically issues a certificate to an individual who has completed the approved program. The standards applied by the state for program approval are higher than the minimum standards applied under the credit-counting system. Both systems may be used simultaneously. For example, the program given by an institution for training English teachers may, in the judgment of the evaluators, warrant program approval, but the program for future teachers of mathematics may not meet minimum standards. In this situation, the future English teacher would be certified automatically by the state; however, the prospective mathematics teacher would have to meet the credit-counting standard. In the states using program approval, institutions are encouraged to keep raising the standards of each program so that eventually all programs within the college or university will have received program approval.

Much progress, therefore, has been made in improving the quality of teachers, especially in the last decade. Working independently, yet cooperatively, the state, the professional associations, and the accrediting bodies have given more and more attention to raising the standards of the prospective teacher's performance, while at the same time working for the improvement of peripheral factors and supporting personnel to provide the best possible education for our children.

SUMMARY

For approximately two centuries, the quality of American teachers was poor, although there were many notable exceptions. The school year in the common schools was only a small fraction of the year so that teaching was not a full-time occupation. At times it was difficult to obtain teachers, so that frequently many poorly qualified people were hired as teachers. Added to these problems was the lack of any specific type of training which would give teachers a better knowledge of their pupils and the learning process. The only basic qualifications for teachers were a knowledge of subject matter, good character, and ability to maintain discipline.

During the early nineteenth century, as the population increased, there was a shortage of elementary teachers. The monitorial system, although it had defects, eased the shortage for a time. Meanwhile, the academies began to offer special courses for teachers and became for many years the chief source of teachers for the common schools.

The first school in the United States established exclusively for the purpose of training teachers was a private school established by Samuel R. Hall in 1823 in Concord, Vermont. The first state-supported normal school was established in Massachusetts in 1839 through the efforts of James G. Carter and Horace Mann. Other states followed the Massachusetts pattern, and by 1900 there were state-supported, as well as private, normal schools located throughout the United States. In addition, many of the larger cities established municipal normal schools. The program offered by the normal schools was on the secondary level, as they offered courses similar to those taught in the academies and a little instruction in the art of teaching with some training in a "model school". Toward the end of the nineteenth century, the normal schools expanded their curriculum, raised standards of admission, and gradually brought the quality of their instruction up to the college level.

The colleges and universities did not show much interest in training teachers for the common schools. A few of them offered education courses before 1850, but during the last quarter of the century, especially after the universities of the midwest began to do so, the establishment of chairs of pedagogy and departments of education for the first time became fairly widespread. The discovery and dissemination of more precise knowledge on child development, principles of learning, methods of teaching, and history and philosophy of education contributed to the introduction of education courses on the college level.

The rapid expansion of secondary education during the twentieth century, and the increasing insistence upon college graduate high school teachers, brought about the expansion of normal schools into state teachers colleges offering four-year degree programs. These single-purpose teachers colleges then developed into multi-purpose state colleges in order to meet the rising demand for college training in occupations other than teaching. By mid-century, most teachers colleges had been converted into state colleges.

Universities and colleges were the traditional suppliers of secondary school and college teachers until the normal schools with established programs for high school teachers challenged their position. As a consequence of this, and the increasing demand for high school teachers, the universities began to establish teacher education programs. By 1900, at least eighteen universities had established chairs, departments, or schools of education. During the twentieth century, universities expanded their programs for teaching as well as non-teaching positions in the field of education, leading to advanced degrees. By mid-century, there were 109 universities offering the doctoral degree in education. As a field, education now attracts more undergraduate and graduate students than any other field.

Various means have been used to improve the quality of teachers. One of the earliest means was the teachers' institute. The first teachers' institute was conducted by Henry Barnard in Hartford, Connecticut in 1839. The early institutes gave instruction in school management and reviewed the common school subjects with teachers who had had no normal school training. As the number of normal schools increased, and as summer sessions at them were introduced, the length of the institutes was reduced from six weeks down to a day or two. Institutes were very popular during the last half of the nineteenth century, but their value was questioned as time went on. They are still held on a county or local level in many places.

As another means of improving the quality of teachers, educators banded together in voluntary associations. A few of them, which were formed during the second quarter of the nineteenth century, were regional in scope. The first nation-wide association was the National Teachers Association, established in 1857 (now the National Education Association of the United States). Professional associations multiplied on the national, regional, state, and local levels. Some of them deal with specific problems, while others deal with every conceivable problem found in the field of education. Their general goal is the improvement of all aspects of the teaching profession. One of the most influential bodies has been the National Commission on Teacher Education and Professional Standards (a department of NEA), which, since 1946, has conducted studies and made recommendations for the improvement of teacher education.

The process of accreditation has done much to improve standards in teacher education. There are national, regional, and state accrediting bodies. The first professional association to accredit teacher education programs was the American Association of Teachers Colleges, which published in 1928 its first list of colleges approved for teacher education.

In 1948, the association broadened its scope and changed its name to the American Association of Colleges for Teacher Education. Six years later, it terminated its accrediting function, and the National Council for Accreditation of Teacher Education replaced it as the only recognized national body for accrediting teacher education programs.

There are six regional accrediting associations in the United States. The regional associations evaluate institutions as a whole, rather than accredit specific programs within an institution. Four of these associations were founded late in the nineteenth century, and the other two in the twentieth century. They cooperate with NCATE in the evaluation of teacher education programs.

At the state level, the state department accredits teacher education programs offered by institutions within the state. Through its certification requirements, the state legally sets minimum standards that must be met by the institutions training teachers. Recently, states have been setting higher standards for institutions that seek "program approval" which would lead to the automatic certification of the institution's graduates in teacher education. The state departments of education cooperate with regional associations and with NCATE in the process of accreditation.

Questions for discussion:

1. What do you consider to be the highpoints of progress in the development of teacher education? Why?

2. During the early years of American education, it was felt that the only qualifications a teacher needed were a good character, knowledge of subject matter, and ability to maintain discipline. What other qualifications do you think a teacher should have? Why?

3. Why did the normal school become obsolete as a teacher-training institution?

4. What are the advantages of belonging to a professional association of teachers?

5. Do you favor unions for teachers? Why?

6. Do you think it is advantageous to have a national accrediting association? Why?

7. Show how the state affects the curriculum of an institution's teacher education program.

For further reading:

Conant, James B., *The Education of American Teachers.* New York: McGraw-Hill Book Company, Inc., 1963.

Cottrell, Donald P., ed., *Teacher Education for a Free People.* Oneonta, New York: The American Association of Colleges for Teacher Education, 1956.

Lindsey, Margaret, ed., *New Horizons for the Teaching Profession.* Washington: National Commission on Teacher Education and Professional Standards, National Education Association of the United States, 1961.

Mayor, John R., *Accreditation in Teacher Education—Its Influence on Higher Education.* Washington: National Commission on Accrediting, 1965.

Norton, Arthur O., ed., *The First State Normal School in America: The Journals of Cyrus Peirce and Mary Swift.* Cambridge: Harvard University Press, 1926.

Richardson, C. A., Helene Brule, and Harold Snyder. *The Education of Teachers in England, France and the U.S.A.* Paris: UNESCO, 1953.

Wesley, Edgar B., *NEA: The First Hundred Years.* New York: Harper & Row, Publishers, 1957.

7

Certification of Teachers

Throughout the preceeding chapters the recurring theme has been the need to improve the quality of American teachers. Even though the quality improved considerably during the twentieth century, the furor over teacher education reached its heighth during the last decade. Prominent critics brought national attention to the education (or, as one critic stated, "miseducation") of future teachers. Much of the controversy centered around certification requirements, because they furnish one of the "quality controls" in education.

When an individual receives his certificate, or license, to teach, he has a written or printed statement declaring that he has met the requirements needed to hold a particular type of teaching position. Throughout the years, there have been many types of certificates, and the requirements have varied with the changing emphases in teacher education.

IN RETROSPECT

The licensing of teachers dates back to colonial America. The teachers in Puritan New England, where they believed in publicly supported schools, were required to obtain a license from the town officials.

The candidate had to pass an examination which was usually conducted by the minister. In the middle Atlantic colonies, where parochial schools predominated, the teachers generally did not need
licenses but did need the approval of church authorities before they
were eligible to teach. A similar situation existed in the southern colonies where the Church of England predominated. Teachers in these
colonies were often required to obtain a license from the Bishop of
London, or from the governor of the colony. Education in all the
colonies, like the examining and licensing of teachers, was a local affair.
The hiring official was chiefly concerned with the candidate's soundness of faith and gave little attention to his knowledge of subject
matter. The examination of candidates was an informal affair, and
frequently persons with doubtful qualifications were hired because better qualified teachers were not available.

This procedure for examining and certifying teachers was used for
approximately two centuries. However, as public education expanded,
and as the district system began to outlive its usefulness, first the county,
and then the state began to assume more authority in education. By the
middle of the nineteenth century, some states had assumed control over
the examination and licensing of teachers, and by the end of the century,
the examination of prospective teachers was made uniform throughout
the state. Later, as the number of normal schools increased, and as liberal
arts colleges began to offer teacher education courses, states began to dis-
pense with examinations for graduates from those institutions. Gradually, the completion of a college program became the major requirement.
"By 1927 every state in the Union was certifying teachers on the basis of
college attendance, though many still offered the option of examination."[1]

Once the college program had been adopted as the basis of certification, the quality of the program again came under close scrutiny. Until
the nineteenth century there were no specific programs for training
teachers. By the end of the nineteenth century, however, the colleges
introduced courses in pedagogy and established chairs, departments,
and schools of education. Gradually the normal schools evolved into
teachers colleges which, in turn, evolved into state colleges that offered
training similar to that of the old liberal arts colleges. During the entire
evolutionary process, the best type of program for the preparation of
teachers was debated by liberal arts colleges and teachers colleges.

---

[1]Stuart G. Noble, A History of American Education (New York: Farrar & Rinehart, Inc., 1938), p. 389.

The old liberal arts colleges had always maintained that secondary school teachers should be college graduates. These schools, therefore, felt that they were the only suitable source of secondary school and college teachers. In actual practice, secondary school teachers in the nineteenth century were graduates of the academies. Very few of them continued their education at the college level. When courses in pedagogy were introduced by the academies and normal schools, the liberal arts colleges hestitated to adopt them, feeling that they were vocational in nature and did not belong in a liberal arts program. Moreover, since the science of pedagogy was still in its infancy, and since these courses were taught by secondary schools (the academies and normal schools), the colleges viewed them as lower-level courses, undeserving of college status. This view has persisted to the present day, for there are still strained relations between some liberal arts faculties and the so-called "educationists" on the staff.

Eventually it became necessary for the liberal arts colleges to introduce education courses into their curricula. Toward the end of the nineteenth century, as the high school movement grew, the normal schools expanded their programs in order to train the secondary school teachers that were badly needed. Bowing to the demand for education courses, and the unexpected competition with the normal schools and state teachers colleges in an area that had been their exclusive province, the liberal arts colleges and universities entered the field of teacher education.

The debate over the appropriate program, however, continued unabated. The liberal arts colleges introduced minimum offerings in teacher education to avoid disrupting their concept of a liberal education. However, the normal schools, and, later, the teachers colleges, continued to introduce new courses as pedagogical information increased. At this point, the liberal arts people criticized the teachers colleges for offering too many "how to teach" courses, claiming that the graduates knew "how to teach" but did not know "what to teach". The liberal arts colleges, with their emphasis on academic disciplines, were criticized, in turn, for offering too much of the "what" and not enough of the "how" to teach. This continuous debate simply emphasized the need for a proper balance between the two programs.

Two important events resulted in some agreement and standardization among teacher education programs. The first was the founding of the various professional organizations concerned with the training of teachers. Through debate, and more recently, experimentation and discussion, the professional organizations arrived at recommendations which received national attention and implementation. These recommendations brought about some agreement even though it was only among the majority of the members of a particular association. The other standardizing influence was the state. As the states assumed control over teacher certification, they prescribed a minimum program for a teacher's certificate. Institutions that wished to train teachers had to introduce a minimum number of education courses if their students were to meet the state requirements. By 1930 state officials began to appoint advisory councils to help them decide the proper requirements for teacher education and certification. At first these councils or committees consisted of professional educators, then the states began to include representatives from academic disciplines. More recently some states have appointed prominent laymen to serve as members. Because they are broadly representative of various interests, these advisory bodies undoubtedly have eased extreme views, and made recommendations that are broadly representative of the diverse groups that have an interest in teacher education. In 1967, 44 states had at least one advisory body in existence.[2]

Accrediting associations have exerted an influence similar to the influence of the state departments of education. They have set standards which an institution must meet in order to be accredited. Since most institutions seek accreditation as a symbol of the quality of their programs, accreditation processes can turn an institution's program in the direction of the standards that have been adopted. The regional associations have usually worked to uphold the liberal arts tradition in education, while the national associations such as the AACTE and the NCATE have tried to introduce into the program enough professional education courses to make a professionally competent teacher, as well as a well-rounded individual.

The debate over the components of a teacher education program is still not ended. G. K. Hodenfeld described its status in 1957 as follows:

> When the Russians sent Sputnik I whizzing about over out startled heads in the fall of 1957, the division between the liberal arts scholars and the teacher educators erupted into an all-out campaign of invective and vituperation. Extremists on one side grabbed the floor (and the headlines) to proclaim that teachers were being taught *how* to teach but not *what* to teach and that, really, if you knew your subject well enough, you could teach it. Extremists on the other side retorted that if you really knew how to teach, you

---

[2]T. M. Stinnett, *A Manual on Certification Requirements for School Personnel in the United States,* 1967 ed. (Washington, D.C.: National Education Association, 1967), Appendix B, pp. 246-252.

could teach anything. Saner folk on both sides pointed out that a good teacher ought to know *what* to teach as well as *how* to teach, but their voices were lost in the din.[3]

The voices of the "saner folk" were heard after the din died down. Professional associations, notably the National Commission on Teacher Education and Professional Standards, brought together the differing factions at the annual NCTEPS conferences of 1958, 1959, and 1960. In these conferences the factions progressed toward mutual understanding and appreciation. Francis V. Lloyd, Jr., one of the conference participants, then superintendent of schools in Clayton, Missouri, later commented:

> A great deal of time has been wasted, in my judgment, in useless bickering, and I am sorry to say that both sides have been equally guilty in running off, crying fire and bloody murder; whereas if they had remained calm and sat together around a table, they would have discovered that in most instances their aims were very similar. The real question, as it has always been since Aristotle first started dealing with students, is what is a proper balance?[4]

What *is* the proper balance between professional education and other disciplines? In 1959–1960, a task force of the NCTEPS reported their findings. The report of the task force, too lengthy to be quoted here, made specific recommendations for the outcomes that should be reached in a teacher education program. The program should include, it was decided, general education, specialization in a teaching field, and professional education.[5] The task force did not give any specific recommendations for the amount of time, in terms of semester hours, that should be spent in each area. Today, it is an accepted fact that a large portion of the curriculum should consist of general education (liberal arts subjects), that a student should major in a field he expects to teach, and that he should have enough professional education courses to provide him with a successful start in his teaching career.

T. M. Stinnett analyzed the teacher education programs of 294 institutions accredited by NCATE in 1957–58, and found a considerable

---

[3]G. K. Hodenfeld and T. M. Stinnett, *The Education of Teachers* (Englewood Cliffs, N.J.: Prentice-Hall, Inc., 1961), p. 4.

[4]*Ibid.*, as quoted on p. 22.

[5]For the specific recommendations see Margaret Lindsey, ed., *New Horizons for the Teaching Profession* (Washington, D.C.: National Commission on Teacher Education and Professional Standards, National Education Association of the United States, 1961), pp. 27-108.

variation in their requirements. The typical semester hour requirements, as represented by median figures, were: 34 hours of professional education for prospective elementary school teachers, and 23 hours for prospective high school teachers; 46 hours of general education for both levels; and, for prospective high school teachers, requirements for a major field varied from 25 hours in foreign languages to 43 hours in agriculture.[6] At the time of the study, 1958, there were not as many liberal arts colleges on the NCATE list as there are now. If the liberal arts colleges had been more represented, undoubtedly the median number of hours of general education would have been higher, and the median number of hours of professional education would have been lower.

This brief discussion on teacher education programs will provide a better understanding of state certification requirements. Teachers' certificates are usually based on the completion of a prescribed amount of general education, specialization, and professional education.

TYPES OF CERTIFICATES

A variety of teachers' certificates have been issued in the past. There have been local, city, county, and state certificates; certificates to cover every level of schooling; certificates that were limited to teaching certain subjects, and certificates that were unlimited. There have been also temporary, emergency, interim, provisional, and permanent certificates. To avoid confusion, we shall arbitrarily classify certificates into three categories: substandard, provisional, and permanent.

The substandard certificate is issued to an individual who has not met all of the minimum requirements for an initial certificate. These certificates are usually issued during a period of teacher shortage, when fully qualified people are not available. For example, if the state requires 24 semester hours for a certificate in mathematics, and a hiring official cannot find a certified teacher, he may hire an individual who has fewer than the required hours. This certificate is issued on a temporary, emergency basis, until a certified person is found, or the temporary employee fulfills his deficiencies and becomes fully certified.

An individual who has completed all of the state requirements for an initial certificate will receive a provisional certificate, in some states. This means that he has fulfilled the requirements of a degree from an approved college, and completed the minimum requirements in general education, professional education and his teaching field. It is a provi-

---

[6]G. K. Hodenfeld and T. M. Stinnett, *op. cit.*, pp. 158-159.

sional certificate because the individual must meet additional requirements before he is eligible for a permanent certificate.

Since it is generally recognized that the training an individual receives before he is issued a provisional certificate is minimal, state certification requirements may prescribe additional courses in order to be eligible for a permanent certificate. Every beginning teacher knows, or soon finds out, that he needs to know much more about his teaching field, and the process of education. The additional requirements, usually prescribed by the state, are of two types: completion of a specified amount of post-baccalaureate college or university training, and a specified number of years of satisfactory teaching on the provisional certificate. Once the individual meets these requirements, he is issued a permanent certificate which usually remains valid until he retires. Sometimes, however, if the teacher with a permanent certificate leaves the profession for a number of years, he may be required to do additional work before he re-enters the field.

Since teaching certificates and state certification requirements vary throughout the states, the prospective teacher should discover the specific requirements of the state in which he hopes to teach early, so that he can adjust his program accordingly. This is particularly advisable if he is receiving his training in a school located in a state other than the one in which he plans to teach.

A summary of Pennsylvania's recent requirements for secondary school teachers serves as an example of certification requirements in operation. The following illustrations are confined to the same state, to avoid any possible confusion.

Pennsylvania Certification Requirements For
Secondary School Teachers Of Academic Subjects, 1968

1. *General education:* 60 semester hours.

   a. Minimum in following fields:
   1. Humanities: 12 s.h.
   2. Social sciences: 6 s.h.
   3. Natural sciences: 6 s.h.
2. *Professional education:* 18 semester hours.

   a. Each of the following areas must be included:
   1. Social foundation of education
   2. Psychology of education and human growth and development
   3. Materials and methods of instruction and curriculum, related to subject matter specialization

4. Six semester hours of student teaching in secondary school, related to subject matter specialization
5. Teaching of reading, which may be incorporated in one of of the above courses

3. *Subject matter specialization.*

   a. English: 36 s.h.
   b. 24 s.h. in any one of the following:
      Foreign language
      Geography and Earth and Space Science
      History
      History and Government
      Mathematics
      Biology
      Chemistry
      Physics
      Physics and Mathematics
      General Science (24 s.h. in any two, or all sciences)
      Earth and Space Science (a course in each of the following must be included: astronomy, geology, meteorology, physical geography)
   c. Comprehensive certificates.
      1. Comprehensive science certificate—40 s.h.
         Must include a minimum of 8 s.h. in each of the following: biology, chemistry, and physics; at least 6 s.h. in earth sciences (astronomy, geology, meteorology); and at least 3 s.h. in mathematics.
      2. Comprehensive social studies certificate—36 s.h. Courses taken must be distributed in each of the following fields: history, geography, government, economics, sociology and/or anthropology.

In addition to meeting the requirements, the applicant must be at least eighteen years old, must have received his training in an approved four-year institution, and must be a citizen of the United States (some exceptions to the citizenship requirement have been made for foreign language teachers).

The Pennsylvania certification requirements correlate with the previous discussion of certification requirements. Approximately one-half of the program consists of general education. There is a minimum of professional education, usually four theory courses, and student teaching, and a heavier concentration on the field of teaching. Through these requirements, the individual, who wishes to teach, receives a well-rounded education, pursues one field in greater depth and receives some professional training.

In the subject matter specialization requirements for Pennsylvania, there are certificates for combinations of subjects, such as physics and mathematics, and comprehensive certificates for a series of courses in a field. This type of certification has some recognized weaknesses. There has been a recent trend to improve the competence of teachers by increasing the number of hours required in their teaching specialty. In Pennsylvania, for example, the number of semester hours required in an academic subject has risen from 18 to, in 1963, 24 semester hours. The English requirement at that time was further raised to 36 semester hours. This revision provided future teachers with a greater depth of knowledge in their teaching specialty. Yet, strangely enough, comprehensive certificates, which are in opposition to this greater depth were retained. For example, an individual could obtain a Comprehensive Social Studies Certificate by distributing 36 semester hours among five or six specified subjects. Once he had received this certificate, he was eligible to teach *any* social studies course taught in the secondary schools. Even though he may have had only 12 semester hours of history as a part of his program, he would be eligible to teach history. Yet the individual who sought certification only in history needed 24 hours in the subject before he could receive his certificate. The result was an incongruous situation in which one individual was not considered qualified to teach history until he had completed 24 hours in it, but another individual was permitted to teach it with only 12 hours of academic credit. The comprehensive certificate (and the combination subject certificate) dilutes rather than strengthens the future teacher's academic preparation.

If the candidate had met all of the foregoing general requirements, and had at least the minimum number of semester hours in general education, professional education, and one of the subject matter specializations, he could apply for a *provisional* college certificate. Teacher-training institutions have a supply of applications. It is the candidate's responsibility to initiate the application when he has completed his program. The following illustration of an application for a teacher's certificate was revised by Pennsylvania in 1968. In that year, its designation as a Provisional College Teacher's Certificate was changed to Professional Personnel Certificate (Instructional I).

There are several items on the application that serve as screening procedures. The candidate must affirm that he is a citizen (with the

Commonwealth of Pennsylvania - Department of Public Instruction

	Date of Application
APPLICATION FOR PROFESSIONAL PERSONNEL CERTIFICATE	

PIHE-280 (9/68)

INSTRUCTIONS: Submit with this application **ALL CREDENTIALS** necessary to verify
                    qualifications for certification (official transcripts, references, evaluations, experience).

Submit to: Bureau of Teacher Education, Division of Teacher Certification, Dept. of Public Instruction, Harrisburg, Penna. 17126

NAME - Last, First, Middle/Maiden Name	SEX ☐ Male ☐ Female	SOCIAL SECURITY NUMBER
HOME ADDRESS - Street, City, State, Zip Code		Do you hold a Pennsylvania certificate? ☐ YES ☐ NO
HOME PHONE & AREA CODE / BIRTHDATE		TYPE CERTIFICATE HELD
NAME OF UNDERGRADUATE COLLEGE/UNIVERSITY STATE		TYPE REQUESTED
DATE GRADUATED DEGREE		REQUESTING ADDITIONAL SUBJECT AREA? ☐ YES ☐ NO

ENTRY BELOW TO BE MADE BY AUTHORIZED COLLEGE OFFICIAL OR SCHOOL SUPERINTENDENT	FOR DPI USE ONLY		
Subject Area or Teaching Field	Date Issued	Type Code	Evaluated By

HEALTH CERTIFICATE (Not Required for Certificate Renewal)

I certify that I am a physician legally qualified to practice medicine in a State of the United States or its capital; that I have examined and find the above-named applicant "neither mentally nor physically disqualified, by reason of tuberculosis or any other communicable disease or by reason of mental disorder from successful performance of the duties of a teacher." (School Code 1209)

STATE IN WHICH LICENSED	PHYSICIAN NUMBER	SIGNATURE OF EXAMINING PHYSICIAN

APPLICATION

I certify that I am a citizen of the United States (or an exchange teacher not permanently employed to teach foreign languages); that I am not in the habit of using narcotic drugs in any form or excessive amounts of intoxicating beverages, (School Code 1209); and that the information in this application is correct.

	SIGNATURE OF APPLICANT

RECOMMENDATION

I certify that the above-named applicant has been a student of this institution, is known as a person of "good moral character" (School Code 1209) and possesses qualities of personality and professional knowledge and skills which will warrant issuance of a teacher's certificate.

COLLEGE CODE	SIGNATURE AND TITLE OF RECOMMENDING DEAN OR AUTHORIZED PROFESSOR
SIGNATURE OF SUPERINTENDENT (When Applicable)	COUNTY-DISTRICT

- READ BOTH SIDES -

exceptions previously noted), and that he is not addicted to drugs or alcohol. A physician must attest that there is nothing wrong with the candidate either mentally or physically which would interfere with his successful performance as a teacher. At this point, the candidate returns the application to his school where the dean or the authorized professor affirms that the individual possesses a good character, has the personal qualities desired in a teacher, and has successfully completed the teacher education program. Then the application is forwarded to the state. If the individual has completed his work in a field in which the institution has received "program approval", the certificate is automatically issued to the candidate. If the program is not approved, a different application is used, accompanied by a transcript. The individual's credentials are inspected, his credits are counted, and, if he has met the requirements, the certificate is issued. In 1969 Pennsylvania like other states began to issue certificates only upon completion of an "approved program". Currently, some states are experimenting with application forms that can be computer-scanned.

Among the various states, a provisional certificate is valid for a limited time, but usually can be renewed for an additional period. If the individual wishes to remain in the profession, he has to work toward semi-permanent or permanent certification. He can attain this standing by meeting two requirements. First, he must give evidence of a specified number of years of satisfactory experience. Second, he must earn a designated number of semester hours of credit beyond the bachelor's degree. These credits can usually be earned in professional education courses, general education courses, or in a specialization. After he has met these additional requirements, some states issue a permanent or life certificate. Other states issue a semi-permanent certificate which requires the teacher to take additional courses periodically.

Since the post-baccalaureate requirements for certification frequently only specify a certain number of hours of post-baccalaureate work, some individuals may be tempted to earn credits cafeteria-style, taking only courses that appeal to them until they have accumulated the necessary credits. Instead, they *should* plan in advance, with the help of a graduate school, a unified program of courses that eventually will lead to a master's degree. It would be a pity for an individual to earn many hours of graduate credit, and then discover that some of these credits are not applicable toward a master's degree.

The details of certification vary considerably from state to state. For an example, which includes all types of school personnel consider the following statement: "The number of school positions for which regular certification requirements are specifically defined ranged in 1962 from one position (Tennessee, Hawaii) to sixty-eight (New Jersey). The total number of differently named certificates issued by all states was 632."[7] Although this large number of certificates represents all types of school personnel, it has created confusion regarding certification requirements, particularly among school people who transfer from one state to another.

The specific requirements for a certificate are fairly uniform on some things and greatly diverse on others. In 1967, 51 states required four years of college for an elementary certificate. The 52nd state required a fifth year of college work. For secondary school certification, 48 states required the completion of four years of college. Four other states demanded the completion of a fifth year. The general education requirement for elementary teachers in 1967 ranged from 16 to 100 hours (most states requiring 40-60), and the professional education requirement ranged from 15 to 36 hours (most states requiring 18-24). At the secondary level, general education requirements varied from 25 to 100 hours (most states ranging between 40-60), and the professional education requirement ranged from 12 to 29 (most states ranging between 18-20). The basic requirements to teach an academic field were also diverse. The majority of states required 24-36 hours to teach English or Social Science, and 18-24 to teach single subjects in the other academic fields.[8]

Examinations as a Basis for Certification

The licensing of teachers by examination was a local matter for approximately two centuries. Beginning in 1825, the counties began to assume authority for examining and certifying teachers, and they remained the chief unit of certification until the close of the nineteenth century. At this time, the state became the chief certifying agency.

Examinations given during the early part of the nineteenth century were brief and oral, covering the candidate's knowledge of elementary subjects, and sometimes including questions on the "art of teaching". The examination was a rough screening device which could not actually identify capable teachers, but at least eliminated the obviously incompetent. Even the incompetent were sometimes permitted to "pass" the examination when teachers were badly needed. Sometimes, too, the examiners were put under pressure to hire certain individuals. The

---

[7]Lucien B. Kinney, *Certification in Education* (Englewood Cliffs, New Jersey: Prentice-Hall, Inc., 1964), p. 18.

[8]Figures in this paragraph are adapted from T. M. Stinnett, *op. cit.*, Table 9, p. 53; Table 10, p. 55; and Table 14, p. 63. Washington, D.C. and Puerto Rico were included in the tabulation of states.

comments of an early examiner in Ohio are interesting in this connection:

> It is an unpleasant duty, on the part of the Examiners, to refuse certification to any one who may submit to their examination. Not infrequently, candidates who have made an exhibition of their ignorance and utter incapacity will importune in the most urgent and pathetic way for certificates. Local directors, sometimes, plead that a candidate be spared rejection, with an importunity like that of Abraham when praying for Sodom. A brawny brother has, more than once, intimated that a sad retribution would, on the first fit occasion, overtake the examiners if his sister should be without a commission; though that girl could not repeat the multiplication table, if it were to save her from the doom of Gomorrah. And, moved by these influences, there is danger that pity or fear will prevail over judgment and a sense of duty.[9]

Politics, favoritism, and coercion were sometimes used to circumvent the results of an examination. The results of the examinations became more objective and less pressured when written examinations were used. Iowa in 1862 passed a law requiring written examinations.

As the number of normal schools increased, and as colleges entered the field of teacher education, the use of examinations decreased because graduates from these institutions were exempt. The examination, however, continued to be used as one of the bases of certification until after World War I because of the shortage of teachers. During the next two decades, however, when the teacher shortage eased, the debate over their use began, studies were made, and the opponents of examinations succeeded. Examinations were all but eliminated. In 1938, Frazier summarized the arguments against the use of examinations as follows:[10]

1. Certification through college credits hastens the elevation of teacher preparation much more than certification through examinations.
2. Certification through college credits provides more assurance of systematic study by the applicant.
3. Minimum requirements are usually lower for certification by examination than by college credits.

---

[9]Lucien B. Kinney, *op. cit.,* p. 47, as quoted from *Fifth Annual Report of the State Commissioner of Common Schools* (Columbus, Ohio: 1858), p. 99.

[10]*Ibid.,* p. 87, as quoted from Benjamin W. Frazier, *Development of State Programs for Certification of Teachers,* U.S. Office of Education Bulletin No. 12 (Washington, D.C.: Government Printing Office, 1938), pp. 40-46.

4. Certification by examination offers minimum stimulus to improvement in service.
5. Certification by examination leads to unfair competition with those who have institutional preparation.

After examining the results of other studies made at the time, Kinney added the following to Frazier's conclusions:[11]

6. Examinations in subject matter are undependable in predicting teaching success.
7. Success in the teacher preparation program is a more reliable criterion for predicting success than is achievement on teacher examinations.
8. The administration of examinations becomes increasingly cumbersome as the number of teachers required increases, and
9. Undesirable local pressure for unmerited certification is often exerted when abuses in examinations are possible.

The evidence was against the use of examinations for certification purposes. Although by 1927 all states were certifying on the basis of the candidate's completion of a college program, some states still allowed the examination to substitute for academic preparation. During the last decade or two some states have required both college preparation and an examination as the basis for certification.

In 1962, Kinney reported the results of a survey made to determine the purposes for which state departments of education could use examinations in the certification process. He found that twenty-two states used examinations for one or more purposes:

Purposes For Which State Departments
Of Education Used Examinations[12]

Purpose of Examination	Number of States in Which Used
Regularizing atypical programs of preparation	5
Issuing provisional credentials	3
Qualifying for special teaching or other fields of service	5
Adding teaching fields	5
In lieu of certain required courses	9

---

[11]*Ibid.*, p. 87.
[12]*Ibid.*, adapted from table on p. 22.

Purposes For Which State Departments
Of Education Used Examinations—cont.

Purpose of Examination	Number of States in Which Used
Determining the grade of certificates	3
As a requirement for certification	2

Each of the twenty-two states used examinations for one to three of the previously mentioned purposes. Only two states used them as a requirement for certification. The most frequent reason for their use in nine states, was to give an examination in place of certain required courses. In his 1967 manual on certification requirements, Stinnett stated that only six states reported use of examinations to qualify for certification.[13] Other states, however, reported using them for some of the purposes mentioned in Kinney's survey.

The formal certification of teachers by examinations has a long history in the United States. During this century, certification on the basis of college work replaced examinations, but attention again seems to be turning toward the use of tests, probably because of the development of standardized tests. All states now certify on the basis of completed college work, but a few of these states have experimented with the use of standardized tests as an *additional* requirement. Some of the better known tests, used for this purpose, are the National Teacher Examinations, the Graduate Record Examination, and the Modern Language Association tests.

Because of their extensive use, a short description of the National Teacher Examinations (NTE) is advisable. These tests are administered by the Educational Testing Service several times annually at regional testing centers located throughout the United States. It measures a candidate's level of achievement in pre-service preparation for the teaching profession. It is not designed to predict success in teaching, nor does it measure intangibles, such as interest, motivation, and personality.

The NTE consist of two sets of examinations: the Common Examinations, and Teaching Area Examinations. The Common Examinations, which give an index of achievement in professional education and general education, may be used for all candidates, regardless of their teaching level or their subject matter specialization. The Teaching Area Examinations measure achievement in the subject or field that the candidate hopes to teach. There are also special tests available for either elementary or secondary school teaching. Candidates may take either

---

[13]T. M. Stinnett, *op. cit.*, pp. 32-33.

the Common Examinations, or the Teaching Area Examinations, or both.

The National Teacher Examinations have been used for several purposes. Some colleges use them to evaluate the preparation of their candidates. These schools occasionally use the results as a basis for recommending certification. Some state departments of education consider the results of the tests a factor in issuing certificates. Similarly, some school districts require candidates for a teaching position to take the tests before considering them for employment. Finally, any candidate may voluntarily take the tests to compare his pre-service preparation with that of other candidates who are about to enter the profession.

The validity of tests as a measure of success in teaching is questionable. Aside from their questioned validity, there remains another strong argument against their use. Once an institution is accredited for teacher education by the state, by a professional association, and by a national accrediting body, its program for training teachers is probably strong enough to make the use of examinations unnecessary. Moreover, only the people who have observed the prospective teacher are in a position to judge the candidate's motivation, personality, and character. These can not be measured accurately by any existing test.

Substandard Certification

When fully certified teachers are needed, but not available, the state and employing officials must hire individuals with lesser qualifications. This situation has occurred throughout our educational history. The shortage of teachers has been more acute during some periods than others. For example, the rapid expansion of education and the population during the nineteenth century, and after World Wars I and II, created an unprecedented shortage of teachers, which resulted in the issuance of a great number of substandard, or emergency, certificates. In 1946–47, the number of emergency teachers was 127,016 (15.2 percent of all teachers employed). The number declined to 69,626 in 1952–53 (7 percent of the teaching force), and then rose again to 96,799 in 1960–61. However, even this higher figure represented only 6.9 percent of all teachers. In 1965–66, the percentage of emergency teachers declined to a low of 4.9 percent, but rose again to 5.1 percent (90,500 teachers) in 1966–67.[14]

Because of the shortage of teachers, the state and other agencies are working in contradictory patterns. While they are raising the standards of the profession through certification and accreditation procedures

---

[14]*Ibid.*, extracted from Table 6, p. 46.

they must admit many people with substandard qualifications. Until the supply of adequately trained teachers is equal to the demand for them, there is no way out of this dilemma. In 1967, the supply of new teachers had exceeded demand in some fields, but the shortage remained in other fields.[15]

Recent Trends in Certification of Teachers

Although there is not yet standardization or complete agreement on certification requirements, the following trends are evident among the various states:

1. An increase in the number of semester hours required in a subject or subject field. Previously it was possible for an individual to receive certification in a subject without having any advanced courses in it. For example, most students were required to take two or three years of English as part of their general education program. After completing this requirement, they often could become certified in the subject. Now, certification requirements usually make it mandatory for the individual to take courses beyond the minimal degree requirements. Even at the elementary level, it is thought that the future elementary school teacher should have a subject matter specialization, especially if he is to join a team teaching program.
2. A decrease in the number of required courses in professional education. This decrease resulted from the compromise reached in the debate over "how to teach" versus "what to teach". Although the requirements in professional education have lessened, enough courses are still required to provide a firm basis for a successful start in teaching. The major in education is changing to the major in a subject or specialized field.
3. Renewed emphasis on the importance of a program of general education to provide a well rounded development. The certification requirements of most states now specify the completion of a certain number of hours in a variety of fields.
4. Wide acceptance of the "approved program" approach to certification. In 1967, forty-five states, and Puerto Rico, had accepted it in varying degrees. This approach has facilitated the issuance of certificates, and, in theory, should raise the quality of teacher education programs.

---

[15]Supply and demand for teachers is discussed in detail in Chapter IX.

5. More demanding requirements for permanent certification. There has been a gradual increase in post-baccalaureate requirements. Some states now require a fifth year of work for permanent certification. There is also a trend to impose additional requirements on individuals who have interrupted their teaching careers for a substantial number of years.

6. Some states now wish to reduce the great number of different certificates in use.

7. There has been an increased use of proficiency tests for purposes related to certification, especially in the teaching of foreign languages.

8. The use of NCATE as a basis for reciprocity in certification, although the advisability of this practice has been questioned. In 1967, 24 states reported "significant" use of NCATE accreditation in reciprocity of certification, and an additional 13 states made "some use of it".[16] Whether or not this trend will continue will depend on the strength of the opposition. Dr. James B. Conant held that because of this practice NCATE has ". . . become a quasi-legal body with tremendous national power."[17] In reply to this argument, it has been pointed out that in past years, there was a wide use of regional accreditation as a basis for reciprocity and that the use of NCATE accreditation is simply an extension of that practice.

Although certification practices have progressed, they still have a long way to go. Some of the problems that need additional attention are: the multiplicity of certificates; the substantial differences in certification requirements among the states; the development of valid criteria for evaluating the programs and products of teacher-training institutions; the further development of reciprocity arrangements among the states; and, since they are experiencing a revival, a critical look at the role of examinations as a basis for certification.

SUMMARY

From the earliest days in American education, teachers have been required to have some form of authorization to teach. In early New England, teachers could obtain licenses from town authorities after passing an examination which was usually conducted by the minister. Other

---

[16]T. M. Stinnett, *op. cit.*, Table 20, p. 83.

[17]James B. Conant, *The Education of American Teachers* (New York: McGraw-Hill Book Company, 1963). Permission granted by Educational Testing Services, p. 69.

colonies required teachers to obtain their licenses from church authorities or from the governor. In the nineteenth century, however, the procedure was changed, and counties began to issue licenses to teach. Gradually the state assumed control of the licensing of teachers, at first granting licenses on the basis of examinations, and later requiring candidates to complete a prescribed course of study. By 1927, all certificates to teach from any state were based on the completion of prescribed college studies.

The prospective teacher's program of studies was the subject of considerable controversy. Some authorities felt that "how to teach" was most important, while other authorities felt that "what to teach" was most important. Although the problem is still unsettled, professional organizations and state departments of education have brought about some agreement on the type of training teachers should receive. Today, it is generally agreed that a teacher's preparation should include a substantial amount of general education, specialization in one field, and enough courses in professional education to give the individual a good beginning in teaching. There are a great many different types of teachers' certificates, which may be arbitrarily classified into three categories: substandard, which are issued on an emergency basis to individuals whose preparation for teaching is incomplete; provisional, issued to teachers who have met all requirements for an initial certificate, but who are going through a probationary period; and permanent, which are given to teachers who have met all educational and experience requirements prescribed by the state.

All states have certification requirements that are stipulated by law. Most states specify the number of semester hours necessary in general education, in specialization, and in professional education. In the past, these requirements were minimal, but in recent years there has been a trend to upgrade the requirements for a certificate. Not only are the states requiring more hours for an initial certificate, but they have also increased the number of hours of post-baccalaureate work necessary for permanent certification.

Until World War I, the written and/or oral examination was the chief basis for certification. Even though by 1927 all the states had adopted the prescribed course of study as a basis for certification, some states continued to use examinations as a supplementary measure. Because the use of examinations was attacked by various authorities, their use became infrequent. Recently, however, they have experienced a revival, in spite of the fact that they are not a valid test for measuring the success of a teacher.

Because of the shortage of teachers since World War II, some compromises have been made in issuing teachers' certificates to individuals who are not fully qualified to teach. In 1946–47, 15.2 percent of all employed teachers were teaching on emergency certificates. As the profession became attractive to more people, this percentage was reduced to 5.1 percent in 1966–67. Even then, there were still 90,500 teachers who fell short of certification requirements.

Although certification practices are still diverse, some general trends have become evident. These include: increase in the number of semester hours required to teach a field; a decrease in the required courses in professional education; renewed emphasis on the importance of liberal arts courses in the training of teachers; the use of an "approved program" approach to certification; increase in the educational requirements for permanent certification; decrease in the number of different types of certificates in use; the use of proficiency tests in some areas of certification; and, the use of NCATE as a basis for reciprocity in certification.

Many problems related to certification still remain. Most important among these problems are the development of valid criteria for evaluating teachers education programs, and the necessity for greater standardization of programs and certificates among the states.

Questions for discussion:

1. What is the value of accrediting associations?

2. Do you think that there should be a national accrediting agency?

3. Should teachers be required to pursue advanced degrees?

4. Should lifetime teacher's certificates be issued?

5. What do you think of examinations as the basis for certification?

6. How can the "approved program" approach in certification lead to higher quality in teacher education?

7. What do you think of Dr. Conant's contention that NCATE has acquired "tremendous national power"?

For further reading:

Conant, James B., *The Education of American Teachers*. New York: Mc-Graw-Hill Book Company, 1963.

Hodenfeld, G. K., and Stinnett, T. M., *The Education of Teachers*. Englewood Cliffs, New Jersey: Prentice-Hall, Inc., 1961.

Kinney, Lucien B., *Certification in Education.* Englewood Cliffs, New Jersey: Prentice-Hall, Inc., 1964.

Lindsay, Margaret, *New Horizons for the Teaching Profession.* Washington, D.C.: National Commission on Teacher Education and Professional Standards, National Education Association, 1961.

Stinnett, T. M., *A Manual on Certification Requirements for School Personnel in the United States,* 1967 Edition. Washington, D.C.: National Education Association, 1967.

8

Basic Qualifications Needed by a Teacher

The word "school teacher" evokes a variety of images and ideas. Depending on the experiences a person recalls from his school life, these visions will range from a warm, kindly, sympathetic individual with a genuine interest in people, to a tyrannical taskmaster who understands little, and cares less, about the welfare and development of his pupils. There can be memories of a teacher *and* pupils working together, or a recollection of a teacher opposing pupils, each eyeing the other with suspicion and resentment.

Students who have pleasant memories of their teachers usually recall individuals who took a personal interest in them, knew their subject thoroughly and came to class well prepared. These teachers were well-adjusted emotionally, and had excellent control of the class and themselves. Students who have unpleasant memories of their teachers usually remember individuals who were either too lax or too strict, who were not conscientious about their work, who did not inquire into their students' problems, or had no sense of humor.

One student, in an education course, recalled a male high school teacher who had no class- or self-control. His classes were endless sessions of boredom as his voice droned on. His pupils' minds wandered, and when he called on them to recite, they either did not hear the question or did not know the answer. After a few negative answers, he would invariably erupt with expletives as his face turned from red to purplish. This teacher obviously did not belong in the profession.

In contrast, another student recalled a female high school teacher who thoroughly enjoyed her work. She worked with her pupils, was strict and demanded high standards of performance, but always remained friendly. The students knew they could approach her with their problems, for she showed a sincere interest in helping them. The students loved and respected her, working hard to meet her standards.

Between the extremely good and the extremely bad teacher there range all variations of ability to teach. In a profession that employs over two million people, it is inevitable that occasional misfits will be hired. However, the ever increasing emphasis on improving the screening procedures and the professional preparation of teachers has helped to eliminate individuals who will not be successful teachers. As this emphasis increases, the number of misfits will decrease.

The factors that make a good teacher cannot be categorized. Successful teachers represent a variety of personalities, levels of mental ability, and types of training. The research programs trying to establish the nature of desirable teacher traits show some similar results, but also show sufficient deviations to preclude a categorical listing of the traits. Personal observations alone will show that this type of listing is not possible, or perhaps even desirable. We can quickly recall that Mr. X was an effective teacher because of his extraordinary ability to dramatize his instruction, but Mr. Y, with a totally different personality, would probably appear ludicrous if he tried to imitate Mr. X. Yet Mr. Y was also a successful teacher. He could reduce ideas to understandable, logical terms that his pupils could easily follow. Similarly, Miss X stimulated her pupils to learn through her vivacious enthusiasm, but Miss Y accomplished the same thing through a quiet sincerity and respect for learning.

If it is true that no two personalities are alike, and that it is possible for people with different traits to become equally effective teachers, who will and who will not make a successful teacher? While no one can predict an individual's success with certainty, his *probable* success will be greatly increased if he possesses certain general traits and qualifications. Although individuals may possess these traits in differing degrees, and although allowances must be made for differences in personality traits, few teachers would be successful without them.

The desirable basic characteristics needed by teachers may be classified into two categories. First, there are those which are based on the individual's natural endowment, such as genuine motivation, above average mental ability, good moral character, acceptance of democratic ideals, good health, favorable personality traits, and good oral expression. The second category includes qualifications that the individual should acquire in his educational training: a background of general education, specialization in a subject or field, and a knowledge of professional education. While it is difficult to separate the influence of one on the other, we shall treat each separately.

PERSONAL QUALITIES DESIRABLE IN A TEACHER

The seven basic personal attributes come from within the individual. Many of them can be improved through training, yet others, such as the individual's mental ability level, remain relatively stable throughout life. Because both his natural endowments and his training are important considerations in a program of teacher education, it is as erroneous to say that "teachers are born" as it is to say that *any* person can become a successful teacher through the training he receives.

The following characteristics are not discussed in the order of their importance. No single characteristic can lead to success as a teacher without the others; however, a lack of any one of them may lead to failure.

Genuine Motivation

People become teachers for a variety of reasons. They may have a desire to help humanity, a love of children, a desire to impart knowledge, or they may want job security, and the prestige of the profession. Unfortunately, some people have no reason at all. They have simply drifted into the profession.

The person who is genuinely motivated toward teaching feels that he has a mission in life. He wants to contribute something to the betterment of humanity. The truly motivated teacher knows that he can help accomplish this through the proper type of teaching. He regards teaching as an opportunity and a challenge. He recognizes his limitations in bringing about major changes, and he knows that he alone cannot change the world. However, he does the best work he can, hoping that there are enough teachers like him to make their combined influence felt.

If an individual belongs in the teaching profession, he enjoys watching his pupils grow. He receives satisfaction, too, in helping them with their individual problems. As his reward, he will see respect, admiration, and gratitude in some of his pupils' eyes, not only while he has them as students, but occasionally when he meets them in later years. Whenever a former pupil achieves something noteworthy, the teacher usually beams with joy about him. If a former student makes a poor adjustment to life, the teacher is unhappy when he learns of it. He experiences these emotions because he is involved in the stream of human development and experiences its joys and sorrows.

Unfortunately, some students have not given enough thought to the motivation underlying their desire to enter teaching. With disturbing frequency, some of them mention that they wish to take courses in education as "insurance", or "something to fall back on". They are primarily interested in other professions or occupations, but feel insecure about reaching their goal. They therefore turn to education as an alternative. Having heard that teaching is a "good field" with steady employment, they apply for admission to teacher education. These individuals, who are selfishly motivated, do not belong in the profession.

It is possible for an individual to have teaching as his secondary occupational goal, and still possess the proper motivation. For example, a student may wish to become a physician, but he is uncertain that he will be able to attend medical school. Having a sincere desire to help society, he feels that teaching could be equally satisfying. The difference between his motivation and the purely "insurance" motivation is obvious.

The proper motivation, then, consists of a desire to help human beings to become all that it is possible for them to become. Unless this type of motivation is present, the individual will receive little satisfaction from teaching. Without this satisfaction his teaching will become sterile, and if he remains in the profession his actions in the classroom will resemble those of an automaton. For this reason, the prospective teacher should view himself as objectively as possible, searching within himself for the reasons that are prompting him to consider teaching as a profession.

Above Average Mental Ability

The complexity of a teacher's work, and the responsibility it entails, make it desirable for a candidate to possess above average intelligence.

If the individual hopes to complete his college work at all successfully, he must have an above average learning ability. In terms of I.Q., with 90 to 109 considered average ability, he should have an intelligence quotient well above 110. The farther above 110 his I.Q., the higher his probability of success in college. However, a high intelligence quotient, in itself, is no assurance of success in college work, or teaching. It is only *one* of the necessary ingredients for success.

During his student teaching, and later in his work as a teacher, the individual becomes involved in many complex classroom activities. He must organize, interpret, and illustrate his material to make it under-standable, thought-provoking, and interesting to his pupils. He must continuously try to devise better ways of doing things, to make the learning situation more effective. He must spend part of his time doing the research that is necessary to expand his knowledge and keep abreast of developments in his field. He is confronted daily with new problems of student behavior, and he must adapt his instruction to the situations as they arise. He must be ready to capitalize on unexpected learning opportunities, and he must be equally prepared to redirect undesirable learning trends among his pupils. Daily he explores the minds of his pupils, trying to lead them to understanding. Obviously, it takes above average intelligence, as well as other abilities, to carry on all these activities effectively.

With the increasing certification requirements, it is necessary for teachers to do graduate work before they are eligible for permanent certification. These post-baccalaureate requirements vary from state to state. Some states may require only a few semester hours of graduate work, while other states specify a master's degree as a condition of permanent certification. Because graduate work calls for a higher degree of mental ability than under-graduate work, the need for above average mental ability in a prospective teacher becomes even more obvious. He *must* be above average in order to complete the necessary training.

Because of these requirements, candidates are screened for their mental ability level before they are admitted to a teacher education program. They are required to make suitable scores on admissions tests, and are expected to show above-average achievement during their training. In schools where teacher education is not offered until the junior year, a candidate must have accomplished above average work during his first two years of college to be admitted to the program. It is unlikely that a poor student would be able to teach others to learn effectively.

Good Moral Character

Obviously, a teacher's character should be beyond reproach. Every teacher exerts an influence on his pupils, helping them to formulate principles which will guide their conduct. Because of his influence, the teacher should *personify* desirable conduct, ideals, and attitudes. Unless he practices the virtues he wishes to inculcate in his pupils, his actions, betraying his words, can produce no other reaction than "he doesn't practice what he preaches". When this happens, pupils can see no reason for accepting the teacher's principles.

The teacher's influence on his pupils will be either positive or negative, depending upon his character, and the way the students perceive it. Character has been defined as "life dominated by moral principles"; therefore, the way in which a teacher influences his pupils will be determined by the principles he accepts and practices. Through his actions and works, the teacher should create a desire on the part of pupils to accept and cultivate virtues such as justice, prudence, fortitude, temperance, honesty, truthfulness, charity, sympathy, and altruism. The development of these qualities not only aids in the proper development of each individual, but also contributes to general social welfare.

There are countless examples of teachers who helped to change their pupils' lives, not only their careers, but also the development of their personalities and characters. There are also examples of teachers who, because they were unsuited for the teaching profession, produced rebelliousness and lawlessness, as forms of reaction in their pupils. These teachers probably failed to practice the virtues of justice, sympathy, or charity.

The teacher's character, then, influences the type of character formed by his pupils. The teacher's beliefs, his concepts of good and evil, virtue and vice, will, to some degree, become a part of his pupils. When we remember that during a lifetime of teaching, a teacher influences thousands of pupils, the importance of good moral character is greatly magnified.

The teacher's moral principles are applied to all of his work and to his relationships with pupils, members of the profession, and people in the community. Education, as a profession, has rules of conduct which have been formulated by its membership. As an example of the scope of these rules of conduct, the 1968 NEA statement of a code of ethics follows.[1]

Code of Ethics of the Education Profession

Approved by the Representative Assembly of the National Education
Association, July 5, 1968.

PREAMBLE

The educator believes in the worth and dignity of man. He recognizes the supreme importance of the pursuit of truth, devotion to excellence, and the

---

[1] National Education Association, *NEA Handbook, 1968-69* (Washington, D.C.: the Association, 1968), pp. 89-91.

nurture of democratic citizenship. He regards as essential to these goals the protection of freedom to learn and to teach and the guarantee of equal educational opportunity for all. The educator accepts his responsibility to practice his profession according to the highest ethical standards.

The educator recognizes the magnitude of the responsibility he has accepted in choosing a career in education, and engages himself, individually and collectively with other educators, to judge his colleagues, and to be judged by them, in accordance with the provisions of this code.

PRINCIPLE I

Commitment to the Student

The educator measures his success by the progress of each student toward realization of his potential as a worthy and effective citizen. The educator therefore works to stimulate the spirit of inquiry, the acquisition of knowledge and understanding, and the thoughtful formulation of worthy goals.

In fulfilling his obligation to the student, the educator—

1. Shall not without just cause restrain the student from independent action in his pursuit of learning, and shall not without just cause deny the student access to varying points of view.

2. Shall not deliberately suppress or distort subject matter for which he bears responsibility.

3. Shall make reasonable effort to protect the student from conditions harmful to learning or to health and safety.

4. Shall conduct professional business in such a way that he does not expose the student to unnecessary embarrassment or disparagement.

5. Shall not on the ground of race, color, creed, or national origin exclude any student from participation in or deny him benefits under any program, nor grant any discriminatory consideration or advantage.

6. Shall not use professional relationships with students for private advantage.

7. Shall keep in confidence information that has been obtained in the course of professional service, unless disclosure serves professional purposes or is required by law.

8. Shall not tutor for remuneration students assigned to his classes, unless no other qualified teacher is reasonably available.

PRINCIPLE II

Commitment to the Public

The educator believes that patriotism in its highest form requires dedication to the principles of our democratic heritage. He shares with all other citizens the responsibility for the development of sound public policy and assumes full political and citizenship responsibilities. The educator bears particular responsibility for the development of policy relating to the extension of educational opportunities for all and for interpreting educational programs and policies to the public.

In fulfilling his obligation to the public, the educator—

1. Shall not misrepresent an institution or organization with which he is affiliated, and shall take adequate precautions to distinguish bteween his personal and institutional or organizational views.

2. Shall not knowingly distort or misrepresent the facts concerning educational matters in direct and indirect public expressions.

3. Shall not interfere with a colleague's exercise of political and citizenship rights and responsibilities.

4. Shall not use institutional privileges for private gain or to promote political candidates or partisan political activities.

5. Shall accept no gratuities, gifts, or favors that might impair or appear to impair professional judgment, nor offer any favor, service, or thing of value to obtain special advantage.

PRINCIPLE III

Commitment to the Profession

The educator believes that the quality of the services of the education profession directly influences the nation and its citizens. He therefore exerts every effort to raise professional standards, to improve his service, to promote a climate in which the exercise of professional judgment is encouraged, and to achieve conditions which attract persons worthy of the trust to careers in education. Aware of the value of united effort, he contributes actively to the support, planning, and programs of professional organizations.

In fulfilling his obligation to the profession, the educator—

1. Shall not discriminate on grounds of race, color, creed, or national origin for membership in professional organizations, nor interfere with the free participation of colleagues in the affairs of their association.

2. Shall accord just and equitable treatment to all members of the profession in the exercise of their professional rights and responsibilities.

3. Shall not use coercive means or promise special treatment in order to influence professional decisions of colleagues.

4. Shall withhold and safeguard information acquired about colleagues in the course of employment, unless disclosure serves professional purposes.

5. Shall not refuse to participate in a professional inquiry when requested by an appropriate professional association.

6. Shall provide upon the request of the aggrieved party a written statement of specific reason for recommendations that lead to the denial of increments, significant changes in employment, or termination of employment.

7. Shall not misrepresent his professional qualifications.

8. Shall not knowingly distort evaluations of colleagues.

PRINCIPLE IV

Commitment to Professional
Employment Practices

The educator regards the employment agreement as a pledge to be executed both in spirit and in fact in a manner consistent with the highest ideals of professional service. He believes that sound professional personnel relationships with governing boards are built upon personal integrity, dignity, and mutual respect. The educator discourages the practice of his profession by unqualified persons.

In fulfilling his obligation to professional employment practices, the educator—

1. Shall apply for, accept, offer, or assign a position or responsibility on the basis of professional preparation and legal qualifications.

2. Shall apply for a specific position only when it is known to be vacant, and shall refrain from underbidding or commenting adversely about other candidates.

3. Shall not knowingly withhold information regarding a position from an applicant, or misrepresent an assignment or conditions of employment.

4. Shall give prompt notice to the employing agency of any change in availability of service, and the employing agent shall give prompt notice of change in availability or nature of a position.

5. Shall not accept a position when so requested by the appropriate professional organization.

6. Shall adhere to the terms of a contract or appointment, unless these terms have been legally terminated, falsely represented, or substantially altered by unilateral action of the employing agency.

7. Shall conduct professional business through channels, when available, that have been jointly approved by the professional organization and the employing agency.

8. Shall not delegate assigned tasks to unqualified personnel.

9. Shall permit no commercial exploitation of his professional position.

10. Shall use time granted for the purpose for which it is intended.

The NEA Code of Ethics shows the dignity and importance of the teaching profession. It calls attention to the great responsibility each teacher has to perform his work "according to the highest ethical standards."

Acceptance of Democratic Ideals

If one of the purposes of our educational system is to perpetuate our democracy, it is obviously necessary to appoint teachers who believe in our way of life. While the constitution guarantees each individual the right to his own opinion and the right to disagree, we could need-lessly endanger these rights by appointing teachers who do not believe in democratic principles. Teachers should foster patriotism, and pride in our democratic way of life. They should point to the accomplish-ments and virtues of the Founding Fathers, and our national heroes. Our short-comings and failures should not be concealed, for pupils should know, and should be told, that all human institutions are fallible. However, this information should be discussed against the backdrop of the advantages of democracy over other forms of government, even when it has failed to provide the ideal for every individual. Teachers imbued with democratic principles will not only preserve, but may also strengthen, our democracy.

Good Health

Contrary to public opinion, teaching is a strenuous occupation. People who refer laughingly, or seriously, to a teacher's short hours and long vacations are uninformed or misinformed about a teacher's work schedule.

A teacher spends five or six hours a day in the classroom in instruc-tional activities. Since he is responsible for keeping his classes active and orderly at all times, he must plan and organize his work carefully. He must know during every minute of each class period what he will say and do, and how he will keep his pupils occupied. Any reader who can recall occasions when it took him several hours to prepare a twenty-minute speech or oral report can appreciate the amount of time needed by a teacher for good class preparation. The beginning teacher will find that it takes him as long to prepare for a class as it does to teach it. As he acquires experience, his preparation time will decrease. Yet even the teacher with many years of experience will find that his preparation is never complete. He must continually reorganize his material, expand his knowledge, and keep abreast of his field.

The teacher's energy is also taxed emotionally. Any conscientious teacher is under some tension while conducting his class, because he is anxious to make his material understandable and interesting. His ten-sion may be increased by discipline problems that demand a high degree of emotional control on his part. After all, the teacher is faced with a group of energetic individuals seeking to release their energy. While usually the activities are channeled toward acceptable goals, occasionally there are cases of student mischief which seem to have the sole purpose of irritating or testing the self-control of the teacher. Since tension and emotional strain cause physical fatigue, it is understandable that teachers feel weary at the end of the day.

There are also time-consuming clerical tasks the teacher must perform. It takes time to make up tests, and more time to grade them. Homework and written exercises must be graded. The teacher keeps various records and must submit reports. These tasks occupy him for hours.

In addition, the teacher may be asked to take charge of, or assist with, an extra-curricular activity such as the school newspaper, the yearbook, club activities, dramatics, advising, or another activity with which he has had experience. Occasionally he may even be asked to help in an area in which he has had no previous experience. Furthermore, he is expected to attend P.T.A., faculty, and professional meetings. All of these activities usually occur after regular school hours.

Although teachers have more frequent vacation periods than people in other professions, they usually use these periods to reduce the backlog of work that has accumulated while school was in session. Similarly, even though teachers have longer summer vacations than other people, they must use this time to continue their education, or to seek summer employment to supplement their modest salaries.

A conscientious teacher, then, is engaged in a variety of activities that are not always apparent to others and may extend beyond school hours. With all of these demands on his time and energy, a person must be in good health when he enters the teaching profession. A person who is not in good health cannot perform effectively as a teacher. Poor health will adversely affect his mental efficiency, disposition, and may even affect his emotional stability. Aware of the necessity of good health, most certification agencies insist that candidates pass a physical examination before they are eligible for a teacher's certificate.

Favorable Personality Traits

Personality has been decribed as "the sum total of what I am". If this definition is correct it would be difficult, if not impossible, to define specifically what is meant by an individual's personality. When we try to describe an individual's personality, we tend to use general statements which involve the whole person. For example, a student may say of his teacher: "I like him. He is a very nice person." This is the student's total impression of the teacher. It is only when he is asked to analyze his reasons for liking the teacher, that the student begins to name specific traits. No matter what specific reasons the student may give for liking a teacher, he likes him because the total impression the teacher makes appeals to him. Total negative impressions are formed in the same way. If we continued to ask students why they liked or disliked certain teachers, we would have a lengthy list of traits, some pertaining to his emotional make-up, others to his ability, or to his physical characteristics. The problem of assessing an individual's personality is further complicated by the fact that our likes, dislikes, and standards influence our judgment. Thus, a teacher's personality may be liked by some, and disliked by others.

Many surveys have been made, asking students to explain why they liked or disliked their teachers. As might be expected, the students gave dozens of reasons. Some traits, however, were mentioned far more frequently than others, so that it is possible to name some traits that make for better relationships with students and to name other traits that have the opposite effect.

A teacher should be able to get along with other people, since he is continuously involved in human relationships. In his relationships with students he should be friendly and approachable, yet maintain the dignity of his position. His pupils should realize through his words and actions that he is willing and anxious to help them with their problems. Puplis who need advice or help, usually ask the teacher who has demonstrated in his daily actions that he was concerned with their welfare and progress.

Students work willingly for, and with, a teacher they like, but they rebel against and refuse to do things for a teacher they dislike. Rapport, therefore, is necessary in the classroom, if effective learning is to occur. Among the teacher-traits that contribute to rapport are friendliness, sympathy, sincerity, justice, enthusiasm, self-control, and a sense of humor. Displaying these qualities should not result in a complete levelling of the teacher-pupil relationship. There should always be a line of demarcation between the two individuals, based on the pupil's recognition of the teacher's authority. The relationship should be "friendly but not familiar." Friendliness generates cooperation on the part of the pupils, familiarity results in the loss of respect for the teacher and his authority.

Although the teacher should be friendly and approachable, he must also be firm and just. He must insist that his pupils comply with his regulations and the regulations of the school. He should not have "pets" who are given preferential treatment, nor should be have "pet peeves" who receive undue severe treatment. His pupils must realize that he means, and acts on, what he says. Firmness and justice, tempered with kindness as the occasion warrants, are indispensable traits for successful teaching.

The teacher must also be emotionally stable. He will encounter many exasperating moments when he should "count to ten" before taking action on a difficult problem. He should not lose control over his emotions, because one emotional outburst, during which he acts imprudently, may irreparably shatter good relationship he has established with his pupils. There are times when it is discreet for the teacher to share in the amusement over a pupil's innocent prank or impromptu remark. A teacher's strategic injection of humor often dissipates the classroom tensions that may arise. Emotional stability and self-control are indispensable assets for any teacher.

There are two emotions that should be eliminated from the classroom: the teacher's anger and the pupils' fear. The teacher who loses his temper does not handle situations rationally, with the result that the pupils may be in a continuous state of anxiety or fear. Fear and anger excite imagination, impair concentration, and affect one's ability to make valid judgments and, therefore, are impediments to learning.

The personality traits possessed by a teacher usually determine the type of relationship that will exist between a teacher and his pupils. For rapport to exist in the classroom, the teacher's personality must be cooperative, friendly, sympathetic, sincere, just, enthusiastic, self-controlled. Above all, he must have a good sense of humor. These traits are essential for success as a teacher. More teachers fail because of personality shortcomings than for any other single reason.

Effective Voice and Oral Expression

Every teacher should have a pleasant, audible voice and clear, grammatical expression. This does not mean that every prospective teacher should be an accomplished public speaker. However, since the chief line of communication between a teacher and his pupils is oral, any pronounced speech defects will adversely affect the receivers.

Teacher trainees often exhibit several problems which, if not corrected, will cause interference in the line of communication. Some of these problems are: peculiarities of pronunciation; mistakes in grammar; speaking in a monotone; speaking too loudly, or too softly; speaking too rapidly, or too slowly. Most of these can be corrected before the prospective teacher finishes his training period. Occasionally, a more serious defect, such as stuttering, is evident. In this situation, if the student still wishes to become a teacher, referral to a psychiatrist and speech therapist may eliminate the problem. If it is not eliminated, the individual frequently is asked to leave the teacher education program.

If minor speech defects are pointed out to the student, he often can plan a program of self-improvement under the guidance of his teachers. This program, with his natural maturation as a college student, usually takes care of his difficulties.

There is at least one other reason why a teacher should have a good voice and effective expression. It is one of the objectives of education to train pupils to express themselves effectively and correctly. Although they may receive this training in a variety of courses and activities, the example of the teacher is also a means toward this end. Pupils consciously or unconsciously imitate many of the things their teacher does, especially if they admire the teacher. If the teacher has good speech habits, the pupils, through imitation, may improve their own skills in communication.

Good voice and correct and effective speech facilitate learning. Also, the teacher's speech acting as a model, may help to raise the pupils' speech habits to a more acceptable level.

These characteristics do not exhaust the list of traits and qualities that have been suggested as desirable in teachers. Among the many other reasons why a teacher may be liked are: neatness, punctuality, courtesy, strictness, reasonableness, adhering to standards, thoroughness, impartiality, high ideals, adaptability, conscientiousness, interest in individuals, knowledge of subject, and ability to teach effectively. Most of these traits, however, are manifestations of the general characteristics that were explained in this chapter. Some of them can be classified as specific manifestations of desirable motivation, high intelligence, pleasant personality, and good moral character. Those that deal with the teacher's knowledge and his ability to teach result from the type of teacher education program he receives.

QUALIFICATIONS ACHIEVED THROUGH SCHOOLING

Although the preceding qualifications are a part of the personality of the future teacher, they may be developed, influenced, or even changed through training. Broad educational background, specialization in subject matter, and professional education, depend mostly upon schooling, although here also certain personal characteristics are evident as, for example, the individual's mental ability level and personality which influence his success during his college training. There is so much interplay between all of these factors that no one factor is uninfluenced by the others. The categorization of these qualifications is therefore, merely a convenience for discussion.

General Educational Background

A teacher should have a broad educational background, aside from specialized training. The terms most frequently used to describe this type of schooling are "liberal education" and "general education". Both terms include study in fields such as English, social studies, philosophy, foreign languages, natural sciences, and mathematics. This type of education helps to develop the individual's ability to seek truth, and live harmoniously with the societies of which he is a member. It has no direct vocational aim. Rather, it helps the individual to understand himself and his relationships with others. Essential to his understanding is a knowledge and appreciation of the values expressed by mankind throughout the years and their application toward the goals of becoming a worthy member of society.

From the practical standpoint, a general educational background results in more effective teaching and better relationships with pupils. Since fields of knowledge are related, overlap, and have implications for one another, a teacher with a broad educational background can understand and explain how his subject integrates with others. He can unify knowledge for his pupils. Drawing on his fund of learning, he can clarify and supplement the material in his own subject. Furthermore, through his educational background, he gains a clearer view of the nature of man and the world, his purpose in life, and, therefore, the purposes of education and how they can be achieved. In addition, he has a better understanding of human relationships, which he can apply in dealing with his pupils.

For these reasons, state departments of education are now emphasizing the necessity for a general educational background. It has become a part of their certification requirements for teachers. In addition, states now insist that a specified number of semester hours in general education should be included in a teacher education program.

Specialization in Subject Matter

Although a teacher should have a broad educational background, he needs to have a greater depth of training in the subject or area that he expects to teach. As a teacher, he should be more conversant with his specialty than with the broad developmental subjects to which he was exposed as a student. If he lacks depth in his specialty, he will only superficially acquaint his pupils with his field, teaching them little or nothing beyond the textbook, poorly explaining and answering material and the students' questions. This, of course, would be unfair to the pupils who look to the teacher for instruction and guidance. It would not take long for a poorly prepared teacher to lose the respect of his students. When this happens, it not only interferes with learning, but also may affect the pupils' total adjustment and attitude toward learning. Furthermore, the teacher, recognizing his inadequacy, will lack the confidence of a good teacher and this, coupled with the frustration he must feel, may discourage him from continuing in the profession.

The prospective secondary school teacher should *major* in the field he hopes to teach. Recently, there have also been recommendations that elementary school teachers receive training in subject matter. With this training the future teacher will be able to meet the demands of his pupils and his conscience. He certainly should choose his major field carefully because he will invest considerable time and effort in it. He should choose a field which has always interested him. His enthusiasm for the subject may kindle an equal enthusiasm in his pupils. Under no circumstances should a future teacher major in a subject just because there is a shortage of teachers in that field. He must love his field; otherwise, his teaching will be lifeless.

Professional Education

The prospective teacher should be exposed to a variety of information and thought-provoking situations that relate directly to the work of a teacher. A good program of professional education will help the beginning teacher to avoid many mistakes that he would otherwise make. It will help him to see and correct mistakes when he begins to teach and greatly increase the possibility of success in his first teaching position.

An introductory course to the field of education is indispensable. Introductory courses have a variety of names, and include a variety of subjects, but certain core elements should be included in the course. A prospective teacher should have at least a general knowledge of: the historical development of our schools; the purposes of education in our democratic society; the problems and controversial issues in education; the qualifications needed by a teacher; the financial as well as the intangible benefits of teaching; the activities of a teacher; professional relationships; organization and control of education; and the financing of education. Of course, any introductory course will suffer the limitation of all survey courses, namely, a lack of depth. Yet a general knowledge in these areas, which the future teacher can later expand, is better than total ignorance. The introductory course is usually the first course, giving the future teacher a perspective on the field, and helping him to decide whether or not he wishes to continue in the field. It will also correct some of his misconceptions about the field, and will help to begin the building of desirable attitudes and ideals.

If the individual decides to continue in the program, he should study learning theories, and the application of these theories in a learning situation. Courses in General Psychology and Educational Psychology usually cover this type of information. These courses help the future teacher to understand the physical and mental powers and processes involved in learning. The student usually studies processes such as memory, association, attention, reasoning, habit formation, motivation, individual differences, emotions, and transfer of training. Obviously, a teacher must know how these processes operate before he can begin to develop them in his pupils. Without this knowledge, he would use a trial and error method and might prevent rather than improve, pupil performance.

A prospective teacher should recognize the different traits that children exhibit at different ages. If he recognizes these traits he can take them into account in teaching and in working with children. Studying the growth and development of children enables a teacher to know what to expect of children at given ages. He is then able to adapt his instruction and relationships to their distinctive traits and levels of development. He learns, for example, that the same approach can not be used with a ten-year-old and a fourteen-year-old. In fact, there is enough difference between the ten-year-old and the eleven-year-old to warrant a complete change in procedures and approach. Information on growth and development is occasionally included in an educational psychology course, but more frequently it is given separate treatment in courses on child development or adolescent development, depending upon the school level for which the individual is preparing.

Methods are the systematic ways in which we try to achieve the objectives in education. An understanding of these methods and an evaluation of their merits, is essential for the future teacher. The individual, in methods courses, is exposed to old as well as new methods and procedures. He will usually discuss lesson planning, questioning, lecturing, reviews, drilling, illustration, assignments, maintaining discipline, evaluation, project, socialized recitation, and programmed instruction. *General* methods courses discuss these things as they apply in the teaching of any subject; *special* methods courses, for example Methods of Teaching English, show how they can be used most effectively in the teaching of a particular subject.

Finally, the candidate's professional training should include the opportunity to go through a period of supervised observation and teaching. During this period the individual puts into practice the theory and knowledge he has learned not only in his professional education courses but also in his general education and area of specialization. All that he has learned throughout his life, in and out of school, may enter into his teaching. Gradually, he assumes full responsibility for the management and instruction of a class. During his whole period of student teaching he receives help in overcoming his weaknesses and further developing his strengths. When his student teaching is over, he has a taste of teaching and working with children. For the first time, he fully realizes the complexities, problems, frustrations, and joys involved in the profession. He is usually ready and anxious to accept his first appointment as a professional employee.

During 1959–60 a task force of the TEPS commission made one of the more prominent statements on the characteristics that are desirable in prospective teachers. After considering the results of other studies made on desirable teacher characteristics, the task force singled out the following basic traits for those who wish to become teachers:[2]

> Emotional maturity
> Effective communication
> Possession of basic skills in English usage and arithmetic
> Moral and ethical fitness
> Academic aptitude or intelligence
> Above average academic achievement
> Ability to work with others
> Knowledge of, and active participation in, democratic principles
> Good health

This listing is similar to that outlined earlier in this chapter, and both listings resemble, but are not identical with, other statements.

The prospective teacher should try to analyze his personal characteristics in relation to those discussed in this chapter. He should discuss his potentialities as a teacher with close friends and with teachers who

---

[2]Margaret Lindsey, ed., *New Horizons for the Teaching Profession* (Washington: National Commission on Teacher Education and Professional Standards, National Education Association of the United States, 1961), pp. 188-192.

know him well. At the end of his self-analysis and discussions with others, he should be able to tentatively judge whether or not he possesses the basic characteristics needed by a teacher. He does, if he: likes people, and they like him; likes to study, and is doing well in his studies; likes to communicate ideas, and has successfully done so; likes to help people with their problems, and receives satisfaction from it; likes to work with groups, and respects the opinions of others; has self-control; and possesses good health. These characteristics provide a suitable foundation upon which to build a teacher education program.

SELECTION AND RETENTION OF TEACHERS

How does the college or university obtain candidates with the desirable characteristics for their education programs? There are a variety of procedures used to screen prospective teachers. Each school engaged in training teachers has a person or group of persons who are responsible for the screening program. As an illustration, let us assume that the chairman of the department of education, or the dean of the school of education is directly responsible for the program. He usually appoints a group of individuals, a "Committee on Teacher Education", to act in an advisory capacity. This committee would recommend policies and procedures to be followed in the teacher education program. They would also recommend the criteria to be used in the selection and retention of students in the program. The recommendations of the committee, before implementation, usually require adoption by some higher institutional authority, such as an academic council or a faculty senate.

When a student decides that he would like to enter the teacher education program, he usually makes a formal application at a specified time in his college program. The time of application varies with the institution, and may occur after the first, second, or even third year, depending upon the nature of the program. The application is made to a person or persons who have been appointed for that purpose, and may have the additional responsibility of evaluating the application.

Some objective evidence for evaluating the application is immediately available. At the time he applies for the program, the candidate may be required to present a doctor's certificate, attesting to his good health. Furthermore, his past academic record is available for ascertaining whether or not his achievement is above average. In addition, the student has a personal interview, during which a general impression of his motivation, personality, and expression may be formed. After his application, and before his admission to the program, further information may be gathered from faculty members. If all the factors appear to be favorable, the applicant is admitted to the program.

This is not an arbitrary procedure. Realizing that they are dealing with complex human beings who are difficult to assess objectively and whose achievements may have been affected by extenuating circumstances, most schools provide for admission to the program with a status that might be designated as "conditional admission". The student who transfers from one degree program to another is a common example of this type of candidate. He may have begun his college career in the field of chemistry, and, finding himself unsuited for it, either failed or did poorly in it. He then transferred to another degree program, in which he did very well. However, his cumulative average remained low because of his poor grades in the initial program. This student would deserve conditional admission to the program with the understanding that he is required to do above average work thereafter. Other examples are the student who begins to do academically well late in his college career and the students who had difficulty adjusting to college life in their freshman year. In these cases, the writer has found that the "forgive the past and look to the future" approach has usually acted as a strong incentive for students to do better work. In some cases, it has even resulted in spectacular spurts of progress. A few students, of course, may continue to do poor work after they are admitted conditionally. These students are dropped from the program. Pupils troubled with shyness, or speech problems, may be admitted conditionally, pending correction of their defects.

Once admitted to the teacher education program, the candidate continues to be closely watched. Whether he has been admitted conditionally or unconditionally, the student must continue to exhibit qualities that are desirable in a teacher. Some screening committees check the academic progress of their candidates at the end of every semester, and hold an interview with the student to determine whether or not he may continue in the program. The candidates' names may be given periodically to the faculty for information relevant to the student's fitness for the profession. The professional education faculty carefully watches his progress toward professional goals. Sometimes pupils are dropped for academic reasons, or for personality shortcomings, or for other reasons. Occasionally some pupils voluntarily drop out of the program.

Student teaching is the climax of the student's teacher education program. Before a student is assigned to student teaching, his qualifications are again given an over-all appraisal. Throughout his student teaching, the candidate is observed regularly by college and school personnel. With their help, the student teacher exploits his strengths and overcomes his weaknesses. Because of the careful, continuous screening that has preceded student teaching, cases of failure are, or should be, rare. Nevertheless, student teaching provides a further screening device that can be used by the institution. If the student does not perform well the school can refuse to recommend him for a teacher's certificate or for a teaching position.

These screening procedures should help to improve the quality of future teachers. Of course, mistakes can be made because of the limitations of human judgment. They can occur in either direction: individuals who might be good teachers may be denied admission to the teacher education program, while, other individuals have become poor teachers because they have been permitted to slide through the program. Yet, the administrators of the program must work with the equipment they have. Most institutions use standardized tests of one kind or another to help them screen and evaluate, the candidates. A 1964 study of the use of these tests by institutions holding AACTE memberships showed that 445 distinct test titles were used among the 443 institutions that responded.[3] Obviously there is *no* valid test presently in existence to measure the effectiveness of a teacher education program. If there were, 445 different tests attempting to measure the effectiveness would not have to be in use. In spite of the limitations of human beings and tests, there exists a level of competence in screening and evaluating prospective teachers that produces teachers of a higher quality than there would be if such procedures were not used at all.

The institutions offering teacher education programs play an important role in controlling the quality of teachers. In these schools the initial selections and decisions are made. Depending upon the effectiveness of screening procedures, only the candidates with suitable qualifications are admitted to and retained in the program. Depending upon the over-all quality of the institutional program, the candidates should receive sufficient training to assure them of reasonable success when they begin teaching.

Screening by the State

The state has the responsibility to hire high quality teachers for the children within its borders. One of the means it takes to accomplish this is through its certification, or licensing, procedures.

---

[3]S. David Farr, *Evaluation and Selection Instruments in Teacher Education Problems,* summary report of the Subcommittee on Testing in Teacher Education, Committee on Studies, American Association of Colleges for Teacher Education, 1964, p. 3.

After the individual has completed his institutional program, he must file an application with the state for a teacher's certificate. This application in itself is a screening device. It shows that the candidate is in good health, has completed the program necessary for the type of certificate he is seeking, and that the institution stands behind him through its recommendation that he be certified.

The first certificate is usually a temporary one. Before a teacher receives a permanent certificate, he must meet other requirements, which serve two purposes: as a further screening procedure, and to raise the level of his qualifications. The successful completion of two or three years of teaching, during which time the individual has received at least a "satisfactory" rating by his supervisors is one of the usual requirements for a permanent certificate. This makes it possible to eliminate incompetent teachers that have somehow managed to get into the profession in spite of all of the precautions that have been taken. The other usual requirement for permanent certification is that the teacher continue to improve his qualifications by completing a specified number of semester hours beyond the baccalaureate degree. Only after he has completed these additional requirements does the teacher receive his permanent certificate.

Follow-up by Institutions

Most schools have a program in which they follow up their graduates to learn how they are performing as first-year teachers. At the end of their first year of teaching, the institution sends a rating scale to the teachers' supervisors, requesting them to rate the first-year teacher on various characteristics. Even a scale as simple as the one on page 251 can give the institution some helpful information.

After all the rating scales are returned, the institution tallies the number of responses in each category. The distribution of the tallies shows the strengths or weaknesses of the teacher education program. For example, if none of the graduates receives a rating of "below average" or "inferior" in personality, the institution's screening techniques for that characteristic are probably good. If a sizeable percentage of graduates are rated below average in "teaching skill", the institution can detect a weakness that needs attention.

The institutional follow-up is a further screening device. If a particular individual receives a below average or an inferior rating by his supervisor, his contract probably will not be renewed. If he then seeks a position elsewhere, he undoubtedly will ask the institution for a

Rating Scale for Graduates Now Teaching

Name of graduate being rated _____

Please check below your rating of this graduate as a first-year teacher:

	SUPERIOR	ABOVE AVERAGE	AVERAGE	BELOW AVERAGE	INFERIOR
Personality					
Teaching Skill					
Knowledge of subject matter					
Motivation for teaching					
Cooperation					
Expression					
Voice					
Over-all rating as a teacher					

SUGGESTIONS OR COMMENTS:

_____
(Signature)

_____
(Official Position)

_____
(Address)

recommendation. The institution, possessing the follow-up information, will hesitate to recommend him (unless the graduate's rating should be considered invalid for one reason or another). Failing to receive good recommendations, the individual may not be able to secure another position and leave the profession. In this way, a poor teacher may be screened out of the profession.

Each segment of the educational community (professional associations, accrediting bodies, state departments of education, and educational institutions) works in cooperation with other segments that are involved in the improvement of the profession, and there are many areas in the field of education that can be improved. The classroom teachers, however, are really the key to the quality of any educational system.

Some students may be overwhelmed with the screening and retention procedures. They may feel that they could not possibly meet the requirements with so many criteria used. These students need not be discouraged, for if they are suited to the profession it will not be difficult for them to meet the requirements. The measures taken to insure quality are for the welfare of the student as well as society. If, in the judgment of professionally competent people, a student does not belong in the profession, it is to his advantage to discover it as early as possible.

SUMMARY

Although it is not possible to state categorically what specific traits, qualities, and characteristics a teacher needs for success, it is feasible to describe the broad qualifications which may increase the chances of success as a teacher. In spite of the fact that teachers are individuals, varying in personality, level of mental ability, and type of training, a general pattern of personal characteristics and training seems to underlie successful performance. Part of this pattern emerges from the personal characteristics of the teacher, and part of it emerges from the type of training he receives.

Seven characteristics come from within the individual: genuine motivation, above average mental ability, good moral character, acceptance of democratic ideals, good health, favorable personality traits, and effective voice and oral expression. Since teaching involves a life of service, the desire to help individuals and humanity should form a substantial part of the reason for becoming a teacher. Organizing, revising, evaluating, and participating in learning situations, and the ability to complete undergraduate and graduate training requirements, make above average mental ability essential in the teacher. Because he will influence the character development of his pupils either directly or indirectly a teacher must be of good moral character; similarly, since one of the functions of our educational system is to perpetuate our democratic society, the teacher's basic philosophy should incorporate democratic ideas and ideals. With all the demands that are made on his time and energy, a teacher's health must be good if he is to carry on his work effectively. In all of his activities, the teacher is dealing in human relationships; he should, therefore, have personality traits which permit him to get along with other people. Finally, since he must communicate effectively with other people, he should have a good voice and use correct grammar.

The type of training the individual receives influences the development of these characteristics. Training, in the form of formal schooling, provides him with further needed qualifications. Through a basic program of general education he acquires an understanding of himself, his relationships with others, and the nature of the world around him. Specialization in a subject or field that interests him, will provide him with the more intensive knowledge necessary to make his material meaningful to his pupils. His professional education program will help him to capitalize on his assets, overcome his weaknesses, and provide him with knowledge, understanding, and methods that will lead to successful performance as a teacher.

Schools take various measures to admit to their teacher education programs only the students who possess characteristics that are considered desirable in future teachers. Before they are admitted, their health, academic record, and personal qualifications are examined. If a candidate has a problem that might be eliminated while he is in training, he may be admitted to the program conditionally, pending correction of his deficiency. During training, the student must continue to exhibit desirable professional traits. He receives periodic evaluations during his academic work and during student teaching.

The legal requirements for certification by the state provide another way of screening candidates. The state may require the institution to certify that the individual has met all requirements, in addition to certification from a physician that the individual is in good health. Also, to provide further screening and to improve the qualifications of teachers, the state issues only a provisional certificate to the beginning teacher. Only after he has demonstrated satisfactory performance on the job, and after he has completed a specified amount of post-baccalaureate work, is he issued a permanent certificate.

An annual follow-up study of graduates by the institution not only helps the institution to determine the quality of its program but also provides information on the performance of graduates. If the performance of an individual is below average during his first teaching position, the institution may refuse to recommend him for subsequent teaching positions, and thus eliminate from the profession, individuals who are not suited for it.

Questions for discussion:

1. Describe the characteristics of the best teacher you ever had. Which characteristic stands out most in your mind?

2. Describe the characteristics of the worst teacher you ever had. Which characteristic stands out most in your mind?

3. Evaluate the statement, "Teachers are born, not made."

4. What would be your answer to a hiring official who asked you why you wish to become a teacher?

5. Analyze the curriculum of your teacher education program. Would you recommend any changes? Why?

6. Summarize the screening procedures used to improve the quality of teachers. Which do you think is most important?

For further reading:

American Council On Education, *College Teaching as a Career*. Washington, D.C.: American Council On Education, 1958.

Haskew, Laurence D., *This is Teaching*. Chicago: Scott, Foresman and Company, 1956.

Highet, Gilbert, *The Art of Teaching*. New York: Alfred A. Knopf Inc., 1954.

Holman, Mary V., *How It Feels To Be a Teacher*. New York: Columbia University, Teachers College, 1950.

National Education Association, *Teaching Career Fact Book*. Washington, D.C.: National Education Association of the United States, 1962.

Ryans, David G., *Characteristics of Teachers*. Washington, D.C.: American Council on Education, 1960.

U. S. Department of Health, Education, and Welfare, Office of Education, *Teaching As a Career*. Washington: U. S. Government Printing Office, 1963.

9

Opportunities and Benefits in the Teaching Profession: Elementary and Secondary Schools

History testifies that there has always been a need for more *good* teachers. Although the gap between the quantity and the quality of teachers has never been closed, the effort to close it has never been greater than in recent decades, even in the face of the acute teacher shortage which has existed for the last quarter-century. Standards and benefits, which make the profession attractive to more and more capable people have been raised. The thousands of people with substandard qualifications, who were hired to meet emergency situations, merely highlighted the need for upgrading all aspects of the profession. Today, even with the existing need for further progress, the opportunities and benefits in the teaching profession are more attractive than ever before.

SUPPLY AND DEMAND

The "population explosion" that occurred after World War II caused an increase in the demand for teachers. The higher birth rate during the war soon started to swell elementary school enrollment. Since the birth rate continued to grow, shortages of teachers and facilities de-

veloped, and soon became a serious problem. New records in enrollment were set every year following the end of the war. Since 1953 each
year has seen over a million more pupils in school than in the preceding
year. An unprecedented number of new teachers are needed to handle
this staggering enrollment, but there are not enough qualified teachers.

A 1953 survey revealed the plight of American education.[1] The
survey, documented by professional associations, showed the supply of
competent teachers diminishing rapidly. Thousands of unqualified
teachers were hired on an emergency basis, which resulted in "educational malnutrition" for the pupils. An extreme example of this situation was the seventh grade teacher who had only a fourth grade
education herself. In some areas, high school teachers who did not
have a college education were teaching on emergency certificates. In
1953, the shortage of qualified teachers was estimated to be 312,000.
Classrooms were overcrowded and in many metropolitan areas, double
sessions were needed to accommodate the bulging enrollment.

Furthermore, teachers were leaving the profession in great numbers.
Overworked and underpaid, they sought employment in better paying
occupations. Between 1940 and 1953, 500,000 teachers left their positions. In the fall of 1953, 200 new teachers in New York City did not
appear for duty on the opening day of school. They had, instead,
accepted higher paying positions in other fields.

One other factor contributed significantly to the teacher shortage.
With the bad conditions in education, fewer college and university
students chose to enter the field of education. In 1920 twenty-two
percent of all college students were enrolled in teacher education; in
1953 the percentage had dwindled to nine. The enrollment in teacher
education at New York University alone fell from 11,010 in 1949 to
7,237 in 1953. At the national level, the number decreased from 115,477
in 1950 to 85,801 in 1954.[2] Clearly a crisis had developed in the supply
of teachers. While pupil enrollment was rising sharply, the number of
teacher trainees was alarmingly low.

Although the number of teacher trainees has shown a steady rise
since 1954, the supply of qualified teachers has lagged far behind the
demand. More new teachers are needed not only to cover the increase
in enrollment, but also to replace retiring teachers, or teachers with
substandard preparation, to relieve overcrowded classrooms, and to
provide special instructional services. These needs have not yet been

---

[1] A Hearst newspaper survey, as reported in the *New York Journal-American*, April
4, 1954.

[2] *Teacher Supply and Demand in Public Schools, 1966*, National Education Association, Research Report 1966-R16, Table 2, p. 15.

met. The NEA for many years has been reporting an annual shortage of well qualified teachers of over 100,000. An estimated shortage of 278,970 teachers was reported by NEA for the school year 1968–69.[3]

Obviously emergency measures had to be taken to at least partially close the gap between supply and demand. During the 1950's, the critical condition of education was widely publicized by various communications media and professional associations. Former teachers were asked to return to the classroom to alleviate the shortage. In some cases, the retirement age was extended in order to retain experienced teachers. A national appeal was made to housewives who were college graduates, but had no professional training in education to consider teaching as a career. There were thousands of women in this category whose families were sufficiently grown up to permit their employment as teachers. Finally, failing to find any of these individuals, people with lesser qualifications were hired on an emergency basis.

These stop-gap measures placed a greater number of teachers in the classroom, but did not alleviate the shortage of *qualified* teachers. During the latter part of the 1950's, professional associations, and the public at large, made teaching a more attractive profession. The public, realizing the importance of having qualified teachers in the classroom, began to view the profession with increasing respect. At the same time, professional associations worked tirelessly to raise the qualifications for certification, and improve the benefits of the profession. Gradually, the number of individuals training to become teachers began to increase. This trend can be seen in the following figures.

Number of College Graduates Prepared To Teach, 1950–1968[4]

1950	115,477
1952	99,159
1954	85,801
1956	97,586
1958	114,411
1960	130,203
1962	142,343
1964	174,133
1966	204,918
1967	227,088
1968	243,442

[3]*Teacher Supply and Demand in Public Schools, 1968*, National Education Association, Research Report 1969-R4, Table 23, p. 50.

[4]*Ibid.*, extracted from Table 2, p. 14.

Within the relatively short time of one decade, 1954–64, the number of college graduates who were prepared to teach more than doubled, and continued to rise sharply after that. However, many of those people who are qualified to teach do not go into the profession. For example, during the decade 1955–65, only 70–75 percent of those annually prepared to teach accepted teaching positions; the number not entering the profession was higher at the secondary school level than at the elementary level.[5]

Paradoxically, although the shortage of teachers has been greater on the elementary level, far more college students prepared themselves for teaching in secondary schools. The shortage of elementary teachers was particularly acute during the post-World War II years, and continued to rise as the population increased. Only when this growth in population reached the secondary schools did their shortage become serious. However, the elementary school situation continued to be the graver of the two. A glance at the table below will show the wide discrepancy in the numbers prepared to teach in those two levels of schooling.

Number of College Graduates Prepared to Teach
in Elementary and Secondary Schools, 1950–1968[6]

Year	Elementary Teachers Prepared	Secondary Teachers Prepared
1950	28,587	86,890
1952	37,649	61,510
1954	36,885	48,916
1956	40,801	56,785
1958	45,318	69,093
1960	52,630	77,573
1962	57,854	84,489
1964	72,581	101,552
1966	77,703	122,208
1967	83,483	137,601
1968 (est.)	89,941	146,511

It is difficult to explain why more people prepare to become secondary teachers. The fact that the percentage of men training to become secondary teachers was three or four times higher than it was on the elementary level would be a major part of the explanation. Further-

---

[5] *Ibid.*, p. 21.
[6] *Ibid.*, extracted from Table 2, p. 14.

more, in the past, salaries were higher for secondary teachers and therefore attracted more candidates. In future years, the number of teachers prepared for each level may be more nearly equal, because of the trend toward a single salary schedule for both levels, and because it is now known that it is beneficial for elementary school children to be influenced by teachers of both sexes. Basing its estimates on recent trends, and applying its quality criterion, the NEA estimated a shortage of 193,200 elementary and 85,700 secondary teachers in 1968–69.[7] Because more individuals train to become secondary teachers, the shortage at that level has been relieved considerably. In 1968, a shortage of high school teachers still existed in the fields of mathematics, sciences, special education, vocational-technical education, women's physical and health education, and industrial arts.

Presently, opportunities are abundant in the teaching profession. In 1967, for the first time in the history of United States public education, the number of instructional personnel[8] in elementary and secondary schools exceeded two million, and the number is still growing. Although the shortage of teachers is most acute at the elementary level, opportunities are still plentiful in secondary school fields. Even in the fields of oversupply, positions are always open for candidates with above average qualifications. It should be remembered, too, that as late as 1967, there were 90,500 full time teachers who had not yet met the certification requirements of their states.[9] Many of these teachers will have to be replaced if they do not move toward certification.

In estimating the demand for classroom teachers in the immediate future, the United States Office of Education presents some interesting data. Their projection shows an annual increase in the demand for teachers from 1,910,000 in 1968 to 2,044,000 in 1977.[10] At the same time they predict a fluctuation in school population. A stabilization in the public school pupil population is anticipated between 1971 and 1975, after which another increase is expected; in private and parochial schools, the decline is expected to occur during 1969, and to remain relatively constant thereafter. Correlating the decline with the demand

---

[7]*Ibid.*, p. 5.

[8]Includes all instructional staff personnel such as librarians, counsellors, principals, supervisors, and psychologists. The actual number of teachers in 1967 was 1,854,700, of which 18,640 were part-time teachers.

[9]*Fall 1967 Statistics of Public Elementary and Secondary Day Schools*, U.S. Department of Health, Education, and Welfare, Office of Education (Washington, D.C.: U.S. Government Printing Office, 1968), p. 2.

[10]*Projections of Educational Statistics to 1977–78*, 1968 ed., U.S. Department of Health, Education, and Welfare, Office of Education (Washington, D.C.: U.S. Government Printing Office, 1969), extracted from Table 25, p. 51.

for teachers, means that fewer new teachers will be needed to care for increase in enrollment. However, it is predicted that a larger number of new teachers will be needed to take care of increased teacher turnover.[11]

FINANCIAL BENEFITS

Many teachers left the profession because they were overworked and underpaid. Many college students turned to studies in other fields for the same reason. The only possible remedy was to make the financial benefits in teaching more competitive with other occupations. Because of the teacher shortage, the profession was in a favorable bargaining position, and vigorously applied itself to the task of improving teachers' salaries.

Salaries

Historically, teachers' salaries have always been low. Even through the nineteenth century, teachers negotiated individually for their salaries which often included food and lodging. The school year was short, which forced teachers to sustain themselves with other occupations when it ended. The length of the school year varied from place to place, and wages varied with it.

Prior to 1800, the wages of a male teacher ranged from four to ten dollars a month. Female teachers usually earned from two to six dollars a month, with board usually included. Even by the middle of the nineteenth century wages had not increased greatly. In 1847, Horace Mann pointed out that in several states the salary of male teachers varied between $12 and $24 a month, while the salary of female teachers ranged from $4.75 to $8 a month. The following half-century saw considerable improvement in teachers' salaries. By 1910, the average salary for men amounted to $68.86 a month, compared to $53.40 a month for women. Throughout the years, salaries were much lower in rural areas than they were in the cities.[12]

Two things contributed to the stabilization and upgrading of salaries, particularly in rural areas. Toward the end of the nineteenth century states began to standardize the length of the school year to eight

---

[11]For detailed statistics, see *Ibid.*, Table 2, p. 10.

[12]Salary figures in this paragraph are from Paul Monroe, ed., *A Cyclopedia of Education*, Vol. V, (New York: The Macmillan Company, 1926), pp. 509-10.

months, which formed a basis for the equalization of salaries. Secondly, states began to establish minimum salaries for all public school teachers within their borders. The first of these laws was passed in West Virginia in 1882. Early in the twentieth century other states enacted similar laws. These laws provided for minimum salaries based on the quality of certificates held by individuals. Initially, rural teachers received the greatest benefit from this legislation, because their salaries lagged behind salaries of teachers in more populated areas. Rural teachers were now assured of at least, a specified minimum salary.

Although the length of the school year and minimum salaries had been standardized, increases in salaries were painfully slow. In 1917, the average salary of a teacher was $525. This rose to about $1,000 in 1920, $1440 in 1930, and $1470 in 1940. The next decade saw the average salary double, to approximately $3,000 in 1949, when the teacher shortage was developing in the United States.[13]

Before describing the current trends in teachers' salaries, the reader should realize that a teachers' salary scale, today, is expressed in terms of a *salary schedule*, which shows the minimum and maximum salary a teacher can earn. The salary schedule is based on the amount of experience and education a teacher possesses. Each state has a mandated salary schedule, which prescribes a minimum salary for all teachers and usually mandates regular increments until the teacher reaches the mandated maximum. The following schedule may be used as an illustration.

Year	Less than A.B.	A.B.	M.A.
1	$5,000	$5,200	$5,400
2	5,200	5,400	5,600
3	5,400	5,600	5,800
4	5,600	5,800	6,000
to	to	to	to
10	6,800	7,000	7,200

If this were a state-mandated schedule, all teachers with less than an A.B. degree would earn a minimum of $5,000 in their first year of teaching and receive an increment of $200 annually until, in their tenth year of teaching they reached the mandated maximum of $6,800. The individual with a bachelor's degree would begin $200 higher on

---

[13]Salary figures from *NEA Research Bulletin* (Washington, D.C.: National Education Association) 36, No. 1 (February, 1958), p. 5.

the scale than a person without the degree, while a master's degree would bring $200 more than the bachelor's degree.

Using this schedule the individual reaches the mandated maximum in the tenth year of teaching. In actual practice, the number of years before reaching the maximum salary fluctuates from state to state. The amount of the salaries also varies among the states, and there may be a greater variety of distinctions made in the amount of education possessed by the individual. For example, there may be separate scales for the following degrees of education:

> 60 semester hours of college work
> 90 semester hours of college work
> A.B. degree
> A.B., plus 15 semester hours
> A.B., plus 30 semester hours
> M.A. degree
> M.A., plus 15 semester hours
> M.A., plus 30 semester hours
> M.A., plus 60 semester hours
> Doctor's degree

Once a state has enacted a salary schedule, no teacher in the state may be paid *less* than the minimum specified. However, any local school district that wishes to, and can afford it, may have a higher salary schedule than the salary schedule enacted by the state. Assuming that the state minimum scale is $5,200–$7,000 for teachers with a bachelor's degree, a local district may establish its own salary schedule at $6,000–$9,000. This higher schedule may be offered to offset the higher cost of living in some areas, and to attract better qualified teachers. Usually there are more applicants in a district that offers a higher salary schedule.

In the past, distinctions were made between male and female teachers, with men earning higher salaries than women because they were more often the sole support of the family. Also in the past, secondary school teachers received higher salaries than elementary school teachers. Recently, however, women have justifiably won salary schedules equal to the schedules of men. An equalization of salaries has also occurred for the two levels of schooling, based on the principle of "equal pay for equal preparation". The prevalent practice today, is a single salary schedule which applies to both sexes and both levels of schooling.

An example of a detailed single salary schedule, adopted by a New York local school district appears on pages 264 and 265. An examination of this schedule shows that allowances are made for past teaching experience, for military service, and for varying degrees of education.

After 1949 the average teacher salary was about $3,000. Salaries continued to advance but more slowly than in other occupations. For example, in 1953-54 factory workers earned more than teachers. In that year, the average employee in manufacturing earned $4,039, compared with an average teacher's salary of $3,605. College graduates accepted positions with corporations at a starting salary higher than the average paid to teachers. Sincere, competent teachers left the profession in large numbers because they "couldn't afford to teach". Those teachers who remained in the profession worked at extra jobs, or had working wives, to support their families.

When parents finally realized that their children were receiving a substandard education because of the shortage of qualified teachers, they became more willing to pay higher taxes. Then, in 1957, when Russia launched Sputnik, Americans became thoroughly alarmed over the quality of our education. The attitude became one of "Something has to be done, and done fast!" One of the basic measures taken to attract competent teachers to the profession was to raise salaries to a level more competitive with other occupations.

National, state, and local professional organizations launched a campaign to upgrade the teaching profession. Television, radio, newspapers and periodicals brought the plight of teachers, and education in general, to every home. Information on teacher's salaries, the teacher shortage and the threat to a quality education, was disseminated to the members of the profession through journals and professional meetings. The combined efforts of these various agencies resulted in a general increase in salaries. In state-mandated schedules, the increases came more slowly and were relatively small. However, many local school districts increased substantially their salary schedules in order to attract better qualified teachers. In turn, other districts also raised their salaries as the competition for new teachers grew. During the latter part of the decade 1950-60, higher salary schedules were enacted and the trend continued into the next decade. Since 1955, teachers' salaries have increased at a higher percentage than the salaries of all other workers.

The average salary of teachers in the United States has risen from $4,520 in 1957-58[14] to $7,320 in 1967-68.[15] This represents a substantial

---

[14]*Ibid.*, p. 5.
[15]*Fall 1967 Statistics of Public Elementary and Secondary Day Schools, op. cit.*, p. 4.

1969–70 TEACHER SALARY SCHEDULE OF THE PATCHOGUE-MEDFORD
PUBLIC SCHOOL SYSTEM
241 South Ocean Avenue, Patchogue, N.Y. 11772

Step	Col. I No Deg.	Col. II BA	Col. III BA+15	Col. IV BA+30	Col. IV-A BA+45	Col. IV-B BA+60
1	6840	7200	7560	7920	8064	8208
2	7200	7560	7920	8280	8424	8568
3	7560	7920	8280	8640	8784	8928
4	7920	8280	8640	9000	9144	9288
5	8280	8640	9000	9360	9504	9648
6	8640	9000	9360	9720	9864	10008
7	9000	9360	9720	10080	10224	10368
8	9360	9720	10080	10440	10584	10728
9	9720	10080	10440	10800	10944	11088
10	10116	10476	10836	11196	11340	11484
11	10512	10872	11232	11592	11736	11880
12	10908	11268	11628	11988	12132	12276
13	11304	11664	12024	12384	12528	12672
14			12420	12780	12924	13068
15						

1. *Prior Experience Credit:* Full credit is given for the first eight years of prior teaching experience; half credit is given for prior experience in excess of eight years.
2. *Military Service Credit:* One step on the schedule is given for service up to eighteen months and two steps for service in excess of eighteen months in the following: U.S. Armed Forces; Peace Corps; National Teacher Corps.
3. *Vertical Movement From Step to Step:* Teachers who begin service in September will move to the following step the next September; teachers beginning service at times later than the beginning month of the school year will be moved to the next step on September 1 or January 1 following completion of 10 months of teaching service in this school system.
4. *Tenure Differential:* After the three-year probationary period and upon tenure appointment, a teacher's salary will be increased by $300.00 over that shown on this schedule. This differential will be added to the base salary of a tenure teacher each year thereafter.
5. *Longevity Differential:* Teachers who have remained in the service of this district for five years on the last step in their salary schedule column will receive a longevity differential of $300.00 the sixth year and each year thereafter.

increase in one decade. Yet, salaries are still far from the recent goal set by the NEA. At its annual meeting in 1968, NEA passed a resolution calling for a minimum salary of $10,500 for qualified degree teachers holding a B.A. degree with a maximum of at least $21,000 for experienced teachers who have earned a master's degree.[16]

Assuming that the present salary trends will parallel the trends in the past decade, the U.S. Office of Education has estimated that the

---

[16]National Education Association, *Today's Education,* 57, Number 7 (October, 1968), 83. This compares with the scale of $8,000–$16,000 that was recommended by NEA at its 1966 meeting.

1969–70 TEACHER SALARY SCHEDULE OF THE PATCHOGUE-MEDFORD
PUBLIC SCHOOL SYSTEM—*Cont.*
241 South Ocean Avenue, Patchogue, N.Y. 11772

Col. V MA	Col. VI MA+15	Col. VII MA+30	Col. VIII MA+45	Col. IX MA+60	Col. X Doct.
8280	8640	9000	9360	9720	10080
8676	9036	9396	9756	10116	10476
9072	9432	9792	10152	10512	10872
9468	9828	10188	10548	10908	11268
9864	10224	10584	10944	11304	11664
10260	10620	10980	11340	11700	12060
10656	11016	11376	11736	12096	12456
11052	11412	11772	12132	12492	12852
11448	11808	12168	12528	12888	13248
11844	12204	12564	12924	13284	13644
12240	12600	12960	13320	13680	14040
12636	12996	13356	13716	14076	14436
13032	13392	13752	14112	14472	14832
13428	13788	14148	14508	14868	15228
13824	14184	14544	14904	15264	15624

6. *Vertical Movement Below Step #12:* Continued salary progression below step
   #12 will take place only on the basis of annual assessment by administrative and
   supervisory personnel of adequacy of professional service as provided for in the
   New York State Teacher Salary Law of 1965.

7. *Horizontal Movement from Column to Column:* Teachers may move from one
   column to another on this schedule on the basis of university and/or local in-
   service courses which have received prior approval of the superintendent of
   schools; salary adjustments on the basis of training will be made only on the paydays which fall on October 15 and May 15 or the nearest paydays thereto.

8. *Columns III, IV, IV-A, IV-B:* These columns are attainable only after completion
   of the bachelor's degree; credits earned prior to date of awarding of the bachelor's
   degree will not be credited toward these columns.

9. *Columns VI, VII, VIII, IX:* These columns are attainable only after completion
   of the master's degree; credits earned prior to date of awarding of the master's
   degree will not be credited toward these columns.

---

average annual salary of instructional staff in public elementary and
secondary schools will increase by approximately $200 annually. Using
the value of the 1967–68 dollar as a basis, the Office of Education has
projected that the average annual salary of instructional staff will
increase from $7,835 in 1968–69 to $9,677 in 1977–78.[17]

Obviously teachers' salaries have become far more attractive and
competitive in recent years. Further increases will occur as lagging districts adopt more appropriate salary schedules. The supply and de-

---

[17]*Projections of Educational Statistics to 1977-78, op. cit.,* Table 41, p. 84.

mand for teachers will determine whether or not salaries continue to progress toward the goal set by the NEA. Although teachers' salaries in the past decades would have risen with other salaries in a prospering economy, it is doubtful that the increases would have been as substantial if a shortage of teachers had not existed. The law of supply and demand seems to have worked effectively in raising teachers' salaries.

Merit Raises Versus Automatic Increments

In recent years, there has been growing controversy over a question which may be expressed as follows: "Should raises be automatic, or should they be given on the basis of merit?" Usually, a teacher receives an automatic increment each year until he has reached the maximum on the salary schedule. However, some people feel that raises should be given only to those people who deserve them.

Those people who favor merit raises support their position with several arguments. They contend that in other occupations raises are given only to those people who merit them. They argue that to give teachers a raise on the basis of their completing a year's work only encourages mediocrity in their performance. The incentive to perform on a high level, or to improve performance, these critics claim, is gone. Moreover, it is said, the teachers who *do* an outstanding job receive no greater reward than those who do not.

Those people who oppose merit ratings point out that teaching is far different from other occupations since it deals with complex human beings. In other occupations it is relatively easy to evaluate the quality of performance: the sales chart shows the dollar volume performance of a group of salesmen; the output of assembly workers can be counted and inspected; or the products of craftsmen can be closely examined. In teaching, however, there is no valid method of evaluating the influences a teacher exerts on his pupils. It may be relatively easy to judge how well a teacher teaches his subject matter, by testing the achievement of his pupils. Yet, a teacher's influence goes beyond teaching subject matter; he helps pupils to build desirable habits, attitudes, ideals, and character. There is no reliable way to measure the degree to which a teacher has influenced his pupils in these important, intangible values. Sometimes, a teacher's influence on a pupil is not evident for many years. Sometimes pupils do not appreciate their teachers until a much later time. Therefore, it is almost impossible to measure all aspects of a teacher's influence. Even ratings on the basis of classroom visits would be subjective, and might place too much power in the hands of the supervisors. Moreover, a system of merit ratings might cause animosity between teachers and their supervisors, and might arouse jealousy among the teachers themselves. Finally, these critics claim that most teachers are conscientious, dedicated people who perform competently, and should receive regular increments. Teachers who are not competent should be dismissed and replaced.

Ideally, the idea that compensation based on merit is valid. However, there are too many intangibles in the teaching profession, to permit a valid implementation of the merit system. The majority of teachers, recognizing these difficulties, have opposed merit ratings. Professional associations have reacted in the same way, but are considering the possibility of devising a valid means of rating teacher-performance. The merit rating system has been used in some school systems but has been unsatisfactory. Some school systems have tried a compromise plan. Under this plan all teachers received increments in salary, with an additional increment for a few teachers who were judged outstanding. The same problems arose, using this plan. In view of all of these difficulties, plans for merit raises have not made much progress to date.

Retirement Benefits

Widespread retirement plans are a product of this century. Until the twentieth century, unless a teacher had saved his money scrupulously, he had no income after he retired. Since teachers' wages were low in the first place, it is unlikely that many teachers ever saved enough to assure themselves of a comfortable retirement.

By the end of the nineteenth century, retirement plans for teachers were adopted locally by cities and some towns, but there were no state retirement plans. The first state-wide retirement plan for teachers was adopted in 1896 in New Jersey. Today, every state has a retirement plan.

The changes in retirement plans during this century alone have been so frequent and so diverse that any attempt to describe them briefly would be confusing. Even now practices vary greatly among the states. Yet a 1964 summary[18] of retirement practices revealed the following trends:

1. Wider adoption of social security benefits for teachers
2. Survivor benefits, providing monthly payments to dependent survivors, if a teacher dies before retirement age

---

[18]"Retirement Statistics, 1964", National Education Association, Research Division, *NEA Research Bulletin,* 42, Number 4 (December, 1964), 99.

3. Lump-sum benefits to survivors, and a refund of the teacher's contributions
4. A fixed benefit formula for determining retirement benefits
5. An increase in contributions made by the teacher, with a consequent increase in benefits
6. A raising of the salary limit upon which contributions are based
7. The investment of retirement funds, to yield higher income for the fund

In 1964, a teacher's contribution to the retirement fund varied from 3 percent to 7 percent except in Delaware, where the state completely financed the pension plan.[19] Usually the teacher contributed between 5 percent and 6 percent of his salary. His contribution was matched with public funds, supplied by the state, or county, or local district, or a combination of these sources. In approximately half of the states, teachers were permitted to make additional contributions (unmatched by public funds) to build additional retirement benefits.

At age sixty-five the teacher usually became eligible for full retirement benefits, but recently the trend has been to permit retirement at age sixty. Normally, the states also specified a minimum number of years of service, ranging from 5 to 35. Some states provided for early retirement, frequently permitting retirement after an individual had accumulated thirty years of service.

If a teacher wished to continue teaching after he reached the retirement age, many states permitted him to do so for a limited number of years. For example, some states permitted voluntary retirement at the age of sixty or sixty-five. If, however, the teacher wished, he could continue to teach until the age of seventy, when retirement became compulsory. Other states authorized their local school boards to determine the compulsory retirement age in their school districts.

Most states now permit a teacher who retires early after serving a specified minimum number of years, to leave his contributions in the fund, and begin to receive a retirement income commensurate with his previous contributions at the age of sixty. Similar provisions are also made for teachers who leave one state to teach in another. Some states include the number of years of out-of-state service in their minimum retirement requirements but also require the teacher to

---

[19]In 1966, Delaware passed legislation permitting teachers to make a voluntary contribution to their pension fund, which would make them eligible to receive double the monthly benefits which were previously possible. *NEA Research Bulletin,* 44, Number 4 (December, 1966), 124.

make up back payments before becoming eligible for full retirement benefits.

Still another problem, physical or mental disability, faces many teachers. All states now make some provision for teachers who become totally disabled and are unable to perform their normal teaching duties. These teachers are eligible for disability retirement benefits after having taught a minimum number of years, usually specified as ten.

The greatest improvements in retirement benefits have occurred since the middle of the twentieth century. Further improvements are still necessary. The erosion of retirement benefits because of inflation needs the states' careful consideration. Future changes may bring about an equalization of benefits throughout the United States. This would offer benefits to those teachers who presently lack them, and also would permit teachers to change states without jeopardizing their benefits.

Social Security

In 1955, public school teachers became eligible for benefits under the United States Social Security Act. This act, first passed in 1935, has been amended periodically to extend its coverage and increase its benefits. The twelfth amendment of the act, made in 1967, extended its coverage to include the medical aid provided by Medicare.

Under the Social Security Act, an employee contributes a specified percentage of his earnings to a government fund which is matched by his employer. This percentage of salary has gradually risen, to defray the cost of providing additional benefits to an ever increasing number of people. The 1967 amendment provided for periodic increases in contributions over a twenty-year period. The contributions of the employee, matched by the employer, were scheduled according to the rates on the first $7,800 of yearly earnings on page 270.

The benefits under the Social Security Act include a retirement income which begins at age sixty-five with full payments, or at age sixty-two with reduced payments. Under certain conditions benefits are also paid to a spouse, and to children under eighteen. The act provides benefits if disability occurs, makes provision for payments to the family in case of death, and, under Medicare, makes payments for hospitalization and medical care. Supplementary medical coverage may be obtained after age sixty-five by contributing an additional four dollars a month, which the government matches.

Social Security Contribution Rate Schedule
For Employees and Employers (Each)[20]

Percent of Covered Earnings

Years	For Retirement, Survivors, and Disability Insurance	For Hospital Insurance	TOTAL
1968	3.8	0.6	4.4
1969–70	4.2	.6	4.8
1971–72	4.6	.6	5.2
1973–75	5.0	.65	5.65
1976–79	5.0	.7	5.7
1980–86	5.0	.8	5.8
1987 and after	5.0	.9	5.9

The retirement benefits outlined in the 1967 amendment, vary according to the amount of an individual's average yearly earnings. At age sixty-five, the individual may receive monthly payments ranging from $55 to $218. However, the maximum of $218 cannot be reached unless an individual has earned an average of $7,800 for a specified number of years. If an individual's spouse is also age sixty-five or over, the combined monthly retirement income may range from $82.50 to $323. Individuals who start their benefits at age 62 receive lesser amounts.

Presently, approximately three-fourths of the states have adopted social security coverage in various ways. In some states, all teachers are covered; in other states coverage is restricted to those districts that voted to come under its benefits. In some states, retirement plans include full amounts of coverage by both the state pension plan and social security; other states use formulas that combine the elements of both plans to determine the retirement income. There has been a growing tendency to provide teachers with the full benefits of both plans.

Sick Leave

In the past, and sometimes even today, a teacher was not paid for the days on which he was absent because of illness. Or, if he were paid

---

[20]U.S. Department of Health, Education, and Welfare, Social Security Administration, *Your Social Security* (Washington, D.C.: U.S. Government Printing Office, April, 1969), Table on p. 34.

at all, he would receive the difference between his pay and the cost of hiring a substitute for him. As a result of this policy, many teachers reported to the classroom while ill, because they could not afford deductions from their wages. This, of course, slowed their recovery, was bad for their morale, and undoubtedly affected their efficiency in the classroom.

City school systems were the first to provide sick leave benefits for teachers. This benefit is also largely a product of the twentieth century. At first, sick leave benefits were provided on an annual basis; if a teacher did not use his benefits in one year, they were lost to him. Eventually, in a few school systems, teachers were allowed to accumulate unused sick leave days, which would pay them for a longer period of time if they had an extended illness. For example, a school system may have allowed ten paid days of sick leave per year. Assuming the district had a cumulative sick leave plan, it may have specified that no more than thirty days of sick leave per year could be taken with pay, regardless of the number of days the teacher may have accumulated. This type of plan gave the teachers an incentive to "save up" their sick leave days and discouraged them from taking days off simply to use up the days they had accumulated during the year. It also provided the teacher with income when he had a prolonged period of illness.

A study made by the NEA in 1927–28 showed that 57.7 percent of the urban school systems made some provision for sick leave benefits, but only 6.9 percent of them had cumulative sick leave policies[21] During the following forty years these benefits steadily increased. In 1965–66 sick leave was provided in 97.6 percent of the school districts having an enrollment of over 300. The number of systems providing for cumulative sick leave had risen to 92 percent.[22] Sick leave benefits today are virtually universal in the public school system. The amount of days of sick leave with pay varies widely, ranging from two to ninety (and an unlimited number in some cases), with a median of 12.3 days. Cumulative sick leave had a range of five to two hundred (also unlimited in some cases), with a median of 69.2 days.[23]

In 1965–66, approximately three-fourths of the states made statutory provisions for sick leave. In most cases, the states provided for a minimum of ten days a year, while nineteen of the thirty-seven states permitted a cumulative sick leave of at least sixty days. In some of these

[21]Marsha A. Ream, "Sick Leave for Teachers," *NEA Journal,* National Education Association, 56, Number 8 (November, 1967), from table on p. 27.

[22]*Loc. cit.*

[23]*Ibid.,* pp. 26-27.

states, if a teacher moves from one system to another, he is permitted to transfer his accumulated sick leave with him.

Sabbatical Leaves

The term "sabbatical year" is derived from an ancient Israelite law under which the people were ordered to allow the land to rest every seventh year. When colleges and universities began permitting their personnel a year off from their teaching duties, they adopted this concept and allowed their professors to become eligible for a "sabbatical leave" every seventh year. The sabbatical leave permits the teacher to "renew" himself intellectually, physically, or emotionally, before returning to perform his duties. This practice became widespread in higher education, but made little headway in elementary and secondary schools until recently.

During this century, as educators gave more attention to improving instruction and the qualifications of teachers, the desirability of sabbatical leaves became more recognized. Many teachers who are anxious to continue their education, cannot spare the time while teaching; those teachers who do take additional courses, take them on a piece-meal basis in evening or summer schools. A sabbatical leave permits them to progress more rapidly toward an advanced degree. Similarly, since a teacher's physical or mental health may be the cause of the deterioration in his classroom performance, a leave of absence could result in the restoration of his health and save a good teacher for the profession. Some teachers may be interested in doing research, but do not have the time for it. Others may want to broaden their experiences through travel, or an exchange-teacher program. Sabbatical leaves allow for these possibilities and at the same time, benefits the school system and the pupils by the professional growth of the teachers.

Sabbatical leaves may add to instructional costs, because a teacher must be hired to replace the one who is on leave. This added cost, and the public's belief that a leave is only a "vacation" for the teacher, has delayed this type of benefit.

At present, the cost of sabbatical leaves is not as great as it first appears since teachers are not granted a full year's leave with full pay. The customary procedure permits leave for a full year with half-pay, or a half-year with full salary. Thus, in the more liberal districts which use this system only a half-year's pay is involved. In many of the less liberal districts, it costs the school districts little or no money when a teacher takes a sabbatical leave. In some areas, the teacher must pay the salary of the teacher who is hired as a substitute. Under this circumstance, the teacher on leave receives the difference between his salary and the substitute's salary. In other districts, the teacher may receive half-salary while he is on leave, but the amount he may receive is limited. For example, a teacher with a salary of $8,500 may be confronted with a ruling which states: "teachers on sabbatical leave may receive half-salary, but not more than $4,000". Therefore, the policies and salaries concerned in the subject of sabbatical vary greatly, and the cost of a teacher's sabbatical ranges from no cost to the district to a cost of half of the teacher's annual salary.

A teacher who is on sabbatical leave is *not* on a vacation. He must have a good reason for requesting a sabbatical leave, and his request must be approved by the board of education. His reason usually falls into one of two categories: further education, or restoration of health. In some areas, the law states that a sabbatical leave may be given "for any reason that the board may decide to be valid". However, a sabbatical leave is never granted for recreational or leisure purposes. When it is granted for educational purposes, the teacher obviously will be working as hard as he would work in his regular teaching position. Furthermore, he may be required to produce evidence of the progress he made during his sabbatical leave.

Many teachers do not apply for a sabbatical leave even though they are eligible for one because their income is reduced while on leave, unless they receive full pay for a half-year. If they receive half-salary, or if they receive the difference between their salary and the costs of employing a substitute, their financial position may be difficult, especially for those who are supporting a family. Therefore, although the benefit is available, they are not able to take advantage of it.

There is a distinct difference between a sabbatical leave and a "leave of absence". A teacher may apply for a leave of absence at any time, for any reason approved by the board of education. If granted, the teacher receives no salary during his leave of absence unlike the sabbatical leave, but his position is kept open to him until he returns. As an example, let us assume that a teacher is not eligible for a sabbatical leave, but has received a private or public grant to continue his education for a year. He may be granted a year's leave of absence by the school board. He will receive no salary from the school during that year, but he will be able to live on the financial grant he received from the government or from a private foundation. After the year of study, he can return to his former teaching position. While a teacher receives some salary during his sabbatical leave, he receives no salary at all while on a leave of absence.

Extracurricular Income

Occasionally, the classroom teacher may supplement his salary with the income he receives from participating in extracurricular activities. School policy, and the extent of his participation determines whether or not he receives compensation for the activities.

All teachers are expected to take charge of certain activities, such as homeroom programs, or student advisement. These are a part of their regular work load. However, if extracurricular activities are extremely time-consuming, the teacher may receive additional compensation for his work. For example, an appointment as an athletics or dramatics coach or moderator of a yearbook or school newspaper, entails a great deal of time and work. This type of appointment usually carries extra compensation with it.

In some instances, teachers have demanded extra compensation for lesser tasks, such as selling and collecting tickets at school events, cafeteria duty, or chaperoning dances. Many school districts have refused compensation, considering these tasks as a part of the teacher's duties. However, some school districts have adopted the policy of paying teachers an hourly rate for out-of-class activities, yet limiting the amount they can earn in this way.

Other Financial Benefits

Although individually they do not contribute greatly to the teacher's income, there are a few more benefits that add to his material welfare. School districts have begun to provide group life insurance for their teachers. Many districts now pay for courses in which teachers enroll to improve their qualifications as teachers. Some school districts now give from one to three years' credit for military experience, which places some of their teachers on a higher level in the salary schedule. Furthermore, an increasing number of school systems have established credit unions, which may offer a higher rate of interest on savings, and still permit borrowing at lower interest rates than are available through usual business channels.

INTANGIBLE BENEFITS

While the monetary aspects of teaching have improved, there are other benefits, not of a material nature, which also add to a teacher's peace of mind and morale. These intangible benefits partially compensate for the gap that still exists between teachers' salaries and the salaries in other professions.

Personal Fulfillment

If teachers were asked why they have remained in a profession which once had extremely poor working conditions, they would frequently reply that the personal satisfaction they received from helping pupils to grow and develop compensated for the working conditions. Many people want to communicate with others, to share knowledge with them, and to help them with their problems. For this type personality, teaching is an ideal profession. In it the teacher can find the expression and fulfillment of some of his life's purposes.

The teaching profession by its very nature helps its members to grow. Frequently teachers have a thirst for knowledge, and love to dwell in the world of ideas. The pursuit of learning, the continuous exchange of ideas, and the search for the new or unknown, continuously contribute to the teacher's development. This is another type of fulfillment the profession offers to those who are intellectually curious and alert.

In the past, then, although they could have earned more money in other occupations, many teachers remained in the profession because they found it personally satisfying and rewarding work. Today, with salaries higher, the teaching profession offers even more to its members, yet future teachers should not consider the improved financial benefits, the chief basis for their decision to teach.

Tenure

Most teachers today, are under tenure; that is, they are assured that they will continue in their positions if they perform competently. A teacher obtains tenure after passing a probationary period. During the probationary period, which usually lasts two or three years, the teacher is rated by his superiors. If his performance has satisfied their standards, then the teacher comes under tenure, and cannot be dismissed except for reasons which are stipulated by law. Tenure practices still vary among the states. Some states have annual tenure under which the teacher cannot be fired in the middle of the year, some have continuous tenure, and others have life tenure. Every state now has procedures for the protection of the teachers' jobs and for action that can be taken by school officials to dismiss incompetent teachers.

Prior to receiving tenure, teachers were never sure that they would be reappointed to their positions. A change in the political power of the school district sometimes resulted in a large-scale dismissal of teachers who were in the opposite political party. Often, personal friends of newly elected school board members were hired to replace competent teachers. Sometimes, without tenure teachers followed the demands and ideas of administrators simply because they were afraid that they would not be reappointed. In effect, teachers were dismissed and re-hired every year, and many teachers were not told until September that they were reappointed. This system, obviously, resulted in an abnormal turnover of teachers and lowered teacher morale.

The National Education Association favored the passage of tenure laws long before they were enacted. As early as 1885, it recommended that a special committee study the question, but the committee only gave a brief report on it two years later. In 1911, another committee was appointed to study the question; it also made several reports during succeeding years. In 1923, another committee, the Tenure Committee of One Hundred, was appointed, and issued annual reports from 1924 to 1928. At the same time, other local and state professional associations added their approval and prestige to securing tenure for teachers. Gradually, the general public began to accept the idea.

By 1946, tenure practices were becoming more common in the United States. In that year, the NEA Committee on Tenure and Academic Freedom explained why tenure for teachers would be beneficial. Their reasons, outlined below, demonstrated that it had benefits not only for teachers, but also for their students and society as a whole. The NEA committee gave the following reasons for tenure:

1. To maintain and improve the educational opportunities of children and youth.
2. To build in the teacher that confidence and freedom which comes with a sense of stability and security as a citizen in a free republic.
3. To protect teachers in preparing children and youth for loyal, effective participation in a democratically controlled society of free men cooperating for the common welfare.
4. To enrich community life by giving permanency and continuity to the service of the teacher.
5. To encourage boards of education to place the welfare of children above the selfish interests of those political or economic groups which may seek to dominate the schools.

6. To guarantee employment conditions, to provide a sense of security which will encourage teachers to attain the highest standards of professional competence.
7. To encourage the most promising young men and women to prepare for teaching as a life work, not as a steppingstone.
8. To set up definite, orderly procedures by which incompetent, unsatisfactory teachers may be dismissed.
9. To protect competent, satisfactory teachers from unjust dismissal.
10. To protect teachers in the exercise of their rights and duties as American citizens.[24]

In 1924, only eleven states had some form of legislation for tenure. This number had increased to 29 by 1942,[25] and 41 in 1955.[26] Today, practically all teachers are protected by some form of tenure.

Once a teacher passes his probationary period he comes under tenure, and can not be dismissed except for serious reasons. The legislation on these reasons varies among the states. However, some of the reasons that are most commonly mentioned are the following:

Immorality
Incompetence
Intemperance
Cruelty
Emotional or mental illness
Violation of school laws
Advocation of, or participation
in, subversive doctrines.

These are serious accusations to be made against a teacher, and would warrant dismissal if they were proven true.

If a teacher is charged with one or more of these offenses, he is notified by the school board. He can, on his request, have a hearing before the board in order to defend himself. Assuming the board still favors dismissal, the teacher usually has other channels of defense available to him. He may first appeal his case to the state superintendent of public instruction, who must, then, arrange a hearing for him.

---

[24]National Education Association, Committee on Tenure and Academic Freedom, *Teacher Tenure: Analysis and Appraisal* (Washington, D.C.: the Association, 1947), pp. 6-7.

[25]Figures for 1924 and 1942 are from William C. Reavis and Charles H. Judd, *The Teacher and Educational Administration* (Boston: Houghton Mifflin Company, 1942), pp. 281-282.

[26]Percy E. Burrup, *The Teacher and the Public School System* (New York: Harper & Row, Publishers, 1967), p. 365.

Finally, if the teacher still is not satisfied with the decision, he may take his case to court. Although this sequence of appeals may vary from state to state, the teacher can protect himself against unfounded or unjust charges.

Under certain conditions a teacher, under tenure, may lose his position through no fault of his own. A distinction is made between the *dismissal* and the *suspension* of a teacher. A teacher may be *suspended* because of a decrease in pupil enrollment, or a consolidation of schools, either of which may cause a surplus of teachers in certain localities. Although there has been a national surge in enrollment for the past two decades, some sections of the country have experienced a steady decline in pupil population because of the exodus of families to more economically attractive areas. Furthermore, the consolidation of school districts has sometimes produced a surplus of personnel, although usually they have been absorbed by the larger districts that have been formed. In any event, if a surplus of teachers occurs in a district, they may be suspended from their positions. Seniority and efficiency ratings are the usual bases for determining suspension or retainment. When a vacancy later occurs in the district, the suspended teacher is given priority over a new applicant in filling the position.

Although tenure has the advantages that were listed by the 1946 NEA Committee on Tenure and Academic freedom, there are some educators who still point to its disadvantages or possible dangers. It protects, they claim, incompetent teachers; teachers who under tenure become satisfied with a mediocre level of performance, and do not extend themselves. Because it is legally binding, some boards of education avoid granting tenure to many good teachers about whom they have even slight reservations. Although tenure practices certainly are not perfect, their advantages outweigh their disadvantages. With the recent emphasis on improving the quality of teachers, and with the more thorough screening of candidates during their training and their probationary period of teaching, it is unlikely that many undeserving teachers will receive tenure. Even at the present time, anyone who has had extensive contact with teachers will affirm that, as a group, they are dedicated, conscientious people.

Steady Employment

The teacher is relatively assured of continuous employment. Tenure provides one aspect of this employment security. There is, however, another aspect of assurance: a teacher's position does not depend on business cycles. In other occupations, because of fluctuations in business, there may be temporary or permanent dismissals of personnel. The teaching profession is not dependent on these fluctuations. Whether the economic picture is cheerful or bleak, there will always be children in school, and, as long as there are, teachers must be retained to teach them. Although the birth rate has now begun to decline, there is no foreseeable drastic decline in school population which would necessitate the dismissal of a large number of teachers. Teaching provides a unique security of employment, because people are unwilling to curtail their children's education, even though they are willing to do without other things if necessary.

Recesses

One of the intangible benefits of teaching which is spoken of, and often joked about, by the lay public are the vacations a teacher receives. These comments are usually supplemented with references to "twelve months' pay for ten months' work".

However, a teacher's contract is for ten months, and he is paid for ten months' work. If he were to contract for twelve months' work, he would naturally receive a higher salary which would reflect the additional time spent in the classroom. Consequently, he does not receive compensation for doing nothing, as the uninformed maintain. Moreover, holiday vacations are an accepted part of the school calendar, and these recesses are take into consideration when salary scales are drawn up.

Nevertheless, a teacher does have more frequent and longer recesses than people in other occupations. As we mentioned in Chapter VIII, most teachers use this "time off" to catch up on their clerical duties and studies, and most new teachers spend their summers in colleges and universities trying to improve their qualifications. However, if they wish to do so, they can occasionally make a recreation period of one of these recesses. This opportunity is not present in most other occupations.

Prestige of the Profession

Finally, the prospective teacher can take pride in the fact that today's teacher is a more respected figure than ever before. Gone are the days of "those who can, do; those who cannot, teach". Today, everyone considers education an important formative force in shaping our society. Every effort is now made to get the right type of persons into the profession, and to exclude those who are unsuited for it. Because the educational qualifications for teaching are more demanding than ever, a new attitude toward the teacher is taking shape, an attitude of increased respect and prestige. This is another compensation offered by the profession.

OPPORTUNITIES FOR ADVANCEMENT

Most teachers remain in the classroom during their entire professional lives, because they enjoy teaching and being with children. Some teachers, however, have the desire, opportunity, and ability to reach administrative positions. For the best qualified of these teachers, there are possibilities for advancement.

After a teacher has taught a few years and demonstrated his worth, he may be appointed a department head. As a department head, he is responsible for the quality of staff and instruction within the department. His duties include formulating policy, making up a budget, interviewing candidates for teaching positions, scheduling classes for teachers, conducting departmental meetings, revising syllabi, submitting reports, and other clerical duties. In addition to these activities, he carries either a partial or a full teaching load.

Another possibility for advancement is an appointment as a supervisor within the school system. There may be supervisors for elementary or secondary instruction, for academic areas, for commercial education, or for vocational or special education. The number of supervisors, and their areas of responsibility, depend upon the size of the school system in which they are employed. They are responsible for improving instruction in their particular field, and may correlate the instructional activities of several school buildings within the district.

Each school building has a principal, who is responsible for the smooth operation of activities in his building. His authority extends over all of these activities, and over the personnel involved in them. He provides the leadership for the school, setting its tone, and determining the standards for teachers, pupils, and other personnel. Since he has frequent contact with parents and other members of the community and business, he must be skilled in personal relationships. The particular duties of a principal are too numerous to describe. He is responsible for faculty, students, building facilities, discipline, in-service training of teachers, scheduling of classes, and extracurricular activities, among other things. Naturally, he should have an adequate staff to help with these activities, and although it is necessary for him to delegate some authority, he bears the ultimate responsibility for what transpires in his school building.

These supervisory positions are the most numerous forms of advancement. Beyond them, some individuals may aspire to become superintendents of schools, on the district or the county level. At the state and federal levels, there are many opportunities for supervisory or executive positions with state departments of education, and with the United States Office of Education.

There are, then, many opportunities for advancement in the teaching profession. Most of them require the individual to have some experience in classroom teaching, and for many of them it is necessary to meet additional educational requirements in the field of supervision. Very often, the decision to leave the classroom is a difficult one for a person who enjoys teaching. Many administrators remark, "My heart is still in the classroom".

SUMMARY

While there has always been a shortage of excellent teachers, the past two decades have experienced an unprecedented gap between the supply of and demand for qualified teachers. Because of the increase in the birth rate after World War II, the situation became especially acute during the 1950's. Fewer college students were training to become teachers at a time when enrollment rose rapidly. It became necessary to hire thousands of unqualified teachers on an emergency basis. Education associations became alarmed, and took measures to make the teaching profession more attractive to qualified people by raising the standards for certification and by increasing salaries. Since 1955, the number of teacher trainees has increased annually. However, there still is an annual shortage of over 100,000 teachers, since additional new teachers are needed not only to take care of increased enrollment, but also to replace unqualified teachers and provide needed additional services. The shortage of qualified teachers has been greatest at the elementary level. In secondary schools, although a shortage still exists, there is an oversupply of teachers of certain subjects.

The improvement of the financial benefits of teaching helped to make teaching more attractive to more people. Historically, teacher's salaries have been low, and have not competed with salaries in other occupations. In 1953–54 the average teacher's salary was lower than the salary earned by factory workers. Efforts to improve salaries have resulted in raising the average from $3,605 in 1953–54 to $7,835 in 1968–69. However, this is still far from the goal set by the NEA in 1968, which calls for a minimum salary of $10,500 for beginning teachers with a bachelor's degree, and a maximum of $21,000 for those with experience and a master's degree.

Each school district has a salary schedule which provides for years of experience and the amount of education a teacher has. The schedule specifies the minimum and maximum salaries that may be received, and raises are automatic after the teacher meets the requirements for advancement. There have been objections to automatic raises. Some people feel that increments should be granted on the basis of merit alone.

Other financial benefits have also been improved in the profession. Retirement funds have been established for teachers, in which the teacher ordinarily contributes 5 percent or 6 percent of his salary, which is then matched with public funds. Ordinarily, the teacher may retire at the age of sixty-five, but some states provide for early retirement after thirty years of service, regardless of teacher's age. All states also provide for disability retirement benefits. After 1955, the majority of the states combined their retirement plans in various ways with the benefits of Social Security. In recent years, most states have also liberalized their policies of sick leave and sabbatical leave. Some of the other financial benefits in teaching are: extra pay for extracurricular activities; group life insurance provisions; payment for courses taken to improve qualifications of teachers; credit on the salary schedule for military experience; and, savings through credit unions.

Besides the financial benefits, there are numerous intangible rewards. The greatest of these benefits is the personal satisfaction received from helping and watching pupils grow and develop. At the same time, the teacher has the opportunity for personal development through a lifetime of study, discussion, and interchange of ideas. The profession offers longer holiday recesses, and a summer vacation of two months. Although most teachers use these periods to work and to study, they can occasionally use one of them for recreational purposes. Today, most teachers are under some form of tenure, and, after passing a probationary period, can not be dismissed except for serious reasons. Adding to the stability of their employment is their independence from the business fluctuations that affect other occupations. A final intangible benefit is the increasing respect and prestige given to members of the profession.

Most teachers find their work so interesting and satisfying that they remain in the classroom for their entire career. However, there are many who are inclined toward administrative work. For these people there are opportunities to advance to positions such as department head, supervisor, principal, or superintendent. Further possibilities for advancement exist at the state and national level, working for state departments of education or for the United States Office of Education. Advancement to any of these administrative positions requires executive ability, and usually, additional schooling in programs of administration.

Questions for discussion:

1. Compare the responsibilities of teachers with the responsibilities of lawyers or doctors.
2. Account for the rapid rise in the supply of new teachers after 1954.
3. Do you think that the salary goal set by NEA is realistic? Why?
4. How do you feel about merit raises for teachers?
5. Discuss the advantages and disadvantages of tenure for teachers.
6. In your opinion, what is the greatest advantage offered by the teaching profession? The greatest disadvantage?

For further reading:

Abraham, Willard, *A Handbook for the New Teacher*. New York: Holt, Rinehart & Winston, Inc., 1960.

Abraham, Willard, *A Time for Teaching*. New York: Harper & Row Publishers, 1964.

National Commission on Teacher Education and Professional Standards, *New Horizons for the Teaching Profession*. Washington, D.C.: National Education Association, 1961.

National Education Association, *Teaching Career Fact Book*. Washington, D.C.: National Education Association, 1964.

National Education Association, annual research reports, *Teacher Supply and Demand in Public Schools*. Research Division, National Education Association.

Stinnett, T. M., *The Profession of Teaching*. Washington, D.C.: The Center for Applied Research in Education, Inc., 1962.

U. S. Office of Education, *Teaching As a Career*. Washington, D.C.: U. S. Government Printing Office, 1963.

U. S. Office of Education, *Teaching Opportunities*. Washington, D.C.: U. S. Government Printing Office, 1964.

10

Opportunities and Benefits in the Teaching Profession: Colleges and Universities

Many persons whose personalities and motivations are unsuited to working with elementary and secondary school pupils, might function effectively and happily in higher education. There are many opportunities for them because college and university enrollment has increased at a rapid rate, creating a shortage of qualified professors. Just as in the case of elementary and secondary school teaching, there have been efforts to make college teaching more attractive and, therefore, ease the shortage of teachers. To a large degree, these efforts have been successful.

SUPPLY AND DEMAND

Although many post-high school programs are classified as "higher education", this discussion will concern only degree-granting institutions of higher learning. This category includes two-year junior and community colleges, four-year colleges, and universities and professional schools. For convenience, only the term "college" will be used throughout this chapter.

The population boom that occurred after World War II also affected college enrollment, although its influence was not felt until the 1950's, when the "war babies" reached college age. From the mid-1950's on, college enrollment has shown a substantial and steady annual increase. In four-year colleges, enrollment has risen from 2,678,211 in 1957 to 5,272,000 in 1967, with a projected enrollment of 7,825,000 by 1977.[1] The rise has been even more spectacular in two-year colleges. Enrollment in these institutions totalled 369,162 in 1957, and rose to 1,075,000 in 1967, with a projected enrollment of 1,859,000 in 1977.[2] If these projected figures materialize, four-year college enrollment during the period 1957–77 will have increased by almost 300 percent. The enrollment in two-year colleges will have increased by approximately 500 percent.

The increase in population is only one factor contributing to the spurt in college enrollment. Another factor is the increase in the percentage of college-age people choosing to go to college. In 1900 of the 18–21 age group, only 4 percent attended college. This percentage now exceeds 40 percent, and there are some predictions that it will soon reach 50 percent. The increase is undoubtedly due to the increased income of the average family and to the many forms of financial aid now available to students. Today, almost any diligent, capable student can discover the means to obtain a college education.

A corresponding increase in the number of college personnel was needed to care for rising enrollment, but difficulties arose. College teaching which demanded higher educational qualifications than teaching at the lower levels of schooling, did not receive adequate pay. Consequently, people with advanced degrees entered other occupations that were financially more rewarding. As enrollment increased, it was necessary to hire college teachers who possessed minimal qualifications. This situation obviously caused great concern over the future quality of college education. There was a definite need for more people with a doctorate degree to enter college teaching.

In 1955, the Ford Foundation began to provide grants to private institutions for the improvement of faculty salaries. This step and the 1957 report of the President's Committee on Education Beyond the High School, highlighted the critical need for raising faculty salaries in order to attract the best qualified persons to the profession. Furthermore the launching of Sputnik in 1957 caused everyone to think in terms of improving our educational system at all levels. The combined efforts of all agencies, including the important work of the professional

---

[1]*Projections of Educational Statistics to 1977-78*, 1968 Edition, U.S. Office of Education (Washington: U.S. Government Printing Office, 1969), extracted from Table 9, p. 17.

[2]*Ibid.*, from Table 10, p. 18.

associations, helped to raise the economic status of college faculties. The improved economic status, in turn, made college teaching more attractive to more people, and therefore, increased the supply of college teachers.

The United States Office of Education has estimated that the total full-time staff and the full-time equivalent instructional staff in colleges amounted to 224,000 in 1957–58, rose to 407,000 in 1967–68, and may reach 572,000 in 1977–78.[3] These figures do not include the additional staff members engaged in administration, services, and research, which have grown from 50,000, in 1957–58 to 116,000 in 1967–68 and may reach 158,000 in 1977–78. The demand for college teachers and other personnel, therefore, is expected to continue to increase in the immediate future. The United States Office of Education has estimated that, to care for increased enrollment and replace those teachers leaving the profession, 211,000 additional teachers will be needed between 1968–73, and another 243,000 new teachers will be in demand during the period 1973–78.[4]

Since the doctorate is the ideally expected educational level for people who teach in college, one way to judge the supply of qualified college teachers is through the number of doctorates that have been awarded annually. Considering the demand for new college teachers with a doctorate, the supply has been sparse. For example, the demand for new teachers in 1966–67 was placed at 48,000, but there were only 18,800 doctorates awarded in that year. The situation is worsened when one considers ". . . that probably not many more than half of those receiving doctorates go into college and university teaching . . ."[5] By the end of the 1950's, the percentage of new teachers with a doctorate degree had declined from 31.4 to 23.8, although the number of doctorates awarded increased annually. Because of this, it became necessary for colleges to hire more new teachers who often did not even possess a master's degree.[6] Clearly, the concern about the quality of higher education was justified.

During the 1960's, the trend began to reverse itself. The percentage of new teachers with doctorates increased slowly, while the percentage of new teachers without a master's degree declined sharply. This trend probably will continue into the future. The increase in the number of

---

[3]*Ibid.*, from Table 35, p. 62.

[4]*Ibid.*, Table 36, p. 63.

[5]Henry C. Herge, *The College Teacher* (New York: The Center For Applied Research in Education, Inc., 1965), p. 12.

[6]In 1957, almost twenty-five percent were in this category.

doctorates, compared with the demand for new college teachers, can be seen in the following estimated figures.[7]

Year	Number of doctor's degrees	Demand for new college teachers
1967–68	22,200	48,000
1968–69	25,100	47,000
1969–70	26,500	32,000
1970–71	27,000	40,000
1971–72	29,200	45,000
1972–73	34,900	48,000
1973–74	38,900	51,000
1974–75	39,300	49,000
1975–76	40,600	49,000
1976–77	42,000	48,000
1977–78	43,900	46,000

According to these figures the gap between the supply and demand of college teachers should diminish. However, a high percentage of those people with doctorates do not go into teaching. Many of them, of course, never had an interest in teaching. Of those who were interested, a substantial number found research work for the government, or for industry, more attractive. The problem of supplying competent college teachers is further complicated by government grants, which enable many excellent, experienced college teachers to do research work and, therefore, limits their availability for teaching assignments.

There has been and will be a great demand for college teachers who hold a doctorate degree. Recruiters in higher education, industry, and government compete fiercely for their services.

> Thus it may be seen that the outside world calls to members and prospective members of the teaching fraternity and lures them away. For the person considering college teaching, the advantage in this situation is obvious: teachers, particularly in science and engineering, are at a premium. It is a seller's market, so to speak, and there is every reason to believe it will remain one.[8]

The competition for the services of the new doctor do not end when he accepts a teaching position. Depending upon his field and compe-

[7]*Projections of Educational Statistics to 1977-78, op cit.*, from Table 18, p. 31, and Table 36, p. 63.

[8]Robert M. Friedberg and Gene R. Hawes, *Careers in College Teaching* (New York: Henry Z. Walck, Inc., 1965), p. 19.

tence, he may be lured away to other institutions, or other types of work. In the past, institutions vied for the services of an individual subtly, or covertly. Today they often do so openly, and sometimes brazenly.

SPECIAL QUALIFICATIONS FOR COLLEGE TEACHING

The general qualifications needed by teachers, outlined in a previous chapter, apply to college teachers. While teachers should possess above average intelligence, a candidate for college teaching should possess *superior* intelligence for a number of reasons. First, the educational training needed by a college teacher is more rigorous and more intellectually demanding than the program of training for elementary or secondary teachers. The college teacher should be capable of completing the work necessary for a doctor's degree. Without this degree, or its equivalent, he will be handicapped throughout his teaching career. Usually, unless he has superior intelligence, he will be incapable of completing the requirements for a doctorate. Secondly, as a college teacher he will be dealing with pupils whose intellectual capacity ranges from "above average" to "superior", or even "near genius". Unless the teacher has superior intelligence, he cannot guide, stimulate, or even cope with minds that exceed his own capacity. Third, the average I.Q. of doctoral candidates in arts and sciences programs is as high as the average I.Q. possessed by students in medical and law schools. Consequently, the individual who is considering college teaching should carefully assess his intellectual capacity.

The college teacher also should have a broad background in general education. Unfortunately, his need for courses in professional education has been largely neglected. For all practical purposes, an individual's formal general education ceases when he receives his bachelor's degree. During his undergraduate program, he began a small degree of specialization by choosing a "major field." He next enrolls in a master's program[9] in a graduate school, where he investigates more intensively the major field he has chosen. Depending on his field of study, and the requirements of the graduate school, he may or may not be required to write a thesis, and pass an examination in a modern foreign language. Following this he enrolls in a doctoral program, where he

---

[9]Some graduate schools by-pass the master's degree, so that the student moves from his bachelor's degree to the doctor's degree. The disadvantage of this plan would be that if the individual is unable to finish his work for the doctorate he is left with the bachelor's degree as his highest degree.

specializes even more within his general field of specialization. In other words, as he advances in his work he follows an ever-narrowing field, in which he eventually becomes a specialist. Usually early in the doctoral program, the candidate is given a qualifying examination, to determine whether or not he should be permitted to continue toward the degree. The Ph. D. candidate often must meet the following requirements: passing an examination in one or two modern foreign languages, and writing an acceptable dissertation on an original topic which has been approved by appropriate university personnel. The requirements for other doctoral degrees may parallel those of the Ph. D., or there may be some modification in the language and dissertation requirements.

Assuming that the student has attended school full-time, he should be able to obtain his master's degree in one year. The doctoral degree frequently requires two years of work to complete the course work, language requirements, and comprehensive examinations. However, the individual still must complete his dissertation. Some individuals can finish it in a year or two; some take several years, while other never complete it. These people who have not completed their dissertations have been designated as A.B.D.,'s, *all but dissertation* in meeting requirements for the doctorate.

Nothing has yet been mentioned about professional education courses as part of the training of a college teacher. In the past, these courses were not required. The individual had little help in facing the pedagogical problems he found in the classroom. Traditionally, it was assumed that the intensive preparation he received in his specialty was sufficient training for college teaching. Many students served as graduate assistants and taught lower level courses, an experience which was often painful to teacher and students alike. Today, in addition to this type of experience, some universities conduct seminars on the problems and procedures in college teaching. Some graduate schools even offer professional education courses that are oriented toward college teaching. On the whole, however, little has been done to improve the teaching ability of college teachers.

The doctorate degree usually requires seven years of formal higher education, in addition to the time the candidate spends on a dissertation. Many individuals who cannot afford to attend school on a full-time basis, accept a college post after completing their master's work, and then work on the doctorate requirements on a part-time basis. These "part-timers" must split their time and energy between a full-time teaching position, family problems, and the part-time graduate courses they are taking. There are bound to be many frustrations along the way, so that, in a sense, obtaining a doctorate is as much a test of perseverance and emotional stability as it is of intelligence.

RANKS AND PROMOTION

Full-time college faculty members are appointed to one of four ranks: instructor, assistant professor, associate professor, or professor. The rank of lecturer designates teachers who have been appointed to teach on a part-time basis. Lecturers are not entitled to the full rights and privileges enjoyed by the other members of the faculty. The requirements for each rank vary somewhat from institution to institution, but the following description is representative of the major considerations in ranking college teachers.

Instructor is the rank of the beginning college teacher, or one who has had some teaching experience in another college. He must have a master's degree in the field he expects to teach.

The appointment usually lasts from three to five years. It is a probationary period, during which the individual must prove his worth to the college. During this time he is expected to offer evidence that he is an effective teacher, that he interacts well with students and other college personnel, and that he is continuing his scholarly development. If he does not have his doctor's degree, he is expected to progress toward its attainment. Further evidence of scholarly development may be presented in the form of research and/or scholarly publication.

The instructor receives a contract on an annual basis. Should he *not* show promise of professional development, his services can be terminated at the end of any year. If he *does* meet the expectations of the college, he probably will be appointed to the rank of assistant professor at the end of the three-to-five-year period. Sometimes, if the individual shows unusual progress and promise, for example, the completion of his doctorate work, he may be promoted to assistant professor at the end of two or three years.

Assistant professors are people who have shown themselves capable of teaching and further intellectual growth. Although practice varies, they may be required to serve as assistant professors from three to five years. During that time they are expected to show further improvement in all areas of their professional development. Usually, they must have a doctorate before they are eligible for promotion. Some institutions may require some degree of research and publication before advancement to associate professor. It is presumed that an individual will have continued to improve as a teacher and counsellor of students and will have made contributions to the college and the community at large.

It is conceivable that an individual may perform effectively in the rank of assistant professor, but may not meet the requirements for an associate professor. In this case, he may remain an assistant professor as long as he remains at the institution. This condition can prevail in colleges that arbitrarily require a doctorate before advancing to associate professor. An A.B.D., under these circumstances, would not be eligible for promotion even though he may have met all of the other requirements for the appointment of associate professor.

Associate professors may be required to serve from three to five years as associate professors, before they are promoted to professors. If an individual has not yet received his doctorate, he must now do so. He must meet the same requirements he met as an assistant professor. However, his teaching ability and contributions to the college must be even greater than before. His teaching must be excellent. His professional growth must include activities such as original research, publication of books or articles in professional journals, and the pursuit of post-doctoral studies. He must show initiative and ability in helping to solve the college's educational and administrative problems.

The rank of associate professor may also be a terminal rank. Many individuals spend the rest of their teaching career as associate professors because they, in the judgment of those who make appointments, never fully meet the qualifications for the rank of professor.

Professors are theoretically, and ideally, fully developed professional persons, who still strive for self-improvement. They have a thorough knowledge of their field and are skilled in communicating with their students. Their relationships with faculty and administration assume a leadership quality, and they are *involved* in the internal problems of the college. They engage in research because they are inquisitive, not because the colleges requires it, and they publish for the same reason. As their talents and time permit, they are active in professional and civic organizations. In other words, they meet the high expectations of people in a position of leadership.

The achievement of a professorship is a well-earned honor. The individual, by this time, has passed through seven years of formal higher education, and the time it takes to do an acceptable dissertation. After beginning his college teaching, it still takes him from twelve to fifteen years of dedicated service and self-improvement to reach the rank of professor.

A *Lecturer* is a part-time college teacher who usually does not have faculty benefits and privileges. He may be hired for a variety of reasons. For example, a college which may not have a full-time faculty member who is qualified to teach a particular course may hire him to teach that one course. Or, a part-time teacher may be hired to handle the overflow of students in a particular subject. Often, authorities in particular fields are invited by the college to give lectures in their specialties. The qualifications among lecturers vary. Although they are not assigned a faculty rank, some lecturers are so well qualified that they would meet the requirements for the rank of professor. Others have the minimal qualifications of an instructor.

Flexibility in Ranking

The qualifications used as criteria in ranking college teachers vary with the institution. Some institutions use higher standards than others. Conceivably, a teacher might qualify as an associate professor in one college, but only as an assistant professor in another.

Within an institution, there is usually some flexibility in ranking teachers. The qualifications of no two individuals are alike. Consequently, the criteria can not be applied arbitrarily. To care for the exceptions, some institutions may waive a requirement by permitting the substitution of its equivalent.

If a new teacher is needed badly, the college may offer him a rank higher than he would normally receive. Or, if the college is in danger of losing a valuable person, it may promote him before he has met the stated experience required for promotion. Some colleges compete with others by offering the individual a higher rank than he holds in his present position. Although these practices are undoubtedly necessary in a competitive market, it adversely affects the morale of faculty members who received their promotions through normal procedures.

FACULTY LOAD

The college teacher signs a contract which makes his services available from September 1 through June 30. His duties, however, usually coincide with the college year, which begins about the middle of

September, and ends around the first week in June. His contract specifies that he will carry a "full load" during that time.

In discussing what constitutes a "full load", it is necessary to distinguish between a full load of classroom teaching, and other duties.
Although practice still varies, twelve semester hours of teaching are
considered a full load, or a normal load, of teaching. The individual
with a full load is expected to teach the equivalent of four three-
semester-hour course each semester. In addition to these classes he
may be expected to counsel students, moderate a club, or serve on
various committees. As he gains more experience, these extracurricular
assignments become heavier. Sometimes the teacher must spend more
hours with them than with classroom teaching. He also is expected to
attend all departmental, faculty, and other all-college meetings. From
time to time, he participates in conventions or professional meetings.

Each college teacher is *expected* to spend a reasonable amount of
time with extracurricular duties. However, if they become overwhelming, his teaching load can be reduced to nine or six semester hours.
For example, departmental chairmen who have many duties, or teachers of graduate courses who are supervising the writing of a number
of dissertations, usually have reduced teaching loads.

There remains the problem of research and publication. Throughout the college community it is believed that research and publication
are necessary for the professional development of an individual. Large
colleges and universities hold this belief more firmly than small colleges. In larger institutions, the "publish or perish" philosophy causes
the output of many publications, some good, some mediocre. Smaller
colleges, although their attitude may be caused by the lack of research
facilities, place greater stress on the quality of teaching than on productive research. However, even though the smaller colleges do not
require publishing, they "like to see" it. The college teacher, therefore,
feels some pressure to publish, no matter where he is teaching. This
produces an undesirable type of motivation for research. Although
true research adds to knowledge, many college teachers grasp at the
thinnest of research lines, just to produce something that will assure
their survival or promotion. It might be more beneficial if institutions
gave research assignments, with reduced teaching loads, only to individuals who want to do original research.[10] This would help many
excellent teachers who have no desire for pure research, but who love
teaching.

---

[10]It is presumed, of course, that all college teachers will continue to strive to do
the research necessary for their doctorate.

The college teacher's schedule of twelve hours a week only appears light. In reality each class requires at least two hours of preparation, which results in a thirty-six hour work week. In addition, many hours are spent in counseling students, attending meetings and extracurricula activities, and in working with committees. More time is spent in making up and correcting tests, and in evaluating term papers and other written assignments. There is no formal work-day, or work-week, for the college teacher. Depending on his various activities, he may work far into the night, including week-ends.

FINANCIAL BENEFITS

College teaching like all teaching offered few financial rewards in the past. The salaries of many other occupations, which required less or equal preparation, offered a much greater financial return. It was not until the middle of the 1950's that the financial plight of college teachers was highlighted, and measures were taken to improve their economic status.

Salaries

During the first half of this century, faculty salaries substantially increased, but a decrease in the purchasing power of the dollar wiped out much of the increase. During the period 1914–1940, the salaries of professors showed an increase of two-thirds to three-fourths while the salaries of instructors nearly doubled.[11] Yet, during that same period, using 1935–39 dollars as a basis, the real median salaries of professors rose only 10 percent, and the real median salaries of instructors less than 25 percent.[12] During and following World War II, the salaries of college teachers failed to meet the increasing cost of living, and the improvement in the salaries of other professions. The real income of all college teachers in 1953–54 (using 1939–40 as a base year) was only 89 percent of what it was in 1939–40.[13] Making a comparison between the 1939 and 1957 real income, Beardsley Ruml has shown that, the real income of college faculties had *decreased* 8.5 percent while the real in-

---

[11]Herbert E. Longenecker, *University Faculty Compensation Policies and Practices in the United States* (Urbana, Illinois: University of Illinois Press, 1956), p. 141.
[12]*Loc. Cit.*
[13]*Ibid.,* pp. 141-142.

come for other occupations increased 79 percent.[14] Herge, summarized the financial plight of college teachers in the 1950's as follows:

> As a result of their low academic salaries, professors have been harassed by professional and economic woes, including: (1) debts; (2) family problems arising from inability to support dependents properly; (3) necessity for extra employment, which restricted time for preparation, research, reflection, relaxation, and informal association with students; (4) curtailment of social relationships outside academic circles, which often led to a closed social, psychological, and political experience; and (5) emotional problems arising from feelings of guilt, insecurity, and frustration.[15]

Something had to be done to alleviate the problems of college teachers. The chief requisite and remedy was more money. In this vein, Jacques Barzun stated: "We must put a premium upon intellect, and a premium is always money. Despite the convention that love of learning lessens the need for material things, brains are attached to organs that require sustenance."[16]

There were other compelling reasons for raising salaries. During the latter part of the 1950's enrollment began to increase, and was expected to double within a decade (which it did). Many new college teachers were needed, but many prospective teachers turned from the profession, because of its financial unattractiveness. Something had to be done, too, to retain those who were already teaching, and to replace those with substandard qualifications.

The Ford Foundation offered perhaps the greatest stimulus to the improvement of faculty salaries. In 1955, the foundation made financial grants to 630 four-year, private colleges, with regional accreditation. The grants, distributed in 1956 and 1957, were to be used exclusively for raising faculty salaries. The work of the Ford Foundation, and the financial plight of college teachers, received wide publicity which stirred others to action.

In 1957, another great impact was made on the public with the publication of the report of the President's Committee on Education Beyond the High School. The committee reported that the low salaries of college teachers were, in effect, subsidizing the education of college students. This subsidy, the committee said, was more than double the amount the institution received from gifts and endowments. It was

---

[14]Henry C. Herge, *op. cit.*, p. 13.
[15]*Ibid.*, p. 14.
[16]Jacques Barzun, *Teacher in America* (Boston: Little, Brown and Company, 1945), p. 283.

pointed out that many students, and their families, were living in luxury, while their teachers lived at the subsistence level. The President's Committee urged that the salaries of college teachers be doubled during the period 1960–70.

With these powerful promptings from the Ford Foundation and from the President's Committee, the salaries of college teachers rose. Professional associations added their weight to this solution of the problem. The American Association of University Professors annually surveyed the progress made in salaries among institutions of higher education, while the National Education Association did so biennially.

To reach the goal set by the President's Committee, college salaries would have to be raised 7.4 percent annually.[17] During the years 1954–1968, this percentage was exceeded only once, when an average annual salary increase of 9 percent was gained in 1956–57. In every other year during that period, the average annual increase ranged from 5–7 percent. There was, then, a steady improvement in salaries, even though the goal was not reached. This abrupt growth may be better illustrated with actual salary figures. During the year 1955–56, when the Ford Foundation grants were made, the median salary for all college teachers was $5,243. This figure rose to $6,700 in 1959–60, and reached $8,163 in 1963–64. The gains made in each teaching rank during that period are illustrated in the table below.[18]

In 1964 when the college teacher's average salary had risen to $9,000,[19] the American Association of University Professors stated that the goal set by the President's Committee had not been met. Although salary increases were regular, the association stated that they were not occurring at the recommended rate of 7.4 percent annually, especially

Median Salaries by College Rank,
1955–56 and 1963–64

1955–56		1963–64	
Rank	Median Salary	Rank	Median Salary
Instructor	$4,087	Instructor	$6,114
Assistant professor	4,921	Assistant professor	7,539
Associate professor	5,731	Associate professor	8,969
Professor	7,076	Professor	11,312

---

[17]Henry C. Herge, *op. cit.*, p. 15.

[18]These figures, and the preceding salary figures in this paragraph were compiled from Robert M. Friedberg and Gene R. Hawes, *op. cit.*, pp. 77, 80.

[19]*Digest of Educational Statistics*, 1965 Edition, U.S. Office of Education (Washington: U.S. Government Printing Office, 1965), from Table 66, p. 88.

in public institutions. Despite this strong statement, annual increases
continued to fall below the recommended percentage. Nevertheless,
the financial position of college teachers today is far better than it was
a relatively short time ago. The annual survey of college salaries by
the AAUP, showed that the average salaries in the 925 institutions that
participated in the 1967–68 survey, were now: instructor, $7,548; as-
sistant professor, $9,516; associate professor, $11,530; and, professor,
$15,341.[20] The amount any one individual earns depends, of course,
upon the place where he is employed, for there is a wide range of
salary scales among institutions. Usually universities have higher salary
scales than colleges. On the average, the salary scales in junior colleges
compare favorably in the lower ranks with those of colleges and universities, but in the rank of professor these schools often fall short of
the others.

Retirement and Related Benefits

College teachers receive the same types of benefits that elementary
and secondary teachers receive. Depending on the policy of their particular college, these may include retirement benefits, social security
coverage, disability benefits, life insurance coverage, protection against
medical expenses, and sick leave benefits. Although some public colleges are under state-financed plans, and some private colleges finance
their own plans, most colleges participate in the coverage offered by
the Teachers Insurance and Annuity Association (TIAA), and the College Retirement Equities Fund, (CREF). These companies offer all
of the benefits previously mentioned except for social security, which
is federally financed, and sick leave benefits, which are determined by
the colleges themselves. Because TIAA and CREF provide these important services to college teachers, their activities will be described
briefly.

TIAA describes itself as ". . . a limited eligibility, non-profit service
organization through which colleges, universities, independent schools,
and other nonprofit and tax-exempt educational and scientific institutions provide retirement and insurance benefits for their staff members." Founded in 1918 under the sponsorship of the Carnegie
Corporation and the Carnegie Foundation for the Advancement of
Teaching, its purpose was to combine the retirement and insurance

---

[20]"On the Financial Prospects for Higher Education: The Annual Report on the
Economic Status of the Profession, 1967-68", *AAUP Bulletin*, 54, 2 (June, 1968),
Appendix, Table 3, p. 197.

plans of many institutions. The combined plan, it was felt, would be more efficient and effective than the individual plans of each institution. By 1967–68 there were 1,858 institutions participating in TIAA, and its belief was justified.[21]

Under TIAA, both the college and the teacher usually contribute a certain percentage (about 5 percent) of the teacher's salary. The retirement contributions vary widely among institutions.

Some institutions bear the entire cost of the teacher's retirement, in some cases paying into the fund a sum as high as 15 percent of the teacher's salary. Usually, however, both the college and the teacher share the contribution into the fund, so that the institution, for example, may contribute 10 percent and the teacher 5 percent. The percentage paid by each varies among institutions, so that various combinations have been used, such as 8%-7%, 7%-3%, 6%-4%.

TIAA, having invested the retirement fund in stable, guaranteed-income producing commodities, provides the teacher with a fixed-dollar annuity at the age of sixty-five.

Recognizing the effects of inflation on the fixed-dollar, TIAA established CREF in 1952, a new company which was financially separate, but under the management of TIAA. CREF allowed participants to elect to receive part of their retirement benefits in the form of *variable* annuity income. Since CREF invests in common stocks, the amount of retirement income fluctuates annually according to the market value of the investments. At the present time, the individual may authorize the school to allocate 25 percent to 75 percent of each premium to either TIAA or CREF, with the balance allocated to the other company. At retirement the individual will have an income which is partly based on fixed dollars (TIAA), and partly based on the current market value of the CREF investments, which offers some protection against inflation.

Besides providing their faculties with TIAA-CREF retirement benefits, some colleges offer one or more of the other benefits provided by TIAA, life insurance, major medical expense insurance, and total disability benefits insurance. In the colleges that have adopted these TIAA plans the cost may be borne by the college, or shared with the faculty.

Sabbatical Leave

In the United States, sabbatical leaves for teachers in higher education were not granted until the end of the nineteenth century. Harvard

---

[21]*TIAA-CREF* Annual Report 1967, p. 9.

was the first college to adopt a system of sabbatical leaves, in 1880. By the turn of the century nine other colleges had also adopted the system.[22] The system made progress slowly during the early twentieth century, but has gathered momentum during the past twenty-five years. Now sabbatical leaves are commonplace in American colleges and universities.

In a study of faculty fringe benefits, directed by Mark H. Ingraham for the Association of American Colleges, it was found that the following reasons for granting sabbatical leaves were most frequently mentioned by 415 responding institutions: further study, research, improvement of teaching, writing, and travel.[23] Most schools believe that the reason for a sabbatical leave should relate to the welfare of the institution, not to the welfare of the individual, although he will almost certainly receive some benefits from it.

Most institutions require six years of experience in one of the professorial ranks before the candidate is eligible for a sabbatical leave, and he is expected to return to the institution for at least one year of service after the leave. The prevalent rate of compensation during the leave is full salary for an absence of half a year, or half-salary for an absence of one year. A few institutions have given compensation equal to two-thirds or three-fourths of the salary during a year's leave. Most institutions also stipulate that the individual may not engage in paid employment during his leave. Frequently the teacher is required to submit a report of his activities, outlining his progress or achievement during the sabbatical.

Sabbatical leaves do not come automatically after six years of service nor are they automatically taken by all teachers. The teacher must submit a reason, and sometimes a plan, which is acceptable to the college. Administrators often have reported that a few teachers cannot think of an acceptable project for a sabbatical leave. Other teachers are too occupied with other tasks or problems to take time off for anything else. Many institutions are restrictive, or have no "full pay" provisions, with the result that only a small percentage of the faculty applies for a sabbatical leave. In some colleges, less than 25 percent of the eligible teachers actually take leaves.[24]

---

[22]Walter C. Eells and Ernest V. Hollis, *Sabbatical Leave in American Higher Education,* U.S. Office of Education (Washington: U.S. Government Printing Office, 1962), p. 1.

[23]Mark H. Ingraham, *The Outer Fringe* (Madison, Wisconsin: The University of Wisconsin Press, 1965), from Table 51, p. 244.

[24]*Ibid.,* p. 77.

Tuition Grants for Children of Faculty

One of the best financial fringe benefits for faculty members who have children is the tuition grant which allows their children to attend college without tuition. Considering that in the past, college faculty members subsidized the education of the students with their low salaries, it is reasonable to expect the colleges to subsidize the education of their children. This benefit is particularly advantageous in private colleges, where tuition fees are high in comparison with state institutions. Over 90 percent of the private colleges in the United States make various types of tuition grants to the children of their faculty members, whereas this is done in only a little over 10 percent of the public institutions. The importance of these plans to individual teachers varies, of course, with the size of their families.

In some cases, cooperative arrangements have been made between colleges which permit the exchange of tuition grants for the children of faculty members. This plan is especially appropriate for colleges that are not coeducational. Under these circumstances exchange arrangements are sometimes made between all-male and all-female colleges. It is also important to parents who feel that there are disadvantages in having a child attend the same school in which his parent is a teacher.

Income from Writing and Lecturing

Some college teachers who have the desire, facility, and ability to express themselves in writing, may try to supplement their income by writing periodical articles or books. Articles or "papers" that are written for professional journals receive little or no financial compensation, but articles written for "popular" periodicals can provide substantial compensation. Books written for a specialized audience, also may receive a limited acceptance. However, in many fields, there are textbooks that have received wide adoption and provide their authors with a steady, supplementary income for a number of years.

Other college teachers have an unusual facility for lecturing. They frequently are invited to make public appearances. Talks given before local P.T.A. groups, professional and civic organizations, usually receive no compensation. However, special-occasion addresses, such as commencements, convocations, conventions, and even after-dinner addresses are sometimes well compensated. Once a teacher has acquired a reputation for lecturing he is sought after and may spend as much time as he wishes in "making the circuit". Today, lecturing has become a big business, with many lecture bureaus which handle the affairs of prominent speakers located in various parts of the country.

Other Sources of Income

There are other ways in which the college teacher may supplement his regular income. If his class load is heavier than usual, he often is paid for the extra teaching assignments. Furthermore, since his contract is usually for work done during the school year, he may earn additional salary by teaching during summer or evening sessions, if he has time. Other time-consuming assignments, such as moderator of the yearbook or school newspaper, or coaching, bring additional compensation. Some college teachers, who are authorities in their field, may be invited by various agencies to act as consultants for which they are well paid.

The economic status of college teachers has greatly improved. Salaries have risen to the point where college teachers can live comfortably, even induling in a luxury or two. Fringe benefits become more widespread and more liberal, providing for income during illness or disability, the education of his children, and retirement income. Probably further improvement in these areas will take place in the immediate future.

INTANGIBLE BENEFITS

Again, the intangible benefits for the elementary and secondary teacher also apply to college teachers but in differing ways and degrees. The college teacher deals with a select population of students, which makes the difference.

Self-Fulfillment

It is probably accurate to say that people who go into college teaching have a desire to bring out the potentialities of human beings and help them with their problems. Moreover, it can be presumed that college teachers, having had at least five years of formal higher education and knowing that they must meet requirements for a doctorate, have a high degree of interest in intellectual pursuits. College teaching provides a satisfying means of following these interests.

The college teacher recognizing that college students are potential leaders receives a great deal of satisfaction from stimulating and developing their intellectual powers. At the same time, because he enjoys the challenge of intellectual exchanges, he finds teaching a pleasureable and broadening experience. In college teaching, he finds the means to foster his own intellectual development as well as that of others. Today's college student is not as passive as his predecessor was. Rather, he is actively questioning traditionally accepted ideas and values, which makes classroom discussion a more stimulating experience for both teacher and student than ever before.

The college teacher cannot permit himself intellectual stagnation. He has a lifelong commitment to intellectual development. As Leonard W. Rice stated:

> It is a remarkable thing to which we commit ourselves when we become college teachers—the commitment to remain intellectually alive at least until we reach retirement. It is like committing oneself to love through sickness and health, poverty and prosperity.[25]

Tenure

The attainment of tenure at the college level takes a longer time than it does on the lower levels of schooling. It is not granted to instructors; it is often granted to assistant professors; and it is assured to associate professors and professors who have met the institution's minimum time requirement. The American Association of Colleges recommended a probationary period of no longer than seven years, before a college teacher receives tenure.

Many institutions are cautious and stringent, in granting tenure. When a college grants a teacher tenure, it, in effect, states that he is the type of person it would like to have associated with it permanently. Some of the factors considered in granting tenure are educational achievement, teaching ability, scholarship, character, and ability to integrate with the college community. Since it takes time to judge these qualifications, some institutions do not grant tenure until the individual reaches the rank of associate professor.

Once he is granted tenure, the teacher's contract becomes continuous, and he can not be discharged except for "due cause". The causes for

---

[25]Leonard W. Rice, "The Improvement of College Teaching", *College Teachers Look at College Teaching* (Washington, D.C.: The American Association of Colleges for Teacher Education, 1965), pp. 37-38.

dismissal usually center around incompetence, immorality, or subversive teaching. Should a teacher be charged with any of these offenses, he has the right to a hearing before an appropriate committee, during which he is entitled to legal and/or professional representation.

Tenure places a serious obligation on the teacher. Although it relieves the teacher of the anxiety of contract renewal, and although he feels freer in exercising academic freedom, he must not relax his standards and efforts. There have been frequent comments about the "yellowed pages of notes" used by some college teachers. In these situations the teacher has not discharged his moral responsibility to keep abreast of his field, and to continuously try to improve his instruction.

Steady Employment

Because college enrollment has risen steadily, there has been, and will be, an increasing demand for qualified college teachers. Consequently, college teachers are assured of steady employment, as long as they perform their work competently. Even for competent teachers without tenure steady employment is certain because of the great need for qualified teachers. College teachers do not need to worry about employment opportunities for many years.

Prestige of College Teaching

The usual public image of a college teacher was one of the "absent-minded professor", who wore baggy clothes, mismated socks, rumpled hair, who forgot to eat his lunch, and who was continuously mumbling abstractions to himself. He was, it was imagined, a person living in an ivory tower, lost in impractical dreams, completely out of touch with reality. This image was fostered by the ridiculous descriptions of college professors presented in novels, motion pictures, and radio and television programs.

There are a few college teachers who fit this old image, but now the public image of the average college teacher has changed. During the past decade, the pace of college life has quickened. Sputnik prompted a hasty appraisal of the effectiveness of our present educational system. The appraisal still has not ended. The importance of education was publicized as never before, and the role of college teachers became one of the focal points of attention. The television program, Continental Classroom, and the television courses offered by some large universities have demonstrated nationally the effectiveness of college teachers. The college teacher emerged in a much different light to the public. Furthermore, college teachers became more involved in social, governmental, and business problems, thus bringing them into direct contact with the public. President John F. Kennedy's consultations with, or appointments of many professors further heightened their prestige and influence. These combined influences showed the college professor to be not only a theorist but also a practical activist, who was interested in solving the problems in the world around him. His public image changed, and he commanded more respect and prestige. Today, college teaching equals law and medicine in prestige. In fact, some studies of student opinions have shown that it outranks those professions in prestige.[26]

Other Benefits in College Teaching

There are other benefits, both financial and nonfinancial, that are found in many colleges and universities. Almost all colleges reimburse their teachers, in part or in full, for travel expenses to attend authorized professional meetings. To recruit new teachers, some institutions offer to pay part or all of their moving expenses. Since housing is often a problem, many colleges own houses or apartment buildings which are rented to faculty members on a priority basis. Reserved parking areas spare the faculty the ever-increasing competition for parking space. Many colleges also give their teachers clerical help in the form of departmental secretaries, secretarial pools, or student assistants. Finally, many colleges permit faculty wives to take courses tuition-free, either on a credit or noncredit basis.

College teaching, then, offers the individual an increasingly attractive salary, ways of supplementing his income, and many fringe benefits, both financial and intangible. For those who are interested in the intellectual challenges found in higher education, college teaching can offer a relatively secure, rewarding life.

Some Cautions

The college teacher, however, does not work under Utopian conditions. There are many frustrations and pressures in this profession also. Some of these are met in the process of acquiring a doctorate, and others are met after achieving it.

Teachers who enter the profession without a doctorate are under continuous pressure to continue their graduate study. Depending on

---

[26]Henry C. Herge, *op. cit.*, p. 7.

the individual's progress toward it when he enters college teaching, he may have to attend graduate school for many years on a part-time basis before he completes the requirements. At the same time, he must carry a full-time teaching load and extra-class activities that are time-consuming. If he is married and raising a family, he is not only further pressed for time, but also subjected to the financial pressures involved in continuing his education. For these reasons, it would be best for the individual to acquire his doctorate before beginning college teaching. Unfortunately, the majority of new teachers are unable to do so.

College teachers who have their doctorate, and some teaching experience, find themselves under a different type of pressure. They are expected to undertake research and to publish their findings: the "publish or perish" pressure. Today, however, an even greater pressure has developed. The pace of educational activities has reached almost hectic proportions.[27] The body of knowledge has grown rapidly, innovations are continuously introduced, and curriculums are revised so frequently that they are often outdated before they are printed. Teachers are urged to show greater involvement in community, state, national, and international affairs. They are caught up in the endless process of self-evaluation and self-improvement, attending seemingly innumerable committee, departmental, faculty, and professional meetings. Proposals for governmental grants are constantly submitted. All sorts of accrediting committees are threading their way through college activities, recommending changes. Today, the cry is "Change!", and it is brought about through democratic involvement of students, faculty, and administration. The college teacher, as he shuttles back and forth between his classes and various activities, may have difficulty defining his role at the college. Although this bewildering sequence of activities may produce good results, the teacher often wonders whether it is necessary to use so much manpower to produce the results. He finds himself wondering whether he is discharging his true function as a college teacher, namely, teaching and guiding his students.

The teacher, if he has a choice, should strike a balance between these activities. He needs time to prepare for classes, and to read, reflect, and do research. If he finds himself neglecting these, he should curtail his other activities. Somewhat exaggerated, but illustrative of the point, is the following statement:

> If a young faculty member fresh from his Ph.D. should ask me for advice, I would tell him to take definite steps to guard his intellectual life from numerous factors that will slowly erode it by

---

[27]This applies as well to other levels of schooling.

dissipating his energy and eating up countless hours best spent in laboratory, library, or classroom. Hundreds of hours are wasted each week in committee-ridden institutions in which large groups meet to decide through the democratic process whether paper or pencils are to be bought with the supply money or whether one general education course is to be substituted for another in a given student's program. Excessive talk in office, halls, coffee shops takes its toll. Naps at noon, tending the baby in the afternoon while the wife is at club, community service, skiing, gardening, adding a basement room, club membership, and a thousand other worthy and pleasant things can eat up one's non-teaching time and if overdone slowly destroy his intellectual power by keeping him from reading, research, expanding his knowledge of his own discipline, and other activities by which he may preserve and strengthen his intellect for teaching. Knowledge, I believe it was Whitehead who said it, is like fish: it doesn't keep.[28]

The leisurely pace of college life is a thing of the past. Now, it frequently parallels the business world: the hurried pace; the insistence on production; and, the competition for advancement. To a degree, this is healthy. However, if the pace becomes too fast, the pursuit of knowledge may become blurred to both teachers and students.

OPPORTUNITIES FOR ADVANCEMENT

The opportunities for advancement in higher education while similar to those in elementary and secondary schools, are fewer, simply because the number of higher education institutions is far smaller. A college teacher may become head of his department and have duties similar to those that were outlined for department heads in secondary schools. Or, he may become a dean, in charge of a specialized area, such as dean of academic affairs, dean of men or women, or dean of student affairs. In universities, deans of the various colleges, or of the schools within the university, are appointed. There are many specialized administrative positions, in the areas of guidance, library work, business, admissions, recruiting, or fund raising, into which the college teacher may move if he wishes to leave the classroom.

SUMMARY

From the mid-1950's on, there has been a steady increase in the demand for college teachers. This demand was caused by the increase in

---

[28]Leonard W. Rice, *op. cit.*, p. 38.

population occurring during and after World War II, and the higher percentage of college-age people who began to attend college.

The increase in college enrollment resulted in a corresponding increase in the demand for college teachers. Yet, prior to 1955, the economic status of college teachers was so poor that it did not attract enough qualified people. Colleges were forced to hire many teachers with substandard qualifications. Concern for the possible deterioration of the quality of a college education grew as the percentage of new teachers with doctorates declined.

In 1955, the Ford Foundation provided the stimulus necessary to improve the financial status of college teachers by offering grants to private institutions for the improvement of their faculty salaries. In 1957, the President's Committee on Education Beyond the High School flatly stated that the salaries of college teachers were so low that they subsidized the education of their students. The President's Committee recommended the doubling of salaries during the decade 1960–70. As a result of these stimuli, the salaries of college teachers rose at a more realistic rate. With this occurrence more people became interested in college teaching, and the shortage of qualified teachers decreased, although demand still exceeds supply.

The prospective college teacher should be an individual of superior intelligence, capable of completing the requirements for a doctor's degree. Without a doctorate, he will lack one of the important requirements for promotion. There are four ranks in college teaching: instructor, assistant professor, associate professor, and professor. In addition, part-time teachers are employed as lecturers. In many institutions, the teacher cannot advance beyond the rank of assistant professor unless he has his doctorate, but in other institutions there is some flexibility in the requirements for promotion.

Ordinarily, twelve semester hours are a full teaching load for the college teacher. If he is asked to teach additional classes, he usually receives extra compensation. In addition to teaching, the college teacher's responsibilities include activities such as: counselling students, research, publication, extracurricular activities, committee work, attending meetings, and community activities.

The financial benefits of college teachers have improved considerably in recent years. The average salaries of college teachers in 1967–68 had risen to the following figures: instructor, $7,548; assistant professor, $9,516; associate professor, $11,530; and, professor, $15,341. Other financial benefits have also improved. Most colleges provide a measure of security for their teachers by subscribing to TIAA-CREF retirement benefits, and, in varying degrees, to other benefits such as disability income, group life insurance, medical expense coverage, and sick leave. Teachers are also eligible for the federally-sponsored social security program. Furthermore, most colleges grant sabbatical leaves for faculty members, and tuition grants for their children. Depending on their abilities and circumstances, college teachers may supplement their income through extra teaching, or other assignments, writing for publication, lecturing, or, working as consultants.

The college teacher shares with other teachers the intangible benefits of the profession. He has the opportunity to express his spirit of service through his work with pupils. He can broaden his knowledge through a lifetime of study. Once he has passed his probationary period, he enjoys the security of tenure and cannot be dismissed except for serious reasons. His security is further strengthened by the shortage of qualified college teachers, a shortage which is expected to continue. Also, as a college teacher, he is a member of a profession which now commands high respect and prestige. Finally, there are some incidental financial and intangible benefits which are provided by many institutions. The college teacher is usually reimbursed for travel expenses to professional meetings; his moving expenses are paid; and he is assisted with housing, parking privileges, provision of clerical help, and permission for faculty wives to take courses tuition-free.

The benefits of teaching in college are greater than ever before. However, the pace of college life has become so fast that the college teacher must guard against becoming involved in too many extraneous details. If he doesn't, he may lose sight of, or lack time for, his primary responsibility as a teacher of students, and as a seeker of knowledge.

Questions for discussion:

1. Do you believe that a doctorate is necessary for successful teaching at the college level? Why?
2. Of what value is the doctor's high degree of specialization in teaching undergraduate students?
3. What do you think should be done about the A.B.D.'s who have given up hope of writing a dissertation?
4. Comment on the requirements for promotion of college teachers.
5. Evaluate the "publish or perish" policy of many institutions.
6. Do you think that the financial benefits of college teachers are now ample? Why?
7. Evaluate the intangible benefits of college teaching.

For further reading:

American Association of Colleges for Teacher Education, *The Improvement of College Teaching*. Washington, D.C.: The American Association of Colleges for Teacher Education, 1965.

Barzun, Jacques, *Teacher in America*. Boston: Little, Brown and Company, 1944.

Caplow, Theodore, and Reece J. McGee, *The Academic Market-place*. New York: Basic Books, Inc., 1958.

Friedberg, Robert M., and Gene R. Hawes, *Careers in College Teaching*. New York: Henry Z. Walck, Inc., 1965.

Herge, Henry C., *The College Teacher*. New York: The Center for Applied Research, 1965.

Highet, Gilbert, *The Art of Teaching*. New York: Random House Inc., 1958.

Ingraham, Mark H., *The Outer Fringe*. Madison, Wisconsin: The University of Wisconsin Press, 1965.

Longenecker, Herbert E., *University Faculty Compensation Policies and Practices in the United States*. Urbana, Illinois: University of Illinois Press, 1956.

11

Local, State, and Federal Roles in Education

In the United States, individual states control the education that occurs within their borders. Much of their authority is delegated to local units within the states, while, at the same time, the federal government supplies the whole educational system with various forms of educational aid. State control of education is based on the Tenth Amendment to the Constitution, which reads: "The powers not delegated to the United States by the Constitution, nor prohibited by it to the states, are reserved to the states respectively, or to the people." Since the Constitution does not mention education it has been regarded as a state function ever since ratification of the Tenth Amendment in 1791. Yet, education remained a local matter for nearly a century after that. The states did not begin to assume leadership in education until the nineteenth century. Although the federal government did not control education, its interest in aiding it dates back to the Ordinance of 1785.

EDUCATION ON THE LOCAL LEVEL

Within a state, the local units which administer education are called "school districts". There may be some confusion in the use of the term, because of the varying district sizes among the states. Towns, townships, cities, counties, or arbitrarily designated territories that do not correspond to any of these units are among the units that have been designated as school districts. In New England, for example, the boundaries of a town or township comprise school districts; in most of the southern states, the county lines form the boundaries of school districts; in Hawaii, because of its small size, the entire state consists of one school district. In most other states, the size of the school district is determined by factors such as the concentration of population and geographical conditions. In any situation, the local administrative unit, regardless of size, is called a school district.

Town Schools and the Origin of Districts

The earliest local unit of public education was the colonial New England town. It will be recalled that the Massachusetts Law of 1642 specifically referred to the selectmen of every *town,* and the law of 1647 referred to *towns* of fifty and one hundred families. Among other things that concerned them, the colonists in their town meetings discussed and decided upon educational matters. This practice gave way to the election of school committees, which were given authority over educational matters, but also were responsible to the town council.

During the eighteenth century, as the population grew, and people moved farther away from town, it was difficult for their children to attend town schools. These "suburban" residents then petitioned the town for permission to use their tax money to establish and administer their own schools. Permission frequently was granted, and the split-off schools then established were known as "districts" or "district schools". Thus, these early school districts in Massachusetts came into existence with the permission of local authorities. During the beginning of the nineteenth century, Massachusetts passed laws which gave school districts legal status, and recognized them as corporate bodies.

Larger Local Units

Sometimes the township, which was an area of thirty-six square miles of territory, rather than the immediate town, served as the local administrative unit. The township unit was used more widely after it was adopted in the Northwest Territory, where the sixteenth section of each township was set aside for educational purposes. From there, the use of the township as the local unit of education spread to other states.

Just as the town was a natural unit of school administration in sparsely populated areas, the city was the natural unit of administration in areas of greater population. It became customary for cities to be designated as school districts, managing their own school affairs on a local level. Even in states using the county as the basic unit of administration, the cities within the counties often are designated as separate school districts. Some of the city school districts have reached staggering proportions. The school population in New York City alone exceeds the school population of many of the individual states.

About a fourth of the states, predominantly southern, adopted the county as the administrative unit within the state. In a few states, which have existing smaller districts, the county is the intermediate unit between the state and the local districts. Under these circumstances the local districts are responsible to the county, which is responsible to the state. In most other states, the county has no authority but acts in an advisory or consultative capacity to the local school districts. There are, then, various possibilities in the flow of authority from the state to the local district, which is demonstrated in the following diagram.

Possibilities in Flow of Authority in State Control of Education

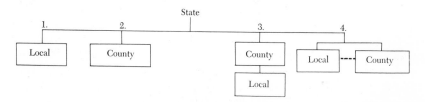

This diagram shows four possibilities in the flow of authority from the state to its school districts. In the first plan, the local school districts (towns, townships, cities) are responsible to and deal directly with the state. In the second plan the county is the smallest administrative unit, and each county is responsible to the state. The third existing plan has both county offices and lesser school districts. The local districts are responsible to the county, while the county in turn, deals with the state. In the final plan, the local school districts deal directly with the state, but receive the advisory and consultative services of the county. In this plan the county has no authority over the local district.

Consolidation of School Districts

The size of school districts varies from the one-room schoolhouse, with one teacher and a few pupils, to the large city school districts, with hundreds of school buildings and teachers, and thousands of pupils.

Each extreme has had its problems. The one-room school, and other small schools lack the facilities necessary for providing a high quality education. Conversely, the large city school districts have been plagued with problems of administration and instruction, as well as inadequate facilities in slum areas.

For many years the problem of the small school has been attacked by the consolidation of schools and redistricting of existing school districts. Small schools have disappeared rapidly, and central schools to which pupils are transported by bus service have taken their place. In this trend toward centralization the number of school districts in the United States has decreased from 127,531 in 1931–32, to 71,094 in 1951–52, and 35,676 in 1961–62.[1] This number was reduced to approximately 21,700 in 1967–68. During the period between 1931–32 and 1961–62, the number of one-teacher schools decreased from 143,391 to 13,333.[2] Presumably, then, the problem of small schools will be solved through their elimination, and the substitution of well-equipped central schools.

However, the trend toward enlarging school districts, and thereby reducing their number can be seriously questioned. In 1960, a well-known textbook writer stated that the current existence of 54,000 relatively independent school districts served as evidence of the democratic control of education in the United States. Six years later, when the textbook was revised, the same statement was made using 28,000 school districts to show that education is democratically controlled. If, however, 54,000 districts show democratic control, do 28,000 (further reduced to 21,704 in 1967–68) indicate that democratic control is slipping away? If not, what figure would indicate the turning point? Furthermore, it is desirable for people to be involved in education at the administrative level. For example, in New York City, plans were formulated to divide the authority in the large district into many smaller units, each with its own board of education. People living in the ghetto areas of cities have requested neighborhood representation in the administration of their schools. The following statement illustrates that local participation is necessary for the preservation of the American tradition in education:

> Whether thru intent or by chance, the autonomous schoolboard
> and school district are the nearest approach to complete local con-

---

[1]Carol J. Hobson and Samuel Schloss, *Statistics of State School Systems, 1961–62,* U.S. Office of Education (Washington: U.S. Government Printing Office, 1964), from Table 5, p. 28.
[2]*Ibid.,* from Table 9, p. 32.

trol that is widely used in our governmental pattern. For this reason, the schoolboard is unique as the firmest and almost the last stronghold where the people have kept the functions of local government under the control of a local agency. The public schools are so much a part of the aspirations of the people that it can be hoped they will never be willing to relinquish this control to any state or federal bureaucracy.[3]

The Educational Policies Commission pointed out another danger in overly large districts, namely, the lack of direct communication between teachers and administrators in formulating policy. Speaking on this point, the Commission stated:

> . . . If the district is too large—in area, in numbers of pupils and teachers, or in both—the teacher may find it impossible to influence decisions being taken in the central office. Yet the major business of the central office is precisely to be sensitive to and aware of the needs of the teacher. Such districts should either be decentralized in important ways or broken up.[4]

The commission also stated, however, that "School districts with too few pupils for an adequate program at reasonable cost should consolidate or establish an intermediate unit."[5]

The real question is "When *is* a school district too large or too small?" There is no ready answer. The size of a school district depends upon population density and geographical location, so that no one specific size can be recommended for all areas. However, a district is too large if the people do not have close contact with their schools and are not represented on the school board, and, secondly, if effective communication is lacking among school personnel because of the size of the district. A district is too small if it is economically unfeasible to provide the variety of programs needed for the full development of pupils.

Local Boards of Education

Each school district is under the jurisdiction of a board of education, which is responsible not only for providing the district with suitable facilities, programs, instruction, and services, but also for determining

---

[3]American Association of School Administrators, *The American School Superintendency,* Thirtieth Yearbook (Washington, D.C.: National Education Association, 1952), p. 110.

[4]National Education Association and American Association of School Administrators, Educational Policies Commission, *The Unique Role of the Superintendent of Schools* (Washington, D.C.: the Commission, 1965), p. 18.

[5]*Loc. cit.*

how these will be financed on the local level. The state, sometimes in specific terms, and other times in generalities determines the extent of the board's authority and responsibility. Even though the local board of education is an agency of the state, and must act in accordance with state laws, it exercises a substantial degree of autonomy in local educational matters.

The number of members on a local school board varies with the size of the district. A survey of local school boards in the United States showed a variation from three to nineteen, with five members constituting the board in a little over half of the districts.[6] Most board members (approximately 85 percent) are elected by the people of the district, while the remainder are appointed by public officials. The term of office varies from one to seven years, and sometimes longer, but the most common length is three years.[7] In 1961–62, there were 155,754 board members serving the 35,676 school districts in the United States,[8] and this number has since decreased because of the continual consolidation of school districts.

The educational qualifications of school board members also vary. Tradesmen and professional people, college graduates and high school dropouts may sit together on the same board of education. White's survey of school board members showed their educational background fell into the following categories: 48.3 percent were college graduates, 44.0 percent graduated from high school but did not complete college, and 7.7 percent had less than a high school education.[9] In larger school districts, almost three-fourths of the board members were college graduates. Some states specify a minimum educational level for those people seeking office as board members.

People are now more aware that the quality of the education their children receive depends largely on the quality of their board of education. For this reason, they now show more concern about the qualifications of candidates for their school board. Some states specify routine requirements concerning age, residence, and educational level. These qualifications are easily assessed. There are other qualifications which are not so easily judged, and therefore need careful study. These include intelligence (which is not necessarily correlated with educational level), character, personality, initiative, emotional stability, and motivation for office. Ideally, the local school board member should be a

[6]Alpheus L. White, *Local School Boards: Organization and Practices*, U.S. Office of Education (Washington, D.C.: U.S. Government Printing Office, 1962), p. 15.
[7]*Ibid.*, p. 12.
[8]Hobson and Schloss, *op. cit.*, from Table 4, p. 27.
[9]Alpheus L. White, *op. cit.*, from Table 7, p. 18.

public-spirited individual who has a special talent to offer. He should be interested in providing a high quality education for the children of the district. For example, a successful business man can apply his talent to the financial aspects of education; a building contractor could offer sound advice on physical facilities and their maintenance; or, a professional person could advise the board on legal, health, or other matters, depending on his field of competence. Reeves offers an exhaustive (and, perhaps, idealistic) list of the qualities that school board members should possess. He stated that a school board member should:

Be interested in the development of children and have a strong belief in the importance of their education in the public schools.

Act with sincerity and without prejudice in the interests of the people of the school district and be willing to subordinate personal, political, and religious interests to the good of the larger group.

Be well balanced and not biased toward or against any particular kind of education—classical or vocational, fundamental or progressive—or toward or against any particular subject or activity of the schools.

Be progressive in improving the public schools but conservative in adopting changes of unproven merit except for the purpose of well-considered experimentation.

Be foresighted and farsighted in helping to plan public education for the future.

Be mature enough to exercise sound judgment and young enough to be interested in the future; age in years is not the criterion of maturity or youth.

Be successful in his profession, business, or trade and be willing and ready to act on expert advice on educational matters when he deems such advice to be sound in general principle.

Be accustomed to making decisions promptly and with dispatch.

Persevere in securing desirable board action and insist on corresponding zeal by the superintendent and his staff in making all adopted actions effective.

Be willing and able to devote time and energy to the work of the school board.

Have a strong loyalty to democratic processes and subordinate personal opinions and desires to the will of the majority.

Be agreeable, courteous, good natured, and tolerant in dealing with persons whose opinions oppose his own.

Be courteous and co-operative and work as a member of a team.

Be capable of withstanding pressure from without in supporting a policy that has been adopted after thorough consideration by the board.

Be courageous and not susceptible to being intimidated nor influenced except by reasons that seem to him to be sound.

Act in a logical and judicious, rather than emotional, manner.

Be open to conviction and subject to change when proved wrong, even after a stand has been taken.

Be decisive, not vacillating.

Have a feeling of loyalty to the board, its several members, and the staff and pupils of the schools.

Be able to face criticism without flinching even if unjust and be willing to stand back of sound principles regardless of the source of opposition.

Be ready to accept responsibility for mistakes made by himself or the board.

Be frank and straightforward, not secretive and devious.

Exercise leadership in the larger community.

Be public spirited and active in promoting the interests of the public.

Be well poised, secure in the respect and esteem of the people of the larger community.

Be discreet and tactful with respect to the school's public relations.

Have a reputation in the community for integrity and good judgment and be worthy of his reputation.[10]

It is doubtful that any school board member possesses all of these qualities, yet all well qualified board members possess some of them. Although there are people who seek election to the board for selfish reasons, most school board members are conscientious, civic-minded persons who generously donate their time and energy for the improvement of education.

The question of compensation for school board members is frequently debated. Those people who propose compensation claim that it would attract better qualified persons, who would be willing to devote more time to the work. Furthermore, they claim that it would add more prestige to the position; and that, since other part-time public officials are paid for their services, school board members also should receive compensation. Their opponents fear that compensation would turn the office into another "political plum" and that it would add greatly to the already high costs of education. Moreover the small salaries, they claim, would attract the incapable rather than the capable. Since he received compensation, these opponents claimed the school board member might feel obligated to undertake activities that belong

---

[10]Charles E. Reeves, *School Boards* (New York: Prentice-Hall, Inc., 1954), pp. 103-04.

to the superintendent of schools, which would result in a conflict of authority. Finally, they claim that enough capable people can be obtained without offering compensation for the work.

In actual practice, some states permit the payment of salaries to school board members, while others prohibit salaries but permit reimbursement for expenses. In 1957, a study[11] showed that twenty-two states prohibited by law any compensation to board members other than reimbursement for mileage and other actual expenses incurred; the other states permitted either state-wide compensation, or compensation in certain districts. In the areas which permitted compensation, three general types of payment were made: an annual salary, a fixed payment for each meeting, or reimbursement for actual expenses.

A quarter of a century ago, the American Association of School Administrators took a firm stand against compensation to school board members, for the previously mentioned reasons. Operating on the premise that board members are civic-minded persons, the Association stated that they receive compensation for their services in a non-financial way:

> Certainly it is true that being on a school board takes time, energy, intelligence, and the ability to deal with people. The reward for such service is threefold: (a) the satisfaction of having rendered a worthy service to the community and to the nation; (b) the opportunity of helping to decide important questions and to form far-reaching policies; and (c) the honor and prestige that come from sharing a responsibility for America's greatest and most important public institution—the public schools.[12]

County Units

In addition to the local school districts, there were, in 1961–62, 1,783 county intermediate units distributed among twenty-six states.[13] Sixteen of these states had county boards of education, with a total membership of 6,860.[14] In twelve states the county school officials have direct responsibility for school administration. In other states, however, they act

---

[11]Morrill M. Hall, *Provisions Governing Membership on Local Boards of Education* (Washington, D.C.: U.S. Government Printing Office, 1957), p. 35. Quoted by Alpheus L. White, *op. cit.*, p. 69.

[12]American Association of School Administrators, *School Boards in Action*, Twenty-Fourth Yearbook (Washington, D.C.: National Education Association, 1946), p. 45.

[13]Hobson and Schloss, *op. cit.*, from Table 3, p. 26.

[14]*Loc. cit.*

only in an advisory and consultative capacity to the local districts. In the twelve county-unit states,[15] each county-unit district has a board of education which has the same type of authority and responsibility as the local school board, but the scope of its activities corresponds to its greater size.

Superintendent of Schools

The local board of education is legally responsible for the administration of the schools within its district. It formulates what it considers to be desirable policies that will provide a high quality education for its children. Yet since the board consists of non-professional people who have other full-time occupations, and since it meets relatively infrequently, it is unable to administer its policies. For administration, the board employs a knowledgeable professional person who is responsible for implementing its recommendations and decisions. This person is the chief executive officer of the district's schools, and generally has the title of superintendent of schools.

The superintendent cooperates with the board. He not only acts on the policies they have already formulated, but also recommends changes in policy, or suggests new policies. He must report to the board the school system's progress, or lack of progress. The superintendent's duties extend over a wide range of activities in the management of the school system. He deals with financial matters, physical facilities, instruction, services, and community relationships. Obviously a person of higher caliber and special qualifications must fill this important position. In the words of the Educational Policies Commission, ". . . the superintendent is a teacher, politician, philosopher, student of life, public relations counselor, and businessman. All these aspects are involved in his central role of leadership."[16]

In larger school districts, the superintendent cannot carry out all of these activities personally. In these situations, he has assistants who are responsible to him for the execution of the special duties delegated to them. His assistants include assistant superintendents, supervisors of instruction, directors of special services, business managers, and principals.

---

[15]These states are: Maryland, West Virginia, Kentucky, Tennessee, North Carolina, South Carolina, Georgia, Florida, Alabama, Louisiana, New Mexico, and Utah.
[16]National Education Association and American Association of School Administrators, *The Unique Role of the Superintendent of Schools, op. cit.,* p. 7.

The executive officer in the county unit is the county superintendent of schools, who is usually elected by the people of the county. His duties correspond to those of local superintendents. He should be the educational leader in his district. He should promote the educational welfare of the pupils, should raise the quality of education in his district, and should work closely with the superintendents of the local districts within his jurisdiction. Unfortunately, when the office of county superintendent is elective, the best qualified people are not always attracted to the position. The position may be unattractive because of partisan politics, or because the salaries are relatively low, and working conditions are poor. Thus, the American Association of School Administrators has stated:

> In many of the states having the intermediate level of county school administration, low salaries are paid, low professional qualifications are required, and severe roadblocks to the development of high educational leadership in rural school communities are retained.[17]

With a few exceptions, most of the states using the county unit do not provide the county superintendent with an adequate professional staff. Consequently, in many areas, the county office can not fulfill its obligations satisfactorily.

THE STATE AND EDUCATION

Because the Constitution does not mention education, the Tenth Amendment permits the states to assume responsibility for it. Several explanations have been advanced to explain the reasons for this. First, many colonists fled to America to free themselves from the oppression they had experienced under the strong, centralized authority of European countries. Therefore, they were hesitant to give the federal government authority over education. Furthermore, the Founding Fathers probably never envisioned the tremendous proportions education would assume and all of its inherent problems. Also, the differences in customs, traditions, beliefs, and educational practices among the colonies, undoubtedly caused them to feel that these could be preserved by leaving education to the individual states.

---

[17]American Association of School Administrators, *The American School Superintendency, op. cit.*, pp. 368-69.

The ultimate authority in the state control of education resides in the people since they adopt a state constitution under which they consent to be governed, and in which the state's authority over education is defined. During the colonial period, and during the early years following the revolution, the states did not assume responsibility in education, leaving it a local affair. By the beginning of the nineteenth century, only a few states had made provisions in their constitutions for education, but by the middle of the century most states had assumed their responsibility.

State constitutions usually specify the extent of public education (elementary and secondary), how it will be organized into districts (town, township, district, city, county) and provide for the control of education through a state board of education, a state school administrator, and local boards of education. Any doubts concerning the meaning of legislation, are interpreted by the courts and the attorney general of the state. The flow of authority in state control of education, then, may be shown as follows.

People
↓
Constitution
↓
Legislature
↓
State Board of Education
↓
State Department of Education
headed by
Chief State School Administrator
↓
Board of Local Unit
(District, County)

If the people are not satisfied with the constitutional provisions for education, they may begin the process used to amend the constitution. Through popular election, they can elect officials who will represent them on educational matters. In states that elect board members and state school officials, the people can express their desires at the polls. At the local level, when local school board members are elected the people can again express their desires at the polls. The efficacy and quality of our educational system depends upon an intelligent and informed citizenry. If the people are interested and aroused, their elected representatives must heed their voices.

State Board of Education

A state board of education, usually consists of non-professional people who are elected in some states, and appointed by the governor in other states. With the exception of Illinois, every state has a state board of education. In 1961–62, the size of the state boards varied from three members in Mississippi to twenty-three members in Ohio, with a total membership of 468 in the United States.[18] In most states, the number of members ranges between seven and nine.

The state board is responsible for the administration of the state's public schools, and for the establishment of broad educational policies which conform with the existing legislation. The board can interpret educational laws, but can not make new laws. The state legislature alone can make new laws.

In addition to the state boards which concern themselves with the general education offered in elementary and secondary schools, there are special boards that are responsible for specific types or levels of education, such as higher education, teacher education, vocational education, and vocational rehabilitation. In some states, the general state board may assume the responsibility for one or more of these special fields.

The qualifications outlined for local school board members also apply to the members of the state board of education. Since they are responsible for providing a high quality education to an entire state, they themselves should be highly intelligent, informed, capable, and dedicated people. Their driving interest should be the educational welfare of all children in the state, and their judgment should be free from prejudice and political influence.

Presently membership on the state board is determined by popular vote, by appointment by the governor, or by *ex officio* status. Appointment by *ex officio* status is declining, and there is growing support for the election of board members by the people rather than by the governor's appointment. As early as 1949, the National Council of Chief State School Officers supported popular election of state boards. The American Association of School Administrators took a similar position, outlining the following reasons for supporting election of state board members:

1. Election contributes more closely to direct representation of the people.

---

[18]Hobson and Schloss, *op. cit.*, from Table 2, p. 25.

2. Election fosters a keener responsiveness on the part of those chosen as board members to local demands.
3. Election of state board members by the people on a nonpartisan basis insures independence of this body from partisan politics— an independence which is not always assured when the members are appointed by the governor. It serves as a strong safeguard to keep education out of state politics.[19]

Burrup summarizes this and other recommendations for the organization of state boards:

> Experience has developed a number of general criteria for the organization of state boards of education. These include the following: (1) the members should have state-wide interest in education—not merely an interest in problems which are found to exist only in their own local area; (2) there should be no *ex officio* members; (3) there should be few, if any, professional educators on the board; (4) members should be elected by popular vote on nonpartisan ballots, and without consideration of political or religious affiliation; (5) terms of office should be overlapping and should endure for a minimum of four years—and preferably longer; (6) the board should have authority which is commensurate with its responsibility—including the power to select its executive officer, assign his duties, establish his salary, set the educational policies for the state, have autonomy over the use of its funds within the accepted budget and allocation of the legislative body, and such other powers as are needed for the functioning of the board within its statutory and implied responsibilities and powers.[20]

The Chief State School Official

Just as the local school board needs a superintendent of schools to carry out its policies, the state board needs an executive officer to carry out its state-wide policies. Every state has a chief state school official, designated as "Superintendent of Public Instruction", or "Commissioner of Education", or similar titles. In 1966, the state board in twenty-three states appointed him, in twenty-two states the people elected him and in the other five states the governor appointed him.

The state superintendent's relationship to the state board depends upon the way he is selected. When he is appointed by the state board, he must carry out the board's recommendations, even though he may

---

[19]American Association of School Administrators, *The American School Superintendency, op. cit.,* p. 357.
[20]Percy E. Berrup, *The Teacher and the Public School System,* 2nd ed. (New York: Harper & Row, Publishers, 1967), pp. 57-58.

disagree with them. If he is elected by popular vote or appointed by the governor, he does not have to implement the state board policies with which he disagrees. Usually, regardless of how he is selected, the chief state school official and the board cooperate and work together closely. Since there is a possibility of disagreement, however, and since it may cause inaction, many authorities favor appointment of the chief school official by the state board of education. Proponents of this plan claim that the people are represented by an elected state board, and that the state board is in a better position to appoint a competent professional person as superintendent.

Some states do not specify the educational qualifications needed by the chief state school official, while other states do in general terms, such as graduation from college, or college graduation and appropriate professional graduate work, or an experiential background suitable for the position. If the superintendent is to work effectively, his background should include graduate work in administration, preferably a doctor's degree, and experience as a teacher and administrator in the public schools.

The state superintendent has many duties and activities. He works and must maintain good relationships with the state board of education, other state officials, federal agencies, and local groups. He is the administrator of the state department of education, which has a staff ranging from less than a hundred members to several hundred members. He must decide disputes emanating from the local districts. Much of his time is spent in advising governmental, professional, and civic groups. In general, he exercises supervision over, and coordinates, all the educational activities of the state. On the average, the chief state school official spends 63.7 hours a week in carrying out his responsibilities.[21] In fact, "He has found that probably no other educational official in the state has more varied or greater demands on his time."[22]

State Department of Education

The state board of education formulates educational policy for the state, while the chief state school official is the executive officer of the board. The state department of education, led by the state superintendent is the actual work-force that implements programs at the state level. The department includes various personnel: administrative, professional, supervisory, clerical, and maintenance. The size of this work-

---

[21]American Association of School Administrators, *The American School Superintendency, op. cit.,* p. 350.
[22]*Ibid.,* p. 348.

force, in 1961–62, ranged from 43 members in South Dakota and Wyoming, to 1,687 members in New York.[23]

The state superintendent is responsible for staffing the department properly. The quality of his staff will determine the effectiveness with which he can implement the state board's recommendations and mandates. For the sake of efficiency, the state department is divided into areas of responsibility. Thus, the state superintendent usually delegates responsibility and authority to several "assistant superintendents" who are in charge of various divisions such as elementary and secondary education, higher education, vocational education, guidance, teacher education and certification, special education, finance, research, and audio-visual education. An assistant superintendent may be responsible for more than one of these divisions, in which case there are division chiefs. Each division is further divided into sections, headed by section chiefs. For example, teacher education and certification may be broken into two sections: a certification section, and a section for accreditation of teacher education programs. This organizational structure of a state department of education may be illustrated in simplified form as follows.

State Board of Education
↓
Chief State School Official
↓
Assistant Superintendents
↓
Division Chiefs
↓
Section Chiefs

The specific activities and services of a state department of education are too many to describe here. However, a partial listing is provided on page 327. Individual states vary in the extent to which they provide these services.

Obviously, the management of a state department of education is complex and entails a great deal of responsibility. Only people of the highest competence should be appointed or elected as state board members and superintendents for it takes that type of person to understand the problems involved in the field of education, and to provide imaginative leadership in solving these problems.

---

[23]Hobson and Schloss, *op. cit.*, from Table 2, p. 25.

SERVICE AREAS OF STATE DEPARTMENTS
OF EDUCATION[24]

Administration of Education in Unorganized Territory

Adult Education

Archives and History

Audio-Visual Materials

Correspondence Schools

Departmental Office Administration

Education and Registration of Nurses

Educational Fair Practices

Exceptional Children and Youth

Film Censorship

Film Production

Finance and Business Administration

Guidance

Higher Education

Instructional Services

Local School Unit Reorganization

Placement Service

Private Academic Schools Elementary and Secondary)

Public Relations

Public Transportation

Records and Reports

Recreation

Research and Statistics

Scholarships

School Attendance and Census

School Health Services

School Law

School Library

School Lunch

School Plant

State and Local Public Libraries

State and Local Public Museums

Surplus Property

Teacher Certification

Teacher Education

Teacher Retirement

Textbooks

Veterans Education

Vocational Education

Vocational Rehabilitation

On all levels of education, in all positions, the *quality* of personnel is the key to providing the best possible education for the children. The leadership, vision, and courage of competent state boards and state departments of education should filter down to local boards and superintendents of schools, and from them to the staffs of individual schools. In a massive venture such as universal education, success can only result from a total effort by each individual engaged in the profession.

The State and Private Schools

While the state exists for the welfare of the individual, it, at the same time, must insure the common good. One way to insure the common

---

[24]Fred F. Beach, *The Functions of State Departments of Education* (Washington, D.C.: U.S. Government Printing Office, 1950), p. 17. As quoted by American Association of School Administrators, *The American School Superintendency, op. cit.,* p. 340.

good is through a system of education that enables each individual to develop his unique potentialities, and still produces an informed citizenry that can contribute to the effective operation of the state. The state, therefore, for its own preservation and welfare, can insist on a minimum amount of education for every person capable of profiting from it. This is provided for in the state constitution and in the educational laws passed by the state legislature. States have legislated basic educational programs and compulsory attendance or education, for children of specified age groups. To carry out this program, the state had to establish a system of public schools.

Yet, millions of children attend private schools. What is the state's relationship to private education in private schools? Can, or does, the state exercise control over these schools? The U.S. Supreme Court decisions in the Dartmouth College Case of 1816, and in the Oregon School Case of 1925 gave the basic answers to these questions. The Darmouth College Case determined that the charter given to a private school constituted a contract between it and the state, and therefore the state could not control the institution. In the Oregon School Case, the Supreme Court ruled that the state could not compel all children between the ages of eight and sixteen to attend public schools. It was held that "The child is not the mere creature of the State"; rather, the parents have first right over the child and are free to choose the type of education, public or private, that they wish for the child.

Although the state has no direct control over private schools, and cannot compel all students to attend public schools, it can insist that private schools give their pupils an education which is equivalent to the minimum standards set for public schools. Thus, all states have compulsory attendance laws which must be observed by the pupils in both public and private schools. Some states have a mandated curriculum which must be taught in both types of schools. They may prescribe safety standards for buildings, or insist that teachers meet certain specified minimum qualifications. Even though the state cannot control private schools, it can make certain that all pupils attending private schools receive the basic education necessary for good citizenship.

FEDERAL PARTICIPATION IN EDUCATION

Although the federal government does not control education, it is interested in it as a means of promoting the general welfare of the people and good government. This interest has existed for nearly two centuries, dating back to the Ordinances of 1785 and 1787. Since then, the federal government has aided education in several ways, sometimes substantially, other times modestly. Since 1958, it has poured an avalanche of dollars into all phases of education and its related services.

Federal participation in education may be divided into four categories: legislation providing land grants for educational purposes; legislation providing money for either temporary or permanent needs in education; the establishment of the United States Office of Education as a national service to education; and, legislation providing education and training for certain groups of people.

Legislation Providing Land Grants

The earliest federal land-grant act was the Ordinance of 1785 for the Northwest Territory, which designated the sixteenth section of each township for the maintenance of public schools. The Ordinance of 1787, which followed this ordinance emphasized the positive relationship between education and good government and provided for the surveying of the territory. The division of a township, and the numbering of the lots which followed the survey, is illustrated below. Each township was thirty-six square miles, and each lot or section was one square mile.

Sections of a Township

6	5	4	3	2	1
7	8	9	10	11	12
18	17	16	15	14	13
19	20	21	22	23	24
30	29	28	27	26	25
31	32	33	34	35	36

The thirteen original colonies were excluded from the land grants, as were a few other states that were admitted to the Union in later years. Ohio, which was admitted to the Union in 1802, was the first state to receive the sixteenth section of a township for educational purposes. Each state admitted thereafter received a similar grant from the federal government for the maintenance of education. In 1850, when California was admitted to the union, the federal government began to grant two sections, the sixteenth and thirty-sixth, to each new state. Later, in 1896, two additional sections, the second and thirty-second, were granted to Utah and to Arizona and New Mexico in 1911. Alaska and Hawaii received special grants when they were admitted as states in 1959. Three states, Vermont, Kentucky, and Tennessee, did not receive land grants, because they were admitted to the Union on the same terms as the original thirteen colonies. Texas received no land because it was an independent state at the time of its admission to the Union, and Maine and West Virginia were not eligible for grants, because they originally were a part of other states. Federal distribution of land grants falls into the following categories:

Received no land grants: 19 states

Received 16th section of townships: 12 states

Received 16th and 36th sections: 14 states

Received 2nd, 16th, and 32nd, and 36th sections; 3 states

Received special grants: 2 states

The Ordinance of 1785 and 1787 also established permanent funds for the maintenance of public schools, as they stipulated that only the income from the land, or from the sale of the land, could be used for the maintenance of public schools. In the states affected by land grants, therefore, the government provided a continuous income for education.

The Morrill Act of 1862 was the second important land-grant act passed by the federal government. This act granted to each state 30,000 acres of land, or its equivalent in scrip, for each of their members in Congress. This act established colleges which would teach agriculture and mechanic arts. Again, only the income, not the principal, of the funds could be used for the maintenance of these colleges.

Eventually sixty-eight colleges and universities received support from the funds of the Morrill Act. Some of these schools were newly established, while others were already in existence. All of the schools provided the vocational training which had been absent from colleges prior to this time.[25] Today, these institutions enroll about 20 percent of all undergraduates, and award nearly 40 percent of the doctorates granted in American higher education.

Legislation providing money grants. The original Morrill Act of 1862 provided land grants for the states. In 1890 the *Second Morrill Act*

---

[25]Land-grant colleges were discussed in greater detail in Chapter V.

which provided funds for land-grant colleges and universities further supplemented it. Under this later act, each state and territory received an initial grant of $15,000, which was increased by $1,000 annually until it reached a total annual grant of $25,000. In 1907, the Nelson amendment increased the initial grants by $5,000 annually for a period of five years. Eventually the acts of 1890 and 1907 produced an annual grant of $50,000 for each state. These amounts were again supplemented by the *Bankhead-Jones Act* of 1935, and its amendments in 1952, which granted to each state an additional flat sum of $20,000, and distributed according to population, another $1,501,500.[26]

The federal government has supplied land-grant colleges with funds in other ways. The Department of Agriculture has cooperated with these schools in research work and the provisions for extension services. The *Hatch Act of 1887* established agricultural experimental stations at land-grant colleges. This law was followed by several other acts which appropriated funds for agricultural experimentation. The *Hatch Act of 1955* consolidated all these previous acts. Under the provisions of the *Smith-Lever Act of 1914*, the Department of Agriculture in cooperation with land-grant colleges and county governments has provided instructional activities, and disseminated research findings, to people of all ages interested in agriculture and homemaking.

While the Morrill Acts provided for vocational education at the college level, the *Smith-Hughes Act of 1917* provided funds for vocational education below the college level. "Less-than-college grade" programs were provided in agriculture, trades and industries, and home economics. Furthermore, provisions were made to train teachers in these fields. Federal grants were made on the basis of a population formula, and the state or local sources had to match the funds. The original grants for these programs were to total $1,860,000 in 1917–18, but this sum was to be escalated to $7,367,000 by 1925–26. In order to receive the funds, the legislatures of the states and territories had to accept the act's provisions, had to appoint a state treasurer to handle the funds, and also had to designate a state board of at least three members to oversee vocational education. The funds of the Smith-Hughes Act were supplemented by other acts in 1929, 1934, 1936, and culminated in the *George-Barden Act of 1946*. Besides supplying additional funds, these acts added programs of training in distributive occupations, fishery trades, and practical nursing. The *National Defense Education Act of*

[26]Clayton D. Hutchins, Albert R. Munse, and Edna D. Booher, *Federal Funds for Education, 1958-59 and 1959-60,* U.S. Office of Education (Washington, D.C.: U.S. Government Printing Office, 1961), p. 44.

1958 which provided for the training of highly skilled technicians in fields important to national defense further amended the George-Barden Act. Presently, vocational education programs exist in all the states, and the District of Columbia, Guam, Puerto Rico, and the Virgin Islands.

Periodically the federal government has provided funds to meet special needs or emergency situations. The *Civilian Conservation Corps*, operated from 1933 to 1943, provided further training for unemployed males between the ages of 17 and 23. During the economic depression of the 1930's, the *Works Progress Administration* programs included repairing old schools, building new ones, and providing financial aid for teachers. Finally, under the *G.I. Bill of Rights*, veterans of World War II were given the opportunity to continue their education or training toward an occupational objective that was commensurate with their interests and abilities. Veterans of the Korean and Viet Nam Wars are provided with similar opportunities.

One of the many effects of the Russian Sputnik was the immediate improvement of our educational practices through the *National Defense Education Act of 1958*. The purpose of the legislation is stated in the Act itself, which reads, in part:

> Sec. 101. The Congress hereby finds and declares that the security of the Nation requires the fullest development of the mental resources and technical skills of its young men and women. The present emergency demands that additional and more adequate educational opportunities be made available. The defense of this Nation depends upon the mastery of modern techniques developed from complex scientific principles. It depends as well upon the discovery and development of new principles, new techniques, and new knowledge. . . .
>
> To meet the present educational emergency requires additional effort at all levels of government. It is therefore the purpose of this Act to provide substantial assistance in various forms to individuals, and to States and their subdivisions, in order to insure trained manpower of sufficient quality and quantity to meet the national defense needs of the United States.[27]

The National Defense Education Act of 1958 provided more than one billion dollars over a four-year period, granting various forms of aid under ten "titles". General provisions were outlined in Title I. Title II provided loan funds to colleges to help deserving, needy students ob-

---

[27]*Ibid.*, as quoted on p. 3.

tain a higher education. Under it students in good academic standing were permitted to borrow $1,000 annually, until reaching maximum of $5,000, which was to be repaid to the college over a ten-year period. Students who became public school teachers could have their indebtedness reduced by 10 percent for each year they taught, up to a maximum of 50 percent. Title III tried to strengthen instruction in science, mathematics, and modern foreign languages at the elementary and secondary level. The act allocated $75,000,000 for this purpose. Under Title IV, students were granted fellowships at graduate schools for the purpose of becoming college teachers. 1,000 fellowships were awarded during the first year, and 1,500 during each of the next three years. Students accepted in this program received a stipend of $2,000 the first year which was increased by $200 during each of the next two years. The graduate school received $2,500 for each student in the program. Title V tried to improve the qualifications of secondary school counselors. For this purpose, institutes were held at various centers throughout the United States. Teachers who attended the institutes from public secondary schools received a stipend of $75 a week, plus $15 for each dependent; teachers from private schools received no stipend, but were permitted to attend the institutes without charge. Similar provisions were made under Title VI, which tried to strengthen instruction in modern foreign languages. Institutes were held, fellowships were offered, and centers were established for foreign language and cultural subjects. Title VII provided funds for experimentation and research or the educational uses of television, radio, motion pictures, and related media; it also provided for the dissemination of this information to schools and colleges. To accomplish this, $3,000,000 was authorized the first year, and $5,000,000 in subsequent years. Title VIII which amended the George-Barden Act, provided vocational training below the college level. The National Science Foundation under Title IX provided for the dissemination of scientific information. It rendered services such as abstracting, indexing, and translating, to facilitate the flow of scientific information. Finally, Title X furnished grants for state departments of education to improve their statistical reports, and their methods of collecting and disseminating their data.

The provisions of the National Defense Education Act ranged through all levels of education, from elementary school to graduate school. It made some provisions for private schools, as well as public schools. Many subjects in the curriculum came under its influence, and the methodology and aids for teaching these subjects received new attention. Considerable emphasis was also given to research, experimentation, and the discovery of more accurate and effective ways of disseminating information received greater emphasis. The cumulative effect most certainly benefited education, and through it, national defense.

The U.S. Office of Education administered the Act of 1958, except for Title IX, which, we noted, operated under the National Science Foundation. The 1958 Act which was originally effective for four years, has been extended and amended several times since then. While the original Act emphasized science, mathematics, and modern foreign languages, it now includes English, reading, history, geography, and civics.

Another act of comparable importance was the *Elementary and Secondary Education Act of 1965*. It was enacted to improve the quality of elementary and secondary education and educational opportunities for children from low-income families. Congress allotted $1,385,082,973 for the act in 1966, the first year of operation. Grants were made under five titles:

Title I:	$1,060,082,973
Title II:	100,000,000
Title III:	100,000,000
Title IV:	100,000,000
Title V:	25,000,000

Because of its impact on education, a brief description of the five titles of the Act follows.[28]

Title I provided local educational agencies with financial assistance for special educational programs in areas having high concentrations of children of low-income families (less than $2,000 annual income). These children do not make average progress in school, presumably because they lack the educational opportunities of children from other income groups. The Act authorized money for the staff, equipment, and facilities necessary to conduct approved programs in public educational agencies. Under Title I, a variety of programs quickly evolved which included areas such as:

Training of teachers and teachers' aides

Development of special curriculums

Special programs for all types of atypical children

---

[28]The provisions of the five titles are summarized from a description of the Act found in ". . . The first Work of These Times . . .", *American Education*, I, Number 4 (April, 1965), 13-20.

Special programs for pre-school children

Programs for potential dropouts

Special laboratories for science, languages, reading

Special audio-visual aids

Under Title II, funds were given for school library resources, text-books, and other instructional materials in both public and private schools. The Act provided for increasing school libraries, for the latest and best teaching aids, and for free, up-to-date textbooks.

Title III provided for supplementary educational centers and services, which would help enrich the curriculum for pupils. These centers were to be developed wherever they did not exist, and were to upgrade existing services. It was hoped that Title III would stimulate the development of exemplary schools, which could serve as models. The benefits of the act applied to all cultural resources, public and private. It was pointed out that programs in guidance, counseling, health, adult education, and special instruction in subjects not taught in the local schools could be offered. The programs could use media such as orchestras, museums, theaters, artists, and musicians. Further services could be provided through the development of regional materials centers, and the use of mobile libraries and laboratories.

Funds for research in education have been meagre. Title IV provided for building national and regional research centers, for expanding present research activities, and for training education research workers. Personnel from state departments, colleges and universities, and local school systems were to conduct the research. Classroom facilities were to be provided for testing their findings.

Title V tried to strengthen State Departments of Education. The services of the departments in areas such as statistical reporting, evaluation of programs, and consultative services were improved in a variety of ways, including an exchange of personnel with the U.S. Office of Education.

Funds have been allocated annually for the Elementary and Secondary Education Act of 1965. The Act was also administered by the U.S. Office of Education, which allocated the funds to the individual states. The states, in turn, were responsible for carrying out the provisions of the Act, which provided for flexible school programs, and urged experimentation and innovation.

In 1965, after supplying the lower schools with funds, Congress again turned its attention to higher education. Two years before, in 1963, the Higher Education Facilities Act provided $1,195,000,000 over a three-year period for grants and loans to institutions of higher learning. These funds were used only for the construction of classrooms, libraries, and laboratories. The *Higher Education Act of 1965* lessened restrictions on the type of construction permitted. The only types of building construction not permitted under the 1965 Act were buildings for sectarian worship, or athletic and recreational facilities which were not part of the educational program, and buildings for events to which admission was charged. The total estimated grants for 1966 were placed at $501,-500,000. Besides providing funds for construction, the Act's eight titles covered the following areas:

Financial assistance to students in postsecondary and higher education through grants, loans, and work-study programs

Programs to solve problems in urban and suburban areas

Grants for library materials

Strengthening developing institutions of higher learning

Establishment of the National Teacher Corps, to teach in impoverished areas

Financial assistance for improvement of undergraduate instruction, through purchase of new teaching equipment, and minor remodeling of present facilities

Graduate fellowships to prepare elementary and secondary school teachers

One of the most recent federal aid to education programs, of special interest to teachers, was the *Education Professions Development Act of 1967*. While several of the previous Acts devoted some attention to improving the quality of teaching, and meeting critical teacher shortage, the Act of 1967 was for this specific purpose. The Act which amended Title V of the Higher Education Act of 1965, extended the National Teacher Corps for three years, and broadened the programs for graduate fellowships that led to teaching as a profession. In addition, the Act sponsored programs for: identifying capable people, and encouraging them to enter the teaching profession; short-term, intensive training, and in-service training, to provide people with the qualifications necessary for teaching; training or retraining personnel in special fields; and, programs or fellowships for training teachers, administrators, and specialists for colleges and universities. Except for programs that were extensions of the Higher Education Act of 1965, the Act of 1967 became effective on July 1, 1968. Appropriations of $395,000,000 were authorized for the fiscal year of 1969. The grants had to be approved by the U.S. Office of Education.

These examples of federal money grants for educational purposes are only a few of the most significant ones,[29] but they show the deep commitment of the federal government in the national effort to improve the quality of education, and offer equal educational opportunities to everyone.

United States Office of Education

The Office of Education recently passed its one hundredth anniversary. During that century it had served under several departments of the government, had undergone a few name changes, and had expanded its functions.

Henry Barnard, who went to Washington in 1838 seeking data on education but could find none,was the first to emphasize the need for a national clearinghouse of educational information. For almost three decades, he worked to establish a national center devoted to education, and in 1867, Congress finally passed an act creating a department of education, to be headed by a commissioner who was to be a presidential appointee. After spending so many years in this effort, it was appropriate that Henry Barnard was appointed the first United States Commissioner of Education.

Until 1869, the Department of Education operated independently of other government agencies. In that year it was placed under the jurisdiction of the Department of the Interior, and remained there for seventy years. In 1939, it was transferred to the Federal Security Agency, and in 1953, it became a unit of the newly established Department of Health, Education, and Welfare. From time to time, too, the name of the department was changed. Originally, it was designated as the Department of Education, but it became the Office of Education in 1869. The following year, it was named the Bureau of Education, and retained that designation until 1929, when it was again called the Office of Education, its present title.

Its original function was to collect and disseminate educational information which would promote efficient school systems throughout the nation. Toward the end of the nineteenth century, the Office undertook the publication of bulletins which reflected the condition of education not only in the United States but also in other countries. As time passed, it became responsible for administering many federal programs of education, such as the National Defense Education Act of 1958, the Ele-

---

[29]For a complete listing of educational programs administered by the Office of Education in 1967, see "1967 Report on Federal Money and Recent Legislation for Education," *American Education,* 3, Number 2 (February, 1967), 14-17.

mentary and Secondary Education Act of 1965, the Higher Education Act of 1965, and the Education Professions Development Act of 1967. In addition to its own activities, the Office has operated programs from other departments of the federal government and recently categorized its activities as follows:

> The Office is engaged primarily in (a) making studies and collecting and disseminating information and statistics dealing with education; (b) administering grants which are distributed to the states on a formula basis; (c) providing consultative services to educational and cultural agencies; (d) contracting with colleges, universities, State and private agencies for studies and research on educational problems; and (e) operating programs under agreement with other Federal agencies.[30]

Future teachers should realize that the Office of Education is a valuable source of information on educational matters. Its *Biennial Survey of Education,* and its annual *Digest of Education Statistics,* present an amazing array of statistical information on education. Furthermore, the Office publishes pamphlets and bulletins on a wide range of topics related to education, besides two monthly periodicals. *American Education* (formerly titled *School Life*) reports on current educational information, trends, opinions, and state and federal legislation in education. *Higher Education* presents similar information directed primarily to a college and university audience.

Provision for Education of Certain Groups

The federal government has shown an interest in aiding, or assuming the responsibility for, the education of special groups of people. These educational programs are more extensive in some departments than in others, but every department is engaged in some educational activity.

The extensive educational activities of the Department of Health, Education, and Welfare's Office of Education have already been described. The Department's budget also includes appropriations for federally aided corporations, namely, the American Printing House for the Blind, Gallaudet College, and Howard University. The American Printing House for the Blind, located in Louisville, Kentucky, has received federal aid since 1879. The HEW department is responsible for allocat-

---

[30]*Handbook, Office of Education,* U.S. Office of Education (Washington, D.C.: U.S. Government Printing Office, 1963), p. 5.

ing to the states the materials produced for the education of the blind. Gallaudet College, incorporated in Washington, D.C. in 1857 as the Columbia Institution for the Deaf, receives annual federal aid for operating expenses and necessary building construction. Howard University which was established in the District of Columbia in 1867 also receives federal aid. These three institutions are only partially supported through federal grants. The Department of HEW also conducts educational and training programs in connection with vocational rehabilitation, food and drug administration, public health service, and social security administration.

The Department of the Interior has the responsibility for providing education for the people in the territories, possessions, and reservations of the United States, and the children of government employees who are working in areas where education is unavailable. When public schools are not available, the Federal government provides educational services for Indian children on reservations, or enters into contracts with public or private schools to provide facilities for them. Since 1955, programs in adult education have been initiated on several Indian reservations, and, since 1956, vocational education now includes Indians between the ages of 18 and 35. Since the employees of certain national parks live in relative isolation, the Federal government provides, or arranges for the education of their children. Similarly, the Department of the Interior makes provision for the education of people living in American Samoa, the Pribilof Islands, and the Trust Territory of the Pacific Islands.

Perhaps the best known school aid program of the Department of Agriculture is the distribution of milk and surplus food to schools. Begun in 1935, the original act and the subsequent acts of Congress which supplement it were consolidated into the National School Lunch Act of 1946. This act was further supplemented by the Special Milk Program of 1954. Both public and private schools, as well as other institutions, are eligible for its benefits through the state departments of education.

The Department of Defense naturally has many educational and training programs related to the defense of the nation. Each military branch conducts its own programs to train its personnel in various military specializations. Each branch also operates its own academy to train military leaders and cooperates with civilian institutions in various educational programs, both graduate and undergraduate. These branches also provide the means for military personnel to continue their education during off-duty hours. The best known of these programs is conducted by the United States Armed Forces Institute (USAFI). The Department of Defense also gives its civilian employees advanced training in their specialities or permits promising employees to improve themselves through work-study arrangements. The children of military and civilian personnel assigned overseas are educated through service-operated schools, in nonservice-operated schools, or through correspondence courses. The Department of Defense also cooperates with medical schools in revising their curricula to include military and civil defense aspects of medicine and surgery. It enters into research contracts with institutions, and provides education for the people of the Northern Mariana Islands in the Pacific.

The other departments in the federal government also offer educational and training programs. Because they are not as extensive or may relate only to specialized training for the personnel of the Department, they are simply summarized in topical forms.

Department of Labor
Programs of apprenticeship training.
Educational program for foreign visitors.
Cooperation with high schools in testing, counseling, and placing students.

Department of State
Educational exchange program.
International cooperation programs.
Interuniversity contracts for assistance to overseas universities.

Department of Treasury
Education of Coast Guard personnel.
Training of Internal Revenue enforcement and management personnel.

Department of Justice
Education and training of prisoners in federal institutions.
Training of law-enforcement personnel in the FBI National Academy, and in Police Training Schools.
Citizenship education for immigrants.

Department of Commerce
Training of foreign technicians in census procedures.
Operation of U.S. Merchant Marine Academy.
Grants to schools giving nautical training.
Training of foreign meteorologists.
National Bureau of Standards Graduate School, and programs in other schools.

There are also numerous independent federal agencies that make important contributions to the education and training of people. In particular areas, Washington, D.C. and the Canal Zone, the federal government is responsible for a system of public education, but most of the financing is accomplished locally. Other federal agencies partially engaged in educational activities include:

Atomic Energy Commission

Federal Aviation Agency

Federal Deposit Insurance Corporation

Library of Congress

National Aeronautics and Space Administration

National Science Foundation

Office of Civil and Defense Mobilization

Small Business Administration

Tennessee Valley Authority

Veterans Administration

Federal participation in education is more extensive than most of us have imagined. Most of these activities constitute specialized training rather than broad education although some of the programs also include broad education. Most of the programs, too, relate directly to the national interest, and are federally controlled. However, recently, larger amounts of federal aid have been more available to our state-controlled educational system.

Federal Aid Versus Federal Control

Heated arguments over federal aid to education have occurred for many years. It has been debated whether or not the federal government should provide *general aid* or *specific aid* to states. With general aid the money can be used for any educational purpose by the states. With specific aid, the money must be used for the purpose designated (school plants, special education, transportation, etc.). Legislation providing general aid has been defeated in Congress because of the fear that general federal aid might lead to federal control. Some people who have opposed general federal aid believe that, if federal aid is given at all, it should be extended to private as well as public schools. Finally, some people simply oppose any type of federal aid to education.

The arguments favoring federal aid are strong. They pointed out that the federal government is responsible for promoting the national interest, welfare, and defense. If the states do not, or cannot, effectively do this, it is argued, it becomes the obligation of the federal government. This was recognized as a national function in the Ordinance of 1787. However, a delicate balance of power is involved, because the states, and not the federal government, control education. Consequently, any federal legislation on education must not infringe upon the rights of the states. The proponents of federal aid state that the balance of power has always been maintained and that this balance will continue into the future.

Other arguments favoring federal aid to education center around the *need* for it. These proponents produce evidence of the differences that exist in educational opportunities among the states. Statistics show the wide differences that exist in expenditures per pupil, and per classroom unit, besides the differences in the expenditures for facilities and teachers' salaries. Also, there are differences in the degree to which individual states try to provide a good education for their children. All of these differences could be eliminated, say the proponents, if federal aid were used to equalize the educational opportunities among the states. Moreover, they claim, federal funds should be used since it is becoming more difficult for state and local sources to raise money for the improvement of education because of the high national taxes.

Opponents of federal aid admit that inequalities exist in the education states provided their children, but they do not feel that federal aid is the only answer to the problem. They believe that many states *can* make a greater effort to upgrade education, and that they can raise the necessary funds. The money needed for more federal aid, they say, would be paid by these people through increased taxes. Why not raise money in the state, and keep it there, instead of sending it to the federal government and having it given back while, at the same time, losing a portion of it through "handling costs"?

The strongest and most widespread argument against federal aid has always been the fear that it will lead to federal control. These opponents claim that requirements for federal aid would gradually give the federal government more power over education. Federal legislation specifies the conditions that the states must meet to share in the aid. Usually the states are asked to submit "proposals" which must be approved by the U.S. Office of Education. Several questions can be raised concerning this practice. Who judges these proposals? On what basis are they judged? To what extent does the judge's personal philosophy of education enter into his decisions? If there is room for interpretation in these decisions, the persons making them could influence educational theory and practice on a national basis. Whether or not this influence is desirable is the basic question underlying the question of federal aid.

Whether or not one agrees with it, we *have* federal aid to education, but new legislation continues to provide special, rather than general, aid. In recent years, special aid has increased and, in certain fields and under certain conditions, it has been extended to private schools. If it is received by the states "with no strings attached", and if it is used wisely, it should alleviate some of the inequalities in educational opportunity. It should improve the quality of education throughout the United States.

SUMMARY

Since education is not mentioned in the Constitution of the United States, it has been considered a state function ever since the Tenth Amendment was ratified in 1791. Although the state controls education, it delegates considerable authority to local units within the state. The federal government, while not controlling education, has aided education in various ways throughout our national history.

The local units which administer education within a state are known as "school districts". The size of a district is determined by the state. It can include towns, townships, cities, counties, or an arbitrarily designated territory. Whatever its size, the district receives its authority from, and is responsible to, the state. In some states, the county acts as an intermediate unit between the local district and the state.

Each local school district has a local board of education which is responsible for providing a high quality education within the district. The local board forms educational policies, and appoints a chief executive officer to administer its educational program. The quality of education in a school district is directly related to the caliber of people who serve as board members and the person appointed as chief executive officer.

There is now a trend toward the consolidation of small districts into larger units. Consolidation can provide better facilities and programs for children, but may cause a lack of communication between the parents and school personnel, and between teachers and administrators because of the size of the district.

The ultimate authority in the state control of education resides in the people, who adopt a constitution and elect the members of the state legislature. The responsibility for education within the state is given to a state board of education. The members of it can be elected by the people, or appointed by the governor, or be *ex officio* members. Election of board members is the method generally supported by professional groups. The state board of education formulates broad educational policies that are in conformity with existing legislation.

The state board has a chief executive officer who enacts its policies. In some states he is appointed by the board, in other states he is elected by the people or appointed by the governor. Since he must work closely with the board to implement its policies, the majority of states permit the board to appoint its own chief state school official.

Each state has a state department of education, which is headed by the chief state school official. The personnel of the state department constitute the work-force which administers educational programs at the state level. Within the state department, the work is divided into areas of responsibility, which are headed by division heads and section heads. Leadership, courage, vision, and intelligence should be possessed by all personnel for the effective implementation of a state program of education.

The federal government has provided aid and services in four general ways: land grants for educational purposes; money grants for specific educational programs; establishment of the U.S. Office of Education; and, the provision of education for certain groups of people.

The earliest federal land-grant act was the Ordinance of 1785, which provided the sixteenth section of each township in the Northwest Territory for educational purposes. Ohio, in 1802, was the first state to benefit from the Ordinance. Beginning in 1850, new states were granted the sixteenth and thirty-sixth sections, and later three states received the second and thirty-second sections as well. All but nineteen states shared in these land-grants.

The Morrill Act of 1862 also provided substantial land grants. It granted to each state 30,000 acres of land, for each congressman, to establish colleges to teach agriculture and mechanic arts. Many of these colleges have now become large multi-purpose state universities.

Throughout the years, Congress passed many acts granting money to support specific programs in education. The original land-grants under the Morrill Act of 1862, were later supplemented several times with money grants for the support of agricultural education. The Smith-Hughes Act of 1917 provided funds for below-college-level vocational education in agriculture, trades and industries, and home economics. This Act also was supplemented by several others which not only supplied additional funds but also extended vocational education to other fields.

During the depression years, the government provided training and educational facilities under the CCC and WPA programs. After World War II, and the following wars, veterans received education and training benefits. The most recent educational acts of the federal government include important bills such as the National Defense Education Act of 1958, the Elementary and Secondary Education Act of 1965, the Higher Education Facilities Act of 1963, the Higher Education Act of 1965, and the Education Professions Development Act of 1967.

The federal government participated in education with its establishment of the U.S. Office of Education. Through this Office, educational information was collected and disseminated, and consultative services were provided. Its function has been expanded to include the administration of grants, and cooperation with various other agencies and institutions in research and educational programs.

Educational activities are carried on by all government departments. The federal government has assumed the responsibility for the education of people residing in territories, possessions, and reservations of the United States and the children of government employees in areas where education is unavailable. It has aided in the education of the blind and the deaf; and it has provided vocational rehabilitation programs. It has distributed milk and food to schools, made transportation available to school children, and has a great number of training and educational programs for the armed forces and for government employees.

Since the states control education, the question has been raised: How much federal aid and federal participation is desirable in education? Opponents of federal aid fear that this aid may lead to federal control of education. Proponents of this aid hold that it is the only means of equalizing educational opportunities throughout the United States. The degree of influence exerted by the federal government in education depends upon the extent of financial aid given and upon the number and kind of stipulations made for its use.

Questions for discussion:

1. Do you think a local school board should consist of nonprofessional educators?

2. Would you specify minimum educational qualifications for members of a school board?

3. Should school board members be compensated for their services?

4. How do you feel about the consolidation of schools into large districts?

5. Should members of the state board of education be appointed or elected?

6. What control does the state have over private schools?

7. Cite examples of federal aid given to the college you attend.

8. Do you believe that federal aid may lead to federal control of education?

For further reading:

American Association of School Administrators, *The American School Superintendency.* Thirtieth Yearbook. Washington, D.C.: National Education Association, 1952.

American Association of School Administrators, *School Boards in Action.* Twenty-Fourth Yearbook. Washington, D.C.: National Education Association, 1946.

Goldhammer, Keith, *The School Board.* New York: The Center for Applied Research in Education, Inc., 1964.

Hutchins, Clayton D., Albert R. Munse, Edna D. Booker, *Federal Funds for Education, 1958-59 and 1959-60.* Washington, D.C.: U.S. Government Printing Office, 1961.

National Education Association and American Association of School Administrators, Educational Policies Commission, *The Unique Role of the Superintendent of Schools.* Washington, D.C.: the Commission, 1965.

Steel, Ronald, ed., *Federal Aid to Education.* New York: H. W. Wilson Co., 1961.

Sufrin, Sidney, C., *Issues in Federal Aid to Education.* Syracuse, New York: Syracuse University Press, 1962.

White, Alpheus L., *Local School Boards: Organization and Practice.* Washington, D.C.: U.S. Government Printing Office, 1962.

U.S. Office of Education, *Handbook, Office of Education.* Washington, D.C.: U.S. Government Printing Office, 1963.

12

Financing Education

In the United States, we have a system of free, universal education through the secondary level. It is free, however, only because the pupils are not charged tuition to attend public schools in the district. To maintain this system of free education obviously costs an enormous amount of money, which someone must provide. That someone is the taxpayer.

This chapter will give brief answers to three questions related to financing education: What are the reasons for the rise in the cost of education? Where does the money come from? For what purposes are the educational dollar spent?

RISING COST OF EDUCATION

It is usually true that the cost of a product is proportionate to its quality. The cost of education is also proportionate to its quality. Much of the increased cost of education can be traced to measures that have been taken to improve its quality. The efforts to improve its quality, the rising enrollment and the shrinking purchasing power of the dollar, have caused expenditures that have reached spectacular proportions in comparison to previous expenditures.

Inflation

The increased cost of education (and the cost of everything else) evolves from the decreasing purchasing power of the dollar during the past few decades. It simply costs more dollars to buy something now than it did to buy its equivalent a decade ago. However, the income of people has outpaced the effects of inflation, therefore they are able to make a greater financial commitment to education.

Increased Enrollment

In 1967–68, enrollment in the public elementary and secondary schools increased to record proportions for the twenty-third consecutive year, a trend which is expected to continue. During each of those twenty-three years, there were over a million more pupils in school than during each preceding year. Private elementary and secondary schools, and all types of institutions of higher learning also increased their enrollments.

To cover this annual increase, additional teachers were needed, and new or additional facilities were necessary. These necessities further added to the cost of education. To illustrate, in 1967–68 the per pupil cost was estimated at $623; an increase of a million pupils added over one-half billion dollars to the expenditures for that year alone. The cumulative effect of this increase in enrollment each year for twenty-three years added billions of dollars to school expenditures.

The increase in enrollment at levels of schooling, public and private, are illustrated in the following enrollment figures.

Enrollment in United States Schools
Selected Years, 1940-1977[1]
(In rounded figures)

Year	Elementary (K-8) Public	Private	High School (9-12) Public	Private	Higher Education Public	Private
1940	18,832,000	2,153,000	6,601,000	458,000	797,000	698,000
1950	19,387,000	2,708,000	5,725,000	672,000	1,355,000	1,304,000
1960	27,616,000	4,643,000	8,485,000	1,035,000	1,832,000	1,384,000
1967	31,600,000	4,600,000	12,300,000	1,400,000	4,816,000	2,096,000
1977	30,800,000	4,500,000	15,200,000	1,400,000	8,018,000	2,650,000

[1]Data for the years 1940-1960 are adapted from U.S. Bureau of the Census, *Statistical Abstract of the United States: 1967*, 88th Edition (Washington, D.C.: U.S. Government Printing Office, 1967), Table 147, p. 109. The 1967 and 1977 figures are estimated ones, from U.S. Office of Education, *Projections of Educational Statistics to 1977-78* (Washington, D.C.: U.S. Government Printing Office, 1969), Table 1, p. 9.

From 1954 to 1967, there was an annual increase of over one million pupils in the public schools. Following 1967, the increase was more gradual. Enrollment in public elementary schools was expected to reach a peak of 32,100,000 in 1970, followed by a slow decline. Yet, public secondary school enrollment is expected to continue increasing throughout 1970. Enrollment in private elementary schools was expected to decline to 4,500,000 in 1969, and then become stable. Private secondary school enrollment is predicted to remain at 1,400,000 until 1977. Enrollment in institutions of higher education is expected to increase throughout the period.

These statistics not only partially explain the rising costs in past years, but also help to demonstrate that costs will continue to rise until 1977, because the total enrollment in the public schools will continue to rise throughout that period. Since there is no foreseeable end to the decreasing purchasing power of the dollar, inflation will continue to add to already rising costs in education.

Attainment of Higher Educational Level

Not only were there more pupils in school each year, but they continued their education for a longer time than pupils previously did. In 1940, only 24.1 percent of persons aged 25 to 29 had four years of high school or more. By 1966 the percentage had increased to 49.9 percent.[2] The percentage of those people with fewer than five years of elementary education correspondingly dropped from 13.5 percent in 1940 to 6.5 percent in 1966.[3] Schools now have a higher retention rate than they had previously since more people wish to achieve a higher educational level which has also contributed to rising costs.

Better School Plants

During the past two decades, much money has been spent building new schools or remodeling old ones. Much of the construction was done to accommodate the increased enrollment, but an equal number of new facilities were built to replace outdated ones. One-room schools, small schools, and other schools unsafe for occupancy or lacking essential facilities, were replaced by school buildings which were structurally sound, aesthetically pleasing, and well equipped.

---

[2]U.S. Office of Education, *Progress of Public Education in the United States of America* (Washington, D.C.: U.S. Government Printing Office, 1968), from Table 11, p. 16.

[3]*Loc. cit.*

Between 1958–59 and 1967–68, 697,000 new public elementary and secondary school classrooms were built. 430,000 of them accommodated the increased enrollment, and 267,000 replaced outdated classrooms. It is estimated that between the years 1968–69 to 1977–78, 710,000 additional classrooms will be constructed. Only 45,000 of these will be needed to accommodate increased enrollment; the other 665,000 will be needed as replacement units. The capital outlay for new buildings, between 1958–59 and 1967–68, was 33.1 billion dollars, while the estimated outlay for the new buildings between 1968–69 and 1977–78 is 43 billion dollars.[4] School construction annually has added roughly over four billion dollars to school costs.

Higher Teachers' Salaries

The nation now has more teachers who are earning higher salaries, than ever before. An increase in the average salary from $4,520 in 1957–58 to $7,320 in 1967–68 has slightly reduced the financial struggle of teachers. The salary for teachers constitutes the largest single expenditure in the school budget, and since there are approximately two million public school teachers, much of the rising cost of education is due to increased salaries. The difference between the average annual salaries previously mentioned amounts to $2,800. With roughly one and a half million teachers in 1957, and two million in 1967, over $7,000,-000,000 more was spent for teachers' salaries in 1967 than in 1957.

Better Equipment, Materials, and Services

Better school plants and more highly qualified teachers further improved the quality of education. Teachers and pupils have been furnished with better materials and media of instruction. Libraries have been updated and expanded. The latest of audio-visual materials have been introduced, including more use of television and language laboratories. Science laboratories have been modernized. Computers have been installed in larger school systems, and courses in data processing have been introduced. More varied instructional programs have been offered to all pupils, and special programs for all types of atypical children have become more prevalent. There is greater concern for providing adequate guidance personnel and facilities. Evening and summer courses, including courses in adult education have been relatively com-

---

[4]The statistics in this paragraph are adapted from *Projections of Educational Statistics to 1977-78, op. cit.,* Table 43, p. 87. Sums are in terms of 1966-67 dollars.

mon. All of these measures have added to the effectiveness and quality of instruction, and, of course, to the cost of education.

SOURCES OF SCHOOL REVENUE

There are three sources of revenue for educational purposes: local, state, and federal. Although the federal government has expanded its aid to education, federal sources provide only a small portion of the total revenue for education. In 1967–68, local sources provided slightly more than half of the revenue, state sources nearly a half, and federal sources less than a tenth. These proportions, of course, have changed over the years.

Local Sources

Although the states control education, they have given local units varying amounts of responsibility for financing educational programs. The states, within limits prescribed by their laws, permit local districts to levy taxes for educational programs. The property tax has been the major source of revenue at the local level, although there are other ways to raise money such as sales, business, and income taxes, license fees, and bond issues.

Not all local districts can equally finance adequate educational programs, because of the differences in their population distribution, and their taxable wealth. Some districts have from ten to twenty-five times the ability of other districts to finance suitable programs of education. Thus, a wealthy district may have an excellent school system, while a neighboring district, lacking local financial support, cannot even provide basic programs without outside aid. To equalize these differences state and federal aid is given to local districts.

For major expenses, such as new building construction, the state permits a local district to borrow money by issuing school bonds. However, the state limits the amount of these bonds to a specified percentage of the assessed valuation of the school district. The issuance of school bonds usually is subject to the approval of the people as expressed through popular vote.

The property tax which is the primary source of school revenue at the local level, has been criticized for several reasons. It sometimes has placed a disproportionate share of the tax burden on those people who own real estate. Money invested in stocks, bonds, and various types of investment plans, is often exempt from property taxes. Furthermore the property tax no longer can produce sufficient revenue for the schools. Because of the sharp rise in school expenditures, a broader tax base is needed. A broader base would not only produce more revenue but would also distribute the tax burden more equitably among all of the people.

State Sources

Through general and special aid, and through leadership and encouragement, the state tries to improve the quality of education throughout its districts. The state and the districts, working together, establish a basic program of education for all children within the state. This program, known as a "foundation program", sets minimum standards that must be met by all of the schools in the state. By this program, the state assures all pupils, who have the necessary ability, preparation for the next phase of their life's work. For example, the state may prescribe a foundation program for all high schools that would enable all college-bound students to meet college entrance requirements. Or, it might prescribe a commercial program that would provide the basic knowledge and skills necessary for entrance into business occupations. Once a foundation program is legislated by the state, the districts are required to provide it. However, the districts are not limited to only the minimum standards prescribed by the state. Districts having the means and desire, may enlarge their programs beyond the minimum level set by the state. The state may try to stimulate financially-able but educationally apathetic districts by withholding aid until they conform to state-mandated programs. Districts that want to conform with state programs but are not financially capable of doing so receive a greater amount of state aid to help equalize educational opportunities.

States derive their revenue for education from two sources. First, approximately three-fourths of the states have permanent school funds that are derived from the early federal land grants. The income from these funds automatically goes to education, but it accounts for only a small percentage of the needed revenue. The second source of revenue is taxation. Special taxes may be levied to raise money for education, or portions of general taxes may be set aside for education. Among the types of taxes that have been used, wholly or partially, to finance education at the state level are: property, income, sales, tobacco, liquor, inheritance, communications, gasoline, and taxes on public carriers.

The state legislature appropriates the money used for education at the state level, and the state department must operate within the limits of the appropriations. The state budget usually provides for general aid or special aid to the local districts. Some states provide an equal amount of general aid to all districts. This is known as a flat grant, or a fixed grant. Other states vary the amount of the grants according to the financial status of the districts. This type of grant is termed a variable grant. Each state uses its own formula to determine the amount of money a district will receive. The formulas usually are based on one or more of the following statistics: average daily attendance (A.D.A.), average daily membership (A.D.M.), school census, number of teachers, levels of schooling, and types of programs offered. The amount of aid granted to a local school district generally depends on the size of the district and the extent of its programs. Besides general aid, states may grant funds for special purposes, such as construction, teachers' salaries, textbooks, lunches, health services, supervision, libraries, audio-visual materials, transportation, and special education.

The degree of state control over the money granted to the local districts varies from state to state. Some states exercise little control, while others specify in detail uses for the money. Too much state control may either dampen or hamper local initiative. Some of the arguments mentioned for and against federal aid to education have also been applied to state aid to local districts. However, legally the state *does* control education. Questions concerning state aid, therefore, should not relate to the desirability of state control, but to the *degree* of control. How much control can the state exercise without endangering local leadership, initiative, interest, and concern for education? Many people feel that the state should establish foundation programs, provide encouragement and aid, yet exercise a minimum amount of control.

There are many problems and factors to consider, in state apportionment of funds to local districts. No two districts are alike in their ability to support an educational program. Most states assure all districts a certain amount of support per child, and then give additional aid to economically distressed districts. In trying to equalize the educational opportunities within their boundaries the states have tried to observe the following principles.

1. Every child should have a relatively equal basic educational opportunity regardless of where he might live in the state or the taxable wealth of the school district which provides his schooling.
2. The state should *encourage* the most efficient organization and operation of the school districts possible.
3. The state legislature has a responsibility to maintain a proper balance among all sources of revenue available to school districts so that no district is penalized or unduly rewarded financially, as compared with other districts.

4. State funds should be apportioned on an objective basis, easily estimated by legislative bodies as to amounts and computed upon definite factors.
5. The state should exercise limited control over local school boards in the administration of their schools.
6. Allowances should be made for some range in revenues among the school districts in recognition of differences in costs not otherwise provided for in the formula and in the scope and quality of local educational programs.
7. The state should encourage local school boards to go beyond basic educational levels in providing quality features and developing experimental educational programs to meet changing needs of local conditions and of the times.[5]

Federal Sources

The federal government also raises money through taxes, and its budget provides funds for education in the amounts, and for the purposes, legislated by Congress. Just as local school districts vary in their ability to finance educational programs, states vary in their ability to finance state educational programs. States possessing rich natural resources and highly industrialized, have three or four times the ability to finance education than states that lack these means of income. In its aid to education for special purposes, the federal government considers these differences and gives more aid to the states with less wealth.

Proportion of Revenue Contributed by Each Source

In early years, American education was almost exclusively a local effort. During the nineteenth century, as the states began to assume the responsibility for education, they took a more prominent role in financing it. Gradually, the proportion of revenue supplied by the states increased. Now some states provide more revenue for education than their districts provide. However, nationally, local districts are still the primary source of school revenue. Because of the rising costs in education and because the sources of revenue at the local level are being exhausted, the states and the federal government have, in recent years, provided higher contributions. It is likely that, before long, local sources will, for the first time in our history, provide less than 50 percent of the revenue for education. This present trend is evident in the following

---

[5]Committee on Educational Finance, National Education Association, *Financing Public Schools* (Washington, D.C.: National Education Association, 1965), pp. 44-45.

figures, which show the percentage of revenue contributed by federal, state, and local sources for selected years.

Sources of Revenue for Education

Percentage Supplied by Local, State, and Federal Sources, Selected Years, 1939-1968[6]

	1939-40	1949-50	1959-60	1965-66	1967-68
Federal	1.8	2.9	4.4	7.9	8.0
State	30.3	39.8	39.1	38.8	40.0
Local	68.0	57.3	56.5	53.3	52.0

These figures show that the percentage of federal contributions has nearly doubled within a decade. State aid increased considerably during the first decade shown, levelled off for approximately two decades, then began to increase again. The revenue supplied by local districts has decreased steadily throughout the period shown. It should be remembered that these contributions represent national averages. The contributions by each source, of course, vary from state to state. For 1967–68, the extremes of the estimated percentage of revenue from each source were:[7]

Federal sources ranged from 3.0% in Wyoming to 29.5% in Alaska (41.9% in Washington, D.C.)

State contributions varied from 3.9% in Nebraska to 84.4% in Hawaii.

Local sources accounted for 5.1% of the revenue in Hawaii, and ranged to a high of 87.5% in Nebraska.

These variations are due to differences in local and state efforts to support education and to differences in taxable wealth in those units. There are, however, special situations which account for some of the extremes. For example, Hawaii's state contributions are high because education is administered entirely by the state.

There are, then, three sources of school revenue: the federal government, the state, and the local district. Most of the money raised by these three sources comes from taxation. The federal government taxes all eligible persons and institutions, and then returns a portion of the money to the states and local districts. It pays for about 8 percent of the

---

[6]Statistics from 1939-1940 through 1965-66 are from *Progress of Public Education in the United States of America, op. cit.* adapted from Table 13, p. 17. Percentages for 1967-68 are from "The Statistics Speak," *American Education*, 4, Number 4, (April, 1968), p. 31.

[7]National Education Association, *Rankings of the States, 1968* (Washington, D.C.: National Education Association, 1968), from Table 84, p. 44; Table 86, p. 45; Table 88, p. 46.

cost of education. Most of the revenue of the states also comes from taxation; the money budgeted for education is used to implement educational programs at the state level. A portion of it is returned to the local districts in the form of state aid to education. State sources pay about 40 percent of the cost of education. Finally, the local districts tax themselves to maintain their schools, and their contributions pay for about 52 percent of the total bill. In the last analysis, however, the individual and corporate taxpayer is the primary source of all school revenue. His tax dollars take national, state, and local routes before a portion returns some type of benefit for him.

EXPENDITURES IN EDUCATION

A short time ago, few people would have envisioned that education in the United States would assume its present proportions. Education has become big business. In 1967–68, there were 43,788,324 public elementary and secondary school pupils taught by 1,837,926 classroom teachers.[8] Administrators, specialists, clerks, aides, maintenance people, school board members, and staffs employed by the states and the federal government have further increased the number of people involved in education. To keep a business of this size running effectively requires a great deal of money.

Total Expenditures

The rapid increase in total expenditures for public elementary and secondary education can be seen in the following figures reported by the U.S. Office of Education.[9]

Year	Amount Expended
1939–40	$2,344,049,000
1949–50	5,837,643,000
1955–56	10,955,047,000
1959–60	15,613,255,000
1965–66	26,195,500,000
1967–68	31,511,051,000 (est.)

---

[8]"Estimates of School Statistics", *NEA Research Bulletin,* 46, Number 1 (March, 1968), p. 14.

[9]*Progress of Public Education in the United States of America: 1967-68, op. cit.,* extracted from Table 15, p. 18.

Expenditures tripled between 1949 and 1959, and doubled in the decade following 1959. Using the twenty-year period, 1949–1969, expenditures have increased by approximately 600%. Projecting into the future, the U.S. Office of Education has estimated that by 1977–78, total expenditures for public elementary and secondary schools would rise to 40.9 billion dollars.[10]

These expenditures do not even include the money spent for public institutions of higher learning, or private schools at all levels. For the year 1968–69, the U. S. Office of Education estimated an expenditure of 4.2 billion dollars for private elementary and secondary schools, 8.0 billion for private higher institutions of learning, and 11.9 billion for public higher educational institutions, in addition to 32.6 billion dollars spent for public elementary and secondary schools.[11] Thus, the total estimated 1968–69 expenditures for education in the United States amounted to the tremendous sum of 56.7 billion dollars.

Per Pupil Costs

A comparison of per pupil costs with per pupil costs of other years is one way to judge the rising costs in education. However, these statistics are reported in different ways. Some sources show per pupil costs based on "average daily attendance", while other sources use "average daily membership" as a basis for computing costs. Per pupil costs are usually expressed in terms of "current dollars", but recently to allow for inflation, some sources have converted "current dollars" into "1966 dollars", or dollars of another year, in order to compare the statistics. Each of these bases produces a different per pupil cost.

Annual per pupil costs have risen steadily throughout the years. Expressed in terms of unadjusted dollars, the annual current expenditure[12] per pupil in average daily attendance (A.D.A.) rose during the past three decades as follows:[13]

[10]*Projections of Educational Statistics to 1977-78*, U.S. Office of Education (Washington, D.C.: U.S. Government Printing Office, 1969), from Table 38, p. 79. Estimate is based on the value of 1966-67 dollars.

[11]*Ibid.*, from Table 38, p. 78. Estimate is based on 1967-68 dollars.

[12]Excluding expenditures for capital outlay and interest on debt.

[13]Figures for 1939-40 through 1959-60 are from U.S. Office of Education, *Digest of Educational Statistics*, 1965 ed. (Washington, D.C.: U.S. Government Printing Office, 1965), Table 5, p. 11. Estimated figure for 1967-68 is from U.S. Office of Education, *Fall 1967 Statistics of Public Schools* (Washington, D.C.: U.S. Government Printing Office, 1968), Table 12, p. 26.

| | Annual Current Cost |
Year	Per Pupil in A.D.A.
1939–40	$88.09
1949–50	208.83
1959–60	375.14
1967–68	623.00 (est.)

The increased cost per pupil is due to inflation, improvement in the quality of education, and to reasons mentioned earlier in this chapter.

These per pupil costs are national averages. Among the individual states, there are considerable differences in the amount expended per pupil. In 1967–68, New York spent an estimated $982 per pupil, which was the highest annual current expenditure per pupil in average daily attendance; Mississippi made the lowest expenditure with a per pupil expenditure of $346.[14] Thus, New York spent 2.8 times as much per pupil as Mississippi. Yet, the people of Mississippi apparently made as great an educational effort, since in 1966, they spent 4.4 percent of their personal income to maintain public elementary and secondary schools, while the people of New York 4.3 percent of their personal incomes.[15] Obviously the use of per pupil expenditures as a measure of educational effort can be misleading.

Another factor to consider in comparing per pupil expenditures is the difference in cost of living in various areas. The per pupil expenditure in a high-cost-of living area will be, of course, much higher than the expenditures in an area where living expenses are lower. Yet the educational effort and the quality of education may be equivalent in both areas. The high cost of living in Alaska is an outstanding illustration of this situation. In 1967–68, the cost of living in Alaska was so much higher than the cost of living in other states that it was necessary to reduce the dollar amounts by one-fourth to make them comparable to figures in other states. Thus, Alaska's 1967–68 per pupil expenditure of $976 was reduced to $732 in terms of the purchasing power of the dollar in other states. Unless this factor is considered, erroneous comparisons with other states will result. Similarly, expenditures may be inflated in states that have large urban populations, where the cost of living is higher than in rural areas. For example, New York City, has a tremendous pupil enrollment, which raises average per pupil expenditure of the state of New York to a much higher level than is really representative of the entire state.

---

[14]*Loc. cit.*

[15]*Rankings of the States, 1968, op. cit.*, Table 104, p. 55.

These illustrations do not dispute the fact that there are differences in expenditures among the states, but rather show that these differences are not always as great as they appear statistically. Nevertheless, even after considering extenuating factors, there are substantial differences among the states in effort and expenditures for education. However, federal and state aid used to establish foundation programs is now fairly constant, and the differences in expenditures are largely due to local efforts.

How the School Dollar is Spent

School districts prepare an annual budget, showing the anticipated expenditures and revenues for the coming school year. The local school board is legally responsible for the preparation of the school budget, but it may delegate the details of its preparation to the district's superintendent, or to its financial officer, or a committee appointed for that purpose.

Usually, two types of budgets are prepared. The first type, the "operating budget", shows the current expenditures and receipts. The other type is known as the "capital outlay budget". It itemizes the long-term expenditures for land, physical facilities, and equipment. The money for the expenditures listed in the budgets comes from three sources: local (property tax, bond issues, etc.), state grants, and federal aid.

In preparing the operating budget, anticipated expenditures are listed under six categories which cover all aspects of the educational program. These categories, and the average percent spent for each, are shown in following chart.

Average Operating Budget Expenditures[16]

Category	Percent Expended
Instruction (salaries of principals, teachers, and other professional help; classroom supplies and textbooks)	78.4
Operation of plant (salaries, supplies, utilities)	10.0

---

[16]Adapted from National Education Association, *Financing Public Schools* (Washington, D.C.: National Education Association, 1965), pp. 47, 51.

Average Operating Budget Expenditures—cont.

Category	Percent Expended
Administration (salaries of super-intendent and office clerks; office expenses)	4.0
Fixed charges (insurance, retire-ment)	3.5
Maintenance (buildings, grounds, and classroom equipment)	3.4
Auxiliary school services (lunch and health programs)	0.7

The largest part of the school dollar is spent for instructional pur-poses, and, within this category, most of the money is spent for salaries (73.2 percent for salaries, 5.2 percent for instructional materials). The recent substantial increases in salary, therefore, account for a major portion of the increased cost of education. Even when the expenditures of the capital outlay budget are combined with the expenditures of the operating budget, instructional costs still account for 55 percent of the money spent.[17]

Expenditures in Relation to Quality of Education

The discussion thus far has implied a direct relationship between the amount of money expended and the quality of education. This rela-tionship is evident, even though exceptions are sometimes cited which seem to weaken the argument. The most important single factor in a good educational program is the teacher, It is the teacher's intelligence, enthusiasm, knowledge, and skill that determine how effectively the school's program interacts with pupils and helps them to develop their particular potentialities. To demand excellent qualifications without offering adequate remuneration is unrealistic. Since it takes many years of education and experience to become a good teacher, many capable young people will not choose teaching if other occupations are more financially attractive. In our previous discussion on the supply and de-mand for teachers, we noted that the supply of competent teachers increased as salaries became more attractive. Therefore, there *is* a relationship between expenditures for salaries and the quality of teach-ers. Although there were many capable teachers in the classroom when

---

[17]*Progress of Public Education in the United States of America, 1967-68, op. cit.,* p. 7.

salaries were low, higher salaries cause a *greater number* of talented people to enter the profession.

Quality education demands a proper environment. Needless hindrances to the learning process, and the development of children, occur when the actual school building is in disrepair, or lacks desirable facilities, or is too small for the school's enrollment. A suitable building not only provides learning materials which facilitate learning but also helps to inculcate the student with a respect for his surroundings, and pride in his school. Proper physical facilities, however, cost money. Consequently, there is again a relationship between the amount of money available and the quality of the education that can be provided.

In our society, where each individual should have the opportunity to develop his potentialities, a quality education implies a variety of programs that take care of individual differences. Since a variety of interests and talents are represented in the school population, a differentiated curricula (such as academic, general, vocational, commercial), would allow each individual to develop in the area for which he is best suited. Special programs are needed for atypical children, such as the physically handicapped, the mentally retarded, and the emotionally maladjusted. Since these programs require additional personnel, facilities, and materials, they can be provided only if adequate financial resources are available.

An adequate supply of money can raise the quality of education. It can provide better qualified teachers, better school plants and facilities, and a variety of programs for individual differences. Money helps to raise the quality of education by providing good libraries, modern laboratories, audio-visual aids, and a wide range of extracurricular activities. While money may not guarantee high quality education, without it, high quality is impossible. In fact, studies have shown that the level of expenditure is the best single measure of the quality of education.[18]

DEGREE OF EFFORT TO IMPROVE EDUCATION

Several questions can be asked about the trend of higher expenditures in education. What has been the reaction of the public to higher taxes? Has the increased revenue been spent wisely? Do greater expenditures mean greater public effort to improve education, or is the increase simply due to higher incomes?

---

[18]U.S. Office of Education, *Profiles in School Support* (Washington, D.C.: U.S. Government Printing Office, 1965), p. 2.

In the 1950's, conditions in education were deplorable. These conditions were publicized widely during the middle 1950's, and remedial measures were begun. After Sputnik in 1957, a crash program was initiated to improve the quality of education. The program, of course, necessitated higher taxes to pay for the rising costs of improvements.

As long as people felt that they were paying for the best possible education for their children, they did not object to the additional tax burden. However, doubts about the large expenditures began to arise. Occasionally critics publicized examples of unwise expenditures, claiming that the "best" was beginning to include frills and luxuries. They charged that, in some schools, the materials used were unnecessarily expensive, and that some physical facilities were too spacious, or even unnecessary. School programs were criticized for offering courses that were not truly educational. Even the quality of the basic programs was questioned.

As a result of the publicity, the public became increasingly concerned about expenditures for education. People became more involved in school affairs. They questioned increased expenditures in school board meetings. If they were convinced that more revenue was not needed, or that money was not spent wisely, they voiced their opposition to increased taxes and school bond issues. Citizens' taxpayer associations carefully watched school expenditures.

This exchange of ideas brought about a desirable involvement of the public in school affairs, and people discovered with occasional exceptions, that they were receiving more for their money than the critics led them to believe. The public became more aware of the many ramifications of school problems. Schoolmen, knowing that the public was greatly concerned, evaluated their proposals more carefully before presenting them to the people. There resulted a healthy system of checks and balances. On the whole, the public accepted higher taxation willingly, if not gracefully. With all the facts laid before them, people saw the need for improvements in education. They realize that better quality in education has to be paid for.

Furthermore, the nation was experiencing unprecedented prosperity, which caused higher personal income and made higher taxes less burdensome. Were people spending a greater percentage of their income for education, or was the revenue raised to pay for increased expenditures simply representing the same percentage of higher incomes? A comparison of the percentage of the gross national product spent annually for education should provide this information. The following figures are based on expenditures for public and nonpublic education at all levels.

Per Cent of Gross National Product
Spent for Education, 1937–1967[19]

Year	Percent
1937	3.3
1947	2.84
1957	4.79
1967	6.65

The percentage of the gross national product which was spent for education in 1967 was double the percentage spent in 1937. Except for the years during, and immediately after, World War II, the percentage rose continuously. It can be concluded that people have made a greater *effort* to support education, because they have spent a higher percentage of their income for education.

The future years will bring further increases in expenditures for education. Will the people accept higher taxes to pay them? They will, if they are convinced of the need for the expenditures. Although the taxpayer is now making a greater effort to support education, he is still able to live comfortably. His contributions to education have not yet forced him to lower his standard of living. This fact is illustrated by the personal consumption expenditures of individuals, as compared with expenditures for education.

Personal Consumption Expenditures
Selected Items, 1965[20]
(In billions of dollars)

Item	Amount spent
Food	85.4
Housing	63.2
Clothing, accessories, jewelry	43.4
Medical care	28.1
New and used cars	26.7
Recreation	26.3
Gasoline and oil	15.1
Alcoholic beverages	12.9
Tobacco	8.4
Personal care	7.5

---

[19]*Progress of Public Education in the United States of America, 1967-68, op. cit.,* Table 16, p. 19.

[20]*Statistical Abstract of the United States: 1967, op. cit.,* extracted from Table 459, p. 323.

These expenditures may be compared with the 26.2 billion dollars spent for public elementary and secondary education in 1965–66. Naturally most of the money is spent for the necessities of life, such as food, clothing, and shelter, but some of the other figures are revealing. For example, in 1965, we spent slightly more for recreation than we did for public schools. Similarly, the expenditures for alcoholic beverages and tobacco equalled about 80% of the total spent for public elementary and secondary education. If it is necessary, obviously, a portion of these expenditures can be re-directed toward education.

Even though we have the ability to finance a quality education, it is probable that opposition to greater expenditures will grow, since additional funds are needed for many other purposes by all levels of government. Tax dollars are needed for military purposes, for combating crime and delinquency, for eliminating slum areas, and for foreign aid. These continuously increasing assessments may make the taxpayer more weary and wary of future expenditures.

In 1968, the United States was still enjoying a prolonged period of prosperity. Yet, in that year, Congress insisted upon cutting the national budget substantially. This cut may have been partially motivated by political reasons, but it *was* a measure taken to reduce deficit spending and inflation. As a result of the budget cut, the amount of federal aid to education had to be somewhat reduced. This, in turn, curtailed state and local educational programs that were dependent on federal aid. It can be seen, therefore, that the groundwork of many years can be undone in an instant through curtailment of federal funds, unless state or local units can shoulder the additional financial burden. A reduction of budgets at the state or local level could have the same effect which explains why it is sometimes undesirable to reduce taxes once they have been levied to provide desirable programs in education.

SUMMARY

The cost of a free, universal education in the public schools has risen sharply during the last two decades for several reasons. During the last quarter-century, the purchasing power of the dollar has decreased, causing equivalent things to cost more now than they did in the past. Increased enrollment in the schools has further added to the cost of education. The rise in enrollment has been particularly sharp since 1950, growing from 19 million in that year to 31 million in 1967. Not only do more pupils attend school, but they stay in school longer, which also has added to the cost of education. To care for the increased enrollment, it was necessary to build new school plants or remodel old ones. In one decade, between 1957–58 and 1966–67, 702,000 new public elementary and secondary school classrooms were built, at a cost of 36.2 billion dollars. A similar expenditure is estimated for the following decade. The largest single item responsible for the rising costs, however, was the increase in teachers' salaries. Between 1957–58 and 1967–68, the average salary rose from $4,520 to $7,320 which added billions of dollars to the cost of education. Finally, as an added cost, pupils have been provided with better equipment, materials, programs, and services than ever before.

The sources of revenue for education are three: local, state and federal. In terms of national averages, the primary source of school revenue is the local district. The state is the secondary source of revenue and federal sources make up the smallest percentage.

Although the state controls education, it delegates to the local district much of the responsibility for financing education. In order to raise money, the state permits local districts to levy taxes. The property tax has been the primary local source of school revenue, but there is a tendency toward the use of a broader based tax in order to raise more money and distribute the tax burden more equitably. With the legal permission of the state, local school districts can also raise money through issuing school bonds.

The state, in cooperation with the local districts, chooses a foundation program, which prescribes the minimum offerings to all children of the state. The state makes some financial contributions to the districts for the support of the foundation program. Some states make flat grants to all districts, other states vary the amount of the grants to conform to the financial resources of the local district. The state derives its revenue for education from permanent school funds and from taxes levied for educational purposes. States vary in the degree of control they exercise over the money granted to local districts. The state's degree of control should not be so rigid that it stifles local initiative and interest in education.

The federal government has provided aid to education through land grants and legislation which allocates funds for special programs. In offering money grants, the federal government tries to consider the differences among the states in their ability to support education and then gives larger grants to states with less wealth. The federal government thus tries to equalize educational opportunities among the states, just as the state does among its local districts.

Historically, the local district has been the primary source of school revenue, but in recent decades the state and federal government have increased their contributions to education. Nationally in 1967–68, local sources provided 52 percent of school revenue, state sources 40 percent, and the federal government 8 percent. Among the individual states, the percentage contributed by each source varied considerably.

Expenditures in education have become enormous. Between 1949–50 and 1967–68, the costs for public elementary and secondary education rose approximately 600 percent, from over five billion dollars to over thirty-one billion dollars. Including public and private schools at all levels, the total expenditures for 1968–69 were estimated at 56.7 billion dollars. The annual current cost per pupil in average daily attendance rose from $208.83 in 1949–50, to $375.14 in 1959–60, and was estimated at $623 for 1967–68. The per pupil cost also varied from state to state. New York was the highest with $982 in 1967–68, and Mississippi was the lowest with $346. The differences in per pupil costs may be attributed to differences in wealth, cost of living, and effort to support education among states.

In determining its fiscal efforts for the coming school year, each school district prepares a budget which shows the expected expenditures and revenues. The "operating budget" shows current expenditures and receipts, while the "capital outlay budget" deals with long-term outlays of money. In the operating budget, expenditures are listed under six categories: instruction, operation of plant, administration, maintenance, auxiliary school services, and fixed charges. In the average operating budget, the greatest outlay of money is for instruction, for which 78.4% of the funds are expended, and the next largest expenditure is 10% for operation of the plant. Within the "instruction" category, 73.2% of the entire budget is spent for the salaries of professional personnel, and classroom supplies and textbooks.

There is a direct relationship between the amount of money spent for education and the quality of education provided. More funds can raise the quality of education by providing better qualified teachers, better school plants and facilities, a variety of programs that provide for individual differences, better libraries, laboratories, audio-visual materials, and a wide range of extracurricular activities. Studies have usually shown a high positive correlation between the amount of money expended and the quality of education provided.

The public has exerted a greater effort to support education. People are spending a higher percentage of their income for education. During the 1950's, when the need for additional expenditures became apparent to all, there were few objections to the higher taxation for educational purposes. However, as expenditures continued to rise, the public asked more questions about the necessity of additional expenditures. With additional increases in school costs forecasted, and many other claims being made on the tax dollar, it is likely that the present questioning attitude will continue.

Questions for discussion:

1. What tax base do you think should be used to raise revenue for the public schools?
2. Should the local, state, or federal government be the primary source of school revenue?
3. Evaluate the property tax as the major source of revenue on the local level.
4. How do you account for the wide differences among states in the amount of money they provide for education?
5. Can you cite examples of school expenditures that have been unnecessary or wasteful?
6. In general, do you think we are "getting our money's worth" for the money spent on education?
7. What factors will determine whether or not we keep increasing expenditures in education?

For further reading:

Barr, W. Monfort, *American Public School Finance*, New York: American Book Company, 1960.

Corbally, John E., *School Finance*. Boston: Allyn & Bacon, Inc., 1962.

Educational Policies Commission, *National Policy and the Financing of the Public Schools*. Washington, D.C.: National Education Association, 1959.

Johns, Roe L., and Edgar L. Morphet, *Financing the Public Schools*. Englewood Cliffs, N. J.: Prentice-Hall Inc., 1960.

Jones, Howard R., *Financing Public Elementary and Secondary Education*. New York: The Center for Applied Research in Education, Inc., 1966.

U. S. Office of Education, *Profiles in School Support*. Washington, D.C.: U.S. Government Printing Office, 1965.

_____, *Progress of Public Education in the United States of America*. Washington, D.C.: U.S. Government Printing Office, 1968.

_____, *State Programs for Public School Support*. Washington, D.C.: U.S. Government Printing Office, 1965.

13

Recurrent Problems in Education

Throughout the preceding chapters, we have discussed the problems and issues that arose as a part of the developments of education in the United States. These debates had centered around administrative objectives and criteria which affect every aspect of teaching, from research to finance. These issues have reccurred throughout the years, but, since they are unsettled, they still rank as current problems.

There are a host of other problems and issues, old yet new, that are related to each aspect of education. In this chapter, recurrent problems are further considered through a discussion of five additional topics: indoctrination and academic freedom; equality of educational opportunity, compulsory education, and the dropout; student unrest; and, the evaluation of student progress. These are diversified, controversial problems which have been experienced by all teachers, and which will confront every beginning teacher. This discussion should offer the prospective teacher further evidence of the magnitude and multiplicity of educational problems. It should help him to begin hypothesizing tentative solutions for them.

INDOCTRINATION AND ACADEMIC FREEDOM

The problems created by different philosophies of education are basic to all other educational problems. Each school of philosophy naturally feels that it possesses the truth and that it is obligated to teach according to its tenets. A teacher's philosophy will be felt by his pupils, because a teacher interprets everything he teaches and all his classroom activity in terms of the philosophy he accepts.

Indoctrination

Although educators know that a teacher's philosophy permeates everything he does, some still claim that a teacher should not indoctrinate his pupils. Because the term, *indoctrinate,* is used in a derogatory sense by some, and because it is misinterpreted by others, the term should be clarified.

The term "indoctrination" is used in two manners. Webster's dictionary defines it as:

> to instruct in the rudiments or principles of learning, or of a branch
> of learning; to instruct in, or imbue with, as principles or doctrines.

In this sense, indoctrination simply means that a teacher instructs his pupils in, or according to, a definite set of principles. Webster's dictionary further indicates, however, that the term is sometimes used to mean "to imbue with an opinion or with a partisan or sectarian point of view." In this narrow definition, indoctrination means that a teacher inculcates his pupils with a biased, one-sided presentation, excluding all other points of view.

If an individual accepts the first definition of the term, it would be difficult to deny that indoctrination does, and should, occur in a classroom. Educators universally agree that every teacher should have a philosophy of education, and that his philosophy will, to a large degree, determine his aims, content, and methods. If he does not have a philosophy, his instructional activities have no direction or meaning. However, the fact that he does teach according to a definite set of principles, does not necessarily mean that he excludes all other philosophies. Every conscientious teacher tries to expose his pupils to several points of view on controversial issues, even though, in the process, his own convictions will invariably stand out.

When educators refer to indoctrination in a derogatory sense, they usually mean teachers who present their material in a one-sided, biased way. These teachers may have such strong convictions, or may, perhaps, know so few other viewpoints, that they see only their own beliefs, unaware of, or ignoring other possibilities. This type of indoctrination is justly condemned. It closes the avenues of investigation to pupils who want to search for knowledge.

Indoctrination always occurs, in either in the broad or the narrow sense. It takes place consciously or unconsciously, directly, or indirectly. It can be seen in the teacher's selection of material, in his explanations and evaluations and even in his mannerisms, gestures, or tones of voice. It is doubtful that a teacher could avoid indoctrination in the broad sense, since his philosophy permeates his entire life and cannot be separated from his activities. He should, however, try to avoid indoctrination in the narrow sense.

The most important element in the whole question of indoctrination is the *type* of indoctrination. There are conflicting philosophies of education, which present opposing explanations of man's origin, nature, and destiny. Some of these philosophies, of necessity, must be false. In the United States, we have accepted a democratic philosophy of education, which recognizes the dignity of the individual, holds certain truths to be self-evident, and maintains that man has God-given, inalienable rights. Our schools try to educate pupils for living in a democratic society, by imbuing them with, or instructing them in, the principles of democracy. In other words, we are *indoctrinating* students with democratic principles. Simultaneously we try to evaluate other forms of government in terms of these principles. In this way, we hope to produce an informed citizenry, capable of intelligent self-government, free yet responsible.

Anti-Democratic Indoctrination

Although most teachers teach the principles of democracy, there is a small minority who teach their pupils principles which are inimical to a democratic form of government. Many publications that have appeared throughout the years have substantiated this fact. It has been shown that many of our pupils are taught concepts such as the following: man is a creature of the state and has no rights except those given to him by the state; personal responsibility does not exist because the individual's actions are determined by forces over which he has no control; the democratic concept that each individual is a sovereign human being is false; spiritual and religious beliefs are cultural fossils; and, undemocratic actions may be used to achieve desirable goals. These teachings are opposed to the personal dignity and responsibility upon which a democratic society rests.

Some teachers instruct their pupils in anti-democratic principles for purely academic reasons; they are convinced that they have the truth, and feel obligated to teach it. There are other teachers, however, whose motives are political as well as academic. They are consciously trying to change our form of government. They frequently will ridicule patriotism, belittle our national heroes, advocate disrespect for law, and try to work with policy-making groups to influence the choice of subjects for the curriculum, and to help select the books for the library. They use "catch phrases" such as the "ruling class" against the "man of the street"; sophistic arguments; and focus on the differences in social status that exist in our schools.[1]

Academic Freedom

Why is this minority permitted to teach things that may undermine our democracy? Often the techniques they use are too subtle to be discovered. But this is not the real answer. The real answer is because they are teaching in a democracy! Just as each person has the freedom to express his thoughts in our society, a teacher has a large degree of freedom in teaching. He may, within limits, teach what he believes to be true. This academic freedom of the teacher to teach the truth as he sees it, is important to the quest for knowledge and the preservation of the democratic way of life. Without a free flow of ideas, the truth could be stifled by various coercive or repressive measures.

Yet, there is a limit to the freedom of expression: it must be combined with *responsible* expression. Freedom of expression does not give a man the right to shout "Fire!" in a crowded theater. There are various restraints on freedom of expression, which are dictated by an individual's conscience, by good taste, and by law. An individual may not, for example, use the right to freedom of expression to slander his neighbor. Even though the teacher has academic freedom, he must use it within the limits of propriety and the law. He has the responsibility of working for the welfare of his pupils, and therefore, the welfare of our democratic society. For this reason, the school laws of many states limit the extent of a teacher's academic freedom. The state can do this legally because it has

---

[1]The testimony of ex-communists provides ample evidence of these activities and teachings.

the right to take measures to secure its welfare, as long as these measures do not violate the Constitution. Similarly, a teacher, in a private institution, his freedom of expression as long as his teachings do not prevent the achievement of the stated objectives of his institution.

Sometimes there is only a fine line separating legitimate self-expression from self-expression which is not legitimate. Freedom of expression must remain a characteristic of our democratic society, but it must not be used to destroy the form of government which protects it. As long as anti-democratic teachers confine their activities to an exposition of theory, as opposed to advocating violent overthrow of the government, they have a right to free expression. Our democracy, in spite of its known shortcomings, is strong enough to survive, in public forum, the battle of ideologies. In classrooms, the work of teachers dedicated to democratic principles should be able to counteract the teachings of a minority who do not believe in those principles and yet profit from them.

EQUALITY OF EDUCATIONAL OPPORTUNITY

A democracy should provide its members with equal educational opportunities. There have been many obstacles which have prevented the achievement of this ideal, and the obstacles are greater than the average nonprofessional realizes. Even though all human beings have the same nature, no two persons are exactly alike in their background and their potentialities. Each person differs from another in his mental, physical, and social-emotional make-up. The very fact that we try to provide equal educational opportunities for approximately 50 million pupils, no two of whom are exactly alike, presents a staggering problem to education. Since the school cannot give individual instruction to all these pupils, various ways of arranging pupils into groups have been devised, and a variety of procedures have been used to provide for individual differences.

Mental Differences

The level of a person's mental ability can be approximated through the administration of any number of mental ability tests. The results of these tests render an intelligence quotient (I.Q.), which may range anywhere from a theoretical zero to approximately 200, depending on the test used. If there were an I.Q. test sophisticated enough to measure fine distinctions, no two individuals in a given school population would have exactly the same scores. However, the number of scores in some ranges would be greater than in others, so that, by treating a number of scores statistically, it has been possible to arrange the scores into broad classifications of mental ability. It is possible to say that a given score is "average", "superior", "below average", when it is compared with the scores of other people in the group. One widely used classification formulated by Terman, follows.

Classification of Mental Ability Scores

Mental Level	I.Q. Score
Gifted, near genius or genius	Over 140
Very superior	120–139
Superior	110–119
Average	90–109
Slow, dull	80–89
Borderline intelligence	70–79
Feeble-minded	Below 70

Since individual instruction is impossible, authorities thought that mental differences could be at least partially accommodated, by grouping students of similar mental ability together (homogeneous grouping), and then adapting the instruction to each group. When homogeneous grouping is used, the students are usually divided into four ability groupings: superior, average, slow, and retarded.

School systems that group superior children together use various I.Q. cut-off scores to classify these students. Some schools may have special programs for children with I.Q.'s of 110 and above, while others may use 115, 120, 125, up to 140, as the lower limits for designating superior children. Once the group has been classified, the children are given instruction in special schools, or special classes within the regular school. Sometimes the superior group is given enriched instruction, during the normal school years; or schools may use the regular curriculum, but permit superior students to finish it in fewer years (acceleration). Some school systems combine both enrichment and acceleration programs for their superior students. Among the specific plans that care for superior children are early admission to school, more rapid progress in ungraded schools, advanced placement, and early admission to college.

The largest number of students fall into the "average" mental ability category, and the school program is adapted to their level. However, some educators feel that so much attention is given to special provisions for atypical children that the student of average ability may become the "forgotten man."

Below average groups include the mentally slow and the mentally retarded. Many school systems provide for the mentally slow through homogeneous grouping. They receive instruction in special schools or special classes. The curriculum for this group consists of "minimum essentials", giving them instruction which is adapted to their more limited capacity. The mentally retarded are classified into two groups: the educable retarded (I.Q. 50-75) and the trainable retarded (I.Q. 25-50). Most large school districts have limited their services to the educable retarded, but recently they have shown concern for the trainable retarded and have begun to establish programs for them. The majority of these schools have employed special classes for the retarded. Others have used special schools, home institutions, or integration with regular classes.

These procedures for taking care of mental differences are based on ability grouping, or the segregation of students by their mental ability. Homogeneous grouping permits each group to proceed at its own rate of learning. Brighter pupils are not held up by slower learners, but instead are challenged to their greatest ability. The slow learners are spared the desperate attempt to keep up with their brighter classmates, an attempt which is frustrating and usually doomed to failure. Furthermore, homogeneous grouping permits a teacher to concentrate all of his activities at one level. It eliminates the split-level classes in which the teacher must divide his time among several ability groups.

Some educators, however, are against homogeneous grouping. They argue that it is better to have all ability levels represented in one classroom (heterogeneous grouping). Homogeneous grouping, they contend, deprives the average and below average students of the more stimulating intellectual atmosphere provided by superior students. Superior children, in turn, are deprived of the opportunity to mingle with all ability levels and therefore will not gain an understanding of the problems of students who are less gifted than they are. It is also argued that this type of segregation by ability is undemocratic, that it may cause "intellectual snobbery" among superior children, and that it may cause feelings of inferiority in slow learners.

Thus, although a great number of plans and procedures have been tried in an effort to provide equal opportunity for the mental development of children, none of them has been universally accepted. Each plan contains disadvantages as well as advantages. The basic questions still remain. Is it better to group individuals by ability level, or should each class represent all ability levels? Should superior pupils be allowed to accelerate, and move through the school program as fast as they can, or should they stay with their own age group, and receive an enriched program of instruction? In recent decades, larger school systems have used procedures based on homogeneous grouping patterns. Smaller school districts, however, which are becoming less numerous, found it economically unfeasible to organize classes according to special groups. It is generally felt that a moderate degree of rapid advancement (acceleration) should not result in problems of social-emotional adjustment, because superior children are usually taller, heavier, and better adjusted than average children. If, however, superior children are accelerated too rapidly, it may result in problems of social-emotional adjustment because they find themselves among classmates who are several years older.

Physical Differences

Pupils are found in all sizes and shapes and different degrees of physical fitness. Again, most pupils are "normal" in their physical development, but there are a great many who have minor physical defects, and a substantial number who have relatively serious handicaps. Since there is a distinct relationship between mental efficiency and physical fitness, pupils with physical defects are also handicapped in the learning process. To equalize their educational opportunities with the opportunities of others, the school must take action to eliminate the defects, or to minimize their effects.

All knowledge originates through the senses, before it is modified and elaborated by other intellectual processes. In school, the greatest number of impressions come through the senses of sight and hearing. A pupil with defective vision or hearing, therefore, is greatly handicapped in learning, because, he either may be deprived of this source of learning, or may receive incomplete or erroneous sensory impressions. These defects must be discovered, and help must be given. Through periodic physical examinations, and through the observation of alert teachers, these defects can be discovered early, and help can be given through prescribing glasses, hearing aids, or an adjustment in the class seating arrangements.

There are other disorders that handicap pupils in learning, such as glandular imbalance, malnutrition, chronic infections, heart disorders, tuberculosis, and physical deformities. Depending upon the defect, the individual may exhibit the following symptoms: excessive fatigue, restlessness, irritability, hyperactivity, loss of weight, excessive weight, headaches, dizziness, and nausea. The possession of any one of these defects, and its accompanying symptoms, prevents the individual from working up to his capacity. Just as in the case of sensory defects, school personnel are alert to the importance of the early discovery of these disorders.

Finally, there are children who have very serious handicaps, such as blindness or deafness. There are others who have severe deformities, either congenital or acquired. These children also must have the opportunity to develop whatever potentialities they have. They are provided with special schools which have special facilities and programs, and they are taught by specially trained teachers.

Differences in Socio-Economic Background

For some pupils, home life is a pleasant experience. They live in a "nice neighborhood", are well clothed and fed, have congenial parents, experience no financial problems, and are accepted by their peers. For other children, growing up is frequently an unhappy experience. They come from slum or "deprived" homes in which there is little to be happy about. Living quarters are crowded and unsanitary, food may be scarce, clothing may be worn out or outgrown, parental harmony may not exist, and each venture into the neighborhood may result in a struggle for survival.

Adjustment to life is an individual thing. Some children, even though they are deprived of many things, are able to achieve inner peace, but other children, whatever their backgrounds, cannot allay their inner conflicts. Some children from the slums become well-adjusted persons, while some children from "privileged" homes become chronic malcontents.

There is no doubt, however, that underprivileged children have more problems than other children. The Negroes and Puerto Ricans who live in the city ghettoes, and the whites who live in poverty pockets, begin life "culturally deprived" or "disadvantaged". They do not have the environmental experiences that are presupposed by the regular school program. Lacking this background, they encounter difficulties as soon as they enter school. To further add to their problems they are sometimes mistaken for slow or retarded learners and are held back. Their problems become still more complicated when they are taught by teachers who have never lived or taught in deprived areas, who are unfamiliar with their problems, and who automatically expect a low level of performance from them. Feelings of inadequacy or inferiority are common concomitants of these experiences. Moreover, the differences they observe between themselves and others in social status and economic position may accentuate their inferiority feelings. These observed differences sometimes result in feelings of frustration and resentment about their position in life. Those pupils who cannot adjust to their problems may resort to abnormal forms of reaction against the chronic state of insecurity they experience in their home, schools, and society.

Recently, governmental agencies have tried to equalize the opportunities for the "culturally and educationally disadvantaged". They supplied those areas with funds for better housing and better educational facilities. Institutions of higher education have developed programs to provide specially trained teachers who will work in poverty areas. The federal government has taken similar measures under the VISTA and Teachers Corps programs. Special educational programs such as Head Start for pre-school children, Follow Through for the early school years, and Upward Bound for those entering college, have been initiated in poverty areas. In addition special textbooks have been written, and curricular adjustments have been made to accommodate the needs of these children. Although these programs have experienced varying degrees of success, it seems necessary to change the whole context of living for the disadvantaged before a high degree of success can be achieved.

Differences in Emotional Adjustment

There are some problems common to all growing children, regardless of their environmental background. Broken homes are found in all levels of society, and, wherever they exist, they threaten a child's feeling of security. All children experience the problems that accompany physical development. They may be too short or too tall; too fat or too thin; they may have skin blemishes, or possess deformities. These physical characteristics cause them embarrassing moments, or may make them unduly selfconscious. The friction and frustration of severing parental authority, the worry of choosing a vocation, the anxiety experienced in heterosexual relationships, the desire for acceptance by the peer group, the fear of failure in school, are all problems common to children.

Fortunately, most children are able to cope with their "growing up" problems, and the school can help them in several ways. Teachers, knowing their pupils as individuals, are alert to their problems. Many of the pupils' relatively minor problems are resolved through conferences with their teachers. Pupils with more serious problems are referred by the teacher to specialists, such as the guidance counsellor, school psychologist, or even a consulting psychiatrist. In large cities, where problems and children with problems are more numerous, delinquent or seriously maladjusted children may be placed in special classes or special schools. In these schools or classes, in addition to group guidance, they receive individual attention by specialists.

These are only some of the problems of trying to provide equal opportunities in education. If we were "men without faces" there would be no problem, for the same education would be appropriate for all. Fortunately, however, we are unique individuals, each contributing to the welfare of society in his own special way. The problem, then, is the provision of equal opportunities for individuals who are "unequal" in their mental capacity, their physical endowment, and in their social-emotional make-up. Although many measures have been taken to try to give each person the opportunity to develop to fullest capacity, no completely satisfactory solution has yet been reached.

COMPULSORY ATTENDANCE

Every state has a compulsory school attendance law, requiring children to remain in school until a specified age. Depending on the state, this age may vary from fourteen to seventeen. Some exceptions may be made legally for children engaged in agricultural employment, or in the case of those who are totally unable to profit by education, but all other children of legal age must be in school attendance, except for very urgent reasons.

A system of compulsory school attendance has obvious advantages. Since the effectiveness of a democracy depends on an educated citizenry, it is in the interest of the state to compel its future citizens to receive at least the basic amount of schooling. Furthermore compulsory education provides equality of educational opportunity to every child who is capable of profiting from it. If school attendance were not required by law, many parents, not recognizing the value of education, would keep their children out of school in order to work at home, on the farm, or in some other way to supplement family income. It is equally certain that, even with parental encouragement to attend school, many children would drop out at an earlier age if attendance were on a voluntary basis. Many talents would be undeveloped and lost, to the detriment of society and the individual.

Critics of compulsory attendance have argued that compulsory attendance laws rest on the assumption that all school children can profit by an education which, at the age of 16 or 17, exposes them to a high school program. Yet, not everyone has the mental capacity to absorb education at that level. Moreover, they have argued, people do not appreciate things they are compelled to do; hence, under compulsory attendance laws, pupils do not appreciate the *privilege* of receiving an education. Also, many children simply do not like school, and would be happier and more productive if they worked. These children, lacking motivation, fail and are held back in school, becoming problems to themselves and to others. There is also the question of standards of school work. Those who oppose compulsory schooling maintain that it lowers the standards of instruction since it must meet the needs of the large average group. As a result, students with high potentialities suffer.

These arguments may have had some validity before there were extensive provisions in the schools for individual differences. Now every child can profit from schooling up to the age of 16 or 17, because each child can usually receive the type of education which is suited to his interest and ability. The standards of instruction have been adjusted to each ability level, and no one group will suffer from inappropriate standards. Pupils of high mental ability are undoubtedly more challenged today than they ever were in the past. Some motivation problems have been solved by vocational and commercial programs which appeal to those students with low interest in academic programs. There are still pupils who are not motivated by any type of school work, but even some of these students have had their problems alleviated through the guidance services of the school. Furthermore, many students who lacked motivation in their earlier schooling, later found appropriate goals and did excellent work. These children might not have remained in school unless they had been compelled to do so. It should be evident that there are far more advantages than disadvantages in a system of compulsory education.

The Dropout

Related to the question of compulsory attendance, and to the provision of equal opportunities in education, is the problem of the dropout. A dropout is a pupil who leaves school before he graduates from high school or from an equivalent program. If he has not finished high school, a pupil is classified as a dropout, even though he has passed the compulsory attendance age.

There have always been dropouts. They are more numerous now, even with compulsory education, simply because the school population is larger now. Even though the actual percentage of dropouts has decreased, their large number causes considerable concern among educational and governmental authorities. It was estimated there were between 7-8 million dropouts during the 1960's alone.

What kind of a person is the dropout? Many studies have been made of their characteristics, and the results have been pooled to form the following description of an "average dropout".

> Although each dropout is an individual whose reasons for dropping out are peculiar to himself, these studies have developed a portrait of an average dropout. He is just past his 16th birthday, has average or slightly below average intelligence, and is more likely to be a boy than a girl. He is functioning below his potential; he is below grade level in reading; and academically he is in the lowest quartile. He is slightly over age for his grade, having been held back once in the elementary or junior high school grades. He has not been in trouble with the law, although he does take up an inordinate amount of the school administrator's time because of truancy and discipline. He seldom participates in extracurricular activities; he feels rejected by the school and, in turn, rejects the school. His parents were school dropouts, as were his older brother and sister. He says that he is leaving school because of lack of interest but that he will get a high school diploma, in some way or other, because without it he cannot get a good job. He knows the reception that awaits him in the outside world, yet believes that it cannot be worse than remaining in school.[2]

There have also been studies to determine the reasons why these pupils drop out of school. Obviously, a variety of reasons were uncovered; among them were: physical illness or disability; mental illness or disability; behavioral problems; lack of motivation, desire to go to work, or to help out at home; pregnancy; marriage; and, difficulty with school work. A large percentage of these dropouts have the mental ability to complete an average high school program, and many of them could even compete successfully with a college program.

Dropping out of school causes problems for both the individual and society. When he leaves school he does not have all the education that is needed to develop his potentialities. He looks for employment without a salable skill, in a society where unskilled jobs are decreasing continuously. Consequently, the unemployment rate is much higher for dropouts than for high school graduates. Should he obtain work, he

---

[2]Daniel Schreiber, "700,000 Dropouts", *American Education*, 4, Number 6 (June, 1968), 6.

must be satisfied with the lower wages that accompany unskilled work. Should he not obtain work, he may become a burden to himself, to his family, and to society, roaming the streets in search for something to occupy him.

Because the number of dropouts is approaching an annual total of one million, the problem has received widespread attention. In large cities especially, intensive efforts have been made to keep potential dropouts in school. In New York City, these pupils have received special guidance, adjusted curricula, and help in obtaining part-time work in the afternoon. Curricular improvements in Columbus, Ohio have reduced the number of dropouts. In Boston, the dropouts of the previous year were contacted by mail, and urged to return to school. Detroit has conducted a wide-spread "stay-in-school" campaign, using all communications media. Attendance officers in Chicago have made personal visits to potential dropouts, a week before school begins, encouraging them to go back to school. These and other measures have been tried throughout the nation.[3] The improvement of guidance facilities, initiation of more vocational programs, publicizing the benefits of remaining in school, provisions for part-time work, remedial classes during the early years of schooling are measures that have received the greatest emphasis. Many people feel that the problems of the dropout originate in the early years of elementary education, when he first experiences difficulties. Unless the problem is corrected there, the difficulties may increase and even become overwhelming as he progresses through school. Early guidance and help are extremely important in forestalling later problems.

The best results have been obtained when all segments of the community worked together. Better results are also obtained when members of the school staff personally deal with dropouts and their parents, because the dropouts, having felt that nobody cared, finally realize that someone is taking a personal interest in them. In addition, many dropouts return to school after they have experienced difficulty finding employment, or when they have become restless from inactivity.

The combined efforts of these intensive programs have saved many pupils from dropping out of school. Yet the number of dropouts remains alarmingly high. They continue to be a cause for concern, because of the individual and social problems that result. It is possible that it is too late to save many potential dropouts by the time they are legally able to leave school. By that time, their attitudes are deeply ingrained,

---

[3]For other measures that were taken, see "A Renewed Effort to Solve the Problem of Dropout," *School Life,* 46, Number 3 (December, 1963), 11-16.

and difficult to change. More extensive guidance facilities at the elementary level, and programs that attack the problem early, such as Head Start and Follow Through, when they are administered effectively, may produce better results.

STUDENT UNREST

During the 1960's, student unrest reached unprecedented proportions. It was not confined to any one geographical area, nor was it affiliated with any one political system or ideology. Rather, it occurred in countries as different as the United States and Soviet Russia. The one common element underlying student unrest, in all countries, was their expressed dissatisfaction with the existing social order.

In the United States, student protests took many forms. There were sit-ins, sit-downs, marches, and demonstrations. The protests were as varied as the activities. Students demonstrated for better food, better housing, civil rights, and higher quality in education. They protested against participation in the Viet Nam war and burned their draft cards, condemning governmental policies. Finally, they expressed a desire for greater independence for themselves, as well as greater representation and participation in policy-making. They challenged the values of their elders, distrusted "anyone over 30", and tried to make their influence felt through the development of "student power." In fact, the protesters expressed dissatisfaction with all aspects of society and disillusionment with the people who were responsible for decision-making.

The actual number of *active* participants in the student protest movement constituted a small percentage of the student body. Within this minority were three types of students: those with high ideals, who sincerely wished to bring about desired reforms; those who were chronically dissatisfied with everything in life; and, those who, wittingly or unwittingly, affiliated themselves with undemocratic organizations, and worked to disrupt democratic ideals. The first group protested in an orderly manner, presented legitimate criticisms, and was instrumental in causing some desirable changes. Students in the third group, working under the principle that "the end justifies the means," often used disruptive, illegal and often violent tactics which usurped the personal and property rights of others.[4] The second group, the chronic fault-

---

[4]In this connection, the influence of Students for a Democratic Society is described by Eugene H. Methoin in "SDS: Engineers of Campus Chaos," *Reader's Digest*, 93, Number 558 (October, 1968), 103-108.

finders, usually incapable of taking constructive action on their own, vocalized without action, or allied themselves with one of the other groups.

Student protests were registered in many phases of education. We will discuss three items which were frequently mentioned as major sources of discontent with the education they were receiving: the quality of teachers, the relevance of instruction, and student desire for independence.

Protests Against Unqualified Teachers

As a whole, students are shrewd judges of teachers. They can easily detect the unprepared, or unmotivated teacher. Recently their dissatisfaction with the quality of education they were receiving was so widespread that it could not be ignored. Student criticism of instruction fell into two categories: they first protested that many of their teachers were of poor quality, and second, even with qualified teachers, they objected to some of the methods of instruction. Both of these criticisms had some validity, and, in both cases, the deficiencies can be traced to the problems created by the continuous upsurge in school enrollment.

In the late 1950's, the shortage of teachers which had existed since World War II began to be felt at the college level. At that time, many educators voiced their concern that the lack of qualified college teachers might lower the quality of a college education in the future. Their "future" is now the present. For nearly a quarter-century, it had been necessary to hire teachers with substandard qualifications to teach in elementary and secondary schools. Students of the present college generation undoubtedly were taught by many of these teachers. When they reached college, they met similar conditions. Many of the best college teachers had given up teaching to do research work or take more lucrative positions in industry. In their place, it was necessary to hire less qualified, inexperienced teachers. To care for the increasing enrollment, larger institutions used an ever-increasing number of graduate students as teachers. Many of these graduate students were not motivated toward teaching. From kindergarten through college, the present college generation has encountered teachers who were not fully qualified for their positions.

It is not surprising, then, that they began to protest against the quality of *some* of their teachers. Unfortunately, they did not realize that anything was being done about it. Previous chapters have described the growing concern of parents, educators, and legislators about the quality of teachers, and the intensive efforts made to improve this quality.

The shortage of qualified teachers remained in spite of these efforts. Hiring officials were faced with undesirable alternatives. They had to hire *someone* because of the overflow in enrollment, and they settled for the best they could find, even though unqualified. Often, if they wished to replace an unqualified teacher, they had to replace him with still another unqualified person. There was no other choice. If this information had been given to students, it undoubtedly might have softened their protests. Meanwhile, the profession must continue its efforts to improve itself.

The students criticized one other aspect of teaching: the exclusive use of the lecture method by some of their teachers. The students rightly believed that a classroom should be a place for the interchange of ideas between a teacher and his pupils. Yet class size must determine whether or not classroom discussion is feasible. When a teacher is assigned sections of students that number in the hundreds, he must use the lecture method. As classes begin to exceed 20-25 pupils, effective communication between the teacher and his students becomes increasingly difficult, and, in large sections, it is impossible.

Again, the increase in enrollment was responsible for the lecture in place of the discussion. Many students of the present college generation found themselves in overcrowded classrooms, first in elementary and secondary schools, and later in college. Many of them may have experienced these crowded conditions *throughout* their schooling, so that they lacked, and very likely missed, the personal contact that usually exists between a teacher and his pupils. It was natural that this type of impersonal classroom atmosphere should be one of the sources of student discontent.

Again, students should have been informed of the extensive efforts made throughout the country to relieve overcrowding. Beginning in the 1950's, new school plants were built at an unprecedented rate, and old ones were remodeled. Better instructional facilities were provided, libraries were expanded, and services were increased. These efforts gradually produced desirable results in the elementary and secondary schools. Class sizes began to approach normal proportions. At the college level, however, although facilities and faculties have been expanded, there has not yet been enough expansion to relieve overcrowding, especially in lower level courses. Some colleges tried to split large lecture classes into small discussion groups for a portion of the time or to use closed circuit television for some courses. Neither method has been a satisfactory solution. The problem is further complicated by the overwhelming financial burden that greater expansion of facilities would create for some colleges.

Student protests against substandard qualifications and impersonal instruction *do* have some validity. Yet, at this point, every known measure has been taken to try to improve these deficiencies. Colleges, unwilling to deprive qualified students of higher education, are admitting an ever-increasing number of students. They have expanded their facilities. New colleges, especially junior colleges, are being founded to handle the overflow of students. Yet, the core of the problem remains: there are not enough qualified teachers available at all levels of schooling. Perhaps today's heavy emphasis on experimentation with new procedures and auto-instructional devices may provide some answers to the problem of working effectively with mass education.

Protests Against Irrelevance

Another recurrent student criticism is related to the curriculum. Many students, protesting against the curriculum, felt that their courses were not "relevant," or that they were not taught in a relevant manner. To some students, relevance implied a direct relationship to vocational goals; to other students relevance pertained to the problems confronting them and society. In general, students considered a course relevant if they realized how it contributed to individual or social betterment.

The relevance of the curriculum, and the subjects that should be included in it, have been debated throughout the centuries by all segments of the educational community, and there have been various curricular emphases. Students understand the relevance of vocational or professional courses, because these courses prepare them for a direct transition into a desired occupation. The usefulness of a liberal education—an education for its own sake, and not for the sake of something else—is not as apparent to them. It is difficult to demonstrate how a liberal education "liberates" an individual's powers, how it promotes a better understanding of himself and of his relationships to others, and how it builds attitudes, habits, ideals, and ways of thinking that can be used during their lives. For this reason most protesters against irrelevance were liberal arts students.

It means little to a student to be told that a course has values that are not immediately apparent, but will benefit him in his later life. He wants to see its value *now*. If he realizes how a course will benefit him, he will be more motivated than he would be if he did not realize its value. The teacher, therefore, must show his students how the course affects their growth and development, how it relates to other fields of knowledge, and how it will help them to live a richer life as human beings. Most teachers try to do this at the beginning of their courses, but many of them then consider it unimportant. A teacher cannot tell his students about the value of a course, and then hope that, as it is taught, they will perceive its relevance. As the course continues, the teacher should continue to show its relevance, value, and usefulness. If it is necessary, he should modify course content to achieve these aims.

The teacher's methods can add to relevance of instruction. He should "begin where the students are," using of, and building upon, the knowledge they already have. Local, familiar examples in illustrations and explanations not only make the instruction more interesting and understandable, but also make it pertinent to every-day living. Similarly, problems and issues of the past compared or contrasted with the present, brings the past alive thus making it more interesting and relevant. These methods can make a course more meaningful to pupils. To the extent that the courses are *not* made meaningful, students are justified in labelling them irrelevant.

Student Desire for Independence

One of the characteristics of adolescence is the desire for independence. As he progresses through this period, the individual gradually frees himself of the authority of his parents, teachers, and elders. This is a normal and desirable process, which should culminate in independent, responsible action. However, there is a delicate balance which should exist in the relationships between adolescents and their elders: a balance between assertion of independence and respect for authority. The adolescent should have as much freedom as he can handle responsibly, but his independence should not override duly constituted authority. At the same time, the authority of elders should not be so oppressive that it stifles the adolescent's legitimate expression of freedom. The development of personal freedom and personal responsibility, should be cultivated in adolescents.

Living in an era when their eighteen-year-old peers were required to serve in the armed forces, sometimes at the sacrifice of their lives, students began to resent being treated as immature individuals more than ever. They reasoned that if they were old enough to be drafted and to be sent into battle, they should not be treated as children by their elders. They asserted that they were mature enough to be free of the paternal control exercised by the colleges, and responsible enough to receive the rights and privileges of citizenship in the academic community. As citizens of the community, they felt that they should have a voice in establishing regulations and policies affecting their welfare.

Once they had adopted these premises, student activists carried their requests to college administrators. They sought changes in regulations and policies that ranged through all phases of the college community life. Among other things they requested more liberal curfew hours, freedom to entertain guests in dormitories, and freedom of association with extramural organizations. In the area of instruction, they requested free expression in the classroom, liberalization of attendance regulations, changes in grading systems, evaluation of teachers and their methods of teaching, more freedom of choice in the curriculum, and the right to bring in guest speakers of their own choice. Regarding administrative matters, they felt that student representatives should sit in on the deliberations of all institutional committees and policy-making bodies. They urged, in fact, greater communication between the student body and the administration.

There were varying reactions and interactions to these student protests. Much of it depended on the manner in which student requests were presented and the flexibility of the college officials. When student requests, protests, or even demonstrations, were orderly, and presented to open-minded administrators, effective communication between the two groups occurred. The reasonable requests of students were either granted or investigated. When, however, radical elements conducted the student demonstrations, which resulted in disruption and violence, as they did at Berkeley and Columbia, resentment and suspicion was aroused in the factions that were created in the student body, faculty, and administration. Threats, violence, and disruption brought no adequate solutions to problems; rather, these actions aggravated old problems, and created new ones.

The protests of sincere students should be heard, for they often have constructive suggestions for needed change. For this to occur, channels of communication must be open at all levels. Administrators, too often pre-occupied with fund-raising and the image of their institutions, forget their responsibilities to their students. They, or their designated representatives, should be accessible to the students. Members of the faculty can improve their relationships with their students by striving for better communication in the classroom and being more available for consultation. The students themselves can strengthen their position by investigating the facts before protesting, by formulating sound counter-proposals, and by opposing radical groups that advocate violence as a means of protest.

A joint committee of the American Association of University Professors, the U. S. National Student Association, the Association of American Colleges, the National Association of Student Personnel Administrators, and the National Association of Women Deans and Counselors studied the question of student rights and freedoms. The committee prepared a Joint Statement on Rights and Freedoms of Students which was approved by USNSA in August, 1967, and by the Council of AAUP in October, 1967. The Joint Statement defines the rights and responsibilities of students in the following areas:

1. Freedom of access to higher education
2. Freedom of discussion, inquiry, and expression in the classroom
3. Protection of students against release of confidential information found in student records.
4. Standards to be maintained in student affairs
5. Off-campus freedom of students
6. Procedural standards in disciplinary proceedings

Although some of its provisions are debatable, the Joint Statement formed a focal point for discussions between students, faculty, and administrators. One outcome of these discussions may be the students' realization that things are not as bad as they originally thought, and the faculty's and administration's realization that matters are not as good as they had hoped. One of the immediate effects of student protests was a beneficial self-examination by all those involved in the educative process.

If student protests continue, it is to be hoped that they will occur in a rational, orderly manner. Many college administrators have already stated that violence and disruption will not be tolerated as a means of protest, and that law enforcement agencies will be used, whenever necessary, to maintain "the regular and essential operation of the institution." Most students who are interested in receiving a good education would support this position. If the small minority continues to protest in an irrational, disruptive manner, it will not be surprising to see student protests against the protesters.

EVALUATION OF STUDENT PROGRESS

One persistent problem experienced by all teachers, and especially new teachers, is how to evaluate the progress of their pupils. Every teacher has a serious obligation to try to grade the achievement of his students accurately, indicating their progress, or lack of it. The grades that a student receives will determine whether or not he will make normal progress in school, and they may act as an incentive, or an inhibiting force, to his progress. They become permanent records, upon which he may be judged in later years. They are a factor in determining whether or not he will gain admission to a college or graduate school. Because they are important, a student may challenge the grades given him, and sometimes receives parental support in his challenge. Even the administrator may ask a teacher to justify his grading practices, either in an individual case, or in relation to school policy. Consequently, the teacher, wishing to be just in awarding grades, and knowing the importance of accurate grades, spends time and thought in evaluating a pupil's progress.

Before he can consider a grade, the teacher must decide whether a grade represents only what a student knows about a subject, or whether it includes an evaluation of his attitude, initiative, cooperation, and other intangible factors. He must decide the importance of a grade given in oral participation, written work, and tests. He must decide which type of test, essay or objective, produces the best results. He will wonder if it is advisable to use "the curve" in grading, and what he should do about borderline cases. These are only a few of the major questions about grading that confront a new teacher. The full implications of these problems can be gained only in a course on tests and measurements. However, we will discuss a few highlights of the problems, so that the prospective teacher may realize that grading a pupil's progress involves many elements that are not superficially evident.

Achievement as the Basis of a Grade

Jack Smith who is a conscientious pupil, works hard, but does barely acceptable work. Fred Jones grasps ideas quickly, but does just enough work to "get by." Should Jack receive a higher grade because of his diligence, and should Fred be penalized because he is lazy? Or, should both receive the same grade, because both have the same achievement level?

Positive and negative answers have been given to these questions. Some people believe that a grade should include effort, punctuality, cooperation, and attitude. Adherents to this practice contend that pupils who exhibit desirable habits and attitudes should be rewarded, while those who do not, should be punished. Moreover, they contend, if the pupils know that these traits will be considered in the grading, it will act as an incentive to them. Opponents of this practice claim that it is impossible to make a valid judgment on the extent a pupil exercises these traits. In evaluating attitude, initiative, or habit only general impressions can be formed, and these are not accurate enough to receive a specific value. If a teacher tries to weight these factors, grading becomes a subjective process, since intangible factors cannot be measured. Furthermore, there is the danger that the teacher's personal likes and dislikes may affect his judgment.

The position most widely held today states that a grade should represent only the student's achievement in a subject. If a school system wishes to evaluate personality and character traits, it may do so by rating these items separately. Grading on the basis of achievement reduces the element of subjectivity that otherwise may be present. It is believed that a pupil's lack of desirable traits automatically reflects itself in the quality of his work. If the pupil is uncooperative and lacks initiative, his achievement level will be lower than if he exhibited the opposite characteristics. If this is true, then the teacher need not give additional consideration to the other factors in making up a grade.

Types of Achievement to Consider

Although there are many specific activities that show achievement on the part of the learner, they can be classified into four general categories: oral participation, written work, demonstration of skills, and tests. Oral work includes the responses to questions asked by the teacher, the questions raised by the pupils, participation in discussions, and delivery of oral reports. Various written assignments including homework, reports, creative writing, workbook assignments, and term papers also must be evaluated. Sometimes it is necessary to evaluate the pupil's proficiency in a skill, such as his laboratory performance in science or langauge, or his operation of mechanical devices such as business machines. Finally, a pupil demonstrates his progress through the scores he achieves on various types of tests. In giving a grade, the teacher must consider as many of these activities as are applicable to the course he is teaching.

Furthermore, the teacher must determine the importance of each activity. Unless there is a school or a departmental policy, the teacher will have to exercise his subjective judgment in weighting each type of activity. His decision will be based on how much of each activity exists in the course. If there is little oral work, but a great deal of written work, he would weight each accordingly; or, if the course is a lecture course, the tests would be given more weight than in other types of courses. Consequently, it is impossible to weight all factors equally in all courses. There may, however, be a school policy which limits the weighting for certain types of performance. For example, the policy may state that final examinations must be weighted no less than 25%, but not more than 50%. The following may be taken as an illustration of how factors may be weighted in making up a final grade.

Weighted Factors in a Final Grade

Factor	Weight
Homework	10
Class participation	10
Projects	15
Unannounced quizzes	10
Major tests	30
Final examination	25
	100%

These percentages can be increased or decreased to meet the requirements of a particular course. Factors may be added or subtracted, depending on the nature of the course. However, there always remains the problem of how much weight to assign to each category. The new teacher, through his own experience, or in consultation with other teachers, will soon learn to make reasonably accurate judgments in this area.

Essay Tests Versus Objective Tests

A large portion of a student's grade is determined by the scores he receives on tests. Here again, the teacher must decide what type of test best measures achievement.

There are two major types of tests: standardized, and teacher-made. Standardized tests are made up by test experts and are published for wide-scale use. They try to measure mental ability, achievement, aptitude, and various aspects of personality; this type of test ordinarily is used in school-wide testing programs, or in guidance. The classroom teacher makes up his own tests to test the achievement of his pupils.

The teacher, to test the achievement of his pupils, may make up either an essay or an objective test. The essay question requires the student to give an extended response in answer to questions that may call for exposition, description, analysis, evaluation, comparison, or contrast. The objective question, is a short response which can be answered with a word, or by selecting the correct answer from given alternatives. The common types of objective items are: true-false, matching, multiple choice, and filling in blanks.

There are many advantages and disadvantages to the essay test. Perhaps its primary advantage is the better evidence it gives of the pupil's ability to express himself, organize material, and manifest his ability in a variety of thought processes, such as analysis, evaluation, generalization, and originality. Advocates also claim that essay tests do not encourage guessing, do not include fake and confusing statements and are easier to make up and to administer. Opponents claim that there is no objective way to score the answers to the test, that only a limited sampling of the student's knowledge is possible, that students may bluff their way through an answer, and that it requires a great deal of time to score them.

The objective test, say its proponents, eliminates the disadvantages of essay questions. Since there is only one correct answer, subjectivity in scoring is eliminated. Moreover, since it takes little time to answer an objective item, it is possible to sample more widely a pupil's knowledge about the subject. Furthermore, with the use of a scoring key, these tests can be corrected in a small fraction of the time it takes to correct an essay test. In reply, opponents say that objective tests are difficult to make up, give pupils no opportunity to express themselves, and do not show how well they can organize and interpret the material. Its items, they claim, tend to confuse pupils and encourage guessing.

While both arguments have merit, some of the dangers of each test can be minimized. For example, the major criticisms of essay tests (subjectivity in scoring) can be almost nullified if the teacher jots down the correct points to an answer and then compares each answer to his key. In addition, each essay question on the test may sample more knowledge than several objective items. The time involved in making up and correcting both tests becomes equal since objective tests take more time to construct, yet less time to correct. The teacher can discourage pupils from guessing on an objective test by using a formula that corrects for guessing.

Both types of tests have their advantages. The type the teacher uses should be determined by the purpose of a particular test. If the teacher

wants to test the knowledge of factual material, the objective test would
be more suitable. If, however, he wants to test the pupil's ability to
apply his knowledge of facts, the essay question is more applicable. It
is likely that the teacher will usually want to test for both. In this situation, he can make up a test which combines both types of items. By
including a large number of objective items, he can sample the material
widely, while, at the same time, he may include a few essay questions
to test the pupil's ability to organize, evaluate, and interpret his knowledge.

Normal Curve Grading

After the teacher has corrected a set of tests, the distribution of
grades may assume any one of an infinite number of patterns. All the
grades may be high, all of them may be low, most of them may be low
with a few high, most of them may be high with a few low, etc. The
teacher now must decide whether he should give each pupil what he
actually earned, or whether he should adjust the grades to allow for
skewed distributions. If the teacher grades the pupils according to a predetermined standard, and leaves the grades as they are, he uses an *absolute* system of grading. If he adjusts the distribution of grades so that
a certain percentage fall into categories of fail, below average, above
average, and superior, he uses the "normal curve" concept of a *relative*
system of grading.

Under the absolute system, the teacher sets the standards of performance for the course. Each pupil is graded in relation to how well
he meets those standards. Under this system, each pupil receives the
grade that he earns, so that it is possible to have within the class more
low grades than high, or more high grades than low. This system,
adherents claim, considers each student as an individual whose grades
should not be determined by arbitrary, artificial distributions of grades
according to predetermined percentages.

The relative system is based on certain assumptions. It assumes that
ordinarily there is a full range of mental ability represented in a class
of students. The assumption is based on the "normal curve" concept,
which holds that any trait that can be measured in a continuous series
will fall into a bell-shaped, "normal" distribution. For example, if a
large random sample of pupils were tested for mental ability, the distribution of their scores would show the following: a small percentage of
individuals either inferior or superior, a larger percentage either below

average or above average, and the largest percentage (roughly two-thirds) average. Those who accept this theory reason that, if there *is* a full range of talent represented in a class, the grades ought to be distributed accordingly. The lowest grades in the class, then, would be classified as "failure", and the highest as "superior." The next lowest and highest, according to given percentages, receive "below average" and "above average" grades, and the remainder receive an "average" grade. The proponents of relative grading also argue that the tests made up by teachers vary in difficulty, so that grades on different tests are not comparable. Relative grading, they say, eliminates this difficulty.

In theory, grading according to the normal curve appears to be logical. However, the normal curve is a mathematical concept which has no counterpart in reality. Consequently, it may be erroneous to base conclusions on its assumptions. Secondly, its assumption that a full range of mental ability is found in any class is more often wrong than not. For example, this assumption would be incorrect whenever homogeneous grouping is used, because the pupils are already classified by mental ability level. Even when heterogeneous grouping is used, and the classes are relatively small, it can not be assumed that all ability levels are present, because chance factors can account for great differences in the groups.

It is, therefore, necessary to use caution in grading students arbitrarily by the use of the normal distribution concept. Some teachers use modifications of the curve without necessarily agreeing with its basic assumptions. Other teachers feel that there is no need to use it. While they agree that no two tests can be perfectly equated for difficulty, they feel that adjustments can be made without actually using the curve. For example, if all of the grades were low on a particular test, the teacher could adjust for its difficulty by adding a certain percentage to each score. This seldom is done, since, after some experience with testing, the teacher settles into a fairly consistent level of difficulty that is appropriate for his students.

Borderline Cases

Sometimes, there are extenuating circumstances, and borderline cases, which cause the teacher to reflect considerably before deciding on a grade. After gathering his evidence, the teacher invariably finds that there are several pupils in borderline categories, between "F" and "D", between "D" and "C", and "C" and "B". Since the student is close to the higher grade, should the teacher award the higher grade to the student, or should he leave him in the lower category?

Some teachers try to be completely objective in grading. They, therefore, would give the student exactly what he earned on the basis of objective evidence. This can be carried to extremes, as illustrated by a student's remark: "If the passing grade were 70, he [the teacher] would even flunk his brother if he made a 69.9." Other teachers favor awarding the next higher grade in borderline cases. This practice has merits, for two reasons. First, there is a margin of error in all testing techniques and practices, and the student's level of achievement can be higher than shown by his test scores. Since this is possible, the student should be given the benefit of the doubt. Secondly, because he received the higher grade instead of the lower one, the student may exert himself more to maintain a higher level of performance than he would if he had received the lower grade.

Another type of case deserves special consideration. There are students who perform consistently on tests, but for a variety of reasons, may have scored so poorly on *one* test that their average was not representative of their normal achievement level. In these cases, the teacher is justified in awarding a grade that corresponds to the individual's usual level of performance. In fact, some teachers, operating on the premise that every pupil is entitled to an "off day" on tests, drop each pupil's lowest score when computing the average. This practice is justified only if enough tests are given to provide an adequate sample of ability without the score that was dropped.

Obviously, there are many problems connected with grading. The new teacher might remember that grades should be based on as much objective evidence as possible, and that if subjective evaluation enters into a portion of the grade, it is better to give the pupil the benefit of the doubt than to give him a grade lower than he deserves. All tests are based on at least two assumptions: that tests can measure reliably and validly what they are supposed to measure, and, that when he is tested, a pupil performs at his full capacity. Usually these assumptions are valid, but there are exceptions. The difficulty lies in the fact that we are never quite sure which pupils are the exceptions.

The problems presented in this and preceding chapters are only a few of the larger ones found in the field of education. There are no universally accepted solutions to most of them, and, therefore, the prospective teacher will find the profession filled with never-ending challenges. Consequently, if he is a dedicated teacher, he will find limitless opportunities to contribute his efforts toward continued progress in the improvement of education.

SUMMARY

Five problems in the field of education, were chosen for discussion in this chapter: indoctrination and academic freedom, equality of opportunity in education, compulsory attendance and the dropout, student unrest, and evaluation of student progress.

Differences in philosophy are the bases of many problems in education. Each philosophy teaches according to its own tenets, which causes conflicting practices in all phases of education. Although all educators recognize the importance of a philosophy of education, some feel that a teacher should not indoctrinate his pupils. In the broad sense, "indoctrination" means that a teacher instructs in, or according to, a definite set of principles. Under this definition, a teacher cannot avoid indoctrinating his pupils. However, in the narrow sense, indoctrination means to instruct according to a partisan or sectarian point of view, to the exclusion of other views. This type of indoctrination is undesirable, because students have a right to be informed about conflicting points of view.

Indoctrination always occurs, either in the broad or the narrow sense. It is the type of indoctrination that is important. In a democratic society, students should be imbued with democratic principles, but, at the same time, they should be able to evaluate, in terms of these principles, other points of view. There is evidence that some teachers indoctrinate pupils with anti-democratic ideas. This may happen because their subtle efforts are undetected, and because teachers have academic freedom to teach the truth as they know it. There are, however, restrictions on freedom of expression which are dictated by conscience, good taste, and law. Freedom of expression must be linked with responsible expression. The influence of the minority who circumvent these restraints can be counteracted by the great majority of teachers who conscientiously imbue their pupils with democratic ideas and ideals.

Another broad problem is presented by the effort to provide equal opportunities in education for all school children. This means that the school system must try to provide for the individual differences of approximately 50 million pupils, no two of whom are exactly alike. To provide for these differences, pupils are sorted into groups that have similar traits and then given instruction adapted to their needs. Of the many different traits found in children the school gives greatest attention to differences in their mental ability, physical make-up, and social and emotional adjustment.

To provide for mental differences, schools use homogeneous grouping, heterogeneous grouping, and/or acceleration. Each of these has its advantages and disadvantages. Larger schools have used a variety of plans based on homogeneous grouping and acceleration, but schools with small enrollments adhered to heterogeneous grouping since it is economically unfeasible for them to implement the other plans.

Recognizing the close relationship between physical condition and mental efficiency, the school takes preventive measures to eliminate this block to learning. Physical defects may take several forms such as defects of the senses, glandular imbalance, malnutrition, or chronic infections. The teacher, through awareness of the symptoms, and the school through periodic physical examinations, can discover these defects early, and initiate help. Children who are severely handicapped, such as the blind, deaf, and severely crippled are usually given instruction in special schools under specially trained teachers.

Recently, much attention has been given to providing equality of opportunity for children who are "disadvantaged" or "culturally deprived." These children, living in slum areas or ghettos, do not have the environmental and experiential background presupposed by the regular school program. To compensate for these deficiencies, several new programs, including Head Start, Follow Through, and Upward Bound, have been initiated under the sponsorship of the federal government. Meanwhile, the federal and state governments try to attack the root of problem by providing these people with better housing and better educational facilities.

The school also makes special provisions for children who are emotionally maladjusted. Most children make a satisfactory adjustment to many situations that cause them anxiety. They have many minor problems which are often easily resolved through conferences with their teachers or parents. Occasionally, however, children have severely traumatic experiences, or chronic anxiety experiences, which cause serious emotional upsets, and may manifest themselves in abnormal behavior. These children may be referred to the counselor or school psychologist. In some cases, they are sent to special classes or special schools, where they may receive group counselling, as well as individual attention.

Many of the problems in education were created by the compulsory attendance laws, which compel children to remain in school for a specified period of time. The opponents of compulsory education feel that it keeps children in school who do not want to be there. Pupils, they claim, do not appreciate an education which they are compelled to have, and the standards of education have to be lowered when *all* children are required to attend school. Most of these objections have been overcome by the provisions that schools have made for individual differences. Furthermore, the advantages of compulsory attendance outweigh any remaining disadvantages, as it assures a basic amount of education for all, which is necessary for the effective operation of a democracy.

In spite of the obvious advantages of receiving an education, many pupils drop out of school before completing high school. Although the schools now have stronger compulsory education laws, the number of dropouts has grown sharply because of the large growth in school population. Concern arose because the dropout experiences personal stresses which he did not foresee, and contributes to social problems. Intensive programs have been implemented in an effort to decrease the number of pupils who drop out of school.

During the 1960's, student unrest contributed to the problems in education. An active minority of students, dissatisfied with all aspects of society, began to demonstrate for changes that they thought would alleviate the problems. They criticized, among other things, the lack of communication between them and college personnel, demanded that the quality of teachers be improved and that the curriculum be made more relevant. They requested a more active part in determining school policies and regulations. Many of their demonstrations were orderly, and produced favorable results. A small number within the minority, however, advocated and used disruption and violence as a means of attaining their aims. These students caused misunderstanding and resentment, and were told that these tactics would not be tolerated. The students who protested in an orderly manner succeeded in bringing about better communication between members of the college community, highlighted their problems, and brought about some of the needed changes.

Teachers have always been faced with the problem of evaluating their students' work accurately. The problem has several aspects. First, the teacher must decide whether a grade should represent achievement only, or whether it should also reflect intangible factors, such as cooperation, initiative, and attitude. The prevalent opinion today is that a grade should represent achievement, and the other factors should be graded separately. Next, the teacher must assign weights to various types of achievement, such as written work, oral work, proficiency in skills, and scores on tests. The weight assigned to each skill will be determined by the degree to which each is utilized in a particular course. The teacher must also decide whether or not to give essay or objective tests. Both tests have advantages and disadvantages, so that the teacher will use the type that best fits his purpose in testing. In grading tests, he must next decide whether to use the absolute system of grading (giving each pupil only what he earned), or the relative system (assigning a certain percentage of grades to each category of grades). Here again, advantages are claimed for both systems, but it should be pointed out that the relative system is an arbitrary, mechanical one, which makes grading wholly impersonal. Finally, in assigning a grade, the teacher will find borderline cases. Giving the pupil the benefit of the doubt is advisable, because it acts as a positive incentive for the pupil to do better work. Furthermore, all evaluation techniques are subject to some error.

Questions for discussion:

1. Evaluate the statement: "It is impossible to teach without indoctrination."

2. Cite specific examples of how you could teach democratic principles to your students.

3. Do you think we are making adequate provision for individual differences in education?

4. How long do you think children should be compelled to attend school?

5. Under what conditions do you think student protests would be justified?

6. Assuming you were an administrator, how would you handle student protests?

7. As a student, what do you dislike about the grading system at your institution?

8. As a future teacher, what system do you think you would use in grading your students?

For further reading:

American Association of Colleges for Teacher Education, *Teacher Education Issues and Innovations*. Washington, D.C.: American Association of Colleges for Teacher Education, 1968.

Baade, Hans W., ed., *Academic Freedom.* Dobbs Ferry, New York: Oceana Publications, Inc., 1964.

Conant, James B., *Slums and Suburbs.* New York: McGraw-Hill Book Company, Inc., 1961.

Educational Policies Commission, *American Education and the Search for Equal Opportunity.* Washington, D.C.: National Education Association, 1965.

Ehlers, Henry, ed., *Crucial Issues in Education.* New York: Henry Holt and Company, 1955.

Frost, S. E., *Introduction to American Education.* New York: Doubleday & Company, Inc., 1962.

Keppel, Francis, *The Necessary Revolution in American Education.* New York: Harper & Row, Publishers, 1966.

Kerber, August, and Barbara Bommarito, *The Schools and the Urban Crisis.* New York: Holt, Rinehart, Winston, Inc., 1965.

Paulson, F. Robert, ed., *Contemporary Issues in American Education.* Tuscon, Arizona: The University of Arizona Press, 1967.

Remmers, H. H., N. L. Gage, and J. Francis Rummel, *A Practical Introduction to Measurement and Evaluation.* New York: Harper & Row, Publishers, 1965.

14

Recent Innovations in Education

Throughout the history of education, there have always been a few individuals who combined their intellectual powers with a fertile imagination and proposed new approaches, or "innovations," in education. An innovation consists of the introduction of something new which may be a better way of reaching a desired goal. Thus, in trying to provide for individual differences, new proposals have appeared continuously. Each proposal has concerned the best way for each individual to achieve his potentialities. For example, in recent years, new plans based on homogeneous grouping were instituted in an effort to achieve that goal. Currently, other innovations, such as programed instruction, nongraded schools, and individually prescribed instruction, have been introduced as methods of tailoring educational practices to the needs of each individual.

Not every innovation is worthwhile. Some of the past innovations proved worthy and have survived to the present. Others were fads or fallacies, which gained momentary attention and popularity because of their novelty. The emphasis on innovation, in recent years, has been greater than ever before. It has been manifested on national, state, and local levels and encouraged by substantial financial grants from the federal government and private sources. Countless experiments with

403

innovative practices have been conducted throughout the country, at all levels of education. By 1968, approximately 2,000 innovative projects had been conducted under the Elementary and Secondary Education Act of 1965 alone. However, the majority of these experiments produced little that was of lasting significance. In fact, after several years of experimenting with new approaches to education, a prominent governmental official concluded that true innovation in education was as rare, and just about as prolific, as the whooping crane. In this chapter, some of the recent innovations that may be promising for the future are discussed briefly.

TELEVISION INSTRUCTION

Television, now on the American scene for several decades, has established itself as a powerful communications medium. Shortly after World War II, its possibilities in the field of education were seriously considered. Since then, many experiments with educational television have been conducted. Today it is possible to enumerate some of the advantages and disadvantages of television as a means of achieving the objectives of education. Its future development and uses, of course, can not be predicted.

There are two types of broadcasting in educational television: open-circuit, and closed-circuit. Programs broadcast open-circuit may be received by any conventional television receiver; these programs include ones that are broadcast by noncommercial educational television stations, as well as the infrequent educational programs of commercial stations. Many colleges have offered credit courses to properly qualified and registered students through open-circuit broadcasting. Closed-circuit instructional television originates locally, usually transmitted by coaxial cable, and can be received only by the audience for whom it is intended. Most instructional television has been the closed-circuit broadcast. In 1965, there were in the public and private schools and colleges alone (aside from industrial, military, medical, and other installations) between four and five hundred closed-circuit educational television facilities in the United States.[1] Through private and federal subsidy, these facilities have risen sharply since then. The following comments are confined to installations of the closed-circuit type.

With the advent of television, educators immediately realized that

---

[1]George N. Gordon, *Educational Television* (New York: The Center for Applied Research in Education, Inc., 1965), p. 14.

the new medium had high potential in the field of education. After World War II, as pupil enrollment swelled and a teacher shortage developed, the possibility of instructing large numbers of pupils by television became apparent. Moreover, since there were outstanding teachers whose classes were limited by the enrollment, it was thought that the services of these gifted teachers could be made available to larger audiences through televised instruction. Yet, educators still did not know whether or not television instruction could be as effective as the instruction of a live teacher in a classroom. Although professional groups were the first to stimulate interest in educational television, the Ford Foundation provided the funds necessary to study all aspects of televised instruction, including experimentation on its effectiveness compared with conventional teaching methods.

During the 1950's, educational institutions began pilot programs, offering selected courses through closed-circuit television. In some cases, the television teacher lectured to a large group in one room. Television receivers were located strategically throughout the room, and each student had a close-up view of the lecturer and his activities. In other cases, the teacher gave his presentation to a group of students in one room, and it, in turn, was televised to students located in several other rooms. In another variation, a broadcast originated in one school building and was transmitted to several other buildings in a school system.

These experiments soon yielded conclusions on the effectiveness of educational television. It did provide outstanding instruction to large numbers of students simultaneously. For demonstrations it was excellent, because each student could easily see the performance. After polling student reaction to televised instruction, the experimentors learned that a high percentage of students accepted it. Students instructed by television scored as high, and sometimes higher, on achievement tests as students who were instructed by conventional methods. Furthermore, television broadcasts could be taped and reused as they were needed. Obviously televised instruction seemed effective initially.

Yet, there were several difficulties in the use of televised instruction. Students began to express dissatisfaction with the lack of personal contact between them and their instructor. Many of them never saw the instructor in person, and began to think of themselves as only "a number" in the instructor's book. They also complained that they could not raise questions nor have class discussions. Other types of problems also became evident. Originally the lack of color was considered a disadvantage in some subjects, but with the advent of color television this problem disappeared. Nevertheless, televised instruction could not provide for individual differences, and it was not equally effective in all subjects. Furthermore, as the novelty of the new medium wore off, problems of motivation and discipline arose. Many classroom teachers, who feared that they might be replaced by televised instruction further opposed it. Finally, the cost of an installation was so high that few institutions could afford it, and since there was no evidence that it *improved* the quality of education, it was not worth the cost.

As these difficulties arose, attempts were made to overcome them. Devices were introduced to try to bring some personal contact between the teacher and the pupils. For example, in one case, the instructor was provided with the names of pupils who were located in other rooms. With the use of a two-way communication system, he could call on students in those areas. At the same time, the communication system permitted students to raise questions at specified intervals. By placing a teacher in each classroom, after the televised lecture was over, questions could be raised and discussions could be held on the lecture material. The problem of motivation was solved by using only the best teachers to give the lectures. These teachers had the ability to make the presentation interesting enough to secure and hold the students' attention. In other classrooms, the presence of monitors or teachers helped to minimize disciplinary problems. All of these measures only helped to alleviate, not eliminate, the basic problems of television instruction.

Although studies have shown that students achieve as much or more through televised instruction as through face-to-face instruction, several qualifications should be made. Although television is effective in some subjects, it has been found to be inferior in others. Also, it is more effective at the elementary level than at the secondary or college level.[2] Moreover, the television teacher is usually freed from other teaching assignments, because he must spend a great deal more time in preparation. Knowing that he is widely observed, he is more highly motivated to achieve exceptional results. This in itself may account for a higher achievement level among his pupils, and camouflage the effects of lack of class participation. A better comparison could be made if an outstanding face-to-face teacher were given the same preparation time, attention, and consideration as the television teacher.

At present, it is agreed that there are certain things televised instruction can and cannot do. It can provide instruction to many students who otherwise might not receive it. It can spread the talent of truly gifted

---

[2]U.S. Office of Education, *Educational Television* (Washington, D.C.: U.S. Government Printing Office, 1965), p. 54.

teachers to a greater audience. It can also be used to supplement or complement the classroom teacher's instruction, by introducing at appropriate intervals specialized topics which may be beyond the competence of many teachers. In addition, the teacher can occasionally use open-circuit educational and commercial television programs that correlate with the material at hand. Yet it does not permit an exchange and free flow of ideas between the teacher and pupils. It cannot adequately provide for answering questions as they arise; it does not adjust to individual differences among pupils, and cannot help pupils with personal difficulties. It cannot supervise the learning of skills. It encourages passivity on the part of the learner, and makes no provision for the development of a pupil's personality. Even in the transmission of knowledge ideal conditions must be present, for it can be truly effective only when the teacher has a desirable television personality, when the curriculum materials are appropriate, and when the methods of teaching are carefully chosen.[3] Finally, an additional problem is created by the reluctance of many capable teachers to even try the medium.

There may be future developments in educational television that will expand its scope as a medium of education. Even then teachers do not need to worry that they will be replaced by a television receiver. No mechanical device can match the effectiveness of a live, enthusiastic classroom teacher who deals with pupils on a personal basis. Television instruction can be valuable to transmit knowledge, and it can be useful as an aid to the teacher, but by itself, it can help pupils to achieve only a very limited portion of the objectives of education.

PROGRAMED INSTRUCTION

Televised instruction is ordinarily directed toward group learning. Programed instruction attempts to offer individual instruction for every pupil. In programed instruction the pupil learns without the aid of a teacher through the use of teaching machines or printed books or pamphlets. The pupil may advance through the materials at a rate which best suits his ability level. Programed instruction assumes that there are many things a pupil can learn by himself, thus allowing the teacher to do more productive things in the classroom. Furthermore, it

---

[3]*Ibid.*, p. 58. See also, Edwin P. Adkins, ed., *Television in Teacher Education* (Washington, D.C.: The American Association of Colleges for Teachers Education, 1960), p. 3.

is based on the principle that individual differences should be taken into consideration in education.

Under programed instruction, the programed materials act as a tutor for each pupil. Its method has been compared to the Socratic method of teaching, in which the tutor makes use of what the pupil knows and proceeds through a series of statements, questions, and answers, to new knowledge and insights. In programed learning, the pupil also proceeds to learn, step by step, new material and receives an immediate evaluation of his every step of progress. The evaluation reinforces his learning, and motivates him to further progress.

Whether it is constructed in book or machine form, programed learning has several characteristics, which follow:

1) The program is built around definitely stated objectives that the pupil is expected to achieve.

2) The material is presented in small, orderly, sequential steps, known as frames, which lead the pupil to the attainment of the objectives. Depending on the type of programed instruction used, these frames may vary in length from two or three sentences to several paragraphs.

3) The steps are so simple that failure is unlikely. The programs are constructed so that most pupils will be able to answer between 90% and 95% of the items correctly. The success experienced by the student is said to reinforce his learning and provide him with motivation for further successful experiences.

4) The pupil must make one or more responses to each frame. If his response is correct, he moves on to the next step. If it is incorrect, he is directed to review the material, or he is referred to additional material, after which he makes another choice. He must make a correct response before moving on to the next step.

5) Periodically, the material previously learned by the pupil is reinserted, as a review and reinforcement. Old material is gradually phased out as additional new material is presented.

6) The pupil studies the program individually, at his own rate of of speed.

7) The program provides for the immediate evaluation of results.

S. L. Pressey first introduced the teaching machine in 1926, as a testing device, but it did not attract lasting attention. In the 1950's, B. F. Skinner's experimentation revived interest in it, and since then, a great deal of work has been done with programed instruction. It has had a variety of names, such as teaching machine, scrambled textbook, programed instruction, auto-instruction, and computer-assisted instruction. Recently, the generic term "programed instruction" has been used to include all of the others.

Two types of programs were developed, the *linear* and the *branching*. In the linear program, developed by Skinner, the program moves in a straight line, one point following another. In response to the questions, the pupil must write a constructed-response answer which tests his recall. The branching program was developed by N. A. Crowder in the form of a "scrambled textbook." In this program the item of information appears on one page, with a multiple-choice question which tests recognition (as opposed to Skinner's recall). Depending on the choice he makes, the pupil is referred to another page, where he will discover whether he is right or wrong. If he is right, he is given the reason why he is, and asked another question. If he is wrong, he is given a further explanation, and then tries another answer. A pupil may start at page 1, move to page 36, back to 15, over to 54, etc., with material, questions, and answers scrambled throughout the book. In the branching program, the pupil is not as tempted to look at the correct answer before giving his own response, as he is in the book form of the linear program where the correct answer appears on the same, or the following, page. The branching program also offers supplementary information to pupils who need it. However, because it is scrambled, the sequences of directions may be confusing to some pupils.

Both linear and branching programs have been used in teaching machines. The linear program is the simpler of the two to adapt to machines, as one item appears after another sequentially in a small window or slot in the machine. The pupil is required to make a response, and through various controls employed by different machines, the next frame does not appear unless the pupil has made the correct response. As the pupil moves from one frame to the next, the machine evaluates and keeps a record of his responses, thus providing the student with immediate feedback on his performance. Because of the high cost of teaching machines, the use of programed books has become more widespread in programed instruction.

The following example, appearing in a short, illustrative brochure by Jay A. Young, exemplifies the procedure followed in programed materials.[4] The material proceeds in sequential manner toward the specific objective of learning a rule of spelling. Also, the pupil must respond to

---

[4]Jay A. Young, *Automated Instruction: An Example* (Wilkes-Barre, Pennsylvania: King's College, 1961), p. 3.

each step. In addition there is a provision for the immediate feedback of the correct answer, which the pupil is asked to keep covered until he has made a response.

Programed Or Programmed?   *A Brief Lesson In Spelling*

1   Consider the word, prefer. This word
has _____ syllable(s).   two

2   In the word, prefer, the _____ (initial/final)   final
syllable is accented.

3   Consider the word, preferred. In this word the final consonant of the root, prefer, is doubled because, according to
the rules of spelling: When the _____ syllable of the root   final
word is accented, the final consonant of the root is _____   doubled
when a suffix which begins with a vowel, such as "ed" is
added.

      Strictly, this rule applies only when the final
      consonant of the root is preceded by a vowel.

4   Consider the word, preferable. In this word the root is
the same as in the previous example. But, in this case, the   initial;
_____ syllable of the root is accented.   or first

5   Therefore, since the final syllable of the root is not accented, the final consonant is _____ doubled, when the   not
suffix "able" is added.

6   Hence, which of the two, programmed or programed, is
correct? _____ is correct, because the root of this word,   Programed
program, is not accented on the _____ syllable.   final

7   To summarize, the final consonant of the root is doubled
when:
a/ The root is accented on the _____ syllable;   final
b/ the suffix begins with a _____; and   vowel
c/ a _____ precedes the final consonant in the root.   vowel
When all three conditions are met, the final consonant of the
root is _____ when a suffix is added.   doubled

      The several exceptions to the rule for doubling the final
consonant cannot be considered in this brief discussion. In
fact, in some other English speaking countries "programed"
itself is an exception. Thus, in England, programmed is preferable. The British have preferred to double the m.

During the last decade, a mass of material has been published on programed instruction, and many refinements have been made in teaching machines. These have been accompanied by experimentation, and the results are still inconclusive. The initial claims for programed instruction were ambitious and, of course, had to be modified.

One of the primary claims for programed instruction is that it provides for individual differences. Initially, many people believed that the same program could be used by pupils from all ability levels, as long as each child had as much time as he needed to learn the program. Other people felt that branching techniques were needed to provide for differences in mental ability. Now it appears that neither method adequately treats individual differences. Some evidence has shown that entirely different programs for the bright, average, and slow are more effective than the same program for all groups.[5] Adjustments are also needed in the size of the steps in learning and in the level of difficulty, if they are to correspond to the traits of a particular group.

Proponents of the reinforcement theory claimed that they had solved the problem of motivation. Their theory of reinforcement extended the experimental findings of the animal world to that of human beings. They believed that just as an animal was conditioned to repeat a task in anticipation of a reward, the success a pupil experienced with each step of a program would constitute sufficient motivation for him to continue. Again, this claim was too optimistic, for the most frequent criticism voiced by students was that, after a time, they found programed instruction boring.[6] The measure taken by programers to insure motivation actually contributed to boredom. Maehr, discussing this point, states that a pupil is better motivated if he finds the task a challenge. Maehr further points out that there is some evidence that students are most persistent with a task when there is only a 50-50 chance of success.[7] If there is little risk of failure (as there is in programs which are purposely constructed for success 90-95 percent of the time), the task may lead to boredom, especially for bright students.

Nevertheless there are ample studies to show that pupils using programed materials can learn as much or more, in less time, as they learn under conventional methods. However, initial experiments with an innovation are carried on by enthusiastic people whose experiments sel-

[5]Lassar G. Gotkin and Leo S. Goldstein, "Programed Instruction in the Schools: Innovation and Innovator," in Matthew B. Miles, ed., *Innovation in Education* (New York: Teachers College, Columbia University, 1964), pp. 243-246.

[6]*Ibid.*, p. 244.

[7]Martin L. Maehr, "Some Limitations of the Application of Reinforcement Theory to Education," *School & Society*, 96, Number 2303 (February 17, 1968), p. 110.

dom "fail". The samples used in the experiments vary considerably, and different evaluative criteria and instruments may be used. Consequently, any generalizations should be viewed with caution. Still, enough evidence is emerging to indicate that programed instruction can be useful in the learning process. It could be used advantageously for a portion of the school program. It would allow pupils to learn by themselves factual and drill type material and review materials previously learned. Also, by using induction and deduction, there is no reason why well-written programs cannot lead pupils through reasoning processes. Programed materials for home study, with the teacher building upon the material during regular school hours has also experienced some success. Programed instruction should be able to enrich the program of studies in small schools by offering courses for which teachers are not available. These courses could be given as supplementary offerings by all schools. In industry and the armed forces, programed materials have been used successfully, but in these cases, the students were *adults* who were motivated toward specific objectives. It is likely that programed instruction will find still another place in adult education programs.

There are still many problems in programed instruction. Its success depends on the quality of the programed material, since it takes the place of a qualified teacher. Actually, unless it can do a *better* job than the teacher, there is little justification for expending large sums of money for programed materials. The problem of motivation still remains. If pupils find this type of learning boring, program writers must develop materials that have more interesting contents and formats. If this is not possible, a student's exposure time to programed materials should be short, so that the deadening effects of boredom are not experienced for prolonged periods of time. Furthermore, the problem of individual differences needs further attention. Well-written programs must be constructed not only for particular grade levels, but also for different learning ability within those levels. In addition, if programs are overused, there will be the usual problems that result from minimizing the function of a live teacher: the lack of personal interaction between the teacher and pupil, and the absence of group discussions and activities.

With the advent of electronic computers, and their subsequent refinements, some complex machines have been designed for computer-assisted instruction. These may become more versatile in their presentation and evaluation of materials than programed books. They can provide for almost instantaneous branching into intricate patterns of additional instruction or explanation. They also can provide reviews and answer questions directed to them. In fact, it is foreseen that, before long, computers may be able to respond to verbal stimuli.[8] These machines are still in an experimental stage, and are extremely costly. Because of their high cost, computer-assisted instruction may not become commonplace in the foreseeable future. However, computers probably will be installed in large information centers. They will be able to provide immediate answers to questions directed to them from the areas they serve. In the field of education, these installations may be provided by schools or colleges on a cost- and time-sharing basis.

TEAM TEACHING

Team teaching began in the late 1950's as a reform measure to ease the teacher shortage and improve instruction. Among the many groups seeking new approaches to educational problems was the Commission on Curriculum Planning and Development, established in 1956 by the National Association of Secondary School Principals. The Commission formulated many proposals for the better utilization of teachers. Among these proposals was what eventually became known as team teaching. The Fund for the Advancement of Education granted money for experimentation and many pilot programs were initiated throughout the United States.

Although it is similar in many ways to the Core Curriculum (an innovation of the 1930's), it is difficult to state precisely what team teaching is, because of the diversity of practices initiated under its name. Team teaching was organized in many different ways, with many different objectives. Therefore in speaking of the team teaching projects that were launched, Shaplin stated:

> Their common properties are difficult to identify, both because each program tends to define itself in very general and, at the same time, exclusive terms and because no clearly recognizable group of projects seems to have the same objectives. Since it is equally difficult to point to one or two projects and say that they are the models for the typical or real team teaching, it is hardly an exaggeration to say that there are as many different types of team teaching as there are different school systems that have undertaken projects.[9]

---

[8]For a concise summary of tentative research findings on computer-assisted instruction, see Robert B. Bundy, "Computer-Assisted Instruction—Where Are We?" *Education Digest*, XXXIV, Number 1 (September, 1968), 5-8.

[9]Judson T. Shaplin and Henry F. Olds, ed., *Team Teaching* (New York: Harper & Row, Publishers, 1964), p. 5.

Because of this diversity of practices, many educators do not even attempt to define team teaching. Some, however, have tried to define it through the common elements that are found among the various projects initiated. Two of these definitions follow.

> Team teaching is a type of instructional organization, involving teaching personnel and the students assigned to them, in which two or more teachers are given responsibility, working together, for all or a significant part of the instruction of the same group of students.[10]
>
> Team teaching may be defined as an arrangement whereby two or more teachers, with or without teacher aides, cooperatively plan, instruct and evaluate one or more class groups in an appropriate instructional space and given length of time, so as to take advantage of the special competencies of the team members.[11]

Combining the common ideas of these definitions, two or more teachers in team teaching combine their special talents to cooperate in the instruction and evaluation of a common group of students over a predetermined period of time. These core ideas have been surrounded by a great variety of practices. A summary of some of these practices should better demonstrate the difficulty of reaching a universally applicable definition of team teaching.

The size of a teaching team may vary from two to ten, or more, members. It may be comprised of teachers only, or teachers and aides, or teachers, aides, and specialists. Teams may teach a single discipline, or departmental lines may be crossed by forming interdisciplinary teams. Whatever its composition, the teaching team, with the approval and cooperation of the administration, plans together the objectives, content, materials, methods, and evaluative procedures of the course. The team members agree on their areas of responsibility, usually under the direction of a designated team leader, or "master teacher". Some teachers may instruct pupils in the presence of other team members, while others may not. Other members of the team may make contributions during, or for a portion of, the class period. If the team includes aides, they may perform the routine duties of the classroom and assist in the evaluation of written work and tests. Flexible schedules may be used, varying the length of class periods to meet the needs of the learn-

---

[10]*Ibid.*, p. 15.
[11]David W. Beggs, ed., *Team Teaching* (Bloomington, Indiana: Indiana University Press, 1964), p. 16.

ing activity. Pupils for team teaching projects may be selected on ability and achievement, or interest, or both. Pupils, at different times, may be instructed in large groups (70 or more pupils), or they may be broken down into small discussion or work groups (12-20 pupils), or assigned to do independent study. Some school systems may try to use existing facilities, while others may create special facilities that use educational technology extensively. These projects may be organized for any level of schooling: elementary school, junior high school, high school, or college. Obviously, if each of these items were taken as a variable, a great number of organizational patterns would be possible. It is quite likely that all of these possibilities were implemented in some way in the array of experiments that were conducted throughout the country.

Team teaching, its proponents claim, results in the more efficient utilization of the special competencies possessed by each teacher. In the elementary school, for example, instead of having one teacher instruct his pupils in all subjects in a self-contained classroom, each team teacher would instruct the same pupils in his specialty. The pupils would benefit from the special training of several teachers, and from the exposure to teachers with different personalities. By using team teaching, the teacher can, at times, instruct many pupils in his specialty, eliminate duplicating his presentation, and extend his instruction to more pupils. At the same time, the team can provide for smaller group instruction, and individual work. In the upper schools, where instruction is departmentalized, each member of a team can be assigned to teach the phase of a subject or field in which he is most competent. In this way, through careful planning, the special talents of teachers can be shared by a greater number of pupils.

Another aspect of team teaching which may make instruction more efficient is the use of teacher's aides. They can free the teacher of many routine time-consuming tasks, enabling him to devote more time to teaching. The aide can collect money from pupils, take attendance, distribute supplies, keep records, and correct papers. In the team teaching concept, this extra time for the teacher can be used for additional planning and instructional activities.

The proponents of team teaching state that it is now possible for them to vary the 50-minute-period, which brings learning activities to a halt at the sound of the bell. Instead, they are able to schedule shorter or longer periods. In addition, flexibility may be promoted by altering existing school plants, or planning of new ones, to accommodate large and small groups and provide for special learning centers. This type of construction, with rooms of different sizes, and opening-out walls between the rooms, makes it possible to adjust facilities to a variety of situations, rather than having only a series of small enclosed areas.

Furthermore, the many planning sessions and conferences held by the team, proponents claim, actually constitute in-service training for teachers. The frequent interchange of ideas, the attempts to solve problems, the adjustment of personalities to each other, all contribute to the professional growth of the participants. In addition, team members learn a great deal from observing the teaching techniques of their colleagues. It is also claimed that the output of teachers is greater when they are observed than when they teach unobserved in their selfcontained classrooms. All of these influences provide a higher quality of instruction for pupils.

In theory, team teaching seems to bring about the more effective utilization of teachers and the improvement of education. Yet, unforeseen problems have arisen, and opponents have raised objections. As soon as funds became available, programs were hurriedly initiated, without sufficient attention to the objectives sought. Because change and innovation were in vogue, some administrators implemented team teaching programs simply to remain in the forefront as progressive educators. Even when the possibilities of team teaching were duly considered the emphasis was often on innovating the innovation. The result, described previously, was a myriad of organizational procedures, each of which was designated as a team teaching program. Hence confusion arose, and still exists, regarding the objectives and procedures of team teaching.

As the various pilot programs began to report the results of their experiments, several problems were discovered. First, flexibility which is an essential feature of team teaching cannot be achieved within the architectural framework of existing schools, and the cost of remodelling would add too much to the already rapidly rising costs of education. The desired flexibility in scheduling is not always possible, because some administrators are not convinced of the merits of team teaching. Because of this, they do not permit the regular school program to be disrupted. Furthermore, some teachers who have participated in the program have felt an undue emotional strain because they knew their colleagues were evaluating them. Other teachers disliked giving up their autonomous role in the classroom, and team teaching necessitated sharing authority and instruction with other teachers. Furthermore, the use of aides and supporting personnel added greatly to the expenditure of manpower and money.

Because of the great variety of procedures used in team teaching, the results of experiments are not, strictly speaking, comparable. Consequently, it is difficult to assess its effectiveness compared to instruction under traditional methods. In spite of this, the reports on team teaching have consistently stated that pupils learn "as much as" and "sometimes more than" pupils instructed in a self-contained classroom. If team teaching is worthwhile, if it is to justify its expense in time and money, if it is to result in the reorganization of the school system, it must offer definite evidence that it is clearly "superior to", not merely "as good as" the procedures now in use. The results of the early studies on team teaching have usually showed no statistically significant differences in student achievement.[12] Maybe team teaching has not yet explored its full possibilities, because of lack of agreement by its proponents. What is needed before there can be further progress in team teaching is a clear formulation of its objectives; agreement on its composition, organization, and procedures of team personnel; careful control of variables; deliberate implementation of acceptable programs; development of valid criteria for its evaluation; and, appropriate training for the personnel of teaching teams.

NONGRADED SCHOOLS

The nongraded school is one in which grade designations have been eliminated, so that there are no Grades 1, 2, 3, on. Instead, the nongraded school, through its organization and operational procedures, permits a pupil to advance through levels of learning at his own rate of speed. Therefore "passing" or "failing" does not exist because there are no grades to pass or fail. Rather, at the beginning of a new school year, the pupil simply begins where he left off the preceding year. This type of progress plan has a variety of names, such as the ungraded primary, primary unit, continuous progress plan, and nongraded high school. Recently, the term "nongraded schools" has been used to include all of these.

The nongraded school is not new. Chapter III, which described the development of elementary education, showed that *all* elementary schools were ungraded until the end of the nineteenth century. Until then, one teacher taught pupils of all age and ability levels in the same classroom. As the school population increased during the nineteenth

---

[12]Judson T. Shaplin and Henry F. Olds, *op. cit.*, p. 326.

century, the graded school evolved as a more efficient organization system to handle large numbers of students. No sooner had the graded school system been adopted, than educators were concerned over the lack of provision for individual differences. We are now at the point where a cycle seems to be completing itself, for we are starting to revert to an organizational plan that was used in schools for the first two centuries of our national existence. Today's teacher, however, has at his disposal many instructional aids that did not exist before.

In our modern educational history, the first, and still existing, nongraded primary school was established in Milwaukee, Wisconsin in 1942, followed by another at Appleton, Wisconsin, in 1947.[13] The growth of nongraded schools was slow until the mid-1950's. After then, experimental schools were established on a fairly wide scale. By 1966, in 12,130 reporting school systems, each with an enrollment of over 300 pupils, it was estimated that 8.1% provided some type of program which was based on a nongraded organization.[14] It was used most frequently in grades 1-3, sometimes in 4-6, and rarely in high school. These programs, especially for disadvantaged children, were initiated more often in larger than in smaller school systems.

The nongraded school organization is intended to provide for individual differences. The work normally done in the first three grades is carefully restructured and sequenced in logical order. With guidance from the teacher, each pupil can make considerable progress working alone. Although there are no grade-level expectations for students or teachers to meet, it is anticipated that the average child can progress through the primary unit in three years, the bright child in two, and the slow child in perhaps four years. The progress of pupils from one level to another is commonly determined by their level of reading ability. For this purpose, schools have established a number of reading levels, ranging from 7-8 levels in most schools, to as high as 20 levels in a few. Regardless of the number, when the pupil has completed the required levels, he has achieved a level of reading ability that was formerly accomplished in grades 1-3. Throughout the program the teacher has tried to adjust instruction to individual needs. He is allowed flexibility in making assignments and used a wide range of materials. Students work individually, or in groups. Movable classroom furniture permits flexibility in grouping children into larger or smaller groups for common learning.

---

[13]Stuart E. Dean, "The Nongraded School," *School Life,* 47, Number 3 (December, 1964), 20.

[14]*NEA Research Bulletin,* 45, Number 4 (December, 1967), from Table 12, p. 119.

Several advantages have been claimed for the nongraded school. Proponents state that the plan provides for individual differences among children, by permitting the teacher to give additional attention to children whenever they need it, and by allowing each child to work at his own rate of speed. It is claimed that, since there are no grade-level expectations, no child receives a "failing grade", thus eliminating the undesirable emotional effects of failure. Instead of repeating the entire work of a grade, the slow pupil simply begins where he left off; at the same time, the bright pupil can move ahead. The flexibility of the plan also permits pupils to be transferred from one group to another during the school year, while pupils entering from another school can be evaluated and placed in an appropriate group at any time. Finally, the flexibility of the plan relieves the teacher of the pressure to keep all of the pupils at the level of attainment prescribed for the particular grade. The teacher does not have to make "pass-fail" judgments for each of the pupils.

Some of the reports of experiments with nongraded schools have been quite favorable. One experiment at the elementary level in Appleton, Wisconsin reported that pupils in nongraded units were a year and a month above the national achievement median by the time they reached junior high school. Other reports from nongraded high schools in Melbourne, Florida and in Middletown, Rhode Island stated that they have a lower dropout rate, and a higher percentage of students going to college, than they had previously.[15] Similar, but not as spectacular, are the results claimed in many other experimental programs with nongrading procedures.

Even though the recent return to nongrading dates back to 1942, it is too early to evaluate it as a movement, because the widespread experimental programs were not undertaken until the late 1950's. There has, however, been enough experience with nongrading to recognize that there are many problems and questions connected with its successful implementation.

One of the primary purposes of the nongraded school is the provision for individual differences among children. Yet, the nongraded school suffers the same limitation as several other innovations, namely, it has concentrated mainly on differences in the rate of progress in learning. The "whole child" needs to be considered in the educational process, but this has not yet been achieved in the nongraded school.

The abolition of the graded structure, and its related system of passing and failing students, is intended to eliminate the feelings of humili-

---

[15]Stuart E. Dean, *op. cit.*, p. 22.

ation, rejection, and inferiority that are often experienced by students who have failed. Although the nongraded school may reduce the incidence, or the intensity, of these feelings, it does not eliminate them. Pupils are still able to recognize their relative progress among their peers and certainly will realize that they are slow learners if they take four years to complete work that others have finished in three years.

With the elimination of grades, and grade expectations, there is a danger of substituting an even more elaborate system of "groups" and "levels" of attainment. For example, instead of Grades 1-3, nongraded schools can substitute a number of levels of performance, such as Levels 1-8, or Groups A, B, on. One terminology merely replaces another, and one graded structure merely substitutes for another. The significant difference between the two systems, however, is that the pupil in the nongraded school is not "failed" and does not repeat a whole year's work as he would in a graded school.

In a nongraded school, it is said that the teacher does not have to try to keep all pupils at a level of performance consistent with grade expectations. Yet, any conscientious teacher in a nongraded school will experience the pressure of trying to have the pupils meet particular levels of performance. Furthermore, the teacher will feel additional pressure from trying to work with different age groups and different ability levels all in the same classroom. At the same time, the teacher must arrange and supervise co-curricular activities that are appropriate for the various groups. It would require an exceptional teacher to do these things effectively without feeling undue pressure.

It is also held that the teacher in a nongraded classroom has greater freedom and flexibility in assigning work to students. But the diversity of students places upon the teacher the *burden* of planning differentiated assignments for each pupil. Not only must the teacher provide for individual differences but also he must continually judge which pupils can be assembled for appropriate group learning. It cannot be denied that the flexibility increases the work and the responsibilities of a teacher.

The division of learning into levels of performance, through which pupils are expected to make continuous progress, poses curriculum problems. Most of the existing curricula, textbooks and learning aids are oriented toward the organization of schools into grades. In a nongraded school, the curriculum and materials must be carefully sequenced to build subsequent learning upon previously learned material. This requires more extensive use of programed learning, a measure that would be viewed with mixed feelings by educators.

Keeping a record of the progress of each pupil imposes an additional burden upon the teacher. This problem could be alleviated through the use of teacher's aides, or the use of computers. Either of these measures, however, would add greatly to the cost of education.

Finally, there is the problem of increased enrollment in the schools. Many innovations have aimed at the more effective use of teachers in instructing larger numbers of pupils. The nongraded school places emphasis on individual instruction. It would seem self-evident that a teacher would have to have smaller classes if he were expected to provide individual help. The nongraded school, if it is expected to operate effectively, requires more personnel than the graded school. Since there has been a shortage of qualified teachers for many years, the staffing of these schools with appropriately trained personnel would constitute a problem.

Nongraded schools have advantages and disadvantages. On the basis of a review of the research reports on nongraded schools, Dean presents the following pros and cons.[16]

Pro. These are some of the reasons given for considering the nongraded school as desirable:
1. It recognizes and provides for individual differences among children.
2. It offers flexibility in administrative structure.
3. It abolishes the artificial barriers of grades and promotion.
4. It permits the pupil to progress at his own rate.
5. It promotes improved mental health in teacher and pupil.
6. It respects the continuity and interrelationship of learning.
7. It stimulates major curricular revision.
8. It is in harmony with the educational objectives of a democratic society.
9. It is administratively feasible for all levels and age groups.
10. It is program oriented, not operationally controlled.

Con. These are some of the reasons the nongraded school is not considered desirable:
1. It leads to soft pedagogy; lacks fixed standards and requirements.
2. It places an impossible burden on the teacher.
3. It replaces grade requirements by reading levels.
4. It results in lack of information on pupil progress to parents.
5. It is difficult to put into practice because teachers are inadequately and insufficiently prepared.

---

[16]*Ibid.*, pp. 22-23.

6. It does not have minimal standards for all children.
7. Its curriculum sequence tends to lack specificity and order.
8. It is only an improved means to an unimproved end.
9. It does not guarantee that improved teaching will result.
10. It suffers from widespread misuse and even abuse of the term "nongraded."

INDIVIDUALLY PRESCRIBED INSTRUCTION

Since the spring of 1964, the University of Pittsburgh, in cooperation with the U.S. Office of Education, has been experimenting with Individually Prescribed Instruction (IPI). This project attempts to develop a program for individualizing instruction in Grades K-6. The project was initiated at the Oakleaf School of the Baldwin-Whitehall Public Schools in the suburbs of Pittsburgh. IPI operates within a nongraded structure, and utilizes some of the principles of programed instruction. However, it extends instructional materials and activities beyond the range of programed instruction.

IPI assumes that each pupil can learn at his own individual pace if he is given learning experiences that are carefully sequenced by degree of difficulty. It further assumes that he can learn these things with little or no outside help. In addition, it believes that, using the same planning procedures that are used in programed textbooks, the entire program of grades K-6 can be planned to transcend grade levels.[17] Instead of classifying subjects grade by grade, the curriculum would be planned into levels of proficiency, beginning with A-level and moving through B, C, etc. As the pupil met the objectives of one level, he would begin the next level, regardless of the time in the schoolyear. Bright pupils would move through the levels faster than the average pupils, while slow pupils would spend as much more time than the average pupils as they needed. Similar to programed instruction, provisions would be made for regular feedback to the student, so that he would know how well he was progressing toward the objectives. With these things in mind, the IPI planners first developed K-6 programs for reading and mathematics, and later for science.

In the Oakleaf Elementary School, pupils were divided into two groups (K-3 and 4-6), but after the first year, three groups were used

[17]C. M. Lindvall and John O. Bolvin, "Programed Instruction in the Schools: An Application of Programing Principles in 'Individually Prescribed Instruction'", in Phil C. Lange, ed., *Programed Instruction,* Sixty-sixth Yearbook of the National Society for the Study of Education (Chicago: The University of Illinois Press, 1967), p. 233.

(K-2, 3-4, and 5-6). Pupils were placed by level, on the basis of place-ment tests, and they were given a pre-test for each unit, which revealed the areas of study needed by them. The teacher then gave each pupil a written prescription of the learning activities he was to undertake. These prescriptions called for activities such as writing, reading, listen-ing to records, working out problems, studying in the library, or carry-ing out simple experiments in science. The teacher in charge of the room provided individual help when it was needed. Teacher-aides who took care of relatively routine matters and helped to score papers as-sisted the teacher.[18] As the pupil moved through the prescribed exer-cises, he frequently took short "curriculum-embedded tests" as a check on his progress. There were, then, placement tests, pre-tests, curricu-lum-embedded tests, and post-tests for each unit. In the IPI program, a pupil can work at different levels within the same subject (such as level B addition, and level C subtraction), or he may be engaged in level C units in reading, and level A units in science. Although most of the work is done on an individual basis, there can be group work with individuals with common problems.

IPI procedures have so far been limited to cognitive learning, but its proponents think that it could be applied to teaching certain affective states, such as the inculcation of values and attitudes. In fact, they claim that the procedures of IPI can be applied to almost any type of educational goal, that its applications are limited only by the lack of ability to define specific goals, and the reluctance of educators to spend the time necessary to develop the needed procedures and materials.[19]

The procedures used in IPI bear a resemblance to the Dalton Plan, which originated in Dalton, Massachusetts, in 1920. For purposes of comparison, the *Dictionary of Education* offers the following definition of the Dalton Plan:[20]

> Dalton plan: a plan of organizing the curriculum, program of studies, and learning activities adopted in Dalton, Massachusetts, in 1920 and organized as follows: each pupil was given monthly assignments, known as *jobs*, in each school subject, each job being divided into about 20 *units*: workbooks and instruction sheets en-abled the pupil to work individually at his jobs, while a *job card* enabled him to record his progress; pupil-teacher *conferences*

---

[18]Experimentation is going on which permits the pupil to score his paper by computer, thus providing immediate feedback.

[19]C. M. Lindvall and John O. Bolvin, *op. cit.*, p. 252.

[20]Carter V. Good, ed., *Dictionary of Education*, 2nd ed. (New York: McGraw-Hill Book Company, Inc., 1959), p. 154.

were held whenever necessary to take the place of recitations; classrooms were known as *laboratories;* pupils were free to plan their own work schedules but were obliged to finish each monthly job before proceeding to the job for the succeeding month; cooperation and group work were encouraged.

The Dalton Plan retained the organization of work into grades, whereas IPI emphasizes levels of performance. Also, undoubtedly there is a more careful planning, or programing, of sequences of work under IPI than there was under the Dalton Plan. The Dalton Plan provided for individual differences by offering superior students supplementary units of work, whereas IPI permits bright students to accelerate their progress through school. In other ways, the two plans used similar procedures: the work was divided into units, instruction sheets were provided, students worked at their own rate of speed, tests were built into the programs, the teacher helped pupils with individual problems, conferences were held when necessary, the work of one unit had to be completed satisfactorily before the next was undertaken (in IPI, the student is required to achieve an 85% level before moving on to the next unit), and provision was made for some group work when needed.

The Dalton Plan failed to survive. It remains to be seen whether IPI will do so. IPI proponents recognize the fact that, to date, the plan has achieved individualization only in the rate of progress that can be made by individual students. However, they maintain that this lack of individualization in other areas is due to the fact that experimentation with it has just begun, and that it is not a limitation of the IPI procedure itself.[21] As experimentation progresses, the adjustment of IPI procedures will become necessary to account for other types of individual differences. Also, if IPI is extended to all subjects, it will expose itself to the criticisms made of other plans which minimize group learning activities.

Up to this point, the innovations discussed were devised as plans that could be applied to a typical heterogeneous school population. Except for educational television, they were directed primarily toward provisions for the mental differences found among school children. In seeking to determine their effectiveness, studies were conducted which compared the innovations with traditional classroom procedures, thus placing the two on an "either-or" basis. In each case, an attempt was made to discover whether the innovation was better than the usual classroom procedures. It was generally found that the innovation was

---

[21]C. M. Lindvall and John O. Bolvin, *op. cit.,* pp. 252-253.

"as good as" traditional methods in stimulating student achievement or progress. These results are not good enough to warrant the reorganization of the school system, nor do they justify the additional expense of implementing an entirely new system of education. An innovation must be clearly superior to existing procedures, before it is implemented on a wide scale.

Instead of the dichotomy that is created between innovative and traditional procedures, perhaps it would be more useful to explore further a union of traditional classroom methods with one or more innovations. For example, instead of comparing traditional procedures with the exclusive use of programed instruction or other innovations, it would be useful to have more information on the effectiveness of programed instruction which has been incorporated into traditional classroom procedures for a part of the time. Neither traditional procedures nor innovative practices are all good or all bad. It is important to salvage the good from each procedure.

HEAD START

The remainder of this chapter will consider innovations that apply to a special segment of the school population, namely, the culturally disadvantaged. Children from disadvantaged families are handicapped when they first enter school, because their limited experiential background does not meet the expectations of a regular school. Very little was done to help these children in past years, but recently an intensive and extensive effort was made to do so.

The problems of the culturally disadvantaged have been heightened by technological developments in our society. In the past, agrarian groups of southern Negroes, southwestern Spanish-speaking Americans, Indians, migratory workers, farmers of Appalachian regions, and Puerto Ricans were able to subsist from the land. However, technological advances, with which they are not familiar, or cannot afford, have prevented them from competing with the more advanced elements of society for a livelihood. Not able to earn a living, they have migrated in large numbers to the cities, where they met a similar problem. They are unskilled, and cannot find employment in a labor market where there is little demand for unskilled workers. Unemployed, or working in low-paid unskilled jobs, they have lived in poverty in slum areas, without adequate food, clothing, shelter, and health services.

The children of these families are disadvantaged not only economically, but also culturally and psychologically. Racial discrimination against the Blacks produced in them feelings of inferiority and despair. They have seen little opportunity to rise above their environment. Children of Puerto Ricans and Mexican-Americans are brought up in the culture of their people, so that many of them cannot speak English when they enter school. Those families who migrated from, or still live in, remote Appalachian regions are so isolated from society that many of their children have never seen commonplace objects such as toys, books, pens and pencils. Many of them are isolated from other children and have consequently never played games. Because of their compartmentalized existence, the disadvantaged compared with other children, are handicapped in all phases of their growth and development: physical, mental, social, and emotional. These deprivations are particularly stunting for young children, for the first five or six years of life are considered the important formative years.

In order to provide disadvantaged children with equal opportunities in education and prepare them for normal entry into the first year of school, it was felt that early childhood education was necessary to supplement whatever educational efforts were being made by their families. Project Head Start was initiated in 1965 by the Office of Economic Opportunity as part of its war on poverty. Children of ages 3, 4, and 5 from disadvantaged families were eligible for the program. It began with approximately one-half million children from the city ghettos and Appalachian poverty areas, and included children of Indians, Eskimos, and migrant workers. Two types of programs were initiated: eight-week summer programs for four- and five-year old children; and, regular school year programs for three-, four-, and five-year olds which lasted anywhere from three to twelve months.

The Head Start program was intended to be a comprehensive program. Children were organized into small, informal classes which were not to exceed fifteen pupils. Supplied with work and play materials, the children were encouraged to develop initiative through learning-by-doing. Each class was conducted by a teacher, who was assisted by two aides. All children received more individual attention than they would ordinarily receive in the larger classes found in regular schools. Since the programs were experimental, and since the background of the various groups was different (Negroes, Appalachian whites, Indians, etc.), considerable flexibility existed in the programs that were initiated. However, all programs had several things in common. They tried to foster initiative and a sense of pride in the children. All the children received health services, which included physical examinations and remedial treatment, and one or two nutritious meals a day. In addition, psychiatric and counselling services were provided for those who needed them.

The program emphasized parental involvement. Parents were invited into the schools, and their cooperation, help, and advice were sought. Some parents worked in the program as teacher's aides, either as volunteers or as paid workers. The educational and counselling services were also extended to the parents, who were interviewed, counselled, and provided with information on budgeting, housekeeping, and the preparation of nutritious meals at low cost. In this way, the efforts of the home supplemented the efforts of the school.

The first national survey of Head Start programs was completed by NEA in 1967. They sampled school districts with enrollments of more than 300 pupils and obtained a variety of information. The following estimated figures were extracted from the statistics provided.

Estimated Head Start Statistics, 1966–67[22]

	Pupils	Teachers	Cost
Summer program, 1966	292,432	15,172	$ 48,241,574
Full year program, 1966–67	57,008	2,920	47,159,157
Other programs	4,248	162	12,092,771
Total	353,688	18,254	107,493,502

These statistics show that Head Start programs were most frequently offered as summer programs. The NEA survey also showed that there was parental participation of some type in 97.2% of the programs,[23] and that the most prevalent practice in financing the programs was one in which the federal government supplied 90% of the funds, with local sources providing 10%.[24]

Head Start began well, as shown by the enrollment figures. A solid commitment to the program continued during the first few years. It was estimated that between the summer of 1965 and the school year of 1967–68, a total of 595,000 children attended Head Start classes during the regular school year, and 1,598,000 attended summer sessions.[25] In 1968, 218,000 children, ages 3-5, were enrolled in full-year Head Start programs.[26]

---

[22]"Head Start in the Public Schools," NEA Research Bulletin, 46, Number 1 (March, 1968), statistics extracted from pp. 3-8.

[23]*Ibid.*, p. 6.

[24]*Ibid.*, p. 7.

[25]Carroll J. Krause, "A Head Start and a Fresh Start," *American Education*, 4, Number 4 (April, 1968), 29.

[26]Minnie P. Berson, "Early Childhood Education," *American Education*, 4, Number 9 (October, 1968), 9.

The Head Start program was further extended in 1967–68. It was felt that it would be beneficial to extend the same type of comprehensive services to children of ages 0-3 and their families. For this purpose, approximately thirty Parent-Child Centers were established in appropriate locations throughout the United States. Each center was intended to serve 100 children and their families. These centers began operating in 1968. In the meantime, an effort was made to develop a Community Coordinated Child Care program (4-C program), with its standards formulated by the Secretaries of Labor, HEW, and the director of the Office of Economic Opportunity.[27] It was hoped that, with federal aid, the states would initiate their own 4-C programs.

Thus, a strong effort was made to provide equality of opportunity for disadvantaged children, first through the Head Start program for children aged 3-5, and then through the Parent-Child Centers for those aged 0-3. The results remain to be evaluated. It is too early to make any statements concerning the Parent-Child Centers, but many general statements have been made about the merits of Head Start. Two evaluative statements appeared in 1966 and may be taken as representative of the diversity of opinion on Head Start. Charles S. Carleton expressed his confidence in the program in the following statement:[28]

> There is no doubt that Head Start is working, that for disadvantaged children it means entering regular school better prepared, with greater self-confidence and with a considerably advanced mental capacity compared to children from the same background without Head Start training.

Carleton cautions, however, that the benefits from Head Start may be erased unless the children are treated understandingly when they enter regular school.

Ivor Kraft, on the other hand, spoke skeptically about the results obtained by Head Start. Although a member of the staff of the Department of HEW, he spoke unofficially about the program as follows:[29]

> To date there is practically no sound research evidence to support the expected achievements of Head Start. The most that can

---

[27]*Loc. cit.*

[28]Charles S. Carleton, "Head Start or False Start?" *American Education*, 2, Number 8 (September, 1966), 20.

[29]Ivor Kraft, "Head Start or What?" The Education Digest, XXXII, Number 3 (November, 1966), 2. Reported from the Nation, Vol. CIII (September, 1966), pp. 179-182.

be claimed for the program is that it "keeps the children off the streets," submits them to medical screening, yields a five- to ten-point gain in IQ, and causes a six-year-old to make a better adjustment to first grade. A seven- or eight-point rise in IQ is not very much, and may be only a gain in "easy" or "cheap" points, a gain in routine practice effects or certain rather low-level manipulative skills.

Kraft maintained that the Head Start program was oversold and misinterpreted. He felt that it was a potentially good program which, if properly planned and managed, could be applied to *all* pre-school children.

Since these statements were made, thousands of children have completed Head Start programs, but it will take several more years to provide the "sound research" necessary to make a valid evaluation of the program. In theory, the program agrees with our desire to provide equal opportunity for all individuals. In practice, a great deal of good has been done for individual children and their families. For the first time, many of them have experienced the hope, and have seen the means, of rising above the limitations of their bleak environment. If the early childhood education programs are used to *supplement* the efforts of the family, they may hold promise for the future.

Follow Through

Children who had completed Head Start programs immediately encountered a common problem. They had trouble adjusting when they began regular school. In their Head Start program, they had considerable freedom of movement and choice. They were in small classes, and were given personal attention. When they entered regular school, they found themselves in larger classes, restricted in their movement, and, of necessity, they received less personal attention. Because of these problems, it was felt that the progress the children made under Head Start might be nullified when they entered regular school, especially if they had an unsympathetic teacher. As an alternative to enrolling in regular school, programs were developed for following through the programs that were begun in Head Start.

In 1967, President Johnson asked Congress to extend the benefits of Head Start to the early school years (ages 6-9). Follow Through was the response to his request. Pilot programs were initiated in 1967–68 in school districts that were known to have strong Head Start programs. The guidelines for Follow Through programs were similar to those for

Head Start: the programs were to be comprehensive, including physical, psycho-social, medical, and nutritional services. As in Head Start, active participation by parents was considered essential to the success of Follow Through. In the pilot programs, the selected school districts were allowed to use their initiative in developing specific Follow Through programs. The programs were to develop the whole child, and it was hoped that they would be designed to build up the child's self-esteem and respect for others. Following a year of experimentation, Follow Through began nationally in 1968–69, with an enrollment of 190,000 children, financed by a federal grant of 120 million dollars.[30]

A report on the pilot program conducted in Detroit has provided some early information on Follow Through. Although no objective evaluation of the program has been made, subjective judgments by teachers have indicated that the pupils are making faster progress than they would in a regular kindergarten. They have shown higher interest in the activities, have had more initiative in finding things to do and have been more verbal, and were less shy.[31]

Through Parent-Child Centers, Head Start, and Follow Through, the federal government has attempted to provide equal educational opportunities for disadvantaged children, aiding them from the fetal stage to the age of nine. Although these programs have self-evident advantages, some questions and problems are being raised. First, it has been pointed out that the symptoms, not the causes, are being attacked. If racial prejudice and poverty pockets were eliminated, and if unskilled workers were given training or retraining, those who are presently disadvantaged could gradually raise themselves to a higher plane of living. While this is true, it should be realized that, during the transition period, there are many children who need help and should receive it. Second, by initiating early childhood education on a broad scale, some critics have claimed that the educational efforts of the home may be replaced by those of governmental agencies, especially since some educators have recommended that *all* children begin their education at the age of four.[32] However, since these present programs are directed toward families that cannot, or will not, discharge their obligations

---

[30]Nolán Estes, "Follow Through," *American Education,* 3, Number 8 (September, 1967), 12.

[31]Harry Salsinger, "Following Up on Follow Through," *American Education,* 4, Number 5 (May, 1968), 13.

[32]The Educational Policies Commission of the National Education Association has recommended that all children be given the opportunity to attend public schools from the age of four.

toward their children, and since these programs will undoubtedly decrease as the number of disadvantaged children decrease, the danger may not be as great as it appears. In the meantime, vigorous efforts should be made to restore the family to its true functions by eliminating the conditions which brought about its deterioration.

SUMMARY

Innovations, new ways of reaching a desired goal, have been proposed throughout the history of education to solve educational problems. Some innovations have left a lasting impression on educational theory and practice, but most of them were either fads or fallacies that have disappeared. Today, more than ever before, we are emphasizing the discovery of new ways of doing things. These efforts are receiving financial support from governmental and private sources. Between 1965 and 1968, approximately 2,000 innovative practices were sponsored by the Elementary and Secondary Education Act of 1965 alone.

Although television has been in use for several decades, its educational possibilities are still being explored. There are two types of broadcasting in educational television: open-circuit, which may be received by any conventional television receiver, and closed-circuit, which can be received only by the audience for whom it is intended. Most instructional television has been of the closed-circuit type.

After World War II, educators began to consider giving instruction to large numbers of pupils through television. During the 1950's, pilot programs were begun in several universities. The results of these programs showed that the services of outstanding teachers could be made available to large audiences; that student achievement was as high through television instruction as it was through conventional methods; that television was particularly effective for demonstrations, because it gave each student a close-up view; and, that it was "accepted" by the students as an instructional medium. However, several disadvantages and problems were also noted: there was a lack of communication between the instructor and pupils, and the students felt the method was too impersonal; it was not equally effective in all subjects, and there was no provision for individual differences; problems of motivation and discipline arose; and, finally, the installation of television facilities was extremely costly.

Programed instruction is an innovation which permits a pupil to progress at his own rate of speed. It uses instructional materials and devices that act as a tutor to the pupil, enabling him to learn many things by himself. The term "programed instruction" includes several procedures which have a variety of names, such as teaching machines, scrambled textbooks, programed materials, auto-instruction, and computer-assisted instruction.

In programed learning, the pupil proceeds in small steps from what he already knows to new knowledge. He receives an immediate evaluation for each step, which acts as reinforcement to his learning and is intended to motivate him to continue his progress. The pupil works by himself, and receives assistance from the teacher only when he needs it. Thus, the procedure is intended to take care of individual differences among pupils.

The primary advantage claimed for programed instruction was that it provided for individual differences. However, there is some evidence developing which indicates that not all pupils can learn the same program effectively. This evidence suggests that different programs are needed for different mental ability levels. It was further claimed that under programed instruction the success experienced by the pupil in each step would motivate him to continue with the next step. Yet, studies have shown that students have found this type of learning boring. Also, over-exposure to programed learning deprives the pupils of the beneficial effects of group procedures.

It is too early to tell, but it appears that, in spite of known shortcomings, programed instruction may be useful to the classroom teacher. It can be used to learn basic material and review previously learned materials. It can be used for a portion of school time, or it can be assigned for home study. In addition, high quality programs can be used as supplementary material in a course. They can enrich the program of a school through additional course offerings that might be studied independently.

Team teaching was another innovation proposed during the 1950's as a way of easing the teacher shortage and improving instruction. Although there is no single definition of team teaching, it is said to embrace the following key concepts: two or more teachers combine their special talents to cooperate in the instruction and evaluation of a common group of students over a predetermined period of time. Members of the team, which may include aides and specialists, plan together all of the details of the course and agree on their areas of responsibility. They are usually under the direction of a team leader.

It has been difficult to evaluate the effectiveness of team teaching because of the variety of procedures that have been used. In general, however, it has been said to utilize the special talents of teachers more effectively, thus improving instruction for larger numbers of pupils. Through the use of aides, the teacher has been freed of many routine duties and has more time to devote to teaching. In addition, since team teaching permits flexible scheduling, it is possible to adjust time and facilities to a variety of learning situations. Finally, proponents have claimed that team teaching provides for the professional growth of teachers through frequent planning sessions and conferences.

As experimentation with team teaching continued, several problems arose. Team teaching procedures could not be implemented in many schools, because the plant did not lend itself to flexibility, and it would be too costly to make the recommended modifications. Another problem resulted from the fact that some teachers did not wish to be observed by their colleagues, while other teachers disliked giving up their autonomous role in the classroom. The problem of financing the program was a serious one too, because the outlay for materials, learning centers, structural changes, and teacher's aides was considerable. It was additionally difficult to justify the adoption of team teaching since early studies showed no statistically significant differences in student achievement between traditional methods and the team teaching approach.

Although the nongraded school is considered a current innovation, it is simply a revival, with a few modifications, of an organizational procedure that was used in our schools until the middle of the nineteenth century. The nongraded school is not organized into grades. Rather, pupils of different ages and different ability levels are in the same room, under the same teacher. It is organized in such a way that pupils work individually at their own rate and at their particular level of ability. In the nongraded school, pupils do not "pass" or "fail". In the beginning of a new year, they resume their work at the point where they left off at the end of the preceding year.

In order to make nongrading workable, it was necessary to restructure the work in a carefully sequenced order, so that the pupil, with guidance from the teacher, could work independently. The work was organized into a number of levels, usually 7–8. Progress from one level to another was usually determined by the pupil's reading ability. The teacher could make varied assignments, arrange for group activities and manipulate movable classroom furniture to suit the needs of the moment.

The nongraded schools, proponents claim, provide for individual differences. Children do not experience the stigma of "failure", as there is no need for children to repeat a year's work. Furthermore, they claim that there is flexibility in transferring pupils from one group to another, and the teacher is relieved of the pressure of meeting grade expectations for all pupils.

Like other innovations, several arguments have been advanced against the nongraded school. It has been pointed out that levels of attainment have been substituted for grades, and that, therefore, the teacher and pupils are subjected to "level expectations" in place of "grade expectations". Moreover, pupils who lag behind others in the nongraded school will be exposed to the same type of emotional reactions as those who fail in the graded school. In providing for individual differences, the nongraded school has considered only differences in rate of progress and neglected other types of differences. Other arguments maintain that the work load of a teacher in the nongraded is greatly increased, that properly sequenced material has not been sufficiently developed, and that the smaller classes of a nongraded school are inconsistent with the demands of increased enrollment and teacher shortage.

Individually Prescribed Instruction combines the nongraded organization with the principles of programed instruction. Under this procedure, the entire work of grades K-6 is planned and sequenced to transcend grade levels. The work is organized into levels of proficiency through which the pupil moves at his own rate of speed. Just as in programmed instruction, the pupil may not begin a new level until he meets the requirements of the preceding level, and he is provided with feedback through periodic tests. Each pupil receives a written prescription outlining his activities from the teacher. Assignments are adapted to the need of each individual. Most of the arguments previously outlined for programmed instruction and nongraded schools can be applied to IPI.

Beginning in 1965, several innovations have been devised for culturally disadvantaged children and their families. The first of these was Head Start which was initiated by the Office of Economic Opportunity as part of the war on poverty.

Children between the ages of 3 and 5 were eligible for the Head Start program. Because they lacked the cultural background necessary for regular school activities, a special program of early childhood education was organized for them. They were organized into small classes, supplied with work and play materials and encouraged to develop initiative through learning-by-doing. A teacher and two aides were in charge of each class, which permitted a high degree of individual attention. In addition, children were provided with health, nutritional, psychiatric, and counseling services. Parental involvement in the program was greatly emphasized. Parents were urged to participate in all phases of the program and were eligible for educational and counseling services themselves. Thus, the effects of the program were felt not only by individual children but also by their families. In 1967–68, Parent-Child Centers were conceived as a way of extending these benefits to children aged 0-3 and to their families.

Children who had completed Head Start programs had difficulty in adjusting to regular school programs. Consequently, experimentation began in 1967–68 with Follow Through, a program for disadvantaged children who were between the ages of 6-9. Follow Through, which was based on the same guidelines as Head Start, began nationally in 1968–69. Thus, three coordinated programs for disadvantaged children, aged 0-3, 3-6, and 6-9, were sponsored by the federal government between 1965–1968. While these programs have merit, it is recognized that measures have to be taken to eliminate the causes of poverty and prejudice and restore the family as a strong, wholesome agency of education.

Questions for discussion:

1. In your opinion, what potentiality does educational television have for the future?

2. Evaluate the arguments given for and against programed instruction.

3. How do you think computer-assisted instruction will be used in the future?

4. If you were a teacher, would you like to be a member of a teaching team, or would you rather be in charge of your own classroom?

5. Compare or contrast the nongraded school with a one-room schoolhouse.

6. What is the teacher's function in an IPI classroom?

7. Are you for or against making public education available to all children from the age of four?

8. What do you think of the special programs for disadvantaged children who are between the ages of 0-3, and 6-9?

For further reading:

Beggs, David W., ed., *Team Teaching*. Bloomington, Indiana: Indiana University Press, 1964.

Educational Policies Commission, *American Education and the Search for Equal Opportunity*. Washington, D.C.: National Education Association, 1965.

————, *Education and the Disadvantaged American*. Washington, D.C.: National Education Association, 1962.

Fry, Edward B., *Teaching Machines and Programed Instruction*. New York: McGraw-Hill Book Company, Inc., 1963.

Gordon, George N., *Educational Television*. New York: The Center for Applied Research in Education, Inc., 1965.

National Society for the Study of Education, *The Changing American School*. Sixty-fifth Yearbook, Part II, 1966. Chicago: The National Society for the Study of Education, 1966.

————, *Programed Instruction*. Sixty-sixth Yearbook, Part II, 1967. Chicago: The National Society for the Study of Education, 1967.

Shaplin, Judson T., and Henry F. Olds, Jr., ed., *Team Teaching*. New York: Harper & Row, Publishers, 1964.

Trow, William C., *Teacher and Technology*. New York: Appleton-Century-Crofts, 1963.

U.S. Office of Education, *Educational Television*. Washington, D.C.: U.S. Government Printing Office, 1965.

————, *New Teaching Aids*. Washington, D.C.: U.S. Government Printing Office, 1962.

Index